"The distinguishing characteristic of a traditional folk game is that although it has rules they are not written. Nobody knows exactly what they are. The players have a tradition to guide them, but must settle among themselves the details of how to play a particular game."

From **ONE POTATO, TWO POTATO:**
The SECRET EDUCATION of AMERICAN CHILDREN,
by Mary and Herbert Knapp.

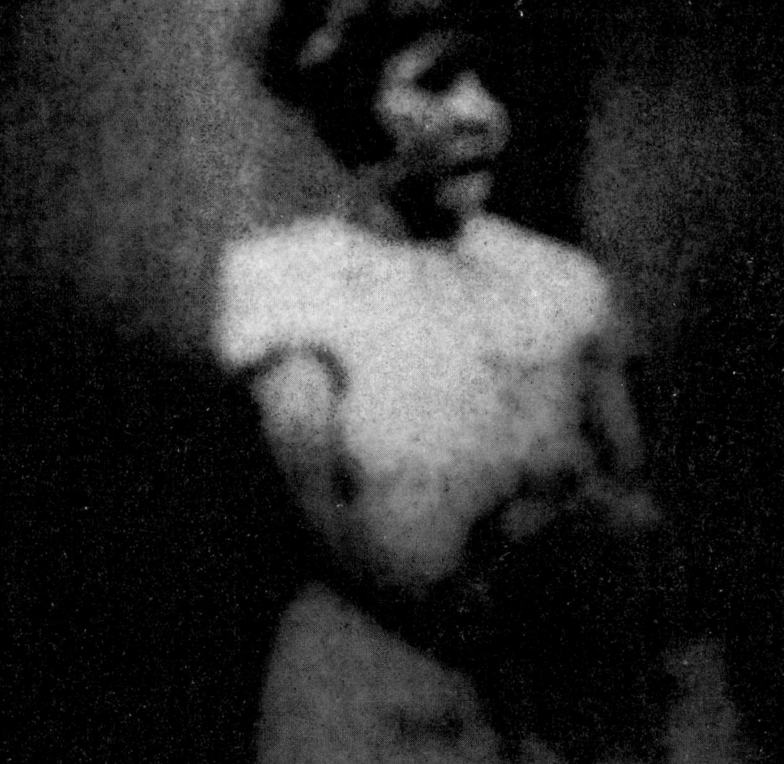

"Well, perhaps you haven't found it so yet," said Alice; "but when you have to turn into a chrysalis - you will some day you know - and then after that into a butterfly, I should think you'll feel it a little queer, won't you?"

"Not a bit," said the Caterpillar.

"Well, perhaps *your* feelings may be different," said Alice: "all I know is, it would feel very queer to *me*."

"You!" said the Caterpillar contemptuously. "Who are *you*?"

From **ALICE'S ADVENTURES in WONDERLAND,**
by Lewis Carroll.

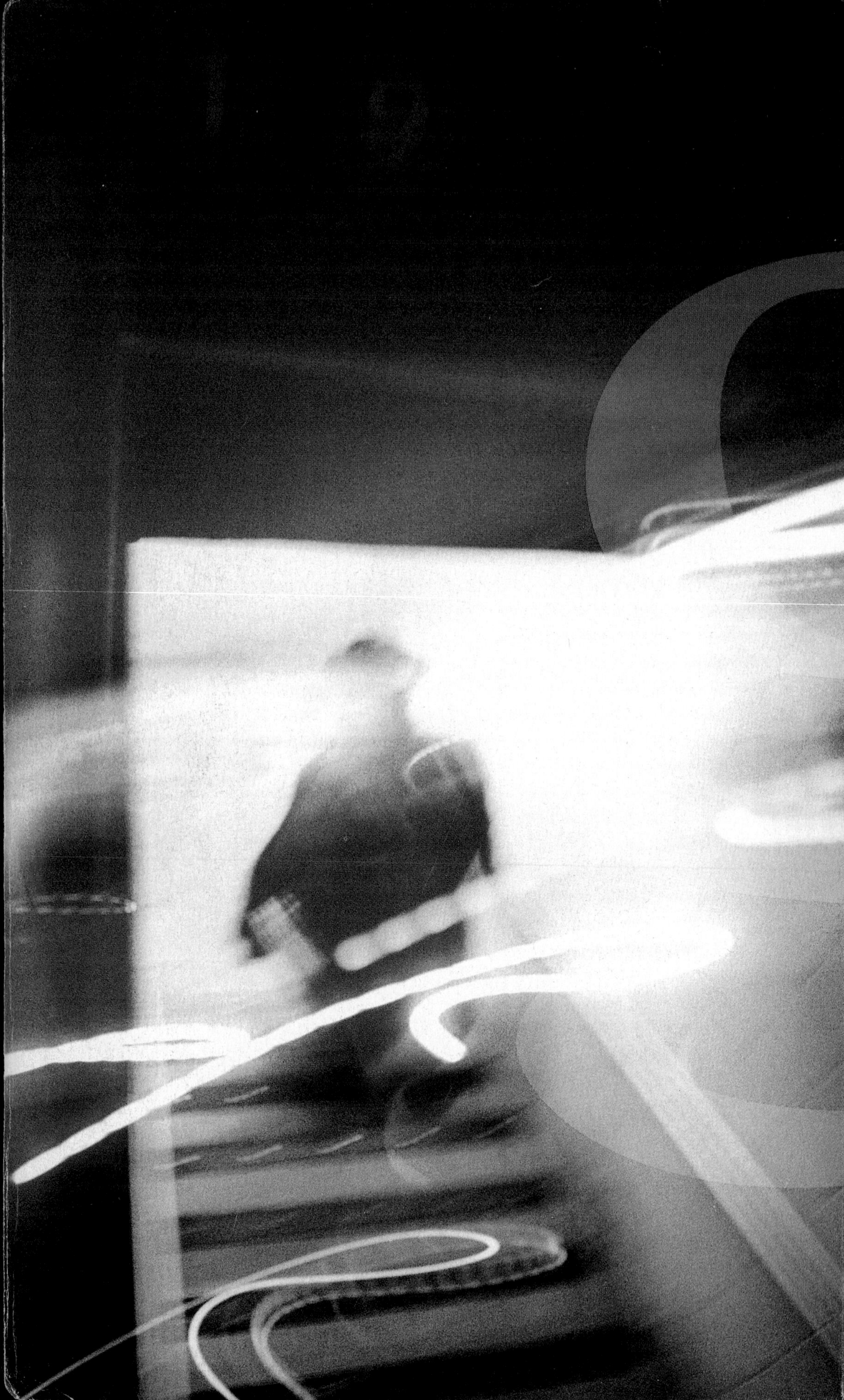

SANDMAN
a game of you

WRITTEN BY
NEIL GAIMAN

ILLUSTRATED BY
SHAWN McMANUS
COLLEEN DORAN
BRYAN TALBOT
GEORGE PRATT
STAN WOCH
DICK GIORDANO

LETTERED BY
TODD KLEIN

COLORED BY
DANNY VOZZO

COVERS BY
DAVE McKEAN

INTRODUCED BY
SAMUEL R. DELANY

FEATURING CHARACTERS CREATED BY
NEIL GAIMAN, SAM KIETH, MIKE DRINGENBERG

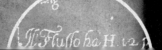

the SANDMAN:
A GAME OF YOU

**Cover and publication design by
Dave McKean.**

DC Comics
1700 Broadway
New York, NY 10019
A Warner Bros. Entertainment Company

DC Comics does not read or accept
unsolicited submissions of ideas,
stories or artwork.

Printed in Canada.
Eighth Printing.

ISBN: 978-1-56389-089-5

SUSTAINABLE
FORESTRY
INITIATIVE

Certified Fiber
Sourcing
www.sfiprogram.org

Fiber used in this product line meets the sourcing requirements
of the SFI program. www.sfiprogram.org PWC-SFICOC-260

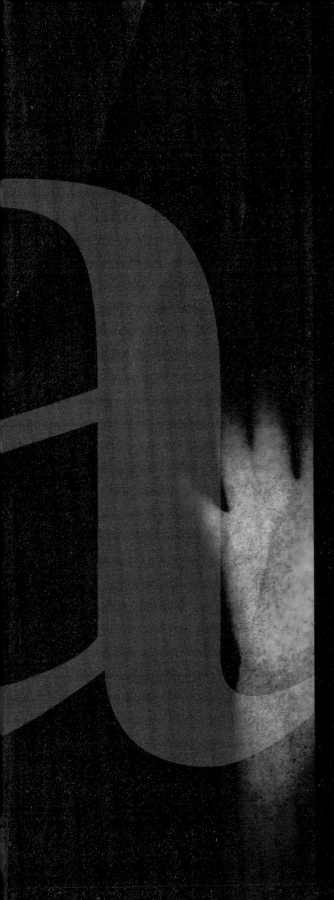

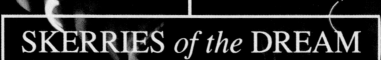

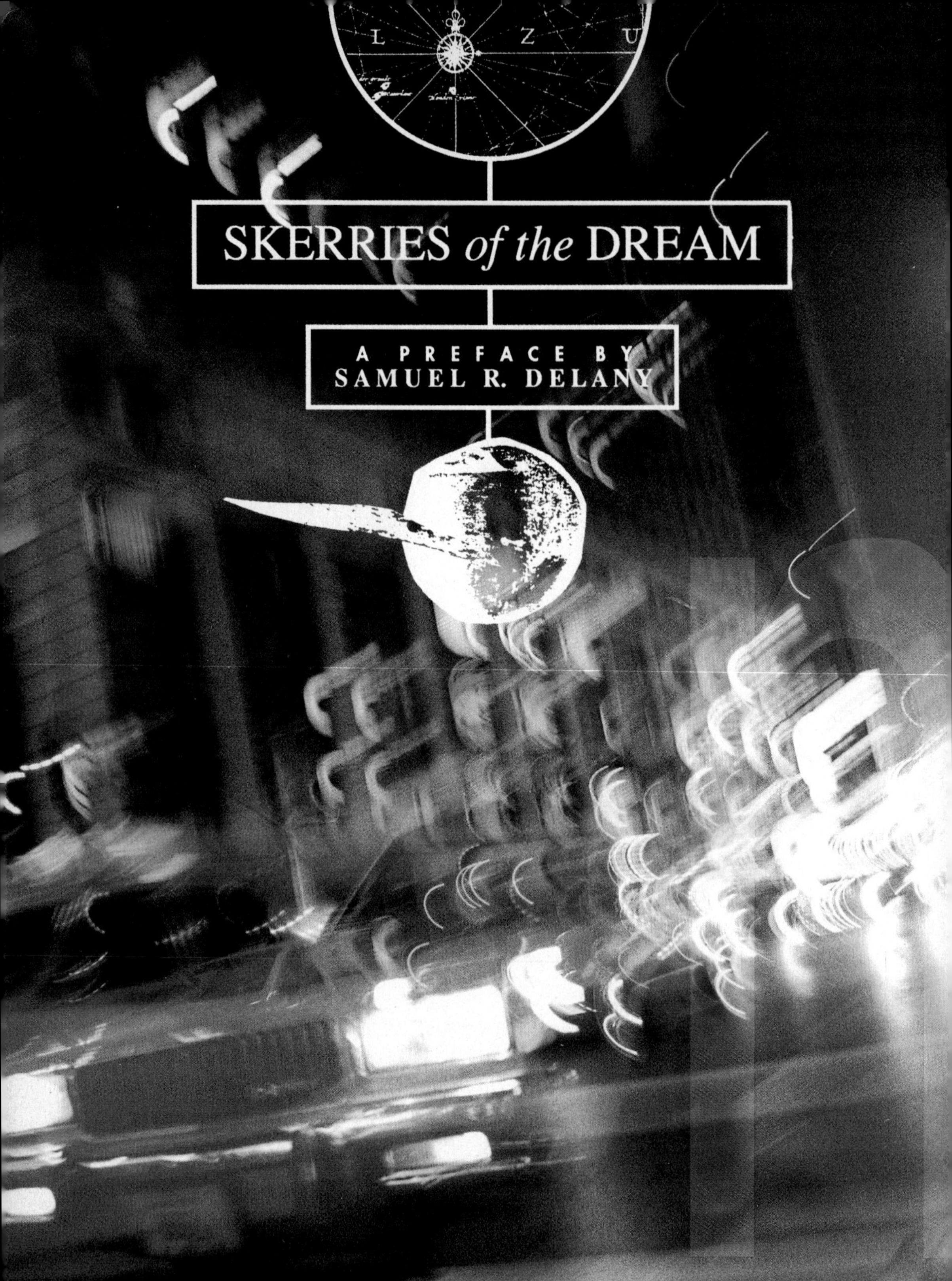

SKERRIES *of the* DREAM

A PREFACE BY
SAMUEL R. DELANY

So the first thing I did was turn to the Oxford English Dictionary and look up "skerry," where I found:

A rugged, insulated sea-rock or stretch of rocks, covered by the sea at high water or in stormy weather; a reef.

It's quite a resonant image, those distant, only partially visible solidities, now and again drowned in dreams —temporarily lost in them. Neil Gaiman plays with it elegantly in the writing; and Shawn McManus (as do Colleen Doran, Bryan Talbot, and Stan Woch) plays with it equally elegantly in the drawings.

THE SANDMAN is one of the most popular comics of our day—and popular with the oddest lot of people. We're all used to the idea of comic books resonating with elemental mythic patterns: the late lamented Superman, the currently thriving Batman, and Wonder Woman. But, when all is said and done, as such myths go, they're pretty brutal things. THE SANDMAN, under the writerly direction of Gaiman, does its work delicately, probing in areas where, often, we might not even have suspected anything mythical lay. It explores always with an ironic cast to the lips. The eyes are narrowed. The approach is always skewed.

Again and again, what it discovers shocks, chills, catches at the heart. It sends us to strange places, to the most distant shores of the imaginative, the mystical, to explore the stuff that can only be figured in dreams...

To talk about these tales in too much more detail, let me warn you, I will have to talk about the plot—what happens in them. Those of you who haven't read them before might better go on and read them now. The analysis that follows will be more fun for a reader already familiar with them. And some of that fun might be, for some of you, spoiled by the odd, upcoming revelation.

Gaiman's **A Game of You**—this particular Sandman series—begins in the snow: need we note that for the comics colorist, depicting snow requires the minimum amount of ink? Take a look: Color there is all but restricted to the shading over the caption boxes. (And that color says: look at the *language* in this tale...) What we have in the opening three pages is two streams of information, all but unconnected, one verbal, one visual. The visual one, by the bottom of the first page, has become shocking: a desiccated corpse!

At the same time the words provide a strangely distanced, even elegant, colloquy between speakers named Prinado and Luz, about the Cuckoo, the Princess, and the Tantoblin—carrying us right past that shock, into the second page, toward a spot of black: a hole in the snow—a hole, a blackness, that grows larger and larger, till, by the bottom of page three, it engulfs the reader, filling its panel.

Need we note that an all-black panel requires the *most* ink possible from the comics inker? (The only color there is restricted to the shading over the caption boxes: look at the language.). But here two eyes blink in that darkness, to look, indeed, in the direction of the words...

What's happening in this three-page prologue is that we are given two simultaneous worlds, as it were, both highly subjective, one represented by words, one represented by pictures. Both are highly formalized—the one represented by words through the deeply conventionalized diction associated with high fantasy, the one represented by pictures through the formal progression from white to black. Both contain violences.

The shocks in one information stream—the starkly drawn ribs of the corpse at the bottom of page one, the verbal shock of "The Tantoblin will not come. I felt him die. The Black Guard found him in the night," even as they fall within the same panel—jar one another; as we move our attention back and forth between one stream and the other, there is impingement, distortion, and interaction that all but obliterates the distinctions the formalities set in place. And that—in case you're wondering—in spite of the abstract language, is a description of what is going to go on through the rest of **A Game of You.**

It's our opening example of how the game will be played:

Two worlds—and elements from each will constantly impinge, cross over, to shock and distort what goes on in the other.

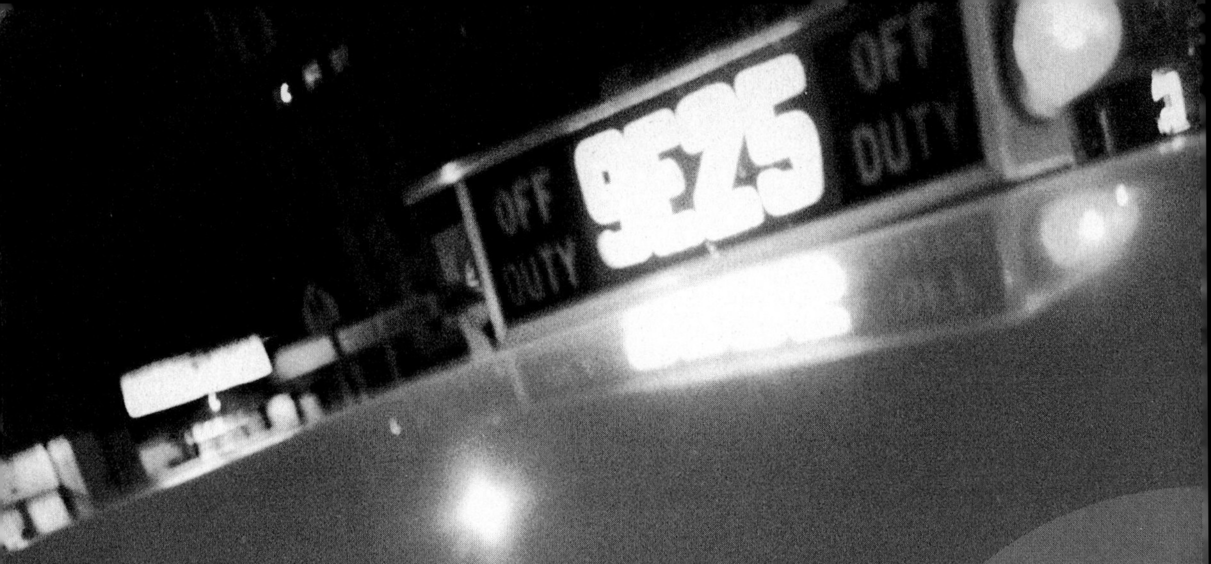
OFF
DUTY
9E25
OFF
DUTY

Also, we're going to get, just incidentally, a tale that covers just about the range of what comics can do—from panels almost pure white to panels almost pure black.

The way to become really frustrated with **A Game of You** is, however, to read one world as reality, the world of Barbie, Wanda, Hazel and Foxglove, and one world as fantasy: the world of Prinado, Luz, Wilkinson, and the Cuckoo. If you try to read one as a simple allegory for the other—if you look in one for a extensional explanation of the other—you will not be a happy camper. Clive Barker, in his introduction to **The Doll's House**, noted that Gaiman's tales tend to take place not in a world where fantasy invades the real, but rather in what Barker called a "far more delirious" form: "In these narratives, the whole world is haunted and mysterious. There is no solid status quo, only a series of relative realities, personal to each of the characters, any and all of which are frail, and subject to eruptions from other states and conditions." The visual shock that comes as the reader leaves page three of **A Game of You** to turn to page four—the transition from the snow-and-shadow world of the Land, where death is an ugly splatter of ink at the bottom of the page in the progression from white to black, to the sheer *messiness* of Barbie's room (a chaos of clothing and wall photos and rumpled bedding wholly organized around the sexuality of Barbie's buns, incidentally) immediately suggests this *is* going to be a two-tiered fantasy, of the real and the imagined.

But hold on to Barker's point. He's been there before...

Consider: in the world that we—certainly—*start* to read as real, the sullen top-floor neighbor harbors a horde of malignant crows inside his rib cage; the quiet girl upstairs with the oversized glasses who drinks soy milk is hundreds of years old; here, it turns out, the moon *cares* whether or not you have a "y" chromosome, and punishes you accordingly. No, *this* is a fantasy world, too.

The world of THE SANDMAN finally takes its power from its intense saturation of irony. Here, the Lord of all Dream has a smart-alec crow for a sidekick called Matthew who calls his boss "boss." It's a world where a stuffed toy animal can scare an old homeless woman into a near heart attack—or betray you to the point of death. In THE SANDMAN a mourner draws the threads of a veil on her face in a restroom with an eyebrow pencil—and, because it's a comic book, we, the readers, can't tell the difference between it and a "real" veil—but all the characters can and comment on it constantly. ("What's that on your face?") It's a world where a "Wundabud" commercial (that's a brand of cotton swab) plays through a storm that all but destroys a neighborhood—in short, it's a world almost as heavily laced with ironies as our own.

he key to this fantasy is Wanda's troubling death (alongside the death of the single black character in the tale)-which drew a whole host of very concerned ideological criticism, when readers first encountered it in issue #36, part five. (And, I confess, Hazel's ignorance of the mechanics of female reproduction seemed to me something one would be more likely to find in the suburban heartland, even at the center on Barbie's Florida childhood—rather than on the third floor of a Lower East Side tenement. But the same reading applies...) Wanda's initial biological sex is of the same visual status as the aforementioned ironic black mourner's veil at he final Kansas funeral: the biologically naive (Hazel), as well as the forces of religion (Thessaly) and the family (Alvin's) now and again speak about it. But we, the readers, just can't *see* it. (The veil is simply *erased* at the end...) And because the comics are a fundamentally visual medium, that palpable invisibility may finally be the strongest statement the story has to make about the topic to the common (comics) reader. It seems to me, as I was saying, that the key to this particular fantasy world is precisely that it *is* a fantasy world where the natural forces, stated and unstated, whether of myth or of chance, *enforce* the dominant ideology we've got around us today, no matter what. (The dominant ideology is the collection of rules and regulations that includes, among many other things, the one that says that in popular narratives, like the *Dirty Harry* films, say, all the members of oppressed groups, blacks, women, Asians, gays, or what have you, have to be killed off at the end, no matter how good and noble they are—so that we can feel sorry for them, then forget about them. The dominant ideology is what's challenged by, among many other things, something like the ACT-UP slogan: "We're here. We're queer. We *won't* go way! Get used to us!") Making the supernatural forces in the tale the enforcers of the dominant ideology is what makes it a fantasy—and a rather nasty one at that.

And it remains just a nasty fantasy unless, in our reading of it, we can find some irony, something that subverts it, something that resists that fantasy, an array of details that turns the simple acceptance of that ideology into a problem—problematizes it, in Lit. Crit.-ese. But, as we said, almost everything in THE SANDMAN has its richness, its ironic spin. I'll mention a couple. But look for more. They're there. Taking the time to tease such subtleties out (and the problem with political readings is precisely that the large and general tend to overwhelm the subtle and specific) makes us stronger readers in the end, not because it makes us *excuse* such political patterns, but because we have to become even *more* sensitive to them, if we are to see how they are affected *by* the subtleties (which are, themselves, just as political).

In life, it will be the subtleties that start to wear away at the major social patterns of oppression, after all. It's the range of subtle subversions that set them up for the big changes that come by as better legislation, economic freedoms, and their material like.

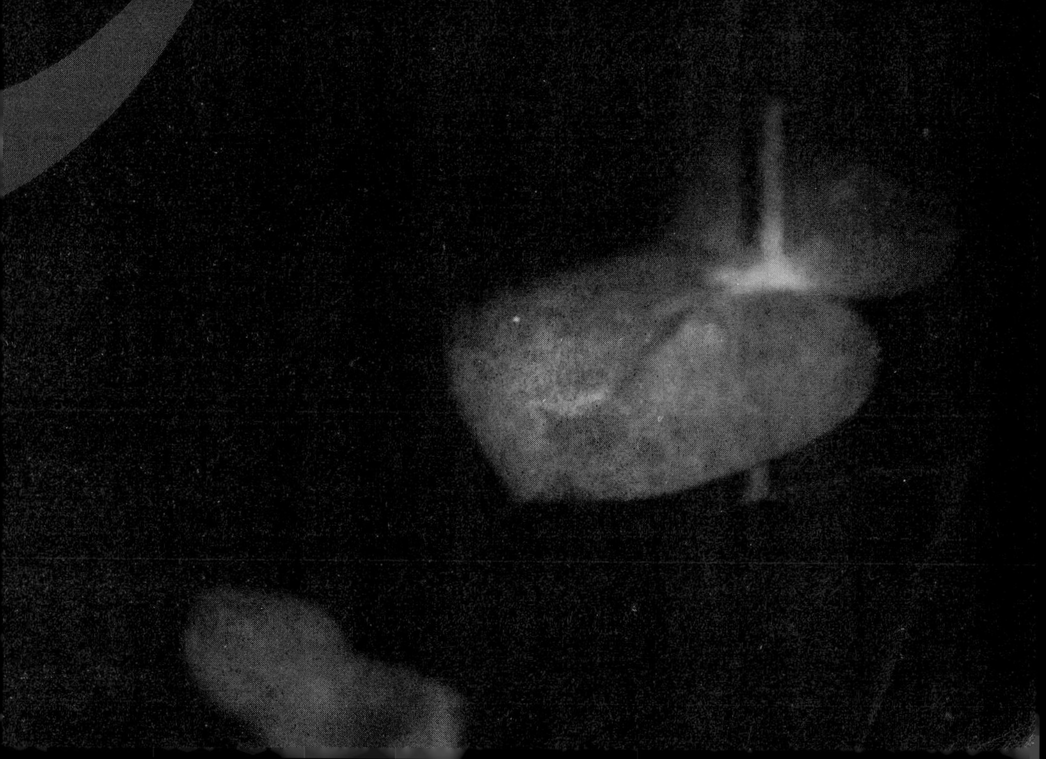

(Notice when major social changes *are* finally legislated and formalized, they tend to surprise everyone *except* those who were paying attention to the details. That's why, in life and on the page, specific details are a good thing to pay attention to.)

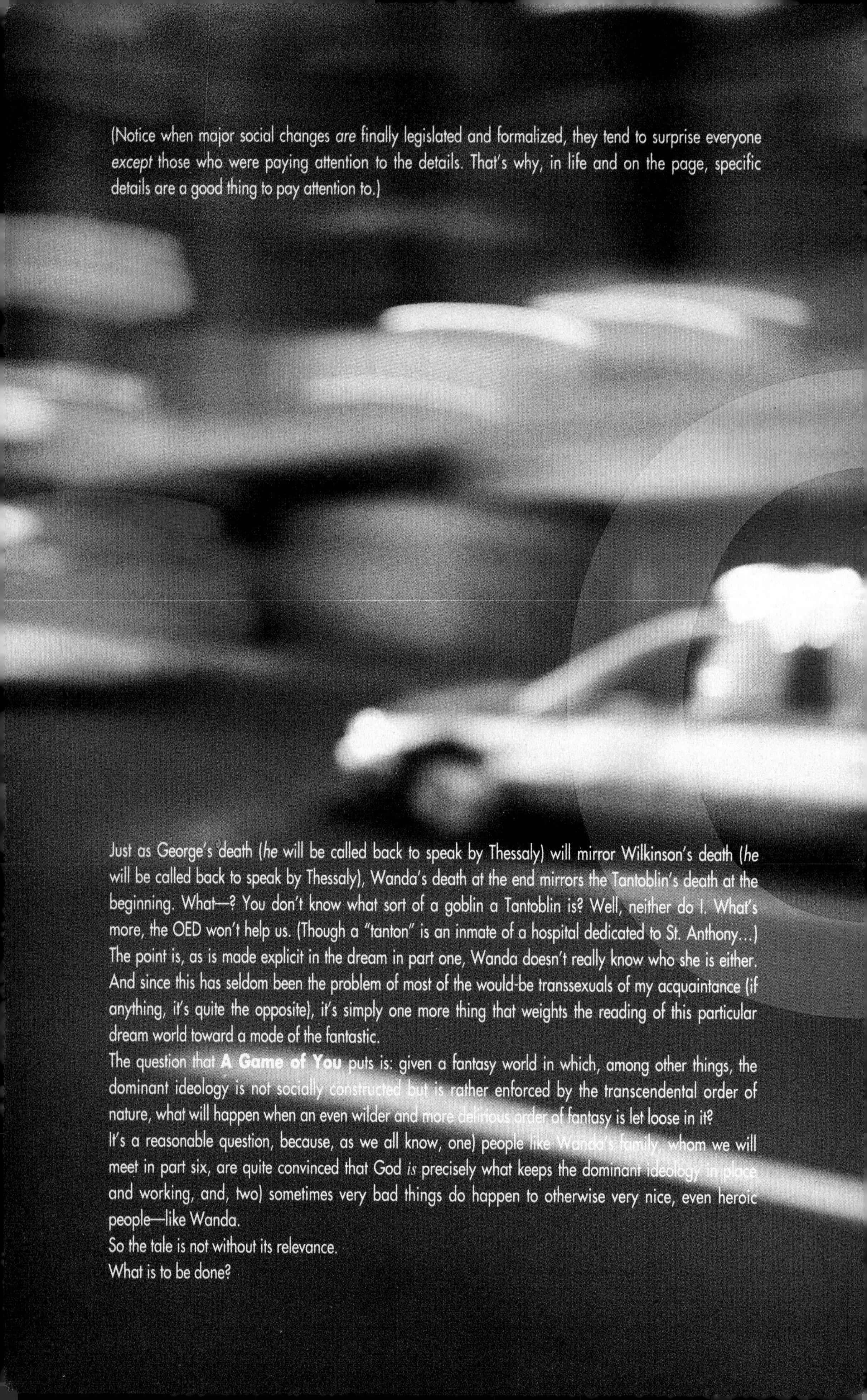

Just as George's death (*he* will be called back to speak by Thessaly) will mirror Wilkinson's death (*he* will be called back to speak by Thessaly), Wanda's death at the end mirrors the Tantoblin's death at the beginning. What—? You don't know what sort of a goblin a Tantoblin is? Well, neither do I. What's more, the OED won't help us. (Though a "tanton" is an inmate of a hospital dedicated to St. Anthony...) The point is, as is made explicit in the dream in part one, Wanda doesn't really know who she is either. And since this has seldom been the problem of most of the would-be transsexuals of my acquaintance (if anything, it's quite the opposite), it's simply one more thing that weights the reading of this particular dream world toward a mode of the fantastic.

The question that **A Game of You** puts is: given a fantasy world in which, among other things, the dominant ideology is not socially constructed but is rather enforced by the transcendental order of nature, what will happen when an even wilder and more delirious order of fantasy is let loose in it?

It's a reasonable question, because, as we all know, one) people like Wanda's family, whom we will meet in part six, are quite convinced that God *is* precisely what keeps the dominant ideology in place and working, and, two) sometimes very bad things do happen to otherwise very nice, even heroic people—like Wanda.

So the tale is not without its relevance.

What is to be done?

For one, Barbie will be restricted to a nominal rebellion—which, perhaps, doesn't seem like much. The first rain will obliterate it, and likely no one in Kansas will ever know. But the idea of the nominal (in name only, having to do with names) is a big factor in **A Game of You.** While a name is always something *you* can choose, it only functions socially as long as I call you by it. (And try calling people names that they *don't* choose to be called by, if you want to see some real social unrest.) The power to choose one's own name is finally the major playing piece in the power game with which the story closes.

But let's look for a moment at another instance of parental naming in the story. Here's Wilkinson on *his* family's naming practices, during the journey through the Land, in part four:

I loved bein' a kid. I was one of seventeen children. We were all named Wilkinson—I suppose it was roughest on the girls, but we all got used to it in the end. I blame the parents, really... I would have liked to've bin an only child. That way when someone shouts Wilkinson, you know if it's you or not. Mustn't grumble. Our parents were the salt of the earth. Lovely people. It was just when they found a name they liked, they stuck with it.

In short, the Land is a fantasy world where there *is* no necessary distinction between male and female names for children—but, apparently, parents are just as sticky about preserving the name they pick as Wanda's parents turn out to be in part six. What we have here is an interesting satirical commentary, given in advance, on the closing moves of the game. (We won't even speculate on what prompted Barbie's parents to name *her*... And when she got together with her disastrous ex-boyfriend Ken, wasn't that just *too* cute...) This is not to say that life in the Land is all skittles and Courvoisier. The god the Land is sacred to is "Murphy," which, before we find out *his* real name, suggests nothing so much as the Murphy of Murphy's Law—that most pessimistic of observations on the Human Condition: "Anything that possibly *can* go wrong, will."

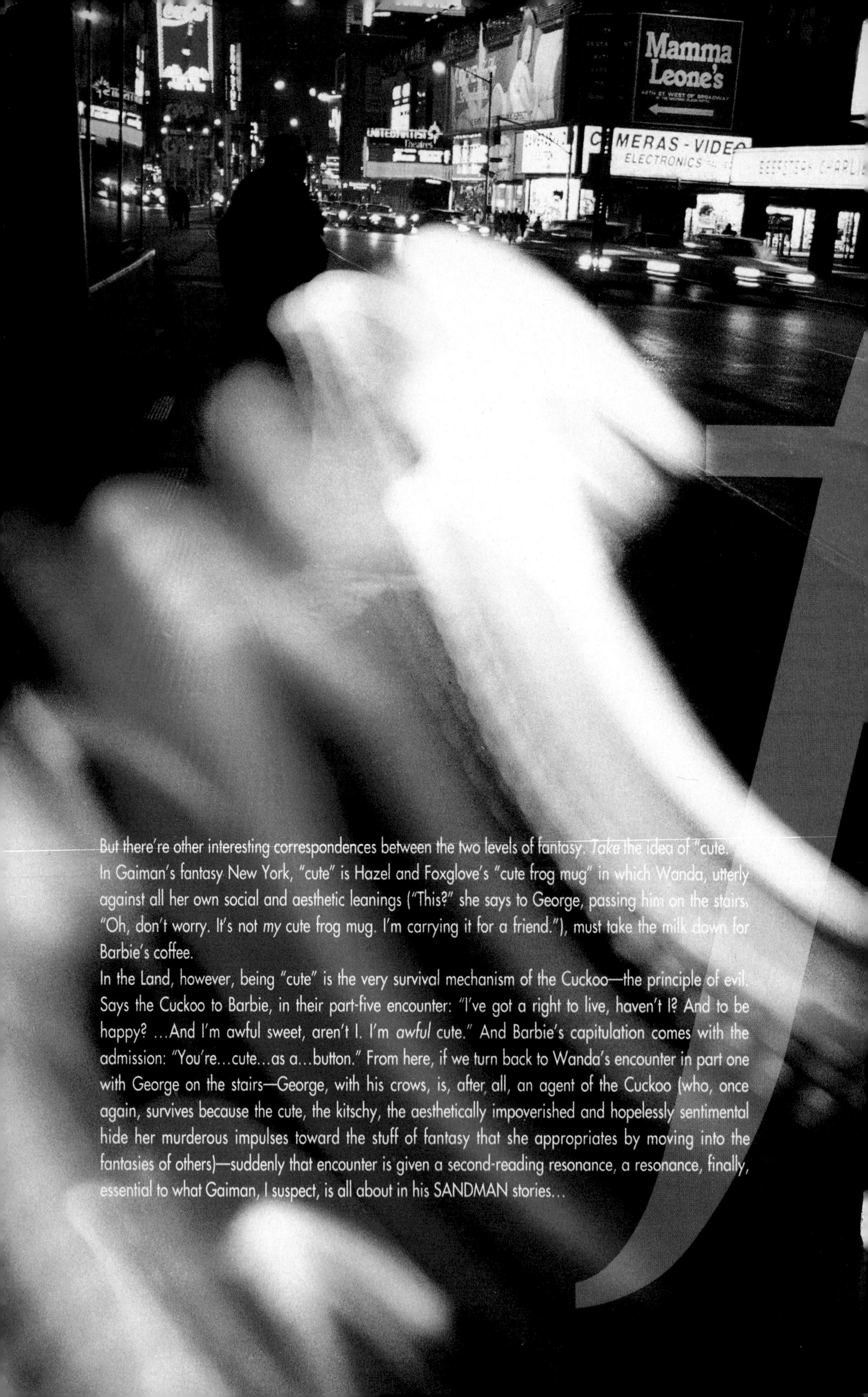
Mamma
Leone's
44TH ST. WEST OF BROADWAY
MERAS - VIDE
ELECTRONICS
Theatres

But there're other interesting correspondences between the two levels of fantasy. *Take* the idea of "cute." In Gaiman's fantasy New York, "cute" is Hazel and Foxglove's "cute frog mug" in which Wanda, utterly against all her own social and aesthetic leanings ("This?" she says to George, passing him on the stairs. "Oh, don't worry. It's not *my* cute frog mug. I'm carrying it for a friend."), must take the milk down for Barbie's coffee.

In the Land, however, being "cute" is the very survival mechanism of the Cuckoo—the principle of evil. Says the Cuckoo to Barbie, in their part-five encounter: "I've got a right to live, haven't I? And to be happy? ...And I'm awful sweet, aren't I. I'm *awful* cute." And Barbie's capitulation comes with the admission: "You're...cute...as a...button." From here, if we turn back to Wanda's encounter in part one with George on the stairs—George, with his crows, is, after all, an agent of the Cuckoo (who, once again, survives because the cute, the kitschy, the aesthetically impoverished and hopelessly sentimental hide her murderous impulses toward the stuff of fantasy that she appropriates by moving into the fantasies of others)—suddenly that encounter is given a second-reading resonance, a resonance, finally, essential to what Gaiman, I suspect, is all about in his SANDMAN stories...

For all we can get out of a careful rereading of Gaiman, the immediate pleasures of these stories to the first-time reader are many. It's the rare reader who does not respond to Gaiman's imaginative breadth, coupled with his simple accuracy of observation. The guarded caring with which his characters live with one another ("Don't take too much," Hazel warns Wanda, giving her the milk for Barbie's coffee) is comic and winning—and, of course, wholly recognizable. But this is a largely linear, melodic pleasure. There is also, however, a harmonic pleasure that accrues as detail resonates with detail. It is a pleasure that increases with careful, multiple readings. It is what makes these stories, in a word, art.

Gaiman's delirious world is held together always by relationships. Nor is his a world of relationships between fixed, solid egos, sure of them-"selves" and clear in their "identity." Each of those relationships, no matter how positive, always has its moment of real anxiety—what relationship doesn't? And all of Gaiman's selves are split, if not deliriously shattered. What he has to say about those relationships is what makes him an artist particularly interesting to our time. The Game of You is, after all, not the Game of I. (That's the "me-first" game—most of us know it only too well—where what I want is wholly above all other considerations and has to be pursued at any cost to anyone else.) It seems to me what Gaiman is saying, with the help of the artists who draw the pictures, is that, in the rich, complex, and socially constructed world around us, you cannot ultimately be what—or who—you want to be without some support from me. Wanda supports Barbie at the beginning of the story. At the end of the story, even though posthumously, Barbie supports Wanda. The element of death, however, makes it a much darker tale than that simple and rather Pollyanna reduction presupposes.

We're not talking simple altruism, here. We're talking about something much deeper, that allows individuals to exist; we're talking about the hidden, shifting, undersea reefs on which every individual stands—rocks that so rarely show clear above the tides of illusion and desire. That's the support we mean, and it always begins in something outside the self.

Gaiman is also saying that, because of death—even a fantasy death that allows articulation and information to come from beyond its borders, when magicked up by a centuries-old moon witch—no one can win the Game of I. Wanda cannot win it. Barbie cannot win it. (Morpheus tells Thessaly that, for all her longevity, she cannot win it either: take a look at the various "immortals'" deaths in Gaiman's more recent SANDMAN series, "Brief Lives...") Nor will I. Nor will you. (Also take a look at Gaiman's moving meditation on the last days of an artist, in his powerful work with Dave McKean, **Signal to Noise.**) Thus, for Gaiman, **A Game of You** is the only game worth playing—because it is the only game where, in the end, there's any chance of coming out ahead.

Even if one wins only by a name written on a stone that will wash away with the next shower, at least that allows something to persist in memory—and thus may lead to something else. But without even the name preserved momentarily in the real world by real action (and here, as I hope we can see, "real" is not the catch-all antonym for fantasy but rather a specific synonym for the political—as it is whenever it's used intelligently), there's no hope at all. Gaiman shows us the most marginal win possible in **A Game of You.**

But it's still won by moments, however small, of real social bravery. And that's what, at the end of **A Game of You,** Gaiman portrays. Thus, in a fantasy world whose tragedies are not real (i.e., not political) but are, nevertheless through that fantasy, deeply recognizable (and readable in any number of real ways), he has given us a triumph.

Amherst
January 17th, 1993

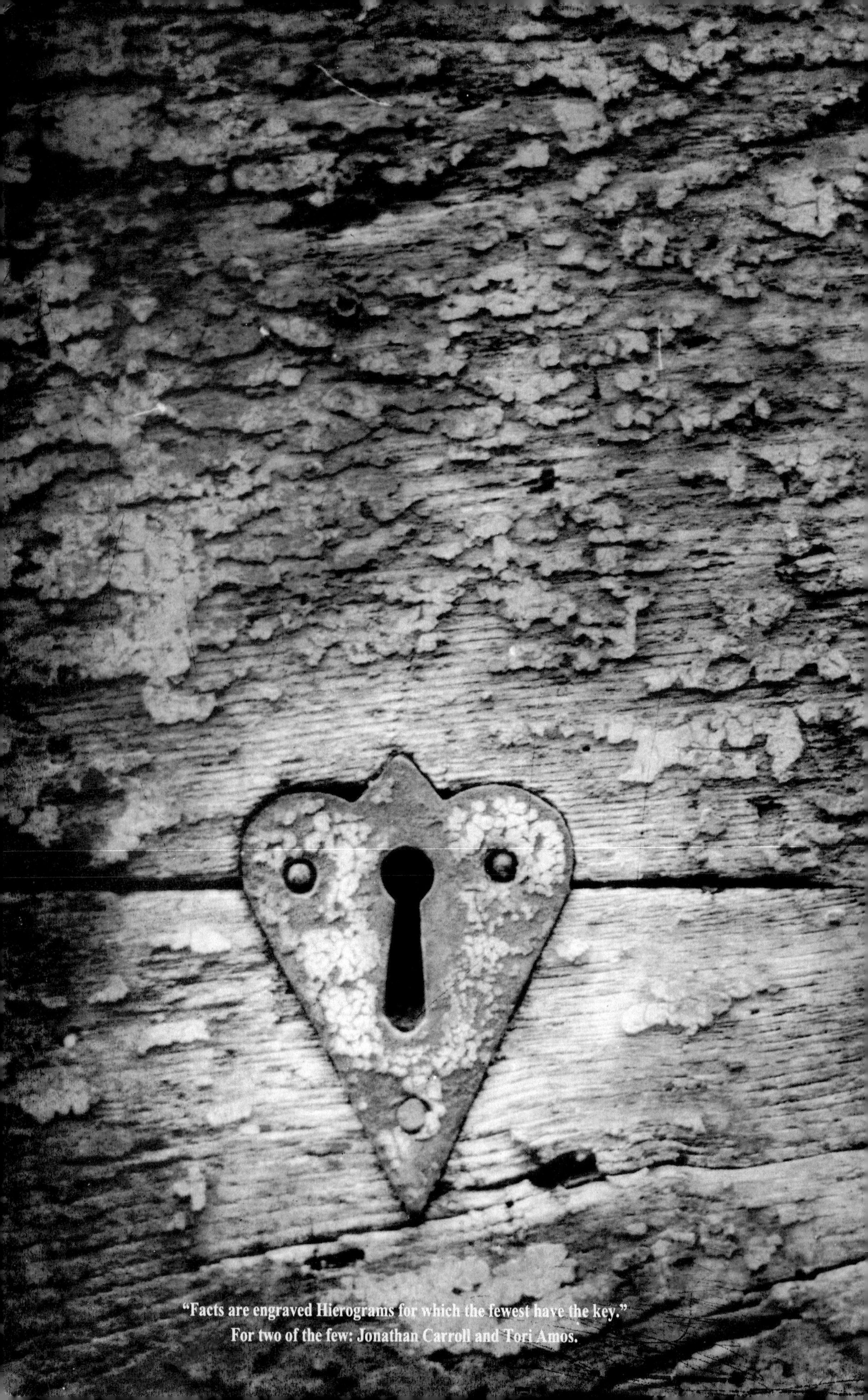

"Facts are engraved Hierograms for which the fewest have the key."
For two of the few: Jonathan Carroll and Tori Amos.

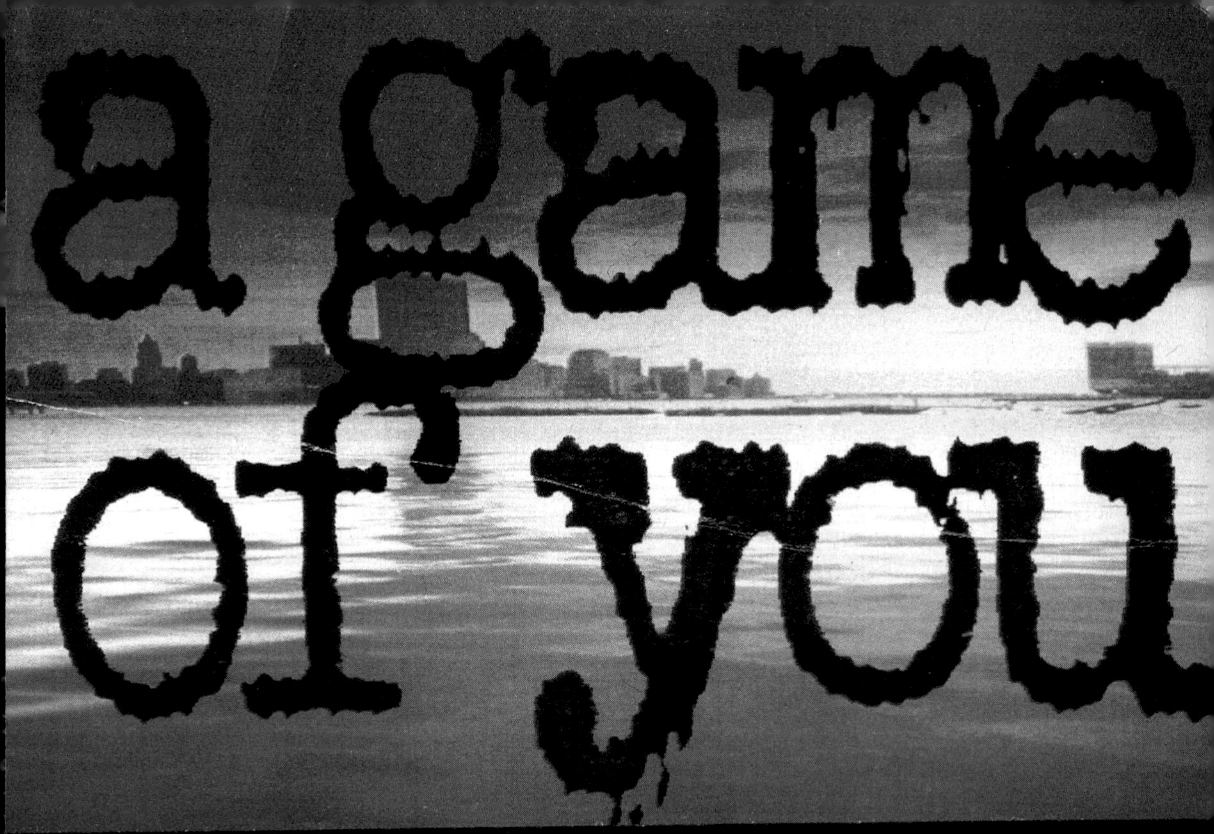
a game
of you

chapter one

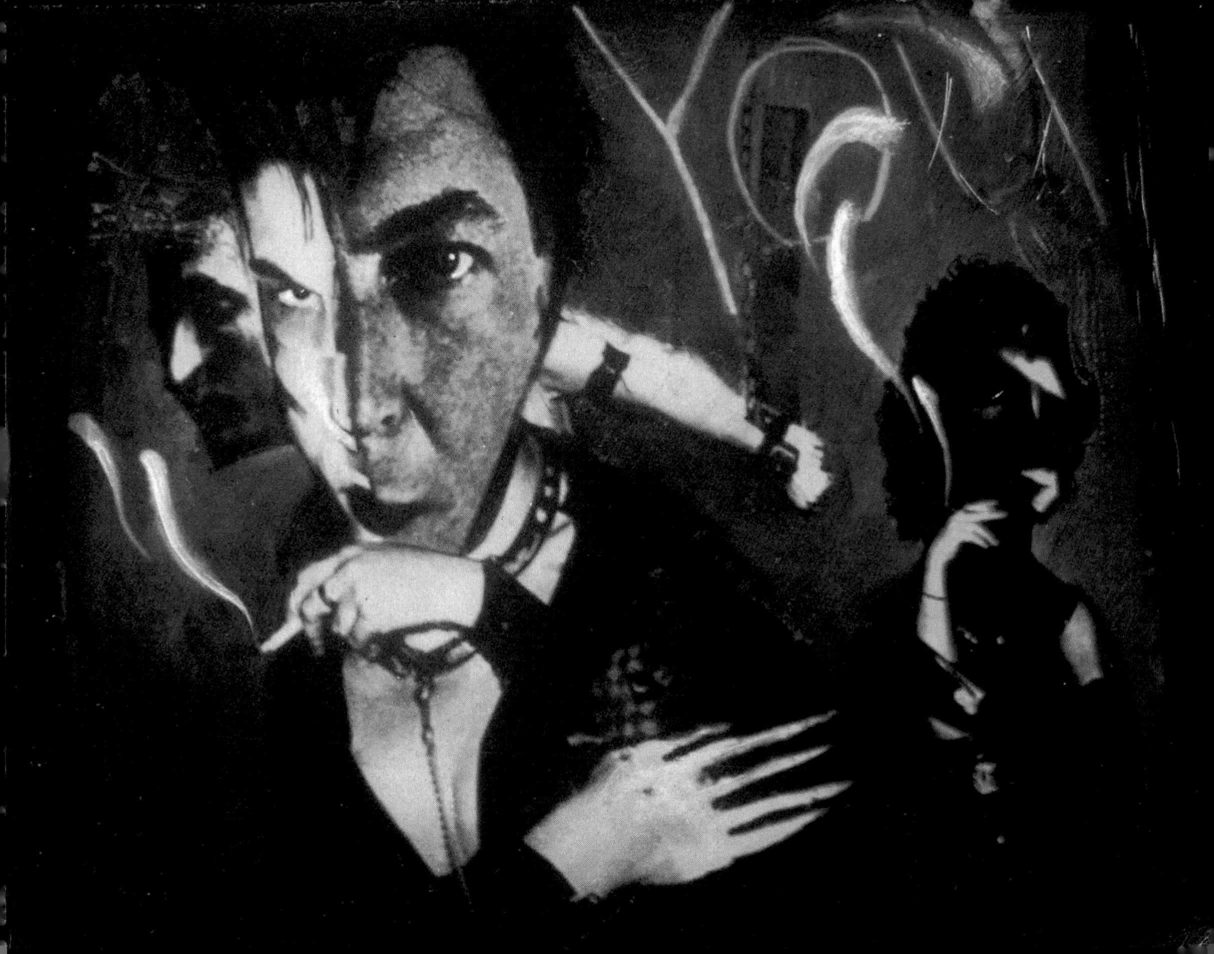
YOU

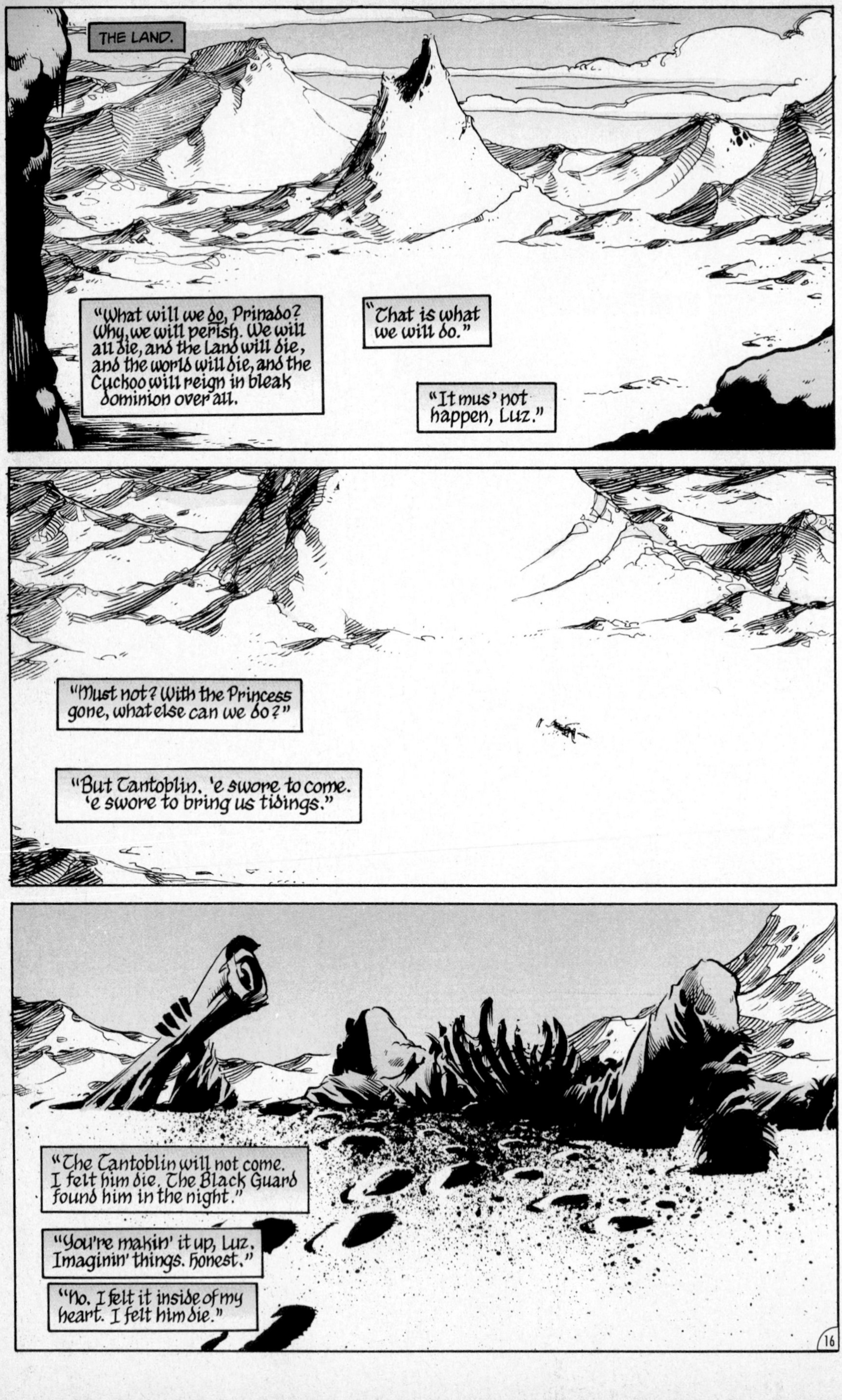
THE LAND.
"What will we do, Prinado? Why, we will perish. We will all die, and the Land will die, and the world will die, and the Cuckoo will reign in bleak dominion over all.
"That is what we will do."
"It mus' not happen, Luz."
"Must not? With the Princess gone, what else can we do?"
"But Tantoblin, 'e swore to come. 'e swore to bring us tidings."
"The Tantoblin will not come. I felt him die. The Black Guard found him in the night."
"You're makin' it up, Luz. Imaginin' things. Honest."
"No. I felt it inside of my heart. I felt him die."
16

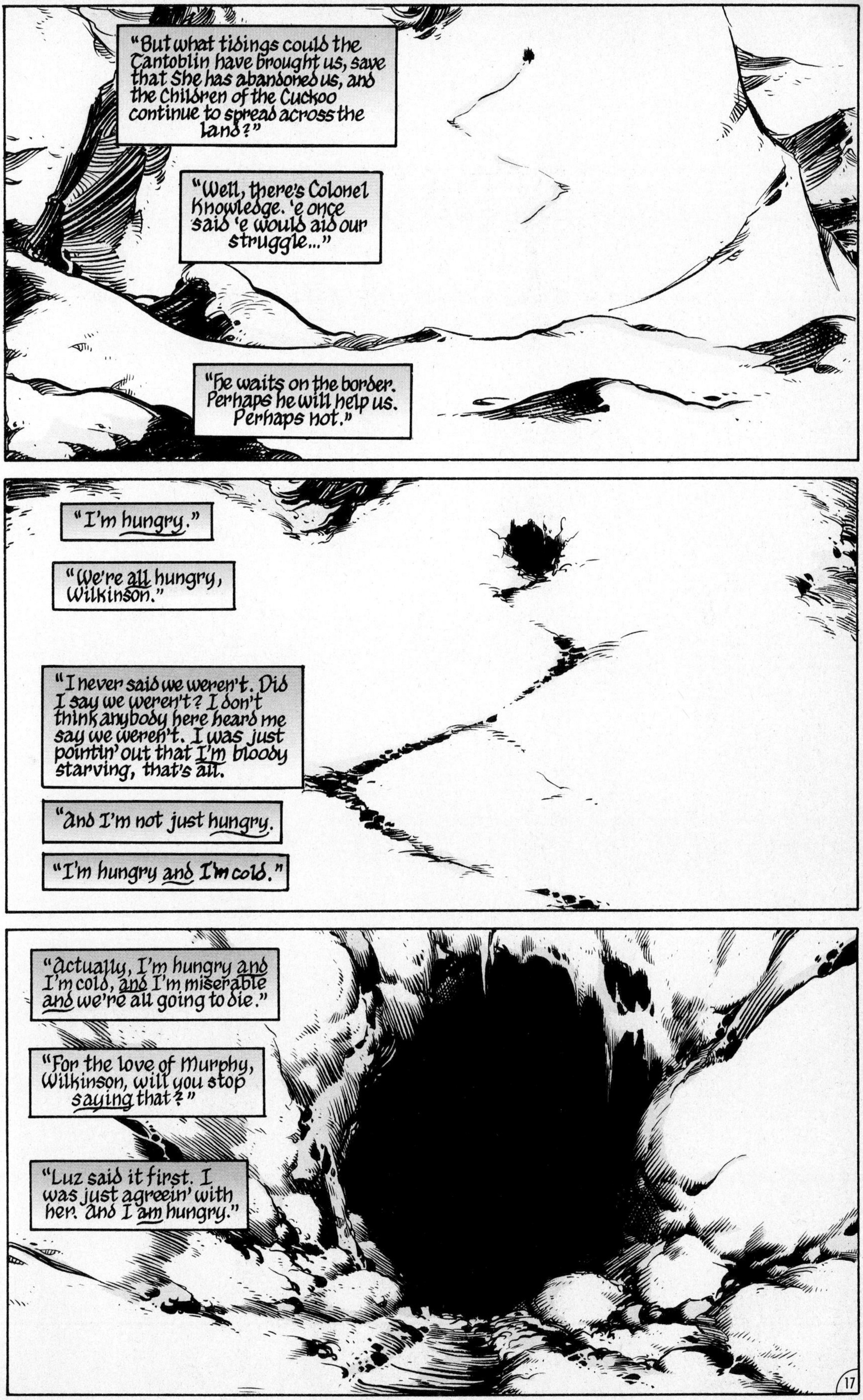
"But what tidings could the Cantoblin have brought us, save that She has abandoned us, and the Children of the Cuckoo continue to spread across the land?"
"Well, there's Colonel Knowledge. 'e once said 'e would aid our struggle..."
"He waits on the border. Perhaps he will help us. Perhaps not."
"I'm hungry."
"We're all hungry, Wilkinson."
"I never said we weren't. Did I say we weren't? I don't think anybody here heard me say we weren't. I was just pointin' out that I'm bloody starving, that's all.
"And I'm not just hungry.
"I'm hungry and I'm cold."
"Actually, I'm hungry and I'm cold, and I'm miserable and we're all going to die."
"For the love of Murphy, Wilkinson, will you stop saying that?"
"Luz said it first. I was just agreein' with her. And I am hungry."

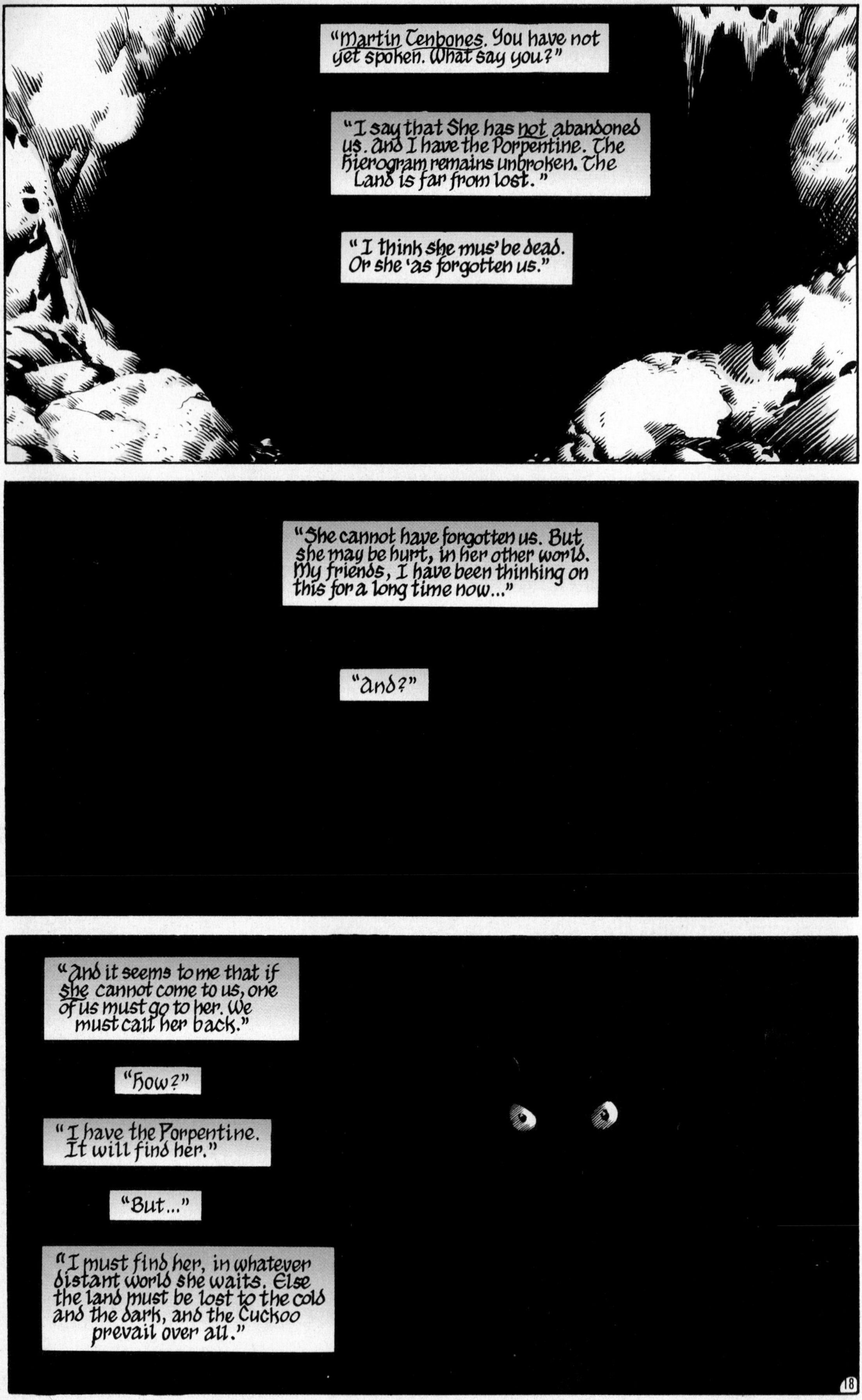
"Martin Tenbones. You have not yet spoken. What say you?"
"I say that She has not abandoned us. And I have the Porpentine. The hierogram remains unbroken. The Land is far from lost."
"I think she mus' be dead. Or she 'as forgotten us."
"She cannot have forgotten us. But she may be hurt, in her other world. My friends, I have been thinking on this for a long time now..."
"And?"
"And it seems to me that if she cannot come to us, one of us must go to her. We must call her back."
"How?"
"I have the Porpentine. It will find her."
"But..."
"I must find her, in whatever distant world she waits. Else the land must be lost to the cold and the dark, and the Cuckoo prevail over all."

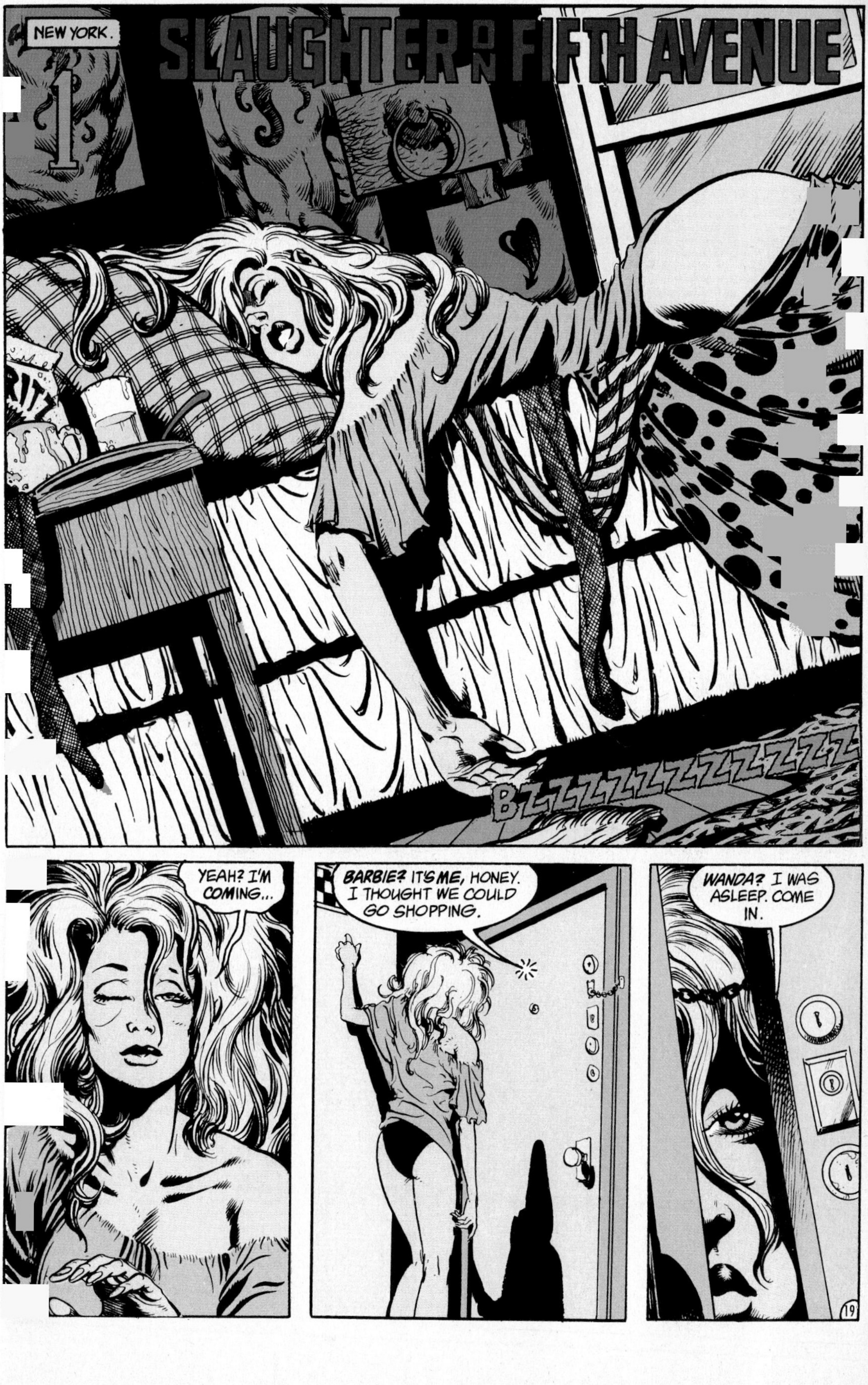
NEW YORK.
1
SLAUGHTER ON FIFTH AVENUE
BZZZZZZZZZZZZZZZ
YEAH? I'M COMING...
BARBIE? IT'S ME, HONEY. I THOUGHT WE COULD GO SHOPPING.
WANDA? I WAS ASLEEP. COME IN.

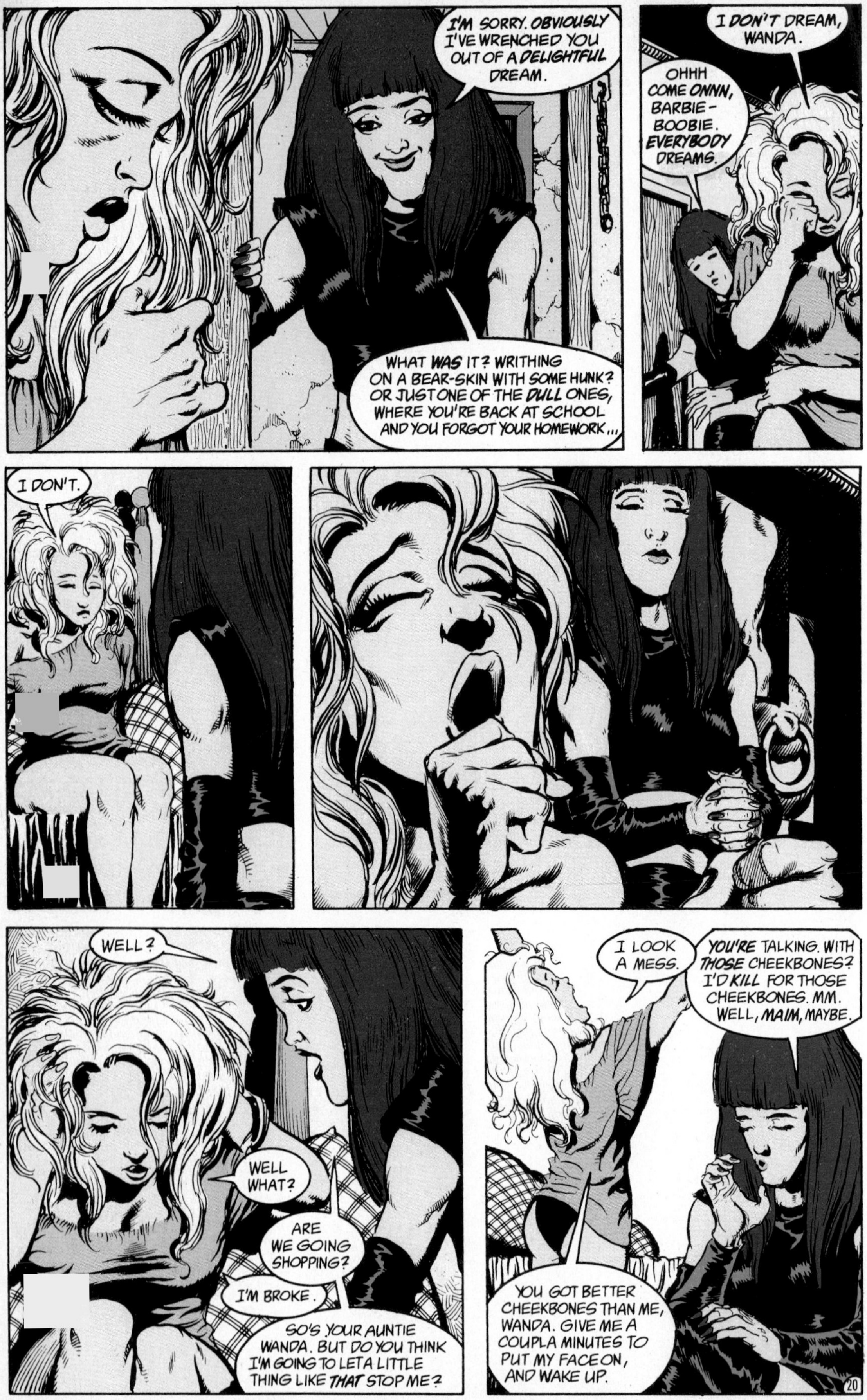
I'M SORRY. OBVIOUSLY I'VE WRENCHED YOU OUT OF A DELIGHTFUL DREAM.
WHAT WAS IT? WRITHING ON A BEAR-SKIN WITH SOME HUNK? OR JUST ONE OF THE DULL ONES, WHERE YOU'RE BACK AT SCHOOL AND YOU FORGOT YOUR HOMEWORK...
I DON'T DREAM, WANDA.
OHHH COME ONNN, BARBIE-BOOBIE. EVERYBODY DREAMS.
I DON'T.
WELL?
WELL WHAT?
ARE WE GOING SHOPPING?
I'M BROKE.
SO'S YOUR AUNTIE WANDA. BUT DO YOU THINK I'M GOING TO LET A LITTLE THING LIKE THAT STOP ME?
I LOOK A MESS.
YOU'RE TALKING. WITH THOSE CHEEKBONES? I'D KILL FOR THOSE CHEEKBONES. MM. WELL, MAIM, MAYBE.
YOU GOT BETTER CHEEKBONES THAN ME, WANDA. GIVE ME A COUPLA MINUTES TO PUT MY FACE ON, AND WAKE UP.
20

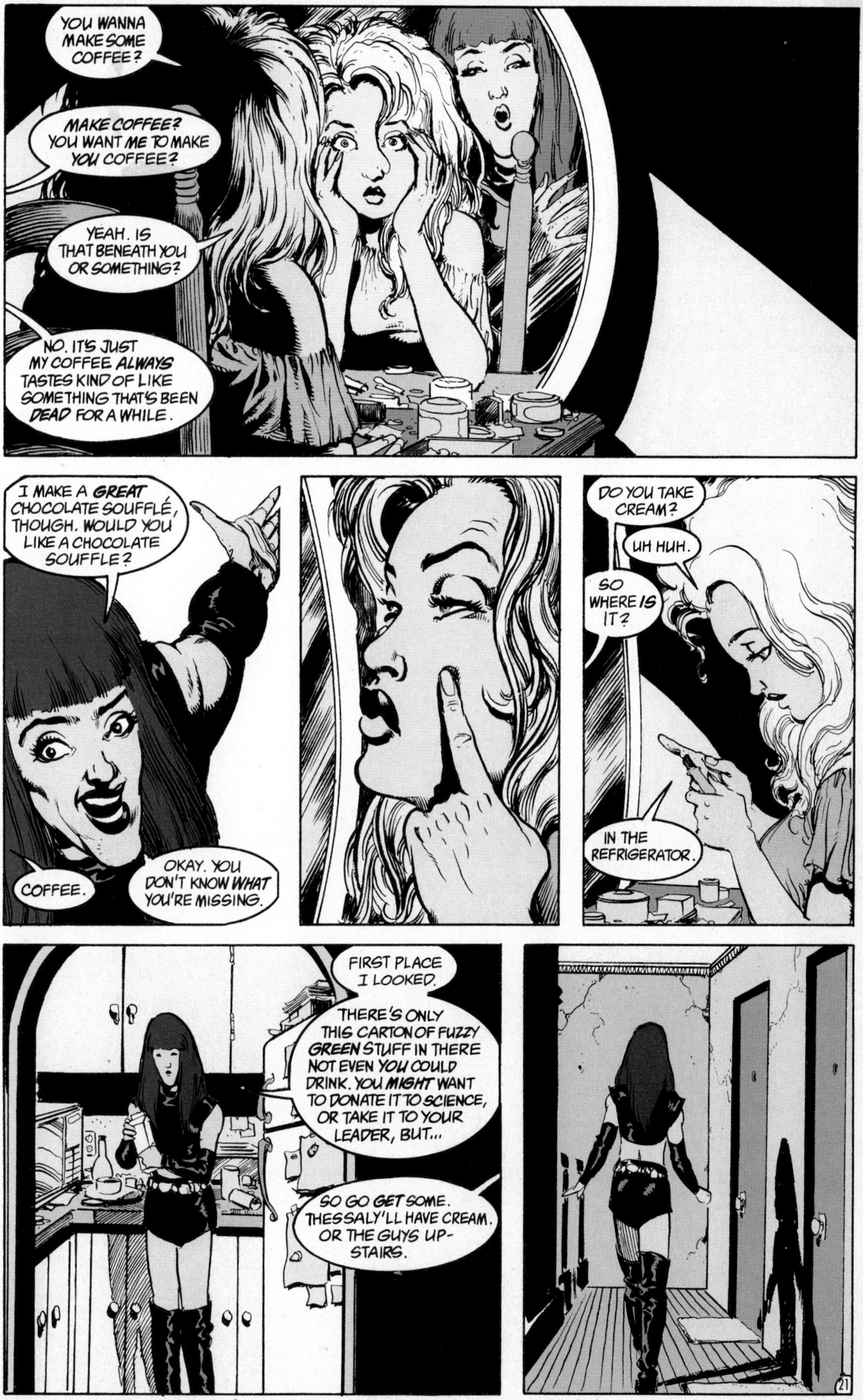
YOU WANNA MAKE SOME COFFEE?
MAKE COFFEE? YOU WANT ME TO MAKE YOU COFFEE?
YEAH. IS THAT BENEATH YOU OR SOMETHING?
NO. IT'S JUST MY COFFEE ALWAYS TASTES KIND OF LIKE SOMETHING THAT'S BEEN DEAD FOR A WHILE.
I MAKE A GREAT CHOCOLATE SOUFFLÉ, THOUGH. WOULD YOU LIKE A CHOCOLATE SOUFFLE?
COFFEE.
OKAY. YOU DON'T KNOW WHAT YOU'RE MISSING.
DO YOU TAKE CREAM?
UH HUH.
SO WHERE IS IT?
IN THE REFRIGERATOR.
FIRST PLACE I LOOKED.
THERE'S ONLY THIS CARTON OF FUZZY GREEN STUFF IN THERE NOT EVEN YOU COULD DRINK. YOU MIGHT WANT TO DONATE IT TO SCIENCE, OR TAKE IT TO YOUR LEADER, BUT...
SO GO GET SOME. THESSALY'LL HAVE CREAM. OR THE GUYS UP-STAIRS.

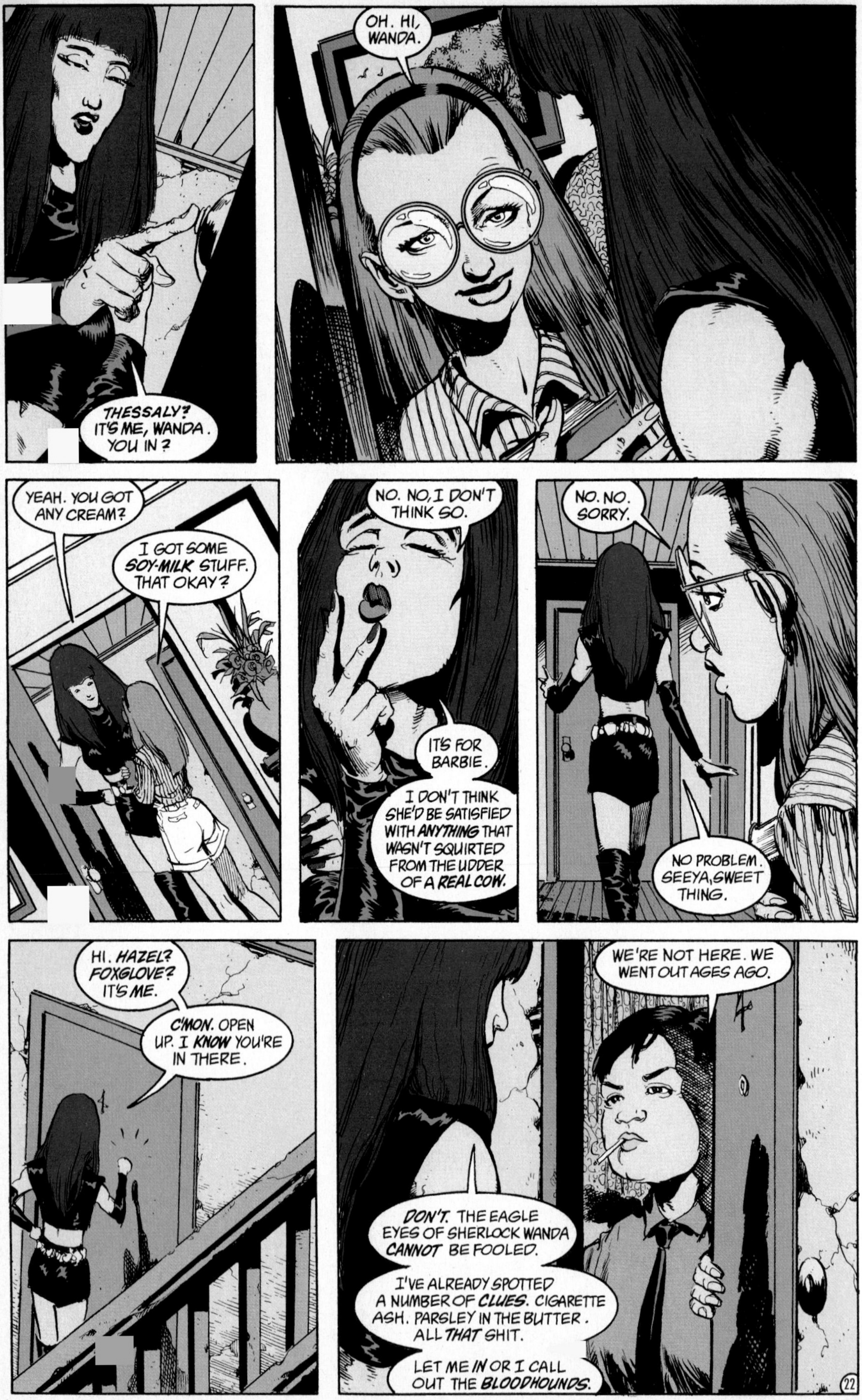

THESSALY? IT'S ME, WANDA. YOU IN?
OH. HI, WANDA.
YEAH. YOU GOT ANY CREAM?
I GOT SOME SOY-MILK STUFF. THAT OKAY?
NO. NO, I DON'T THINK SO.
IT'S FOR BARBIE.
I DON'T THINK SHE'D BE SATISFIED WITH ANYTHING THAT WASN'T SQUIRTED FROM THE UDDER OF A REAL COW.
NO. NO. SORRY.
NO PROBLEM. SEEYA, SWEET THING.
HI. HAZEL? FOXGLOVE? IT'S ME.
C'MON. OPEN UP. I KNOW YOU'RE IN THERE.
WE'RE NOT HERE. WE WENT OUT AGES AGO.
DON'T. THE EAGLE EYES OF SHERLOCK WANDA CANNOT BE FOOLED.
I'VE ALREADY SPOTTED A NUMBER OF CLUES. CIGARETTE ASH. PARSLEY IN THE BUTTER. ALL THAT SHIT.
LET ME IN OR I CALL OUT THE BLOODHOUNDS.
22

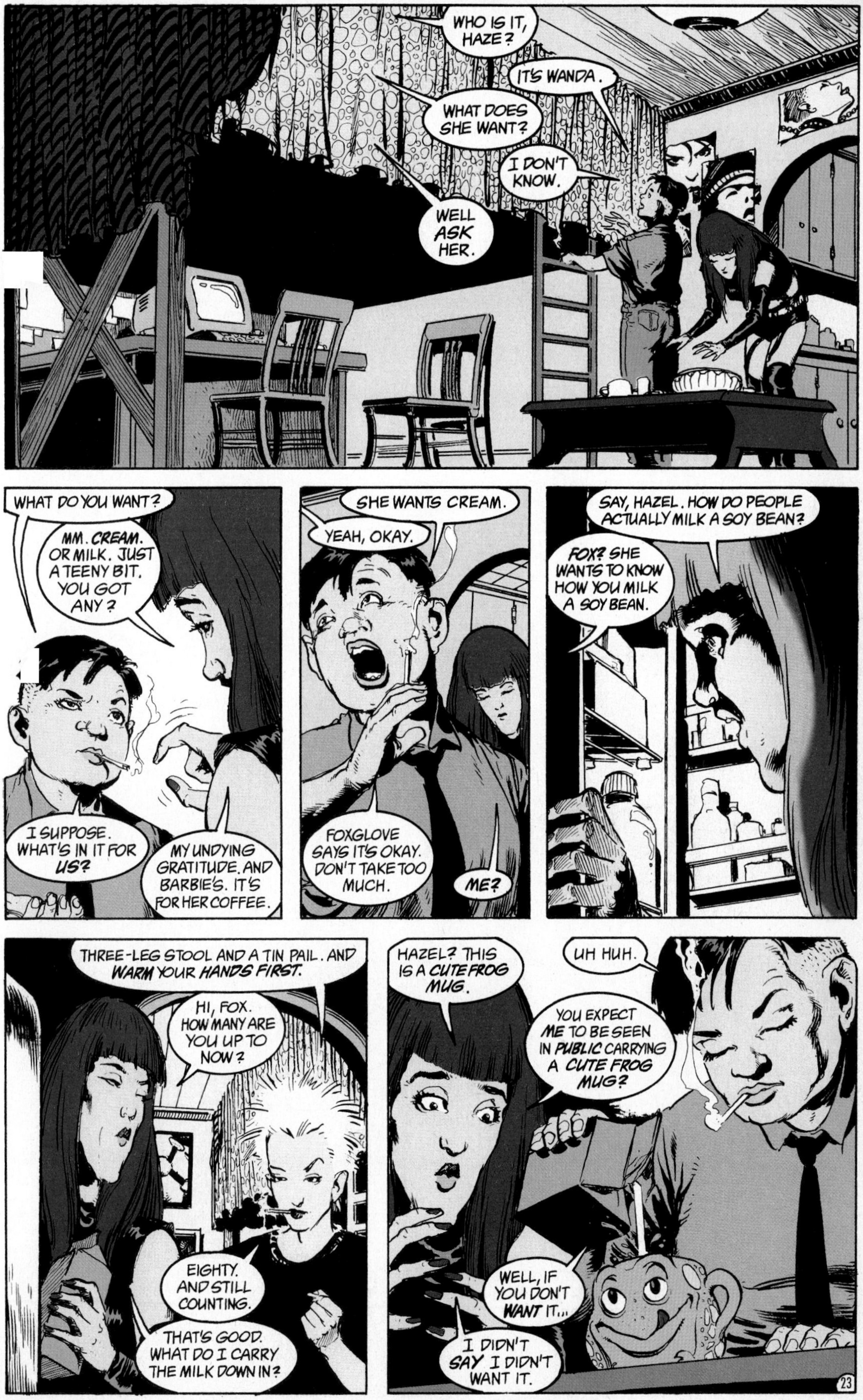
WHO IS IT, HAZE?
IT'S WANDA.
WHAT DOES SHE WANT?
I DON'T KNOW.
WELL ASK HER.
WHAT DO YOU WANT?
MM. CREAM. OR MILK. JUST A TEENY BIT. YOU GOT ANY?
I SUPPOSE. WHAT'S IN IT FOR US?
MY UNDYING GRATITUDE. AND BARBIE'S. IT'S FOR HER COFFEE.
SHE WANTS CREAM.
YEAH, OKAY.
FOXGLOVE SAYS IT'S OKAY. DON'T TAKE TOO MUCH.
ME?
SAY, HAZEL. HOW DO PEOPLE ACTUALLY MILK A SOY BEAN?
FOX? SHE WANTS TO KNOW HOW YOU MILK A SOY BEAN.
THREE-LEG STOOL AND A TIN PAIL. AND WARM YOUR HANDS FIRST.
HI, FOX. HOW MANY ARE YOU UP TO NOW?
EIGHTY. AND STILL COUNTING.
THAT'S GOOD. WHAT DO I CARRY THE MILK DOWN IN?
HAZEL? THIS IS A CUTE FROG MUG.
UH HUH.
YOU EXPECT ME TO BE SEEN IN PUBLIC CARRYING A CUTE FROG MUG?
WELL, IF YOU DON'T WANT IT...
I DIDN'T SAY I DIDN'T WANT IT.

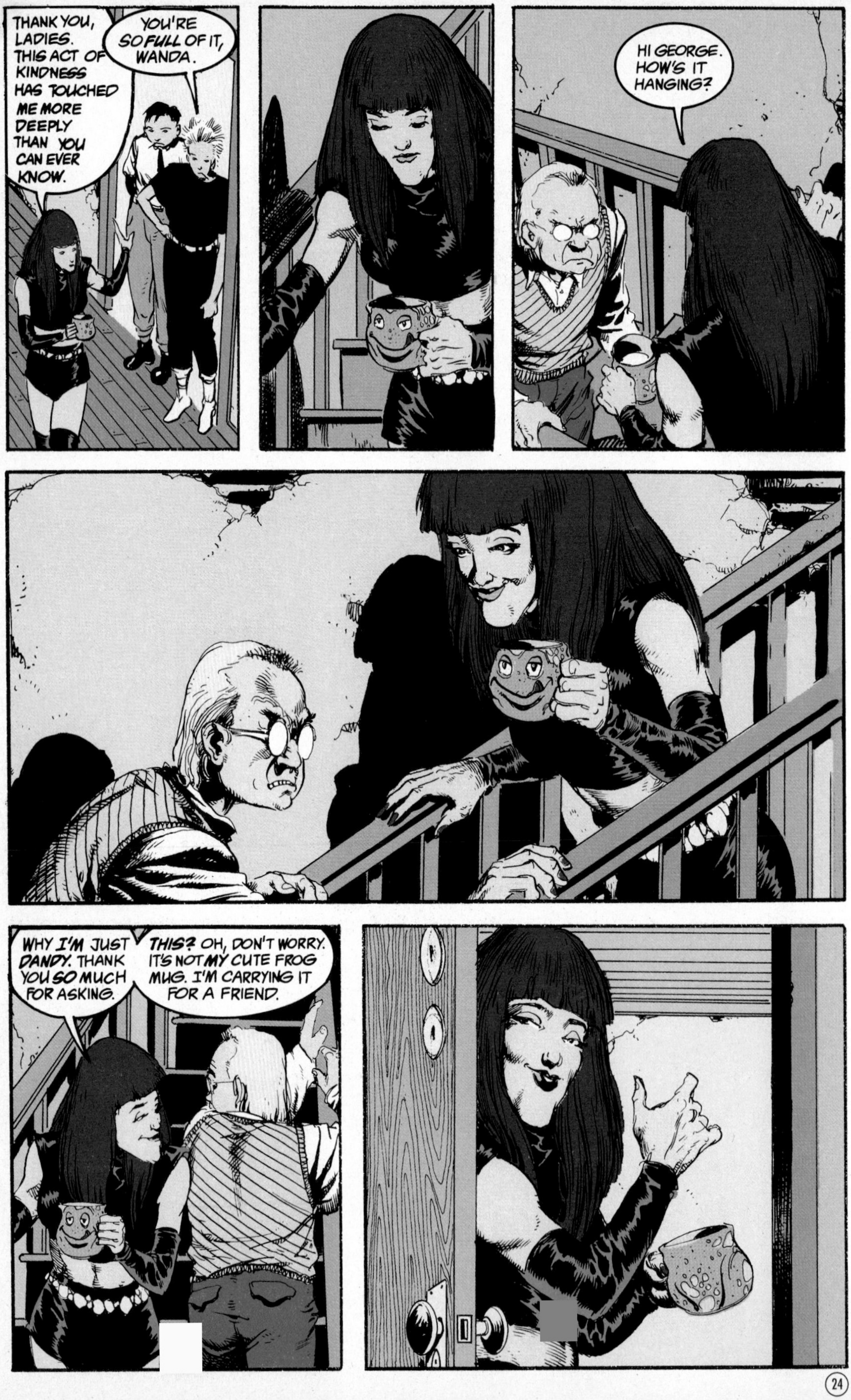
THANK YOU, LADIES. THIS ACT OF KINDNESS HAS TOUCHED ME MORE DEEPLY THAN YOU CAN EVER KNOW.
YOU'RE SO FULL OF IT, WANDA.
HI GEORGE. HOW'S IT HANGING?
WHY I'M JUST DANDY. THANK YOU SO MUCH FOR ASKING.
THIS? OH, DON'T WORRY. IT'S NOT MY CUTE FROG MUG. I'M CARRYING IT FOR A FRIEND.

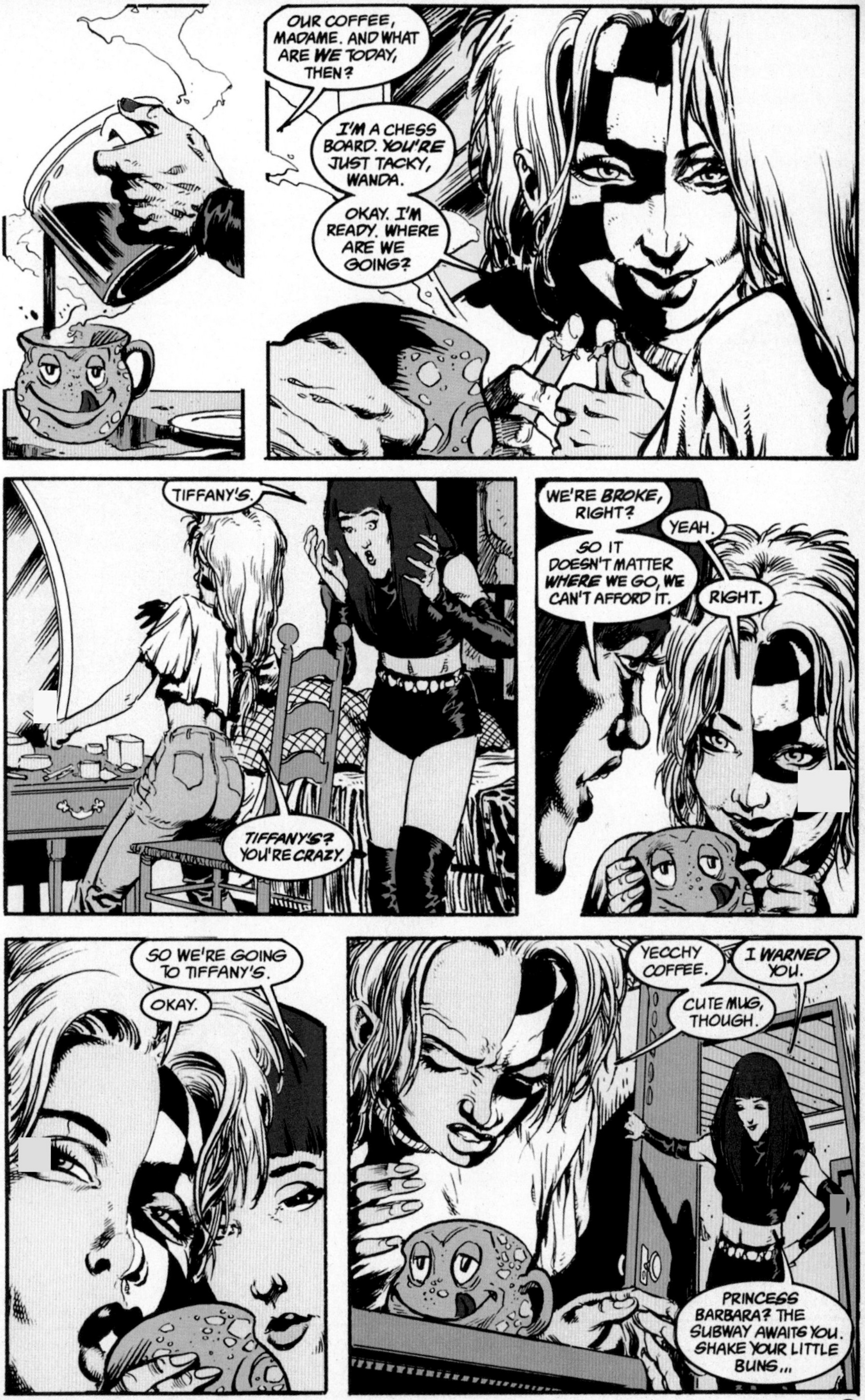
OUR COFFEE, MADAME. AND WHAT ARE WE TODAY, THEN?
I'M A CHESS BOARD. YOU'RE JUST TACKY, WANDA.
OKAY. I'M READY. WHERE ARE WE GOING?
TIFFANY'S.
TIFFANY'S? YOU'RE CRAZY.
WE'RE BROKE, RIGHT?
YEAH.
SO IT DOESN'T MATTER WHERE WE GO, WE CAN'T AFFORD IT.
RIGHT.
SO WE'RE GOING TO TIFFANY'S.
OKAY.
YECCHY COFFEE.
I WARNED YOU.
CUTE MUG, THOUGH.
PRINCESS BARBARA? THE SUBWAY AWAITS YOU. SHAKE YOUR LITTLE BUNS...

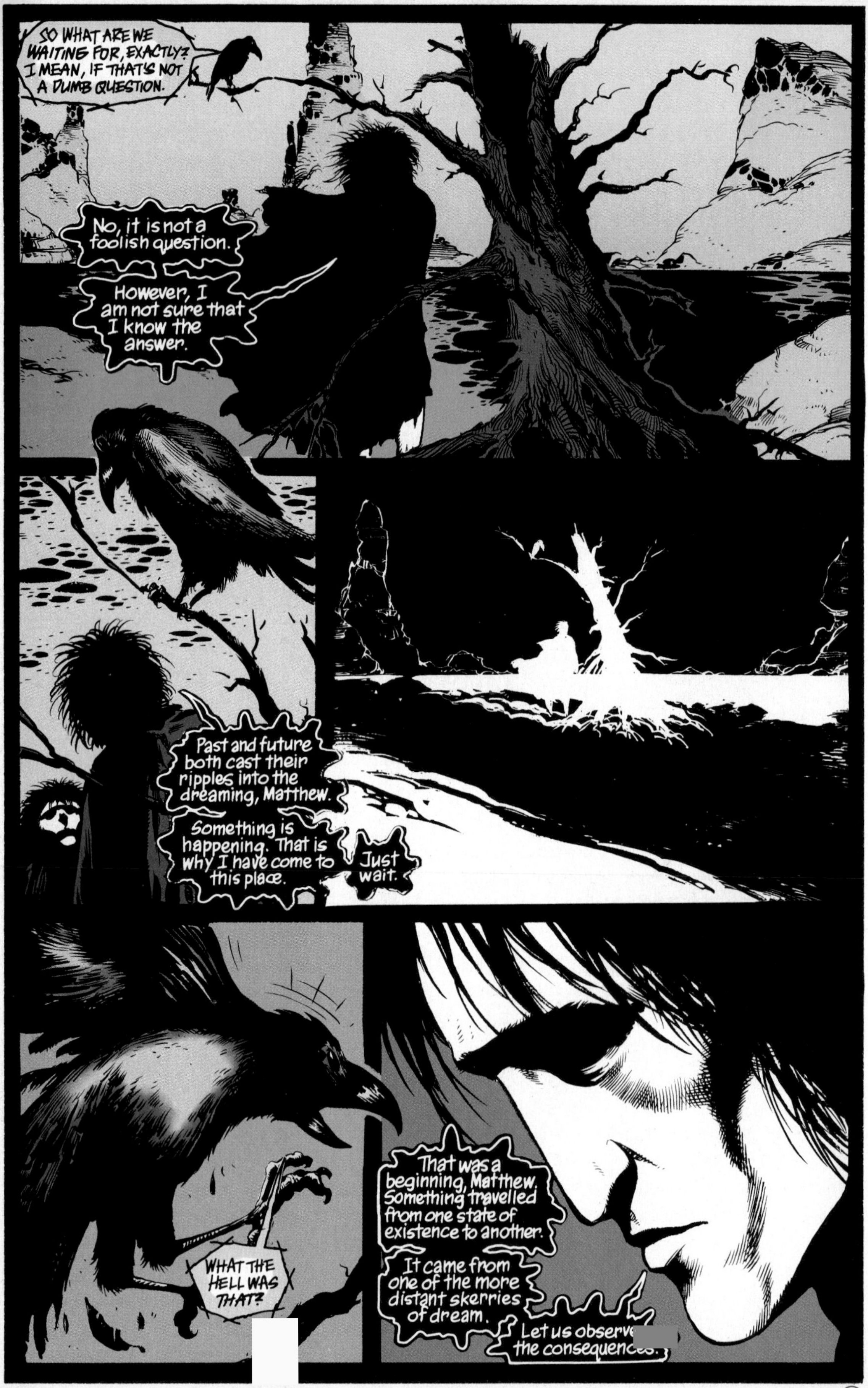
SO WHAT ARE WE WAITING FOR, EXACTLY? I MEAN, IF THAT'S NOT A DUMB QUESTION.
No, it is not a foolish question.
However, I am not sure that I know the answer.
Past and future both cast their ripples into the dreaming, Matthew.
Something is happening. That is why I have come to this place.
Just wait.
WHAT THE HELL WAS THAT?
That was a beginning, Matthew. Something travelled from one state of existence to another.
It came from one of the more distant skerries of dream.
Let us observe the consequences.

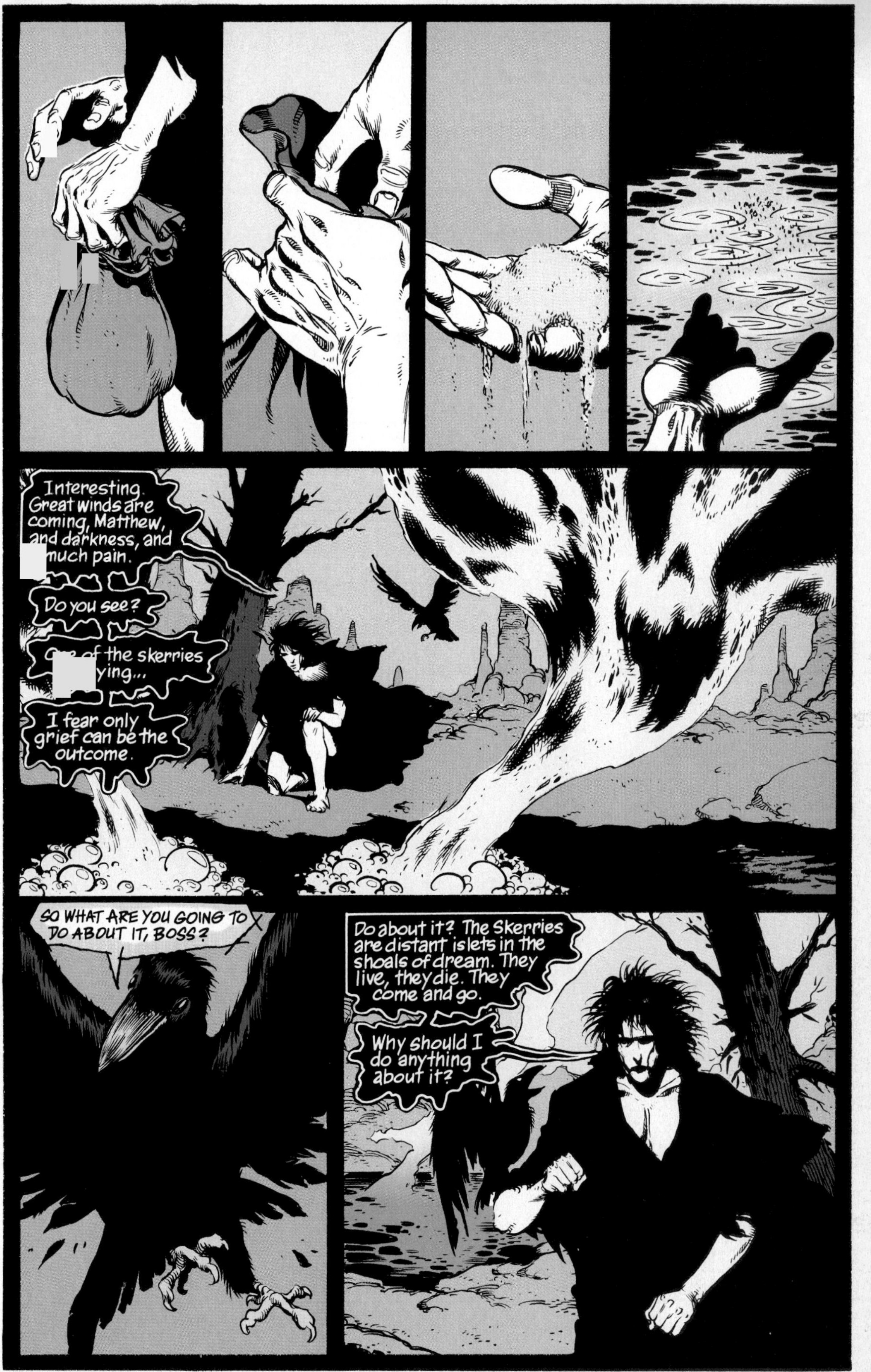
Interesting. Great winds are coming, Matthew, and darkness, and much pain.
Do you see?
of the skerries ying...
I fear only grief can be the outcome.
SO WHAT ARE YOU GOING TO DO ABOUT IT, BOSS?
Do about it? The Skerries are distant islets in the shoals of dream. They live, they die. They come and go.
Why should I do anything about it?

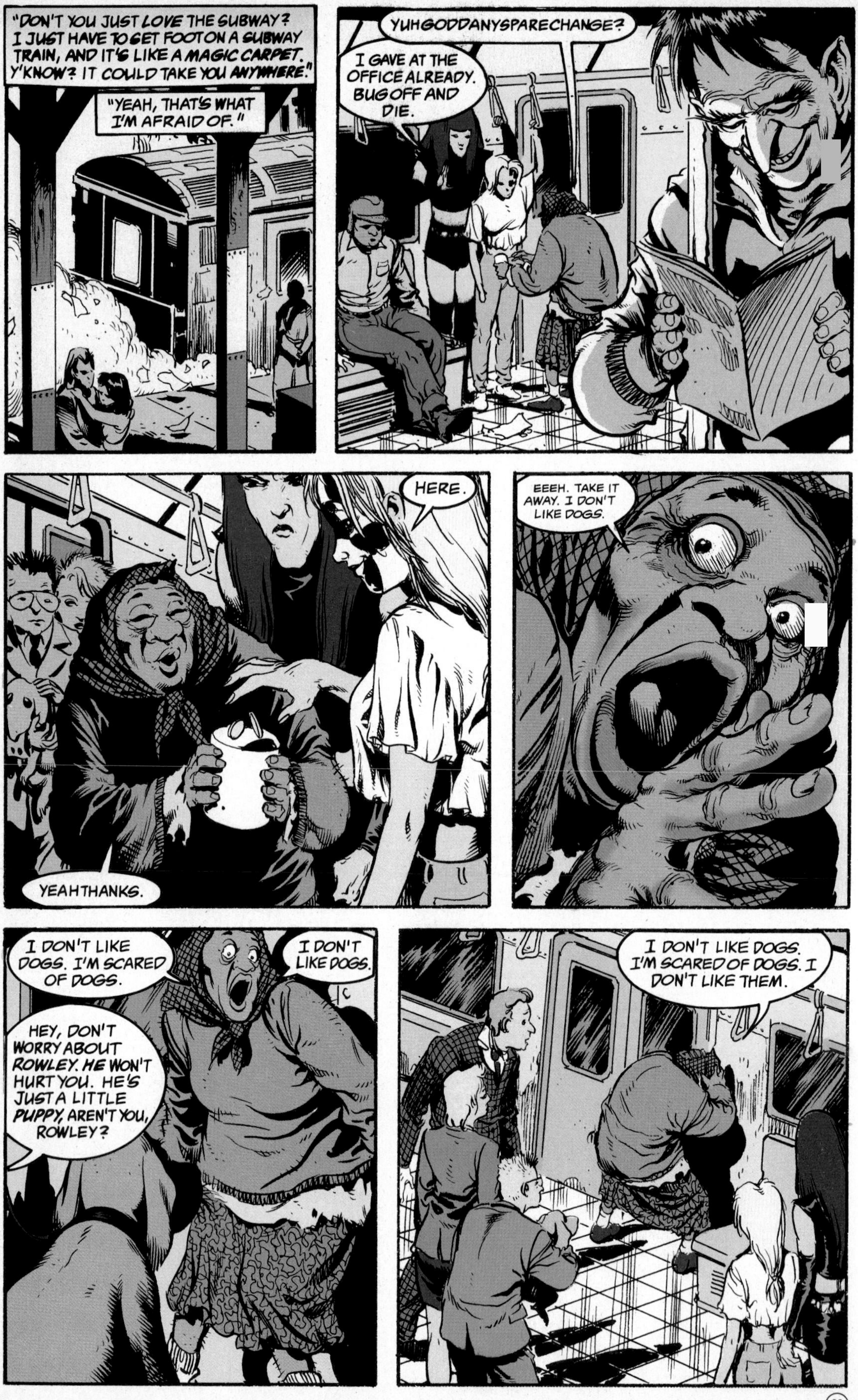

"DON'T YOU JUST LOVE THE SUBWAY? I JUST HAVE TO GET FOOT ON A SUBWAY TRAIN, AND IT'S LIKE A MAGIC CARPET. Y'KNOW? IT COULD TAKE YOU ANYWHERE."
"YEAH, THAT'S WHAT I'M AFRAID OF."
YUHGODDANYSPARECHANGE?
I GAVE AT THE OFFICE ALREADY. BUG OFF AND DIE.
HERE.
YEAHTHANKS.
EEEH. TAKE IT AWAY. I DON'T LIKE DOGS.
I DON'T LIKE DOGS. I'M SCARED OF DOGS.
I DON'T LIKE DOGS.
HEY, DON'T WORRY ABOUT ROWLEY. HE WON'T HURT YOU. HE'S JUST A LITTLE PUPPY, AREN'T YOU, ROWLEY?
I DON'T LIKE DOGS. I'M SCARED OF DOGS. I DON'T LIKE THEM.

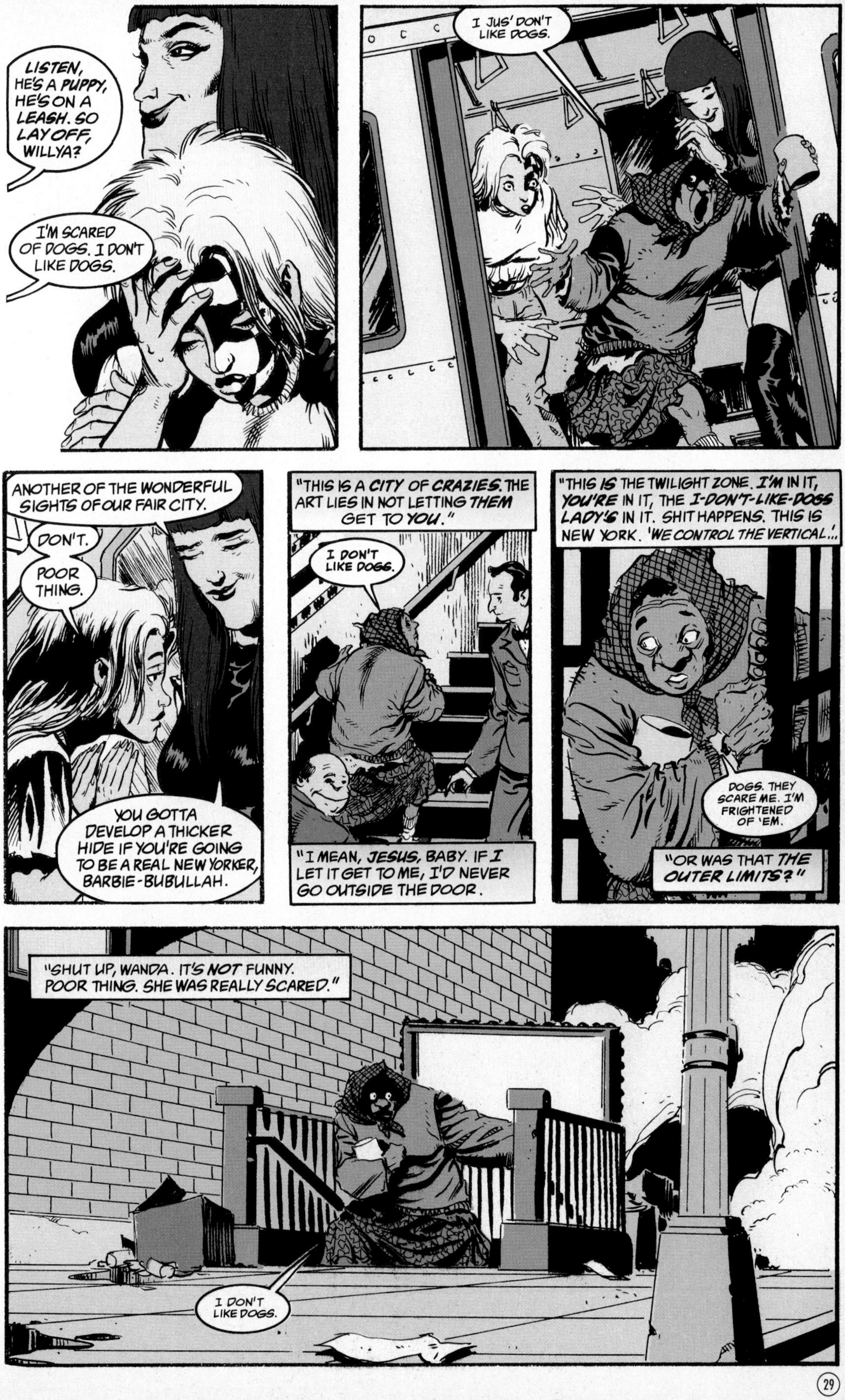
LISTEN, HE'S A PUPPY, HE'S ON A LEASH. SO LAY OFF, WILLYA?
I'M SCARED OF DOGS. I DON'T LIKE DOGS.
I JUS' DON'T LIKE DOGS.
ANOTHER OF THE WONDERFUL SIGHTS OF OUR FAIR CITY.
DON'T.
POOR THING.
YOU GOTTA DEVELOP A THICKER HIDE IF YOU'RE GOING TO BE A REAL NEW YORKER, BARBIE-BUBULLAH.
"THIS IS A CITY OF CRAZIES. THE ART LIES IN NOT LETTING THEM GET TO YOU."
I DON'T LIKE DOGS.
"I MEAN, JESUS, BABY. IF I LET IT GET TO ME, I'D NEVER GO OUTSIDE THE DOOR.
"THIS IS THE TWILIGHT ZONE. I'M IN IT, YOU'RE IN IT, THE I-DON'T-LIKE-DOGS LADY'S IN IT. SHIT HAPPENS. THIS IS NEW YORK. 'WE CONTROL THE VERTICAL'...
DOGS. THEY SCARE ME. I'M FRIGHTENED OF 'EM.
"OR WAS THAT THE OUTER LIMITS?"
"SHUT UP, WANDA. IT'S NOT FUNNY. POOR THING. SHE WAS REALLY SCARED."
I DON'T LIKE DOGS.

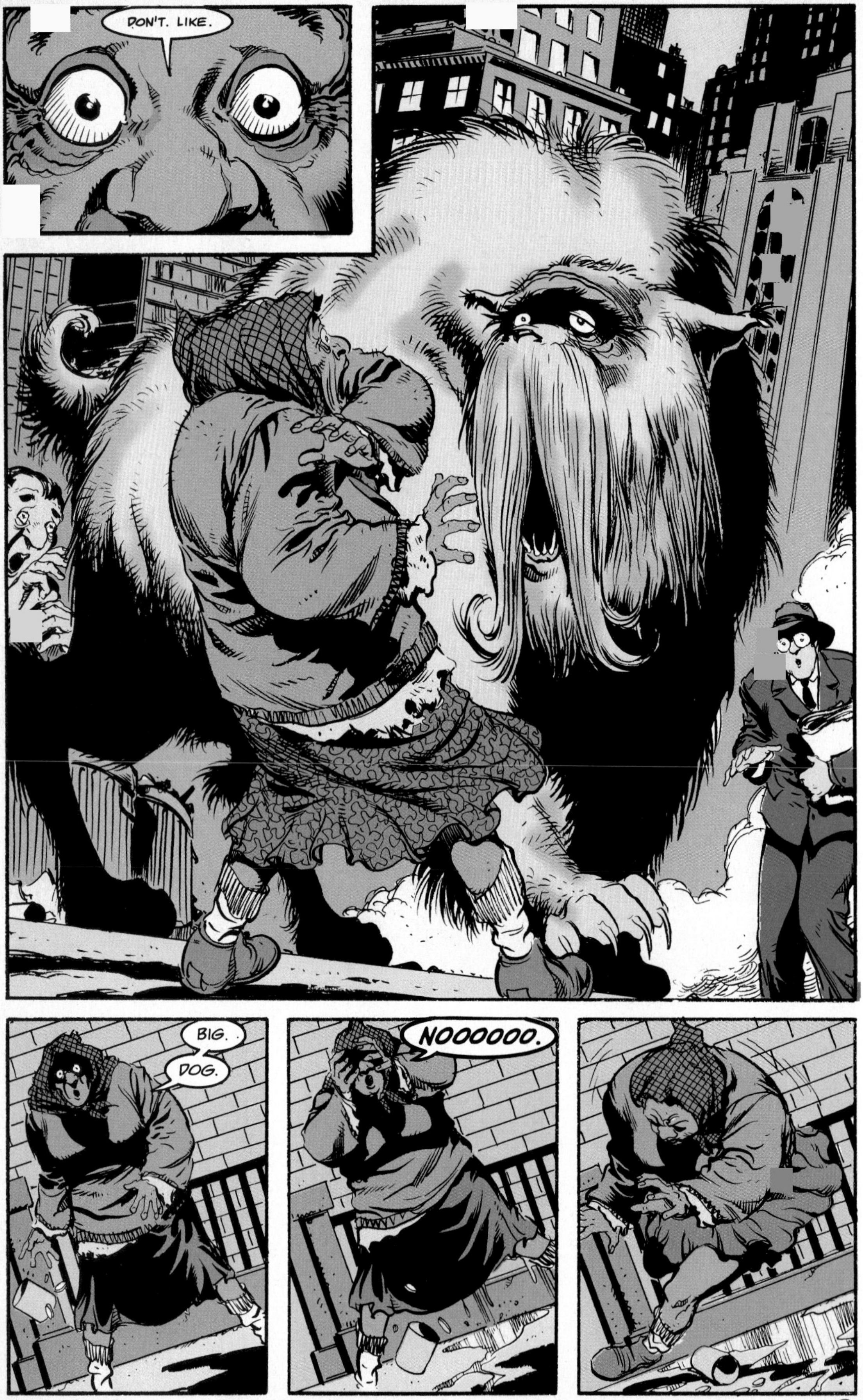
DON'T. LIKE.
BIG.
DOG.
NOOOOOO.

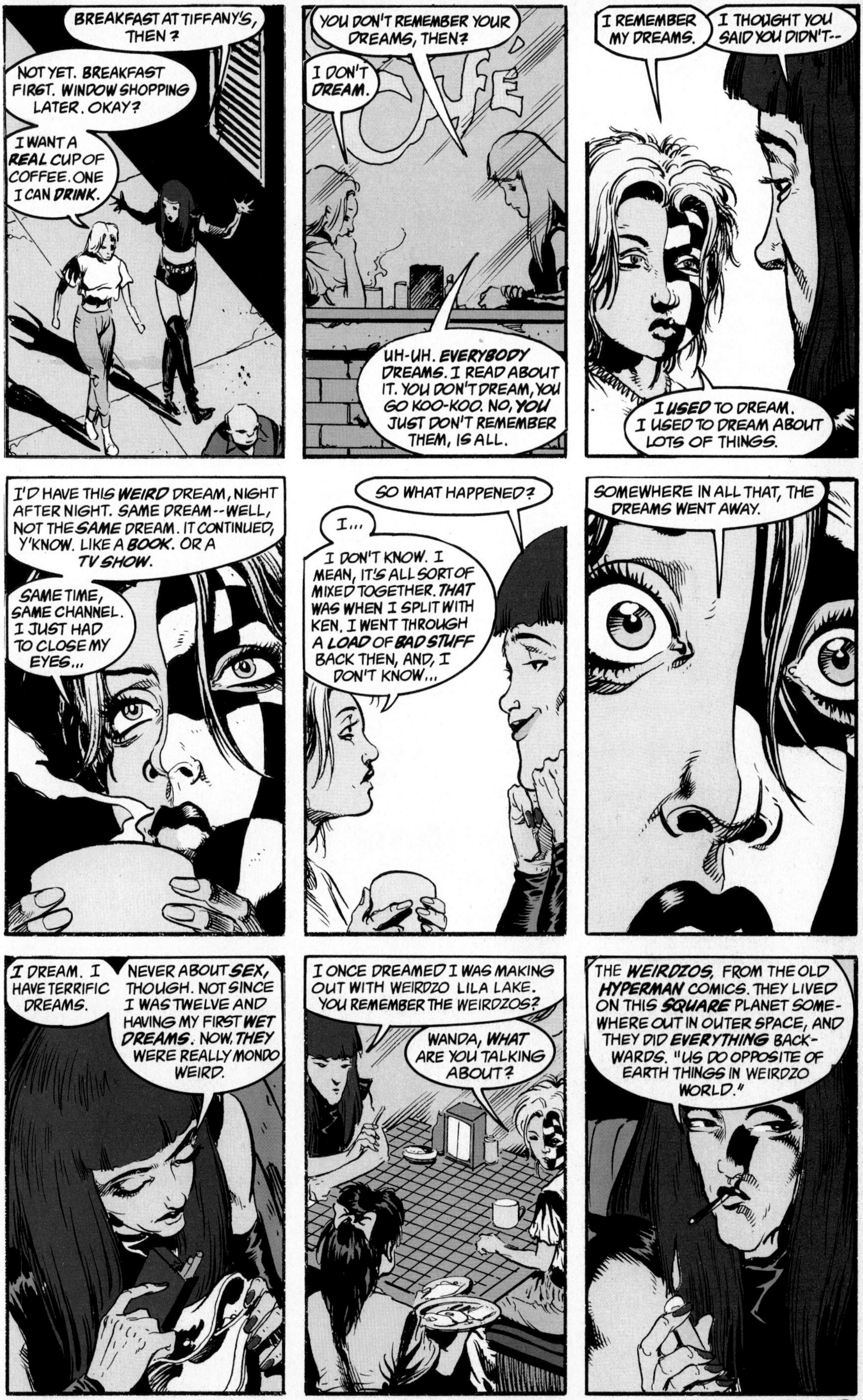
BREAKFAST AT TIFFANY'S, THEN?
NOT YET. BREAKFAST FIRST. WINDOW SHOPPING LATER. OKAY?
I WANT A REAL CUP OF COFFEE. ONE I CAN DRINK.
YOU DON'T REMEMBER YOUR DREAMS, THEN?
I DON'T DREAM.
CAFE
UH-UH. EVERYBODY DREAMS. I READ ABOUT IT. YOU DON'T DREAM, YOU GO KOO-KOO. NO, YOU JUST DON'T REMEMBER THEM, IS ALL.
I REMEMBER MY DREAMS.
I THOUGHT YOU SAID YOU DIDN'T--
I USED TO DREAM. I USED TO DREAM ABOUT LOTS OF THINGS.
I'D HAVE THIS WEIRD DREAM, NIGHT AFTER NIGHT. SAME DREAM--WELL, NOT THE SAME DREAM. IT CONTINUED, Y'KNOW. LIKE A BOOK. OR A TV SHOW.
SAME TIME, SAME CHANNEL. I JUST HAD TO CLOSE MY EYES...
SO WHAT HAPPENED?
I...
I DON'T KNOW. I MEAN, IT'S ALL SORT OF MIXED TOGETHER. THAT WAS WHEN I SPLIT WITH KEN. I WENT THROUGH A LOAD OF BAD STUFF BACK THEN, AND, I DON'T KNOW...
SOMEWHERE IN ALL THAT, THE DREAMS WENT AWAY.
I DREAM. I HAVE TERRIFIC DREAMS.
NEVER ABOUT SEX, THOUGH. NOT SINCE I WAS TWELVE AND HAVING MY FIRST WET DREAMS. NOW, THEY WERE REALLY MONDO WEIRD.
I ONCE DREAMED I WAS MAKING OUT WITH WEIRDZO LILA LAKE. YOU REMEMBER THE WEIRDZOS?
WANDA, WHAT ARE YOU TALKING ABOUT?
THE WEIRDZOS, FROM THE OLD HYPERMAN COMICS. THEY LIVED ON THIS SQUARE PLANET SOMEWHERE OUT IN OUTER SPACE, AND THEY DID EVERYTHING BACKWARDS. "US DO OPPOSITE OF EARTH THINGS IN WEIRDZO WORLD."

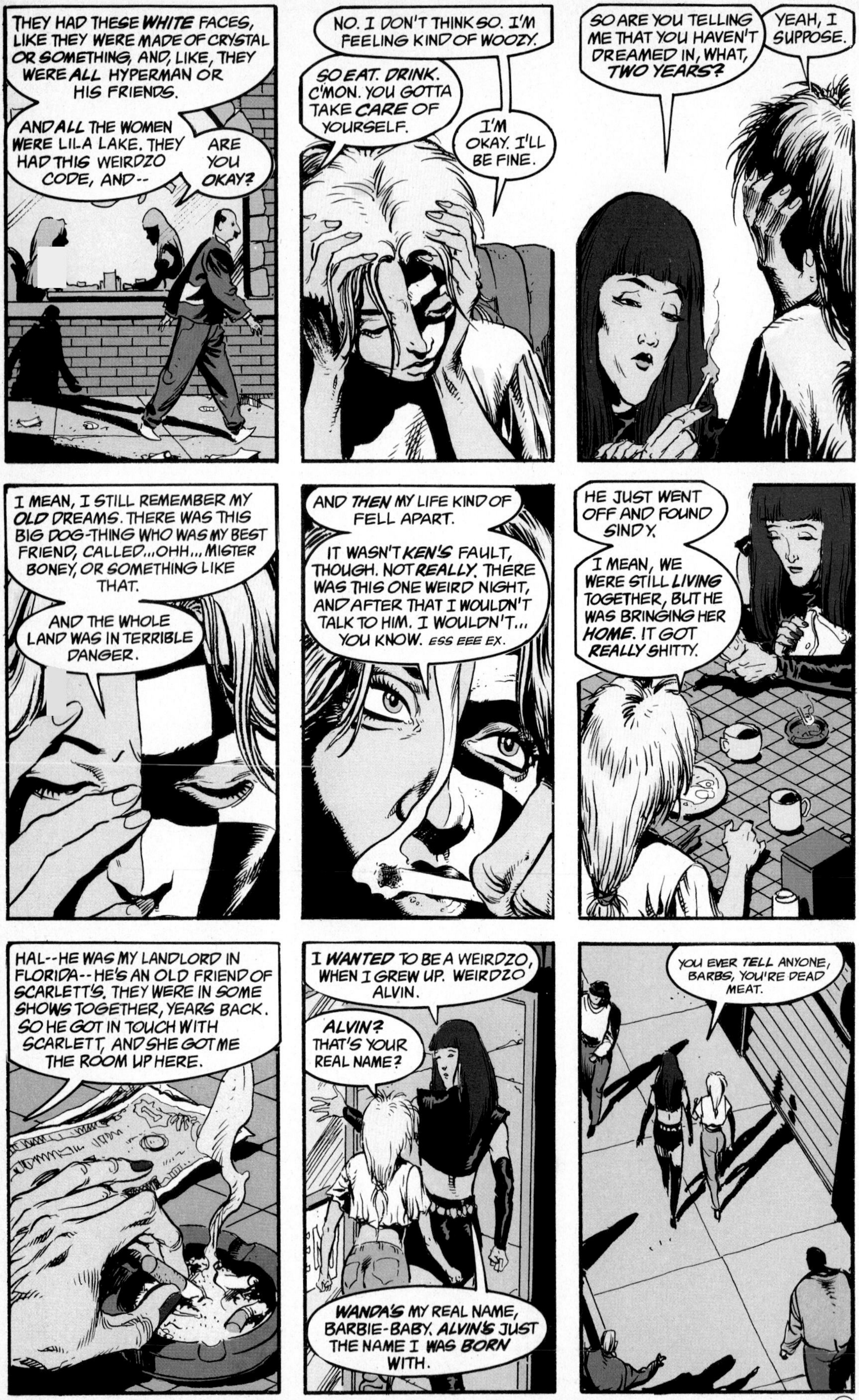
THEY HAD THESE WHITE FACES, LIKE THEY WERE MADE OF CRYSTAL OR SOMETHING, AND, LIKE, THEY WERE ALL HYPERMAN OR HIS FRIENDS.
AND ALL THE WOMEN WERE LILA LAKE. THEY HAD THIS WEIRDZO CODE, AND--
ARE YOU OKAY?
NO. I DON'T THINK SO. I'M FEELING KIND OF WOOZY.
SO EAT. DRINK. C'MON. YOU GOTTA TAKE CARE OF YOURSELF.
I'M OKAY. I'LL BE FINE.
SO ARE YOU TELLING ME THAT YOU HAVEN'T DREAMED IN, WHAT, TWO YEARS?
YEAH, I SUPPOSE.
I MEAN, I STILL REMEMBER MY OLD DREAMS. THERE WAS THIS BIG DOG-THING WHO WAS MY BEST FRIEND, CALLED...OHH... MISTER BONEY, OR SOMETHING LIKE THAT.
AND THE WHOLE LAND WAS IN TERRIBLE DANGER.
AND THEN MY LIFE KIND OF FELL APART.
IT WASN'T KEN'S FAULT, THOUGH. NOT REALLY. THERE WAS THIS ONE WEIRD NIGHT, AND AFTER THAT I WOULDN'T TALK TO HIM. I WOULDN'T... YOU KNOW. ESS EEE EX.
HE JUST WENT OFF AND FOUND SINDY.
I MEAN, WE WERE STILL LIVING TOGETHER, BUT HE WAS BRINGING HER HOME. IT GOT REALLY SHITTY.
HAL--HE WAS MY LANDLORD IN FLORIDA--HE'S AN OLD FRIEND OF SCARLETT'S. THEY WERE IN SOME SHOWS TOGETHER, YEARS BACK. SO HE GOT IN TOUCH WITH SCARLETT, AND SHE GOT ME THE ROOM UP HERE.
I WANTED TO BE A WEIRDZO, WHEN I GREW UP. WEIRDZO ALVIN.
ALVIN? THAT'S YOUR REAL NAME?
WANDA'S MY REAL NAME, BARBIE-BABY. ALVIN'S JUST THE NAME I WAS BORN WITH.
YOU EVER TELL ANYONE, BARBS, YOU'RE DEAD MEAT.

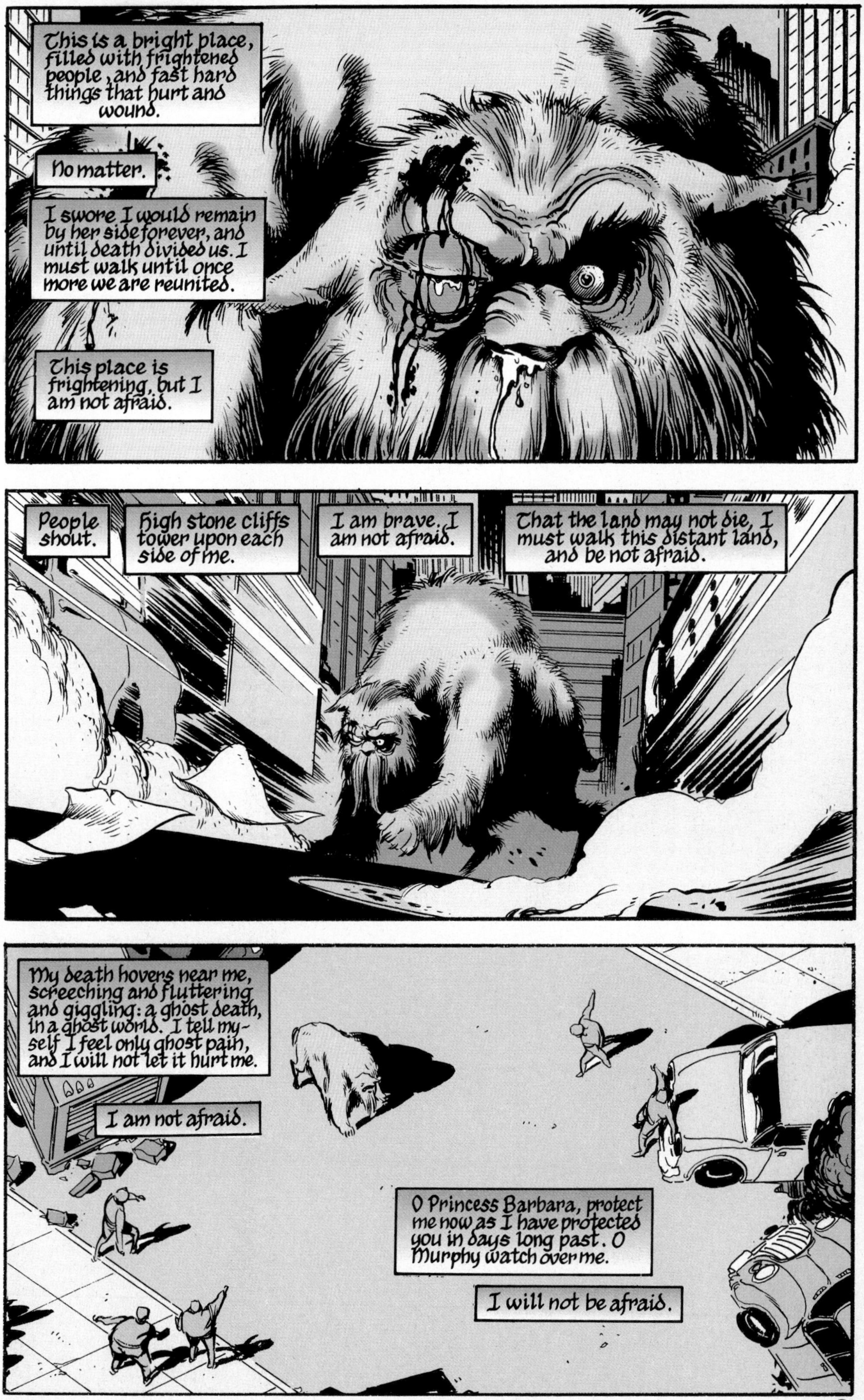
This is a bright place, filled with frightened people, and fast hard things that hurt and wound.
No matter.
I swore I would remain by her side forever, and until death divided us. I must walk until once more we are reunited.
This place is frightening, but I am not afraid.
People shout.
High stone cliffs tower upon each side of me.
I am brave. I am not afraid.
That the land may not die, I must walk this distant land, and be not afraid.
My death hovers near me, screeching and fluttering and giggling: a ghost death, in a ghost world. I tell myself I feel only ghost pain, and I will not let it hurt me.
I am not afraid.
O Princess Barbara, protect me now as I have protected you in days long past. O Murphy watch over me.
I will not be afraid.

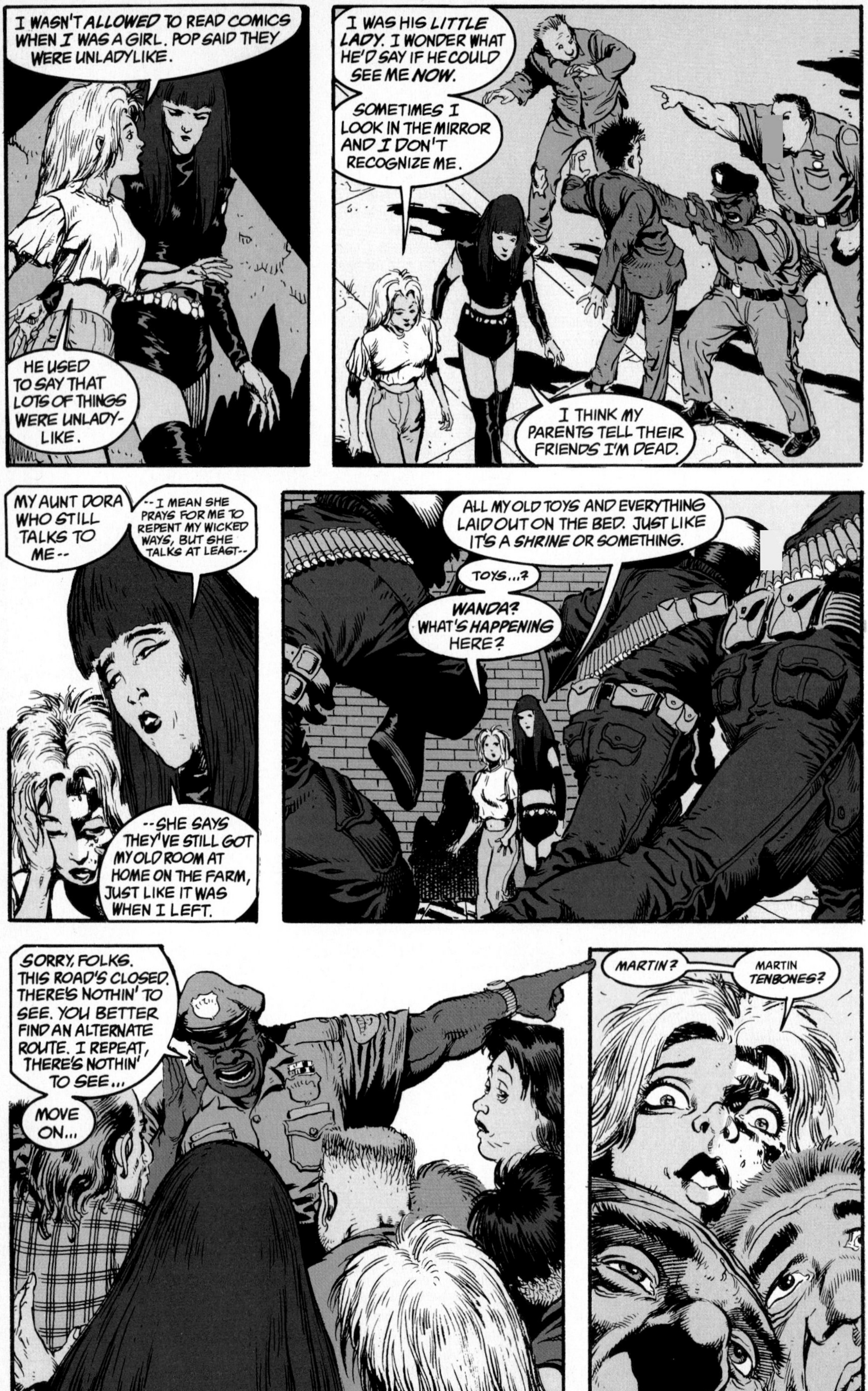
I WASN'T ALLOWED TO READ COMICS WHEN I WAS A GIRL. POP SAID THEY WERE UNLADYLIKE.
HE USED TO SAY THAT LOTS OF THINGS WERE UNLADY-LIKE.
I WAS HIS LITTLE LADY. I WONDER WHAT HE'D SAY IF HE COULD SEE ME NOW.
SOMETIMES I LOOK IN THE MIRROR AND I DON'T RECOGNIZE ME.
I THINK MY PARENTS TELL THEIR FRIENDS I'M DEAD.
MY AUNT DORA WHO STILL TALKS TO ME--
--I MEAN SHE PRAYS FOR ME TO REPENT MY WICKED WAYS, BUT SHE TALKS AT LEAST--
--SHE SAYS THEY'VE STILL GOT MY OLD ROOM AT HOME ON THE FARM, JUST LIKE IT WAS WHEN I LEFT.
ALL MY OLD TOYS AND EVERYTHING LAID OUT ON THE BED. JUST LIKE IT'S A SHRINE OR SOMETHING.
TOYS...?
WANDA? WHAT'S HAPPENING HERE?
SORRY, FOLKS. THIS ROAD'S CLOSED. THERE'S NOTHIN' TO SEE. YOU BETTER FIND AN ALTERNATE ROUTE. I REPEAT, THERE'S NOTHIN' TO SEE...
MOVE ON...
MARTIN?
MARTIN TENBONES?

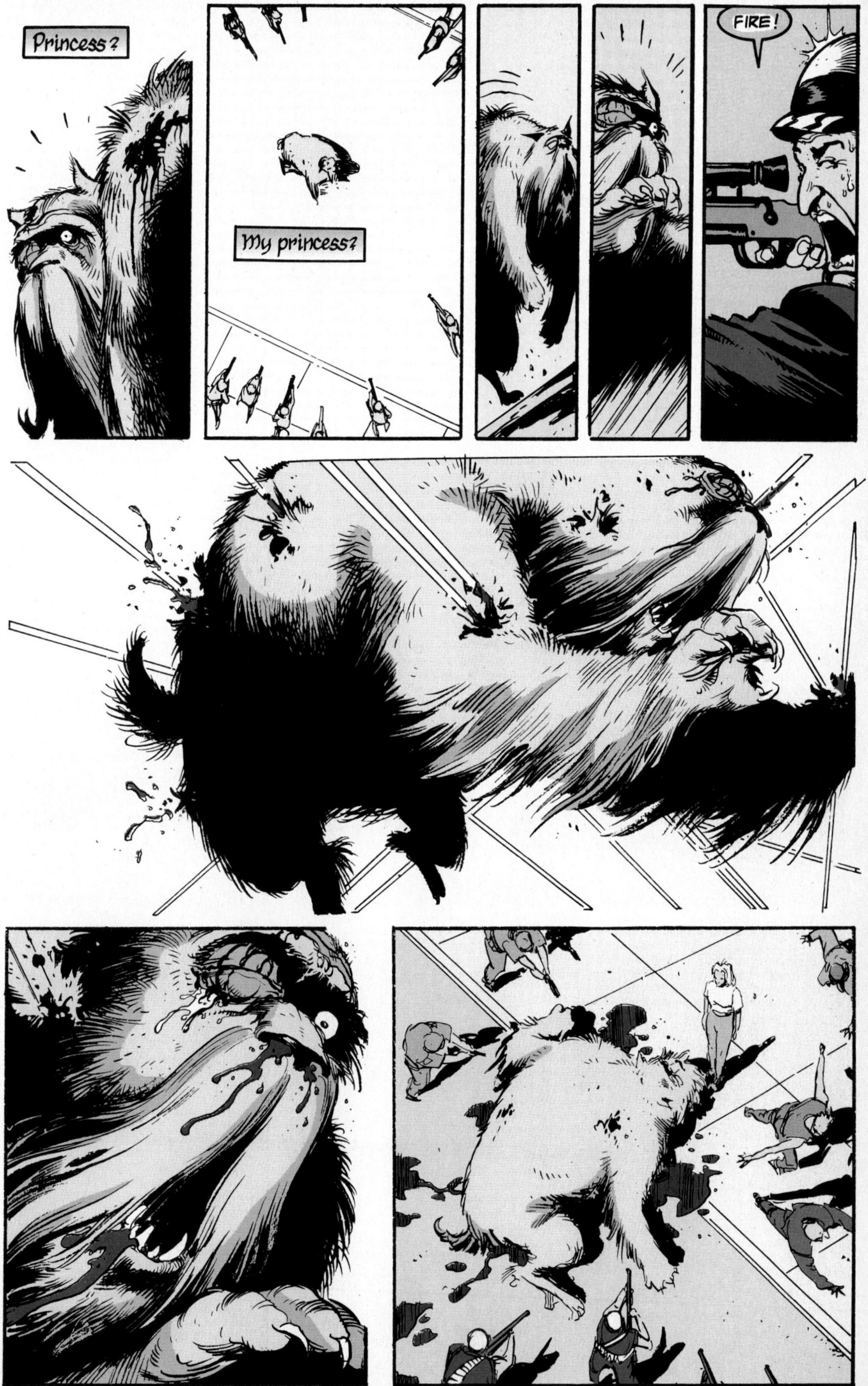
Princess?
My princess?
FIRE!

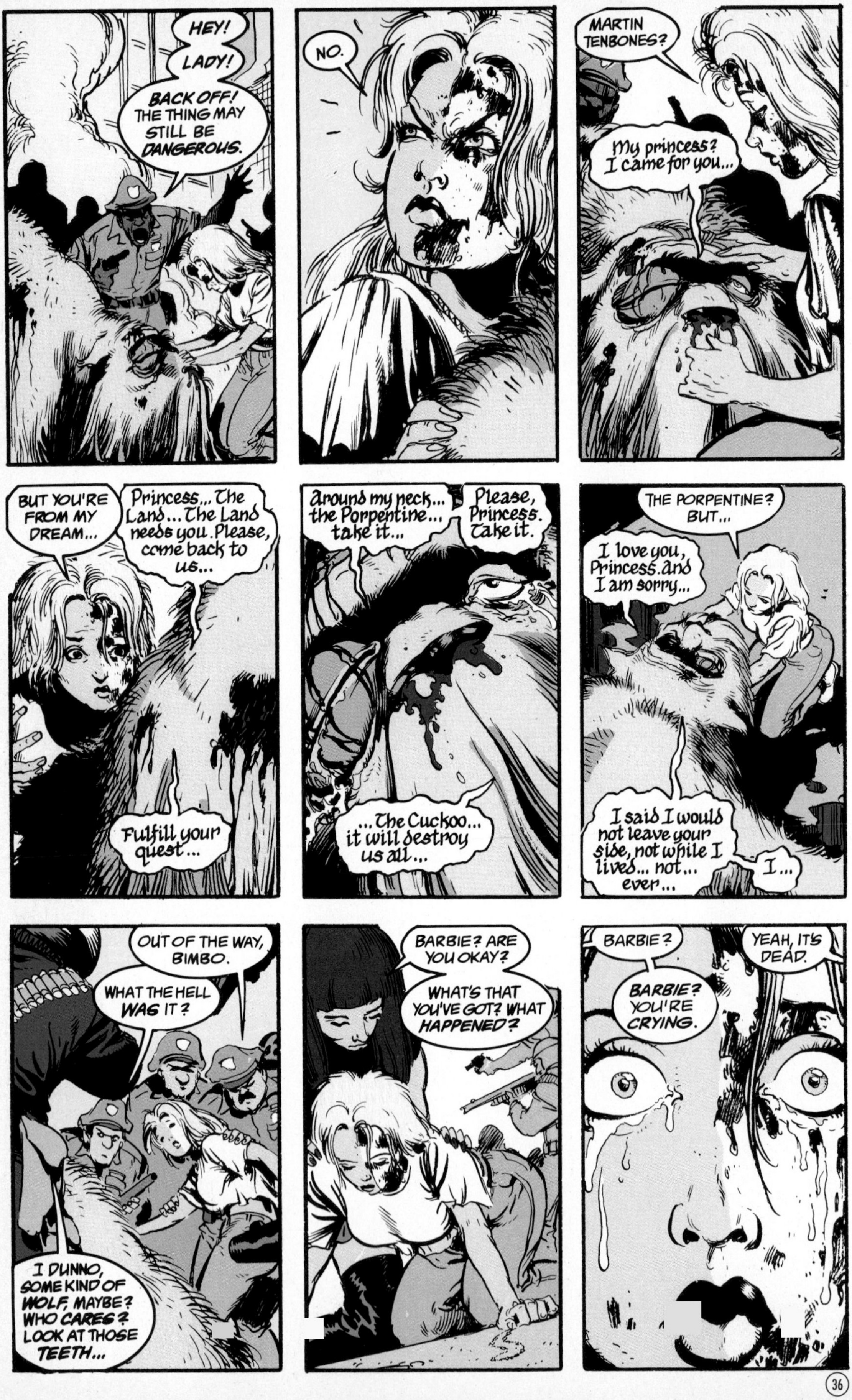
HEY!
LADY!
BACK OFF! THE THING MAY STILL BE DANGEROUS.
NO.
MARTIN TENBONES?
My princess? I came for you...
BUT YOU'RE FROM MY DREAM...
Princess... The Land... The Land needs you. Please, come back to us...
Fulfill your quest...
Around my neck... the Porpentine... take it...
Please, Princess. Take it.
...The Cuckoo... it will destroy us all...
THE PORPENTINE? BUT...
I love you, Princess. And I am sorry...
I said I would not leave your side, not while I lived... not... ever...
I...
OUT OF THE WAY, BIMBO.
WHAT THE HELL WAS IT?
I DUNNO, SOME KIND OF WOLF, MAYBE? WHO CARES? LOOK AT THOSE TEETH...
BARBIE? ARE YOU OKAY?
WHAT'S THAT YOU'VE GOT? WHAT HAPPENED?
BARBIE?
YEAH, IT'S DEAD.
BARBIE? YOU'RE CRYING.

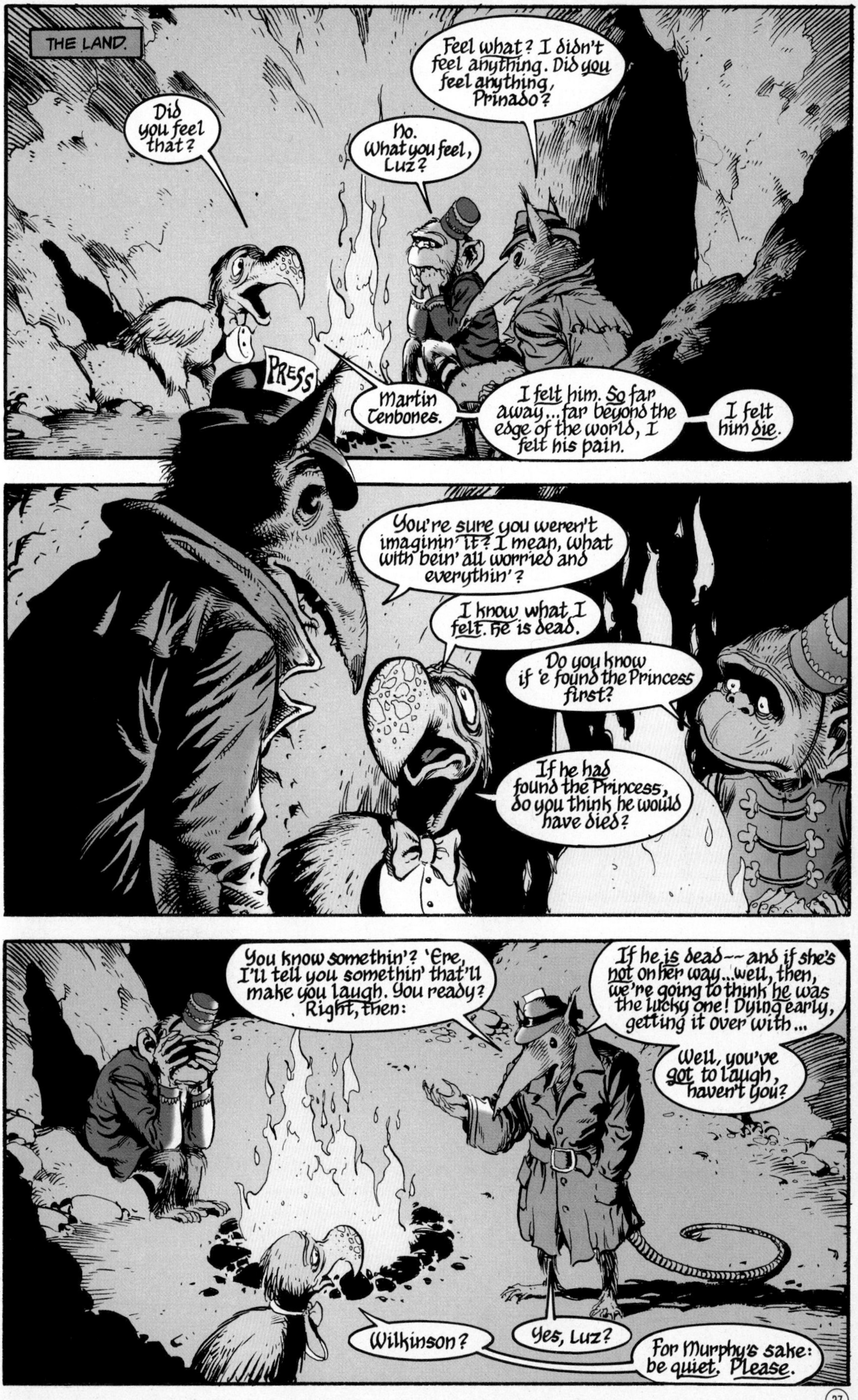
THE LAND.
Did you feel that?
Feel what? I didn't feel anything. Did you feel anything, Prinado?
No. What you feel, Luz?
PRESS
Martin Tenbones.
I felt him. So far away... far beyond the edge of the world, I felt his pain.
I felt him die.
You're sure you weren't imaginin' it? I mean, what with bein' all worried and everythin'?
I know what I felt. He is dead.
Do you know if 'e found the Princess first?
If he had found the Princess, do you think he would have died?
You know somethin'? 'Ere, I'll tell you somethin' that'll make you laugh. You ready? Right, then:
If he is dead-- and if she's not on her way... well, then, we're going to think he was the lucky one! Dying early, getting it over with...
Well, you've got to laugh, haven't you?
Wilkinson?
Yes, Luz?
For Murphy's sake: be quiet. Please.

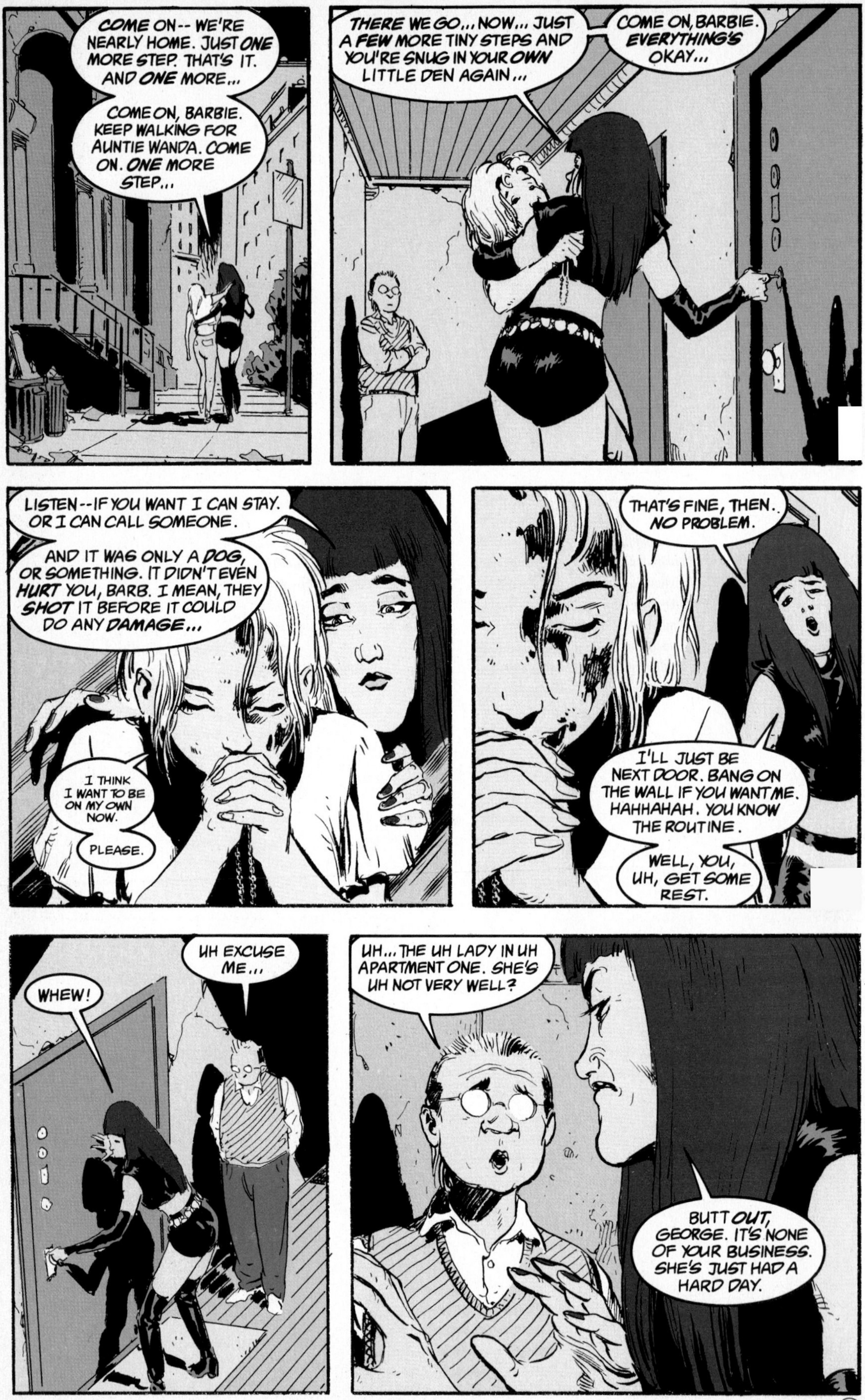
COME ON-- WE'RE NEARLY HOME. JUST ONE MORE STEP. THAT'S IT. AND ONE MORE...
COME ON, BARBIE. KEEP WALKING FOR AUNTIE WANDA. COME ON. ONE MORE STEP...
THERE WE GO... NOW... JUST A FEW MORE TINY STEPS AND YOU'RE SNUG IN YOUR OWN LITTLE DEN AGAIN...
COME ON, BARBIE. EVERYTHING'S OKAY...
LISTEN--IF YOU WANT I CAN STAY. OR I CAN CALL SOMEONE.
AND IT WAS ONLY A DOG, OR SOMETHING. IT DIDN'T EVEN HURT YOU, BARB. I MEAN, THEY SHOT IT BEFORE IT COULD DO ANY DAMAGE...
I THINK I WANT TO BE ON MY OWN NOW.
PLEASE.
THAT'S FINE, THEN. NO PROBLEM.
I'LL JUST BE NEXT DOOR. BANG ON THE WALL IF YOU WANT ME. HAHHAHAH. YOU KNOW THE ROUTINE.
WELL, YOU, UH, GET SOME REST.
WHEW!
UH EXCUSE ME...
UH... THE UH LADY IN UH APARTMENT ONE. SHE'S UH NOT VERY WELL?
BUTT OUT, GEORGE. IT'S NONE OF YOUR BUSINESS. SHE'S JUST HAD A HARD DAY.

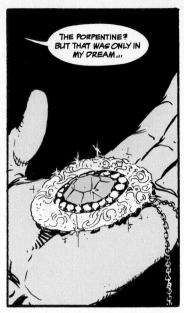

THE PORPENTINE?
BUT THAT WAS ONLY IN
MY DREAM...

IT'S ALL COMING BACK... MARTIN
TENBONES... AND THE PORPENTINE...
AND THE LAND...

AND
THE SCARY
THING...

THE
CUCKOO.

NO.

PLEASE
NO. IT ISN'T
REAL...

IT
WAS ONLY A
DREAM.

WHAT'S
HAPPENING
TO ME?

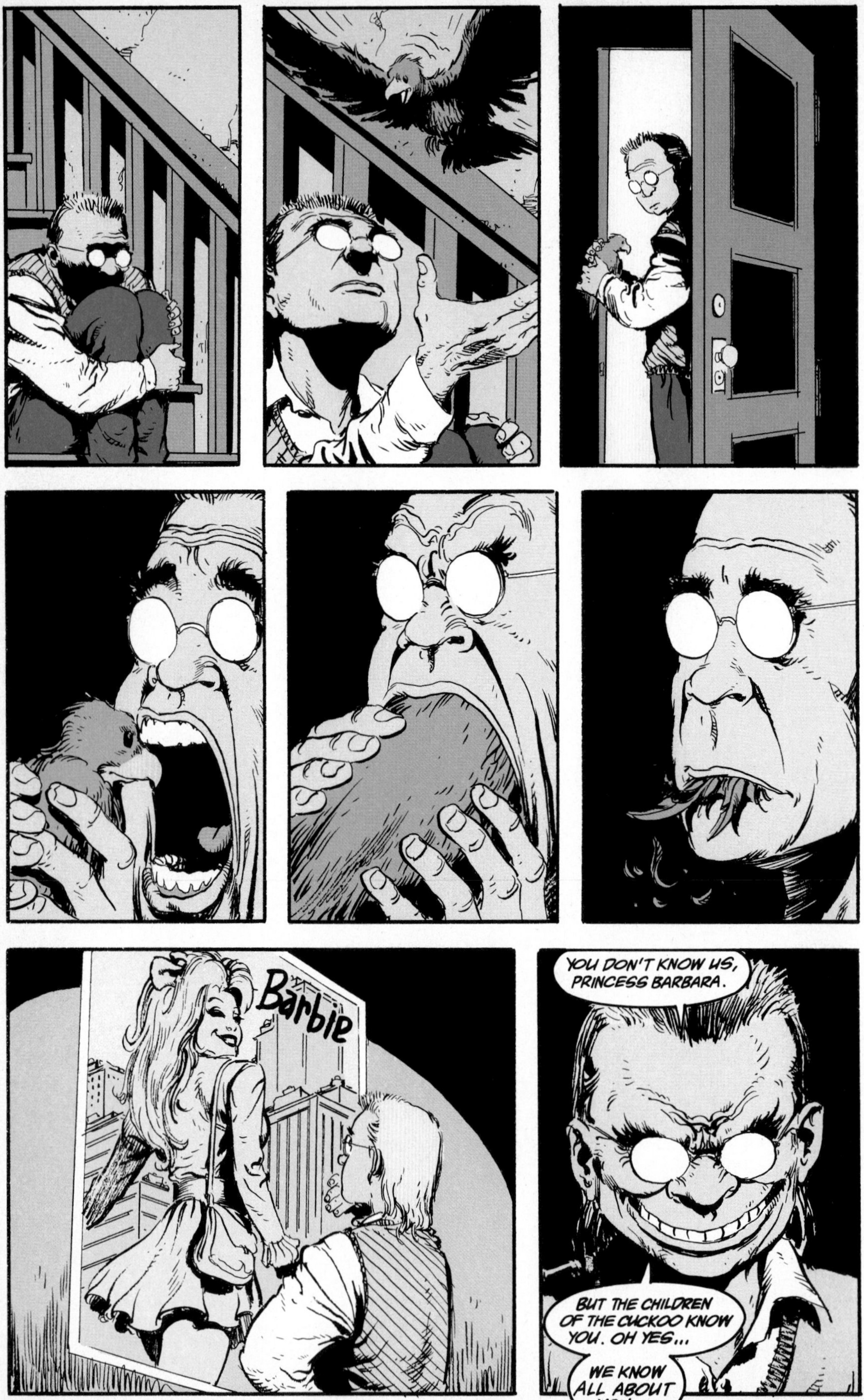
Barbie
YOU DON'T KNOW US, PRINCESS BARBARA.
BUT THE CHILDREN OF THE CUCKOO KNOW YOU. OH YES...
WE KNOW ALL ABOUT YOU.

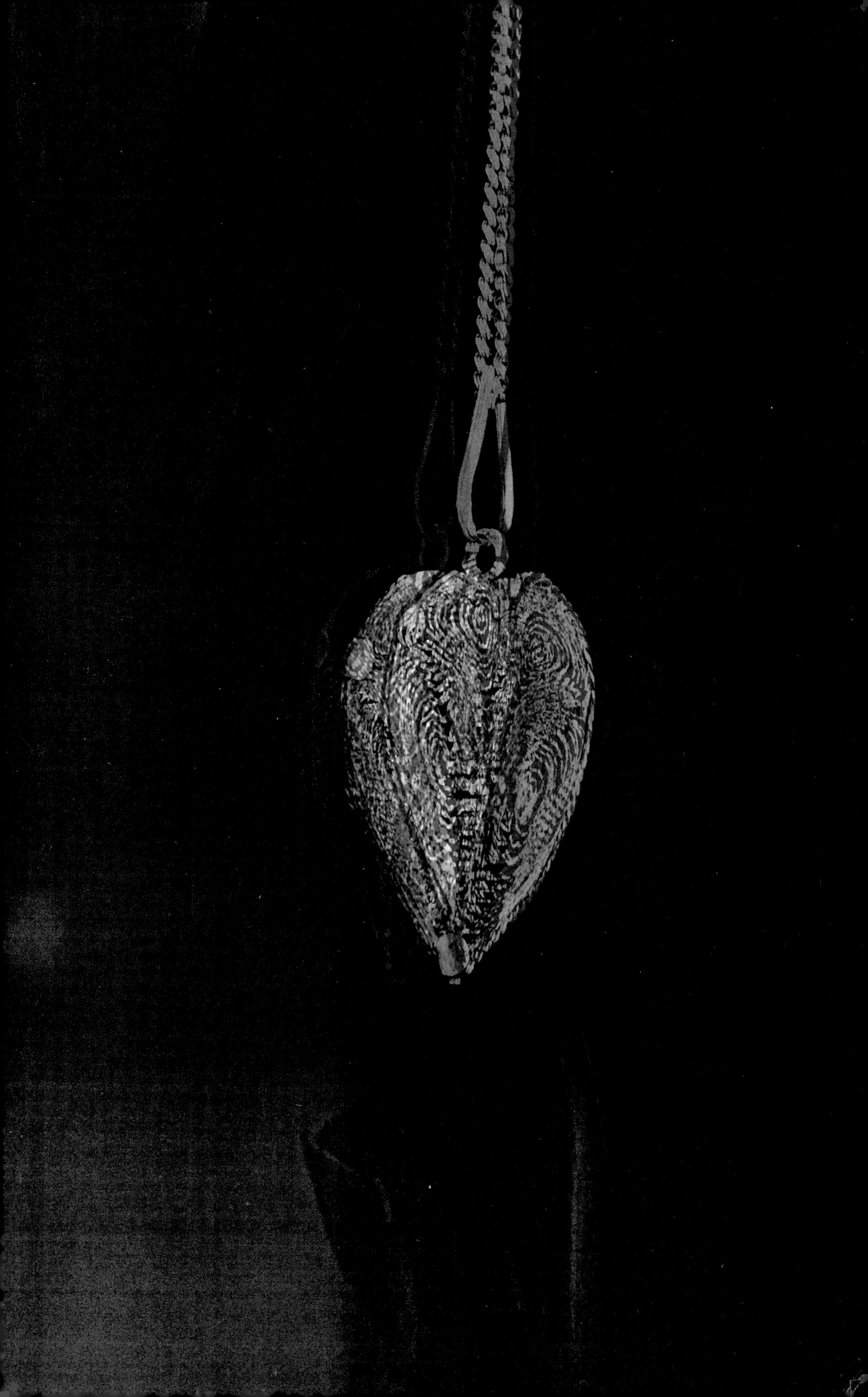

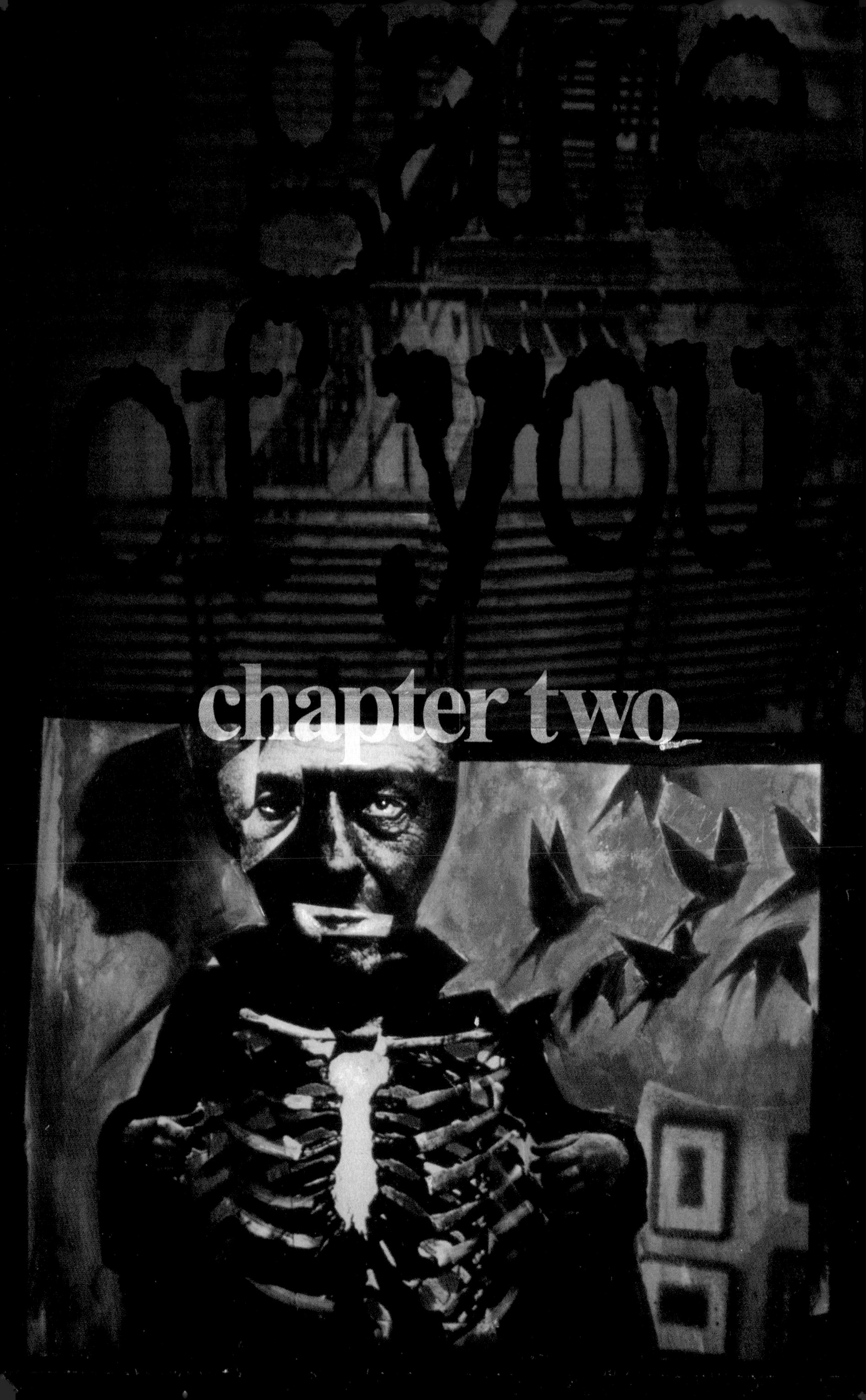
of you
chapter two

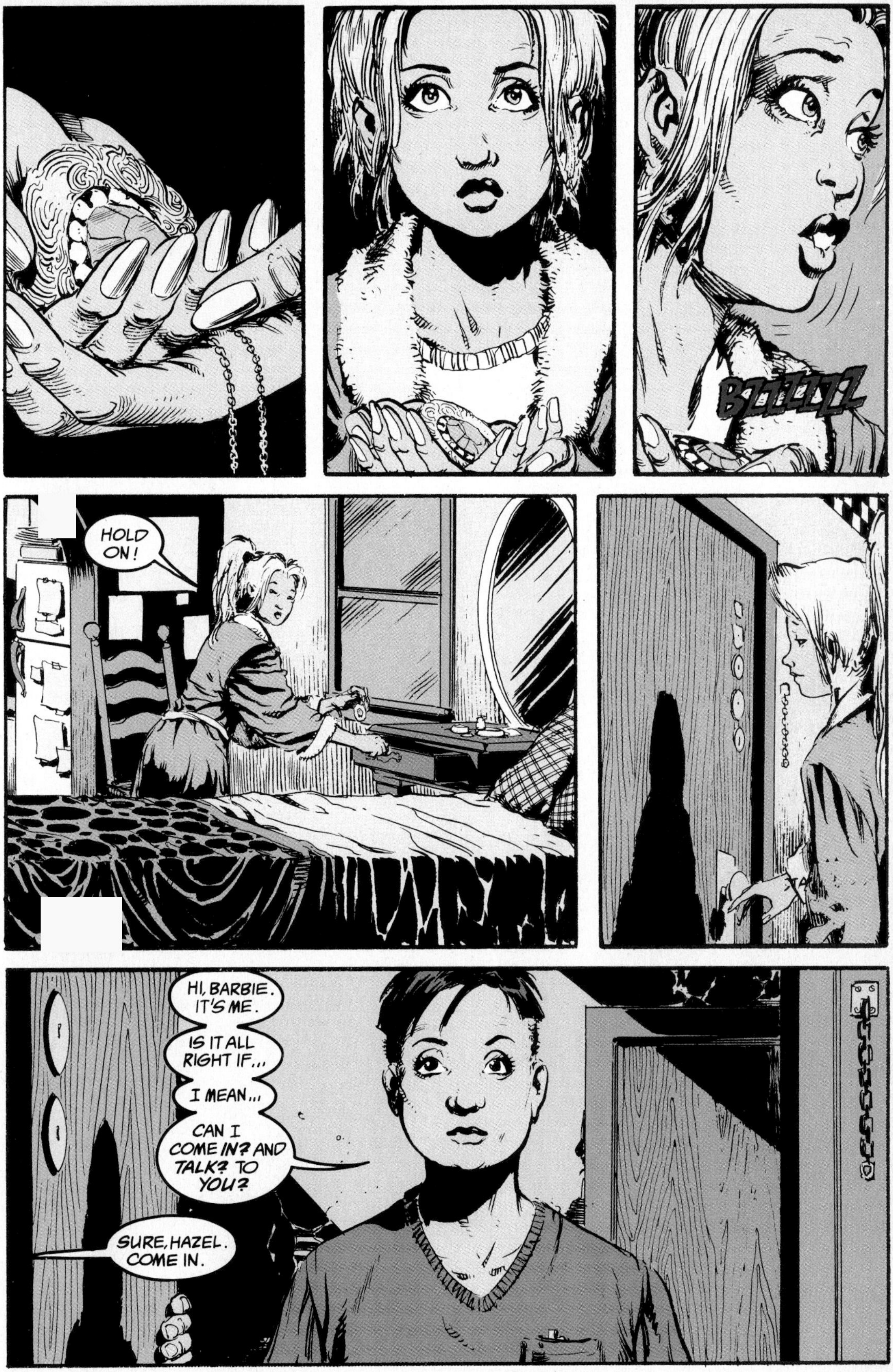
BZZZZZZ
HOLD ON!
HI, BARBIE. IT'S ME.
IS IT ALL RIGHT IF...
I MEAN...
CAN I COME IN? AND TALK? TO YOU?
SURE, HAZEL. COME IN.

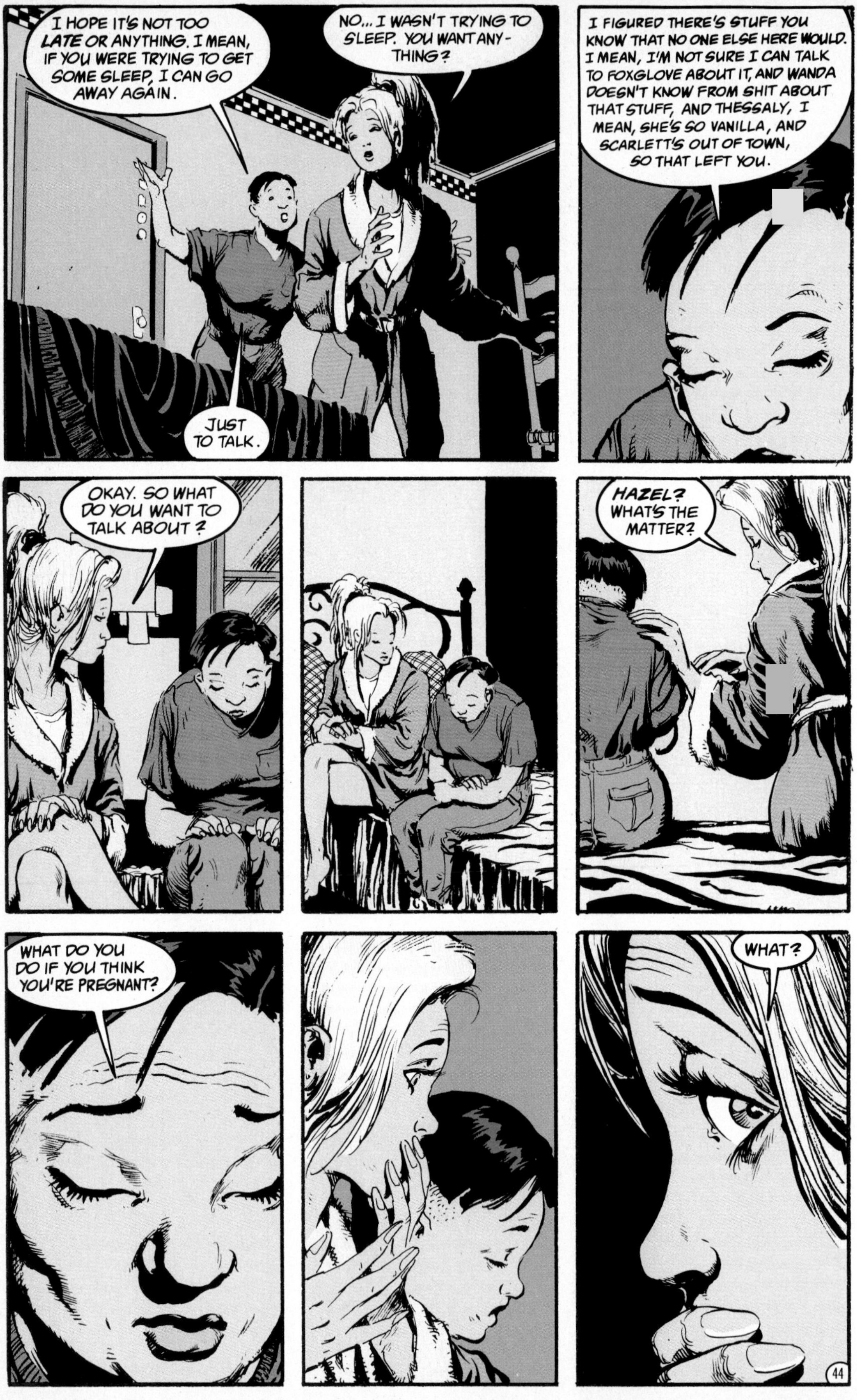

I HOPE IT'S NOT TOO LATE OR ANYTHING. I MEAN, IF YOU WERE TRYING TO GET SOME SLEEP, I CAN GO AWAY AGAIN.
NO... I WASN'T TRYING TO SLEEP. YOU WANT ANY-THING?
JUST TO TALK.
I FIGURED THERE'S STUFF YOU KNOW THAT NO ONE ELSE HERE WOULD. I MEAN, I'M NOT SURE I CAN TALK TO FOXGLOVE ABOUT IT, AND WANDA DOESN'T KNOW FROM SHIT ABOUT THAT STUFF, AND THESSALY, I MEAN, SHE'S SO VANILLA, AND SCARLETT'S OUT OF TOWN, SO THAT LEFT YOU.
OKAY. SO WHAT DO YOU WANT TO TALK ABOUT?
HAZEL? WHAT'S THE MATTER?
WHAT DO YOU DO IF YOU THINK YOU'RE PREGNANT?
WHAT?

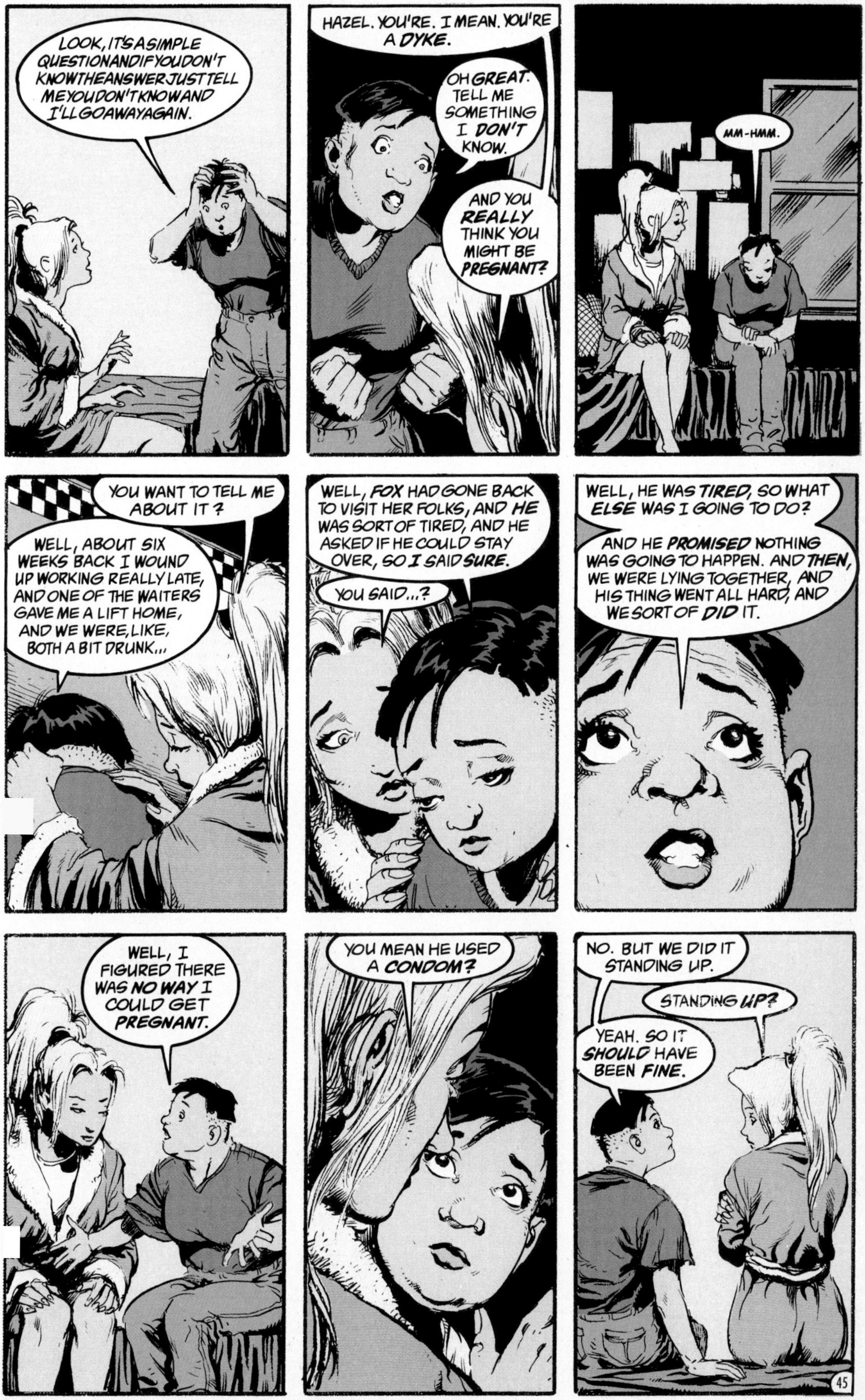
LOOK, IT'S A SIMPLE QUESTION AND IF YOU DON'T KNOW THE ANSWER JUST TELL ME YOU DON'T KNOW AND I'LL GO AWAY AGAIN.
HAZEL. YOU'RE. I MEAN. YOU'RE A DYKE.
OH GREAT. TELL ME SOMETHING I DON'T KNOW.
AND YOU REALLY THINK YOU MIGHT BE PREGNANT?
MM-HMM.
YOU WANT TO TELL ME ABOUT IT?
WELL, ABOUT SIX WEEKS BACK I WOUND UP WORKING REALLY LATE, AND ONE OF THE WAITERS GAVE ME A LIFT HOME, AND WE WERE, LIKE, BOTH A BIT DRUNK...
WELL, FOX HAD GONE BACK TO VISIT HER FOLKS, AND HE WAS SORT OF TIRED, AND HE ASKED IF HE COULD STAY OVER, SO I SAID SURE.
YOU SAID...?
WELL, HE WAS TIRED, SO WHAT ELSE WAS I GOING TO DO?
AND HE PROMISED NOTHING WAS GOING TO HAPPEN. AND THEN, WE WERE LYING TOGETHER, AND HIS THING WENT ALL HARD, AND WE SORT OF DID IT.
WELL, I FIGURED THERE WAS NO WAY I COULD GET PREGNANT.
YOU MEAN HE USED A CONDOM?
NO. BUT WE DID IT STANDING UP.
STANDING UP?
YEAH. SO IT SHOULD HAVE BEEN FINE.

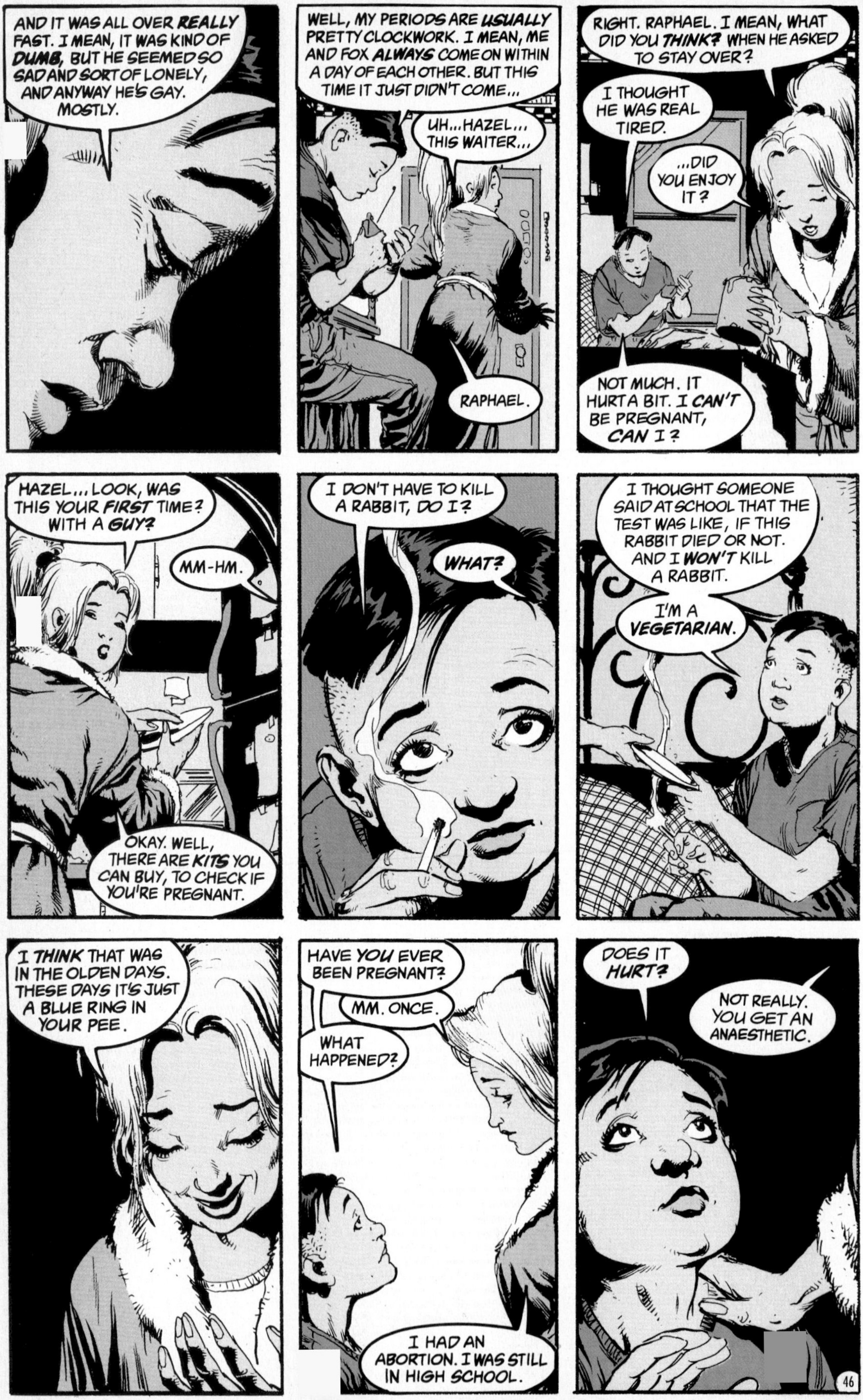

AND IT WAS ALL OVER REALLY FAST. I MEAN, IT WAS KIND OF DUMB, BUT HE SEEMED SO SAD AND SORT OF LONELY, AND ANYWAY HE'S GAY. MOSTLY.
WELL, MY PERIODS ARE USUALLY PRETTY CLOCKWORK. I MEAN, ME AND FOX ALWAYS COME ON WITHIN A DAY OF EACH OTHER. BUT THIS TIME IT JUST DIDN'T COME...
UH...HAZEL... THIS WAITER...
RAPHAEL.
RIGHT. RAPHAEL. I MEAN, WHAT DID YOU THINK? WHEN HE ASKED TO STAY OVER?
I THOUGHT HE WAS REAL TIRED.
...DID YOU ENJOY IT?
NOT MUCH. IT HURT A BIT. I CAN'T BE PREGNANT, CAN I?
HAZEL... LOOK, WAS THIS YOUR FIRST TIME? WITH A GUY?
MM-HM.
OKAY. WELL, THERE ARE KITS YOU CAN BUY, TO CHECK IF YOU'RE PREGNANT.
I DON'T HAVE TO KILL A RABBIT, DO I?
WHAT?
I THOUGHT SOMEONE SAID AT SCHOOL THAT THE TEST WAS LIKE, IF THIS RABBIT DIED OR NOT. AND I WON'T KILL A RABBIT.
I'M A VEGETARIAN.
I THINK THAT WAS IN THE OLDEN DAYS. THESE DAYS IT'S JUST A BLUE RING IN YOUR PEE.
HAVE YOU EVER BEEN PREGNANT?
MM. ONCE.
WHAT HAPPENED?
I HAD AN ABORTION. I WAS STILL IN HIGH SCHOOL.
DOES IT HURT?
NOT REALLY. YOU GET AN ANAESTHETIC.

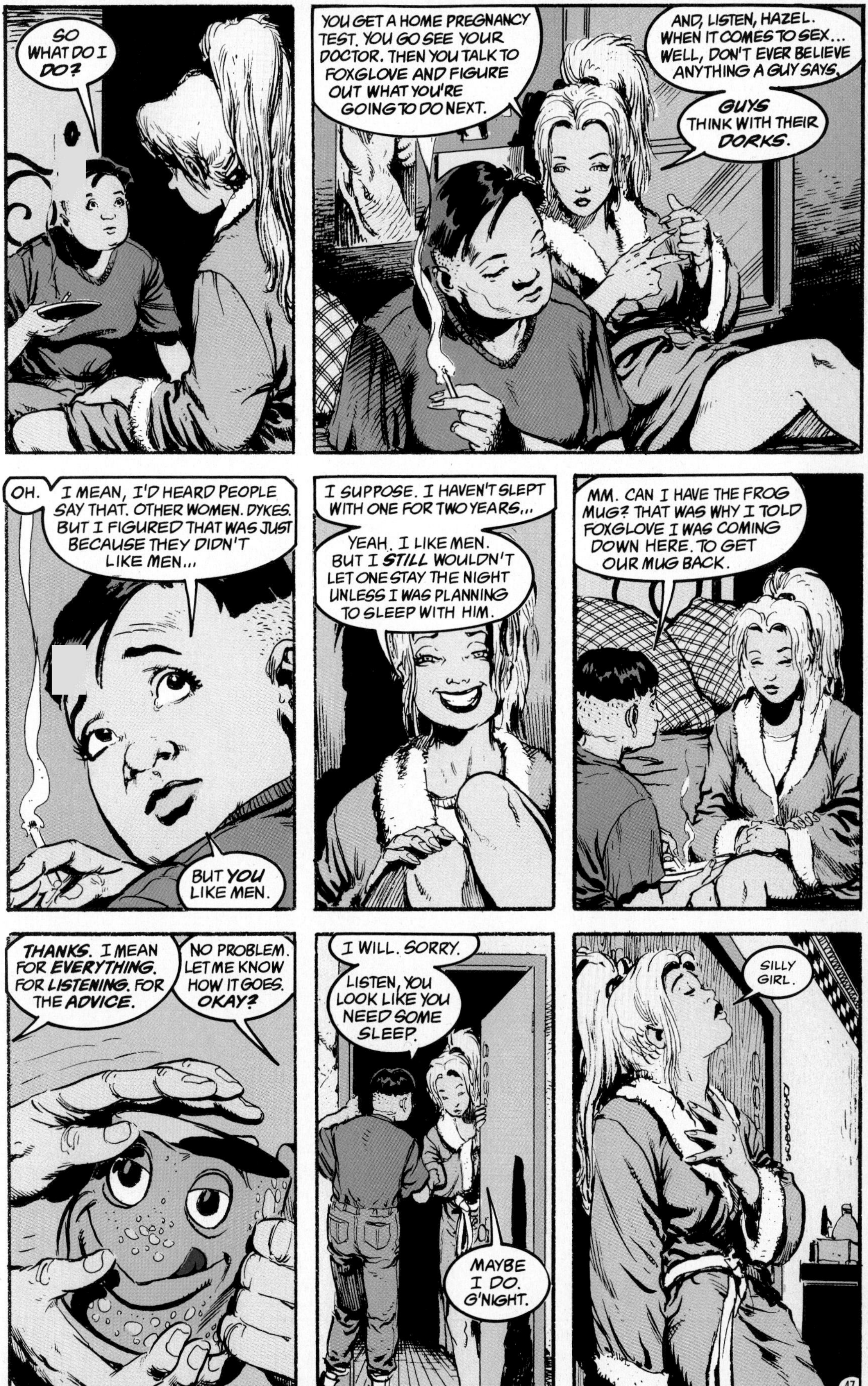
SO WHAT DO I DO?
YOU GET A HOME PREGNANCY TEST. YOU GO SEE YOUR DOCTOR. THEN YOU TALK TO FOXGLOVE AND FIGURE OUT WHAT YOU'RE GOING TO DO NEXT.
AND, LISTEN, HAZEL. WHEN IT COMES TO SEX... WELL, DON'T EVER BELIEVE ANYTHING A GUY SAYS.
GUYS THINK WITH THEIR DORKS.
OH.
I MEAN, I'D HEARD PEOPLE SAY THAT. OTHER WOMEN. DYKES. BUT I FIGURED THAT WAS JUST BECAUSE THEY DIDN'T LIKE MEN...
BUT YOU LIKE MEN.
I SUPPOSE. I HAVEN'T SLEPT WITH ONE FOR TWO YEARS...
YEAH. I LIKE MEN. BUT I STILL WOULDN'T LET ONE STAY THE NIGHT UNLESS I WAS PLANNING TO SLEEP WITH HIM.
MM. CAN I HAVE THE FROG MUG? THAT WAS WHY I TOLD FOXGLOVE I WAS COMING DOWN HERE. TO GET OUR MUG BACK.
THANKS. I MEAN FOR EVERYTHING. FOR LISTENING. FOR THE ADVICE.
NO PROBLEM. LET ME KNOW HOW IT GOES. OKAY?
I WILL. SORRY.
LISTEN, YOU LOOK LIKE YOU NEED SOME SLEEP.
MAYBE I DO. G'NIGHT.
SILLY GIRL.

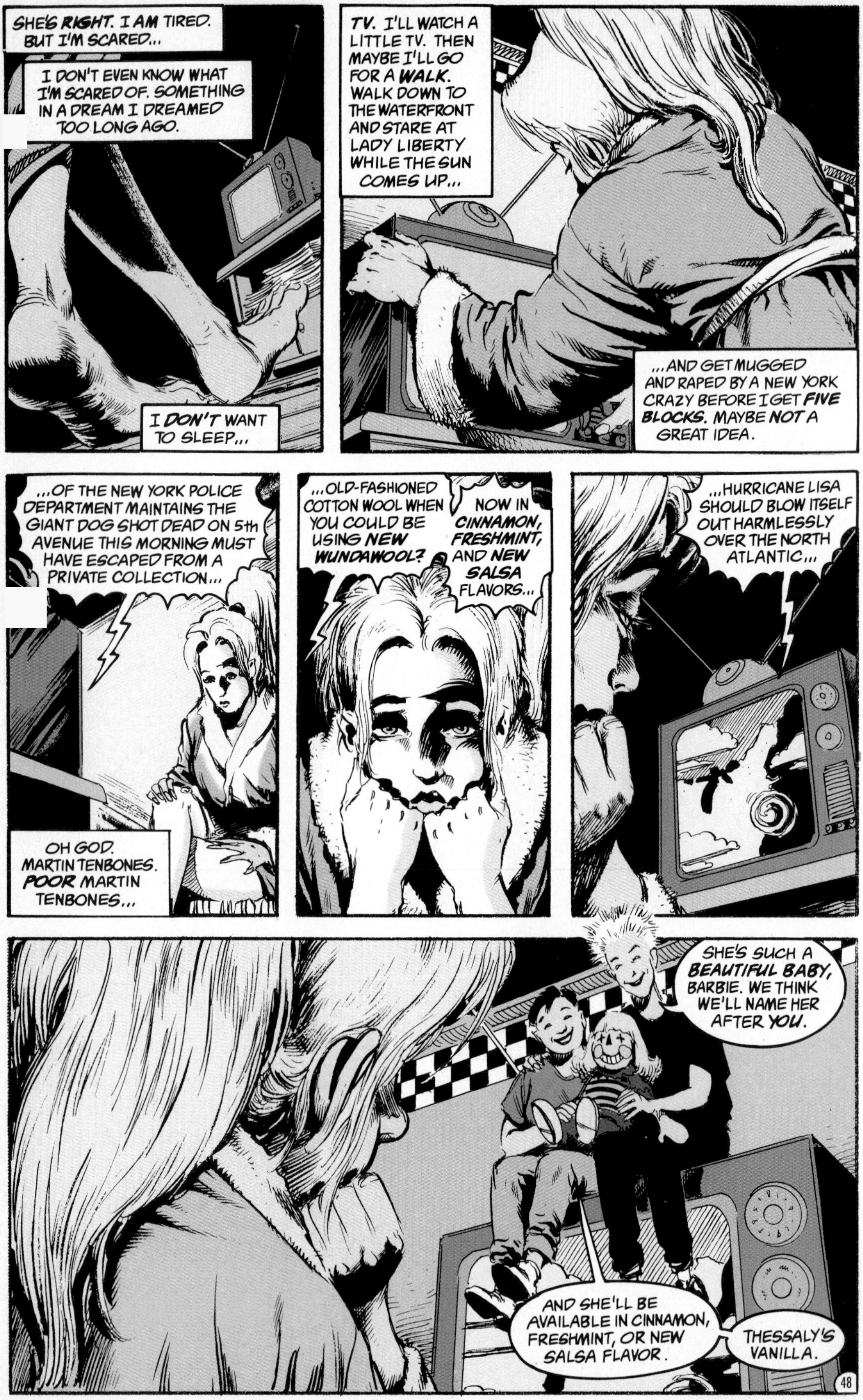
SHE'S RIGHT. I AM TIRED. BUT I'M SCARED...
I DON'T EVEN KNOW WHAT I'M SCARED OF. SOMETHING IN A DREAM I DREAMED TOO LONG AGO.
I DON'T WANT TO SLEEP...
TV. I'LL WATCH A LITTLE TV. THEN MAYBE I'LL GO FOR A WALK. WALK DOWN TO THE WATERFRONT AND STARE AT LADY LIBERTY WHILE THE SUN COMES UP...
...AND GET MUGGED AND RAPED BY A NEW YORK CRAZY BEFORE I GET FIVE BLOCKS. MAYBE NOT A GREAT IDEA.
...OF THE NEW YORK POLICE DEPARTMENT MAINTAINS THE GIANT DOG SHOT DEAD ON 5th AVENUE THIS MORNING MUST HAVE ESCAPED FROM A PRIVATE COLLECTION...
OH GOD. MARTIN TENBONES. POOR MARTIN TENBONES...
...OLD-FASHIONED COTTON WOOL WHEN YOU COULD BE USING NEW WUNDAWOOL?
NOW IN CINNAMON, FRESHMINT, AND NEW SALSA FLAVORS...
...HURRICANE LISA SHOULD BLOW ITSELF OUT HARMLESSLY OVER THE NORTH ATLANTIC...
SHE'S SUCH A BEAUTIFUL BABY, BARBIE. WE THINK WE'LL NAME HER AFTER YOU.
AND SHE'LL BE AVAILABLE IN CINNAMON, FRESHMINT, OR NEW SALSA FLAVOR.
THESSALY'S VANILLA.

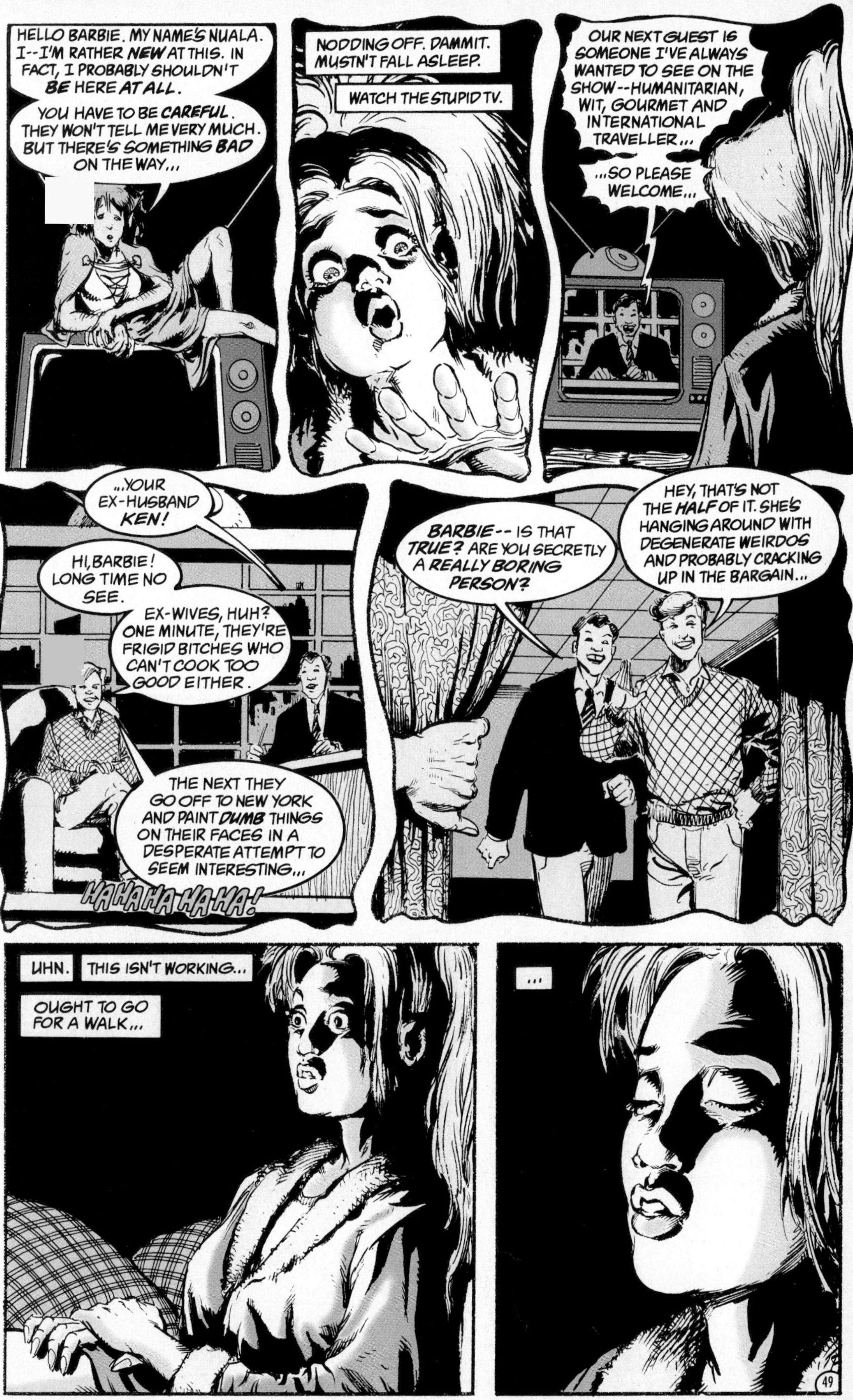
HELLO BARBIE. MY NAME'S NUALA. I--I'M RATHER NEW AT THIS. IN FACT, I PROBABLY SHOULDN'T BE HERE AT ALL.
YOU HAVE TO BE CAREFUL. THEY WON'T TELL ME VERY MUCH. BUT THERE'S SOMETHING BAD ON THE WAY...
NODDING OFF. DAMMIT. MUSTN'T FALL ASLEEP.
WATCH THE STUPID TV.
OUR NEXT GUEST IS SOMEONE I'VE ALWAYS WANTED TO SEE ON THE SHOW--HUMANITARIAN, WIT, GOURMET AND INTERNATIONAL TRAVELLER...
...SO PLEASE WELCOME...
...YOUR EX-HUSBAND KEN!
HI, BARBIE! LONG TIME NO SEE.
EX-WIVES, HUH? ONE MINUTE, THEY'RE FRIGID BITCHES WHO CAN'T COOK TOO GOOD EITHER.
THE NEXT THEY GO OFF TO NEW YORK AND PAINT DUMB THINGS ON THEIR FACES IN A DESPERATE ATTEMPT TO SEEM INTERESTING...
HAHAHA HAHA!
BARBIE-- IS THAT TRUE? ARE YOU SECRETLY A REALLY BORING PERSON?
HEY, THAT'S NOT THE HALF OF IT. SHE'S HANGING AROUND WITH DEGENERATE WEIRDOS AND PROBABLY CRACKING UP IN THE BARGAIN...
UHN.
THIS ISN'T WORKING...
OUGHT TO GO FOR A WALK...
...

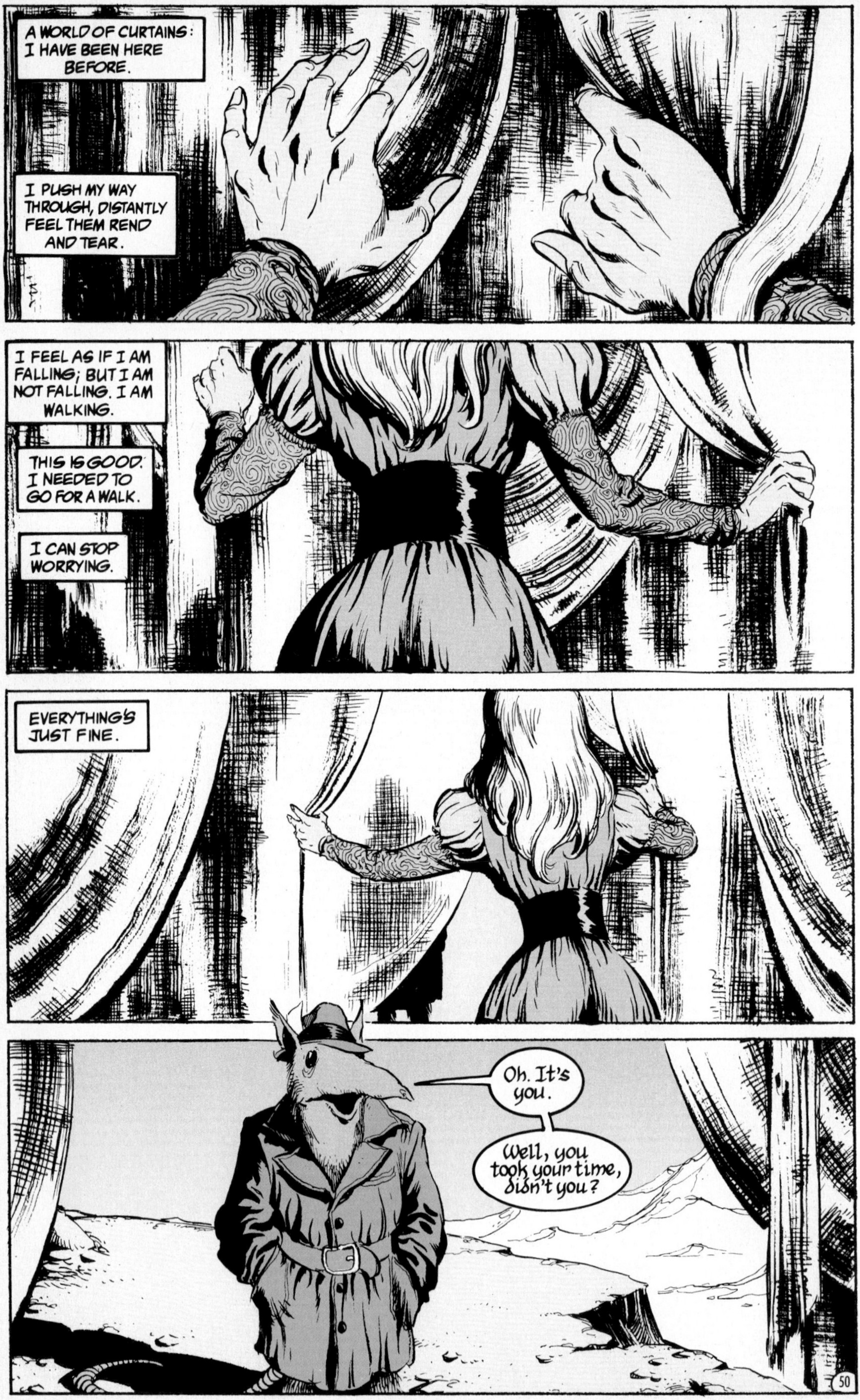

A WORLD OF CURTAINS: I HAVE BEEN HERE BEFORE.
I PUSH MY WAY THROUGH, DISTANTLY FEEL THEM REND AND TEAR.
I FEEL AS IF I AM FALLING; BUT I AM NOT FALLING. I AM WALKING.
THIS IS GOOD. I NEEDED TO GO FOR A WALK.
I CAN STOP WORRYING.
EVERYTHING'S JUST FINE.
Oh. It's you.
Well, you took your time, didn't you?

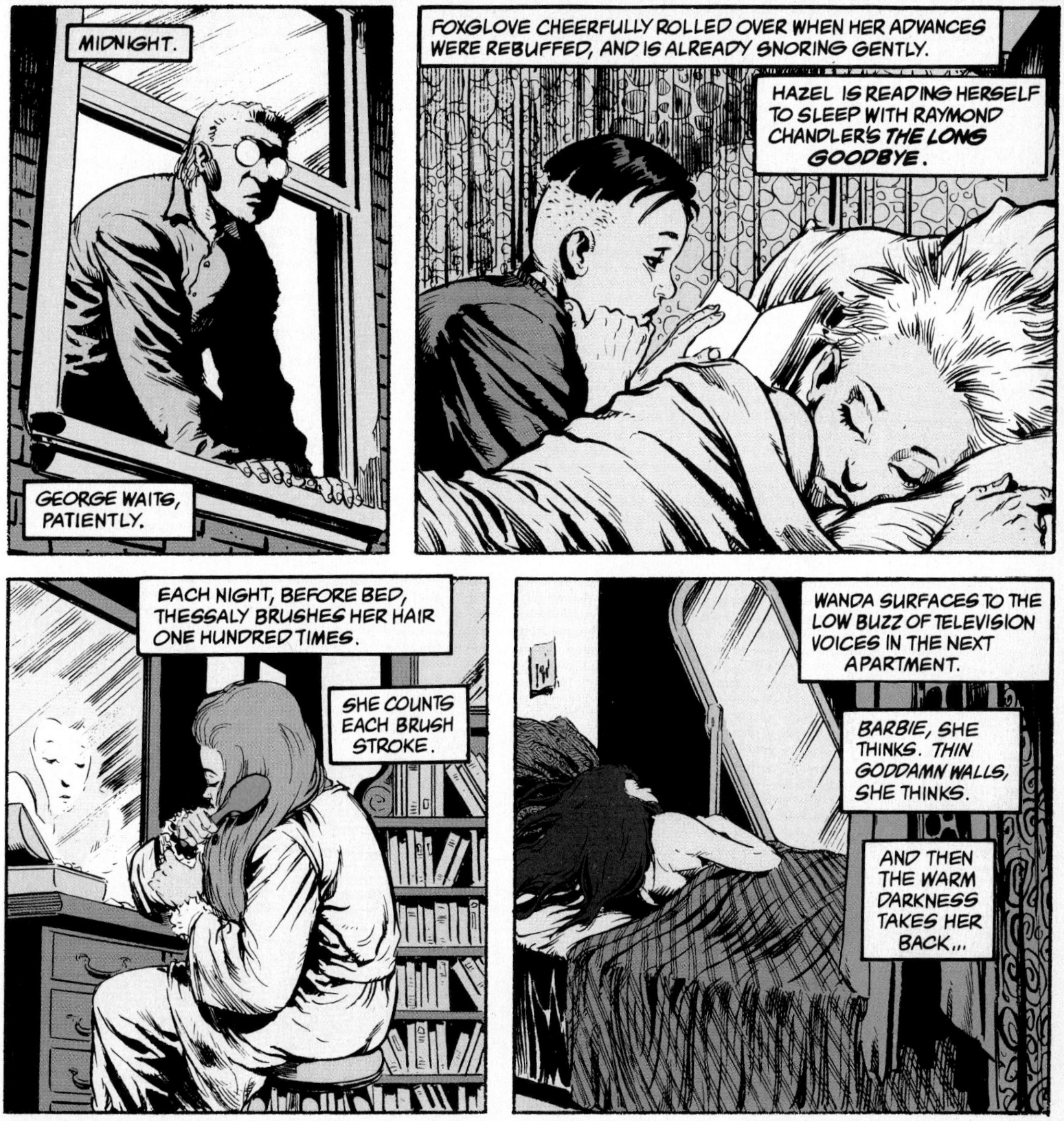
MIDNIGHT.
GEORGE WAITS, PATIENTLY.
FOXGLOVE CHEERFULLY ROLLED OVER WHEN HER ADVANCES WERE REBUFFED, AND IS ALREADY SNORING GENTLY.
HAZEL IS READING HERSELF TO SLEEP WITH RAYMOND CHANDLER'S ***THE LONG GOODBYE***.
EACH NIGHT, BEFORE BED, THESSALY BRUSHES HER HAIR ONE HUNDRED TIMES.
SHE COUNTS EACH BRUSH STROKE.
WANDA SURFACES TO THE LOW BUZZ OF TELEVISION VOICES IN THE NEXT APARTMENT.
BARBIE, SHE THINKS. *THIN GODDAMN WALLS,* SHE THINKS.
AND THEN THE WARM DARKNESS TAKES HER BACK...

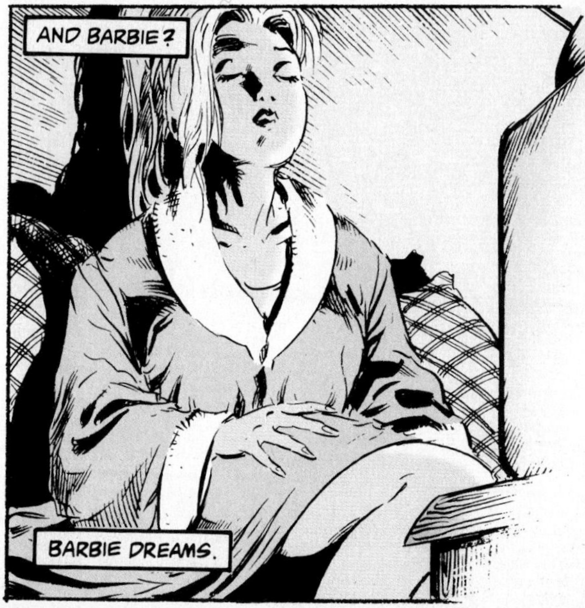
AND BARBIE?
BARBIE DREAMS.

2
LULLABIES OF BROADWAY

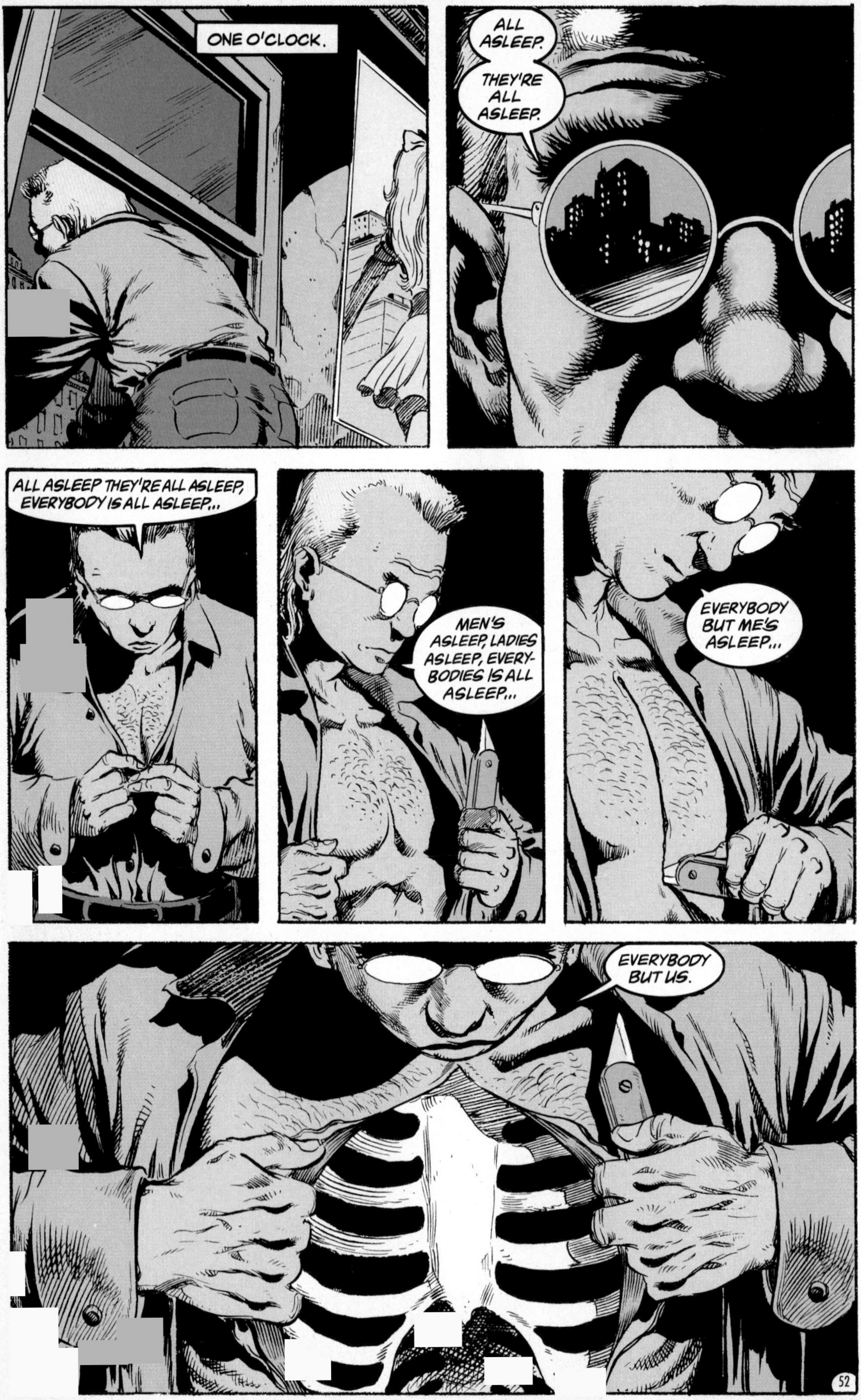
ONE O'CLOCK.
ALL ASLEEP.
THEY'RE ALL ASLEEP.
ALL ASLEEP THEY'RE ALL ASLEEP, EVERYBODY IS ALL ASLEEP...
MEN'S ASLEEP, LADIES ASLEEP, EVERYBODIES IS ALL ASLEEP...
EVERYBODY BUT ME'S ASLEEP...
EVERYBODY BUT US.

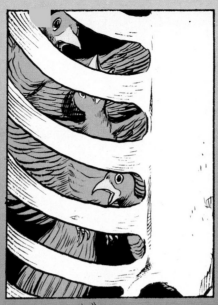

IT'S TIME, MY BROTHERS.

FLY.

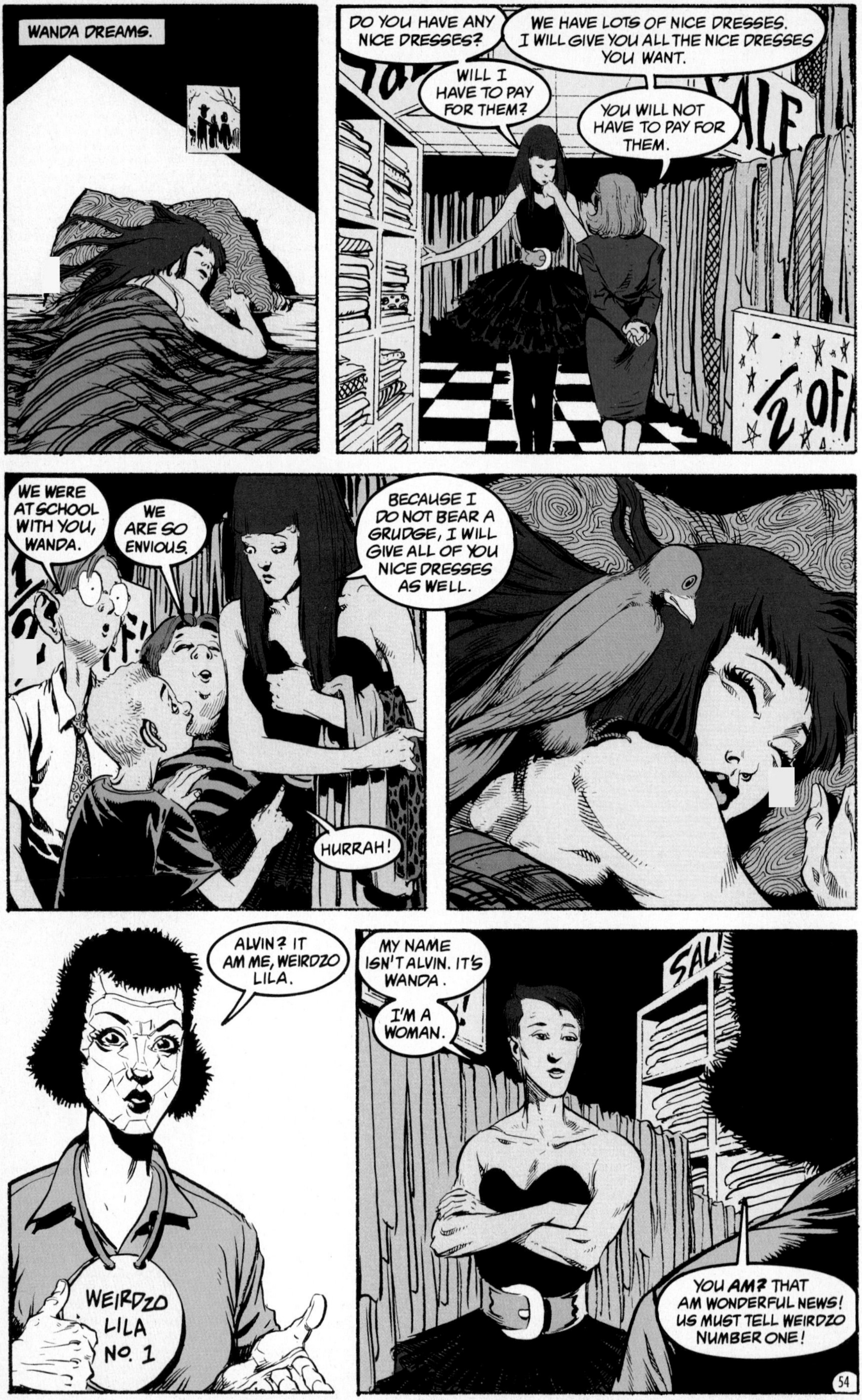
WANDA DREAMS.
DO YOU HAVE ANY NICE DRESSES?
WE HAVE LOTS OF NICE DRESSES. I WILL GIVE YOU ALL THE NICE DRESSES YOU WANT.
WILL I HAVE TO PAY FOR THEM?
YOU WILL NOT HAVE TO PAY FOR THEM.
WE WERE AT SCHOOL WITH YOU, WANDA.
WE ARE SO ENVIOUS.
BECAUSE I DO NOT BEAR A GRUDGE, I WILL GIVE ALL OF YOU NICE DRESSES AS WELL.
HURRAH!
ALVIN? IT AM ME, WEIRDZO LILA.
WEIRDZO LILA NO. 1
MY NAME ISN'T ALVIN. IT'S WANDA.
I'M A WOMAN.
YOU AM? THAT AM WONDERFUL NEWS! US MUST TELL WEIRDZO NUMBER ONE!

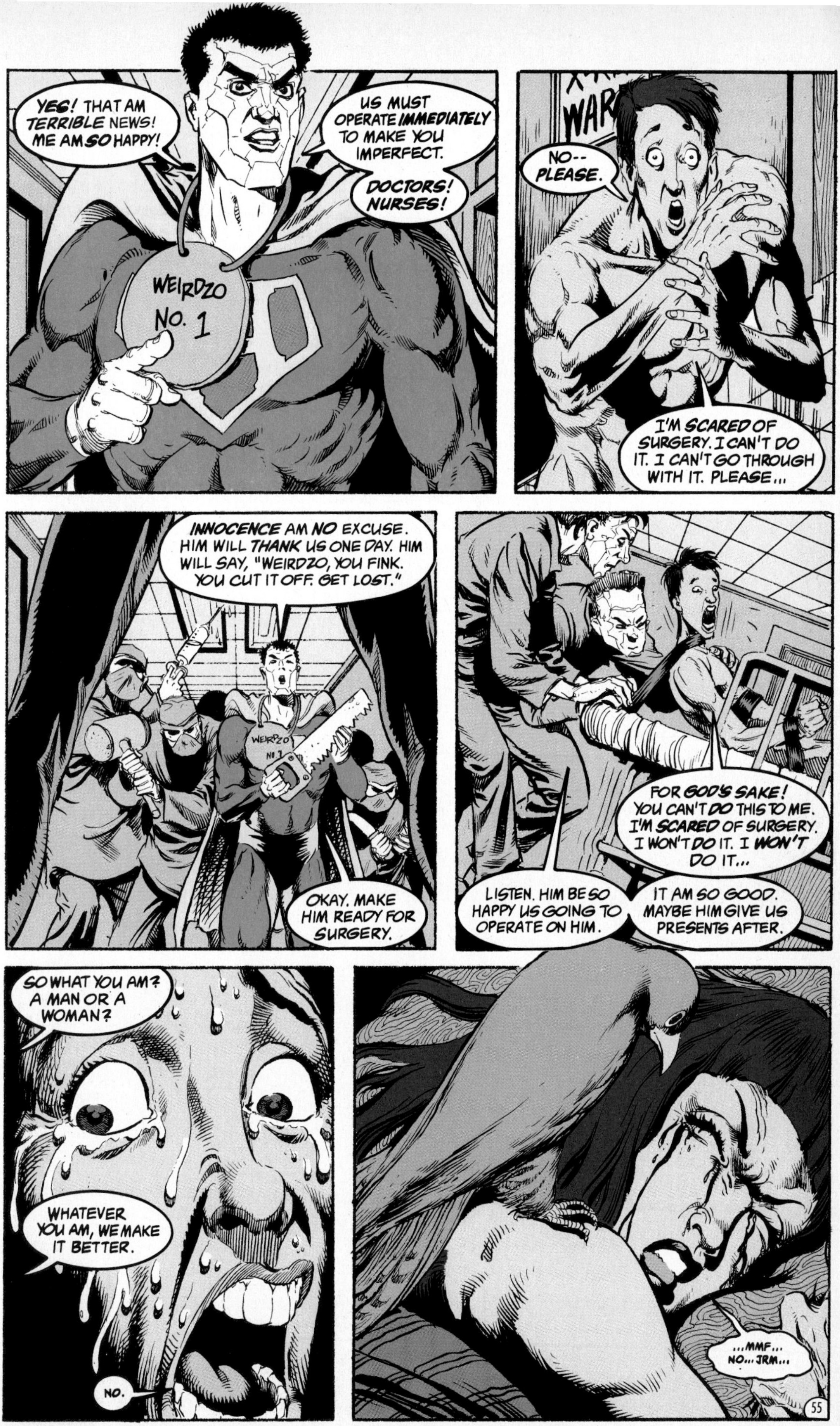
YES! THAT AM TERRIBLE NEWS! ME AM SO HAPPY!
US MUST OPERATE IMMEDIATELY TO MAKE YOU IMPERFECT.
DOCTORS! NURSES!
WEIRDZO NO. 1
NO-- PLEASE.
I'M SCARED OF SURGERY. I CAN'T DO IT. I CAN'T GO THROUGH WITH IT. PLEASE...
INNOCENCE AM NO EXCUSE. HIM WILL THANK US ONE DAY. HIM WILL SAY, "WEIRDZO, YOU FINK. YOU CUT IT OFF. GET LOST."
WEIRDZO NO 1
OKAY. MAKE HIM READY FOR SURGERY.
FOR GOD'S SAKE! YOU CAN'T DO THIS TO ME. I'M SCARED OF SURGERY. I WON'T DO IT. I WON'T DO IT...
LISTEN. HIM BE SO HAPPY US GOING TO OPERATE ON HIM.
IT AM SO GOOD. MAYBE HIM GIVE US PRESENTS AFTER.
SO WHAT YOU AM? A MAN OR A WOMAN?
WHATEVER YOU AM, WE MAKE IT BETTER.
NO.
...MMF... NO... JRM...

HAZEL DREAMS.

I'm on a train journey across a country I don't know. I don't know if I speak the language or not.

I don't know if I have a ticket.

A ticket inspector tells me that there is something wrong with my ticket. I have to go with him.

I didn't know that there were steps on trains.

He tells me there are cellars under all trains in this country. I have to go down.

The present I won with my ticket is in the box. I go to open it.

The baby smells of formaldehyde, not unpleasantly. It is cold and slightly clammy to the touch.

The autopsy scar is sewn together with black silk thread. It has been dead exactly seventy years.

It is perfectly preserved.

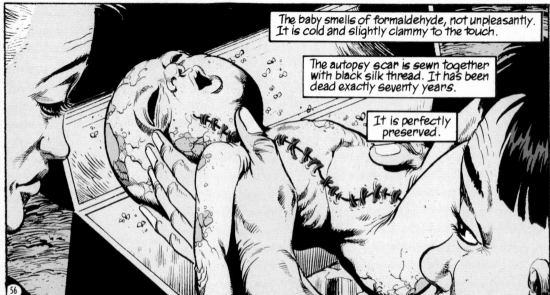

Foxglove is waiting for me, with her baby.

I cannot remember her baby's name. I cannot remember how old it is.

It's a boy, though. I remember that.

My baby is cold, so we put them together in a crib, to warm it up.

We love our babies.

My baby begins to move. I am unspeakably proud of it.

Now it smells of roses.

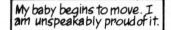

NO...

I know what it's going to do. I want to hide. I want to turn away. I want to stop looking.

I can't.

I hear Fox keening for her son. I cannot move.

And I know: once it's finished with Fox's child...

(Stop it, says Fox. Stoppit stoppitstoppitstoppit...)

Then it will come for us...

FOXGLOVE SLEEPS WITHOUT DREAMING.

DONNA?

DONNA CAVANAGH?

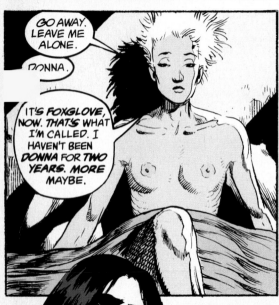

GO AWAY. LEAVE ME ALONE.

DONNA.

IT'S *FOXGLOVE*, NOW. *THAT'S* WHAT I'M CALLED. I HAVEN'T BEEN *DONNA* FOR *TWO YEARS*. MORE MAYBE.

DONNA'S SOMEBODY ELSE. DONNA'S *DEAD*.

DONNA.

DON'T *CALL* ME THAT! WHO'S TALKING, ANYWAY? WHO *IS* THAT?

IT'S ME. JUDY.

JUDY?

YOU CAN'T BE JUDY. YOU'RE *DEAD*.

YEAH. *DEAD* AS A DODO. IT'S A REAL *SHIT*, ISN'T IT?

AND IT'S *YOUR* FAULT. YOU KNOW THAT?

MINE...?

SURE IT IS. IF *YOU* HADN'T TAKEN OFF, *I* WOULDN'T HAVE BEEN HANGING AROUND IN THAT DAMNED *DINER*...

AND I'D STILL BE ABLE TO TASTE, AND FEEL, AND DREAM...

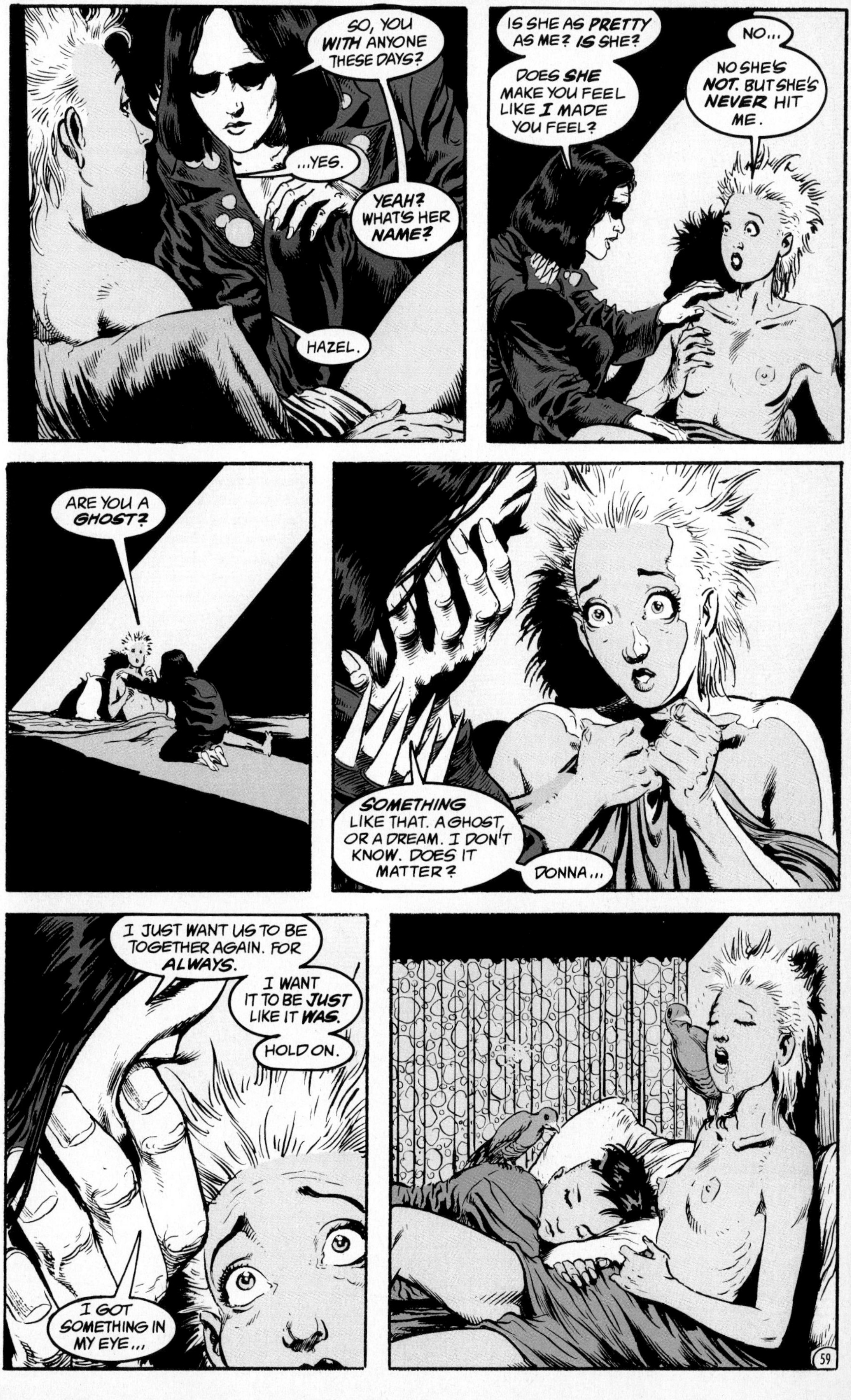
SO, YOU WITH ANYONE THESE DAYS?
...YES.
YEAH? WHAT'S HER NAME?
HAZEL.
IS SHE AS PRETTY AS ME? IS SHE?
DOES SHE MAKE YOU FEEL LIKE I MADE YOU FEEL?
NO...
NO SHE'S NOT. BUT SHE'S NEVER HIT ME.
ARE YOU A GHOST?
SOMETHING LIKE THAT. A GHOST, OR A DREAM. I DON'T KNOW. DOES IT MATTER?
DONNA...
I JUST WANT US TO BE TOGETHER AGAIN. FOR ALWAYS.
I WANT IT TO BE JUST LIKE IT WAS.
HOLD ON.
I GOT SOMETHING IN MY EYE...

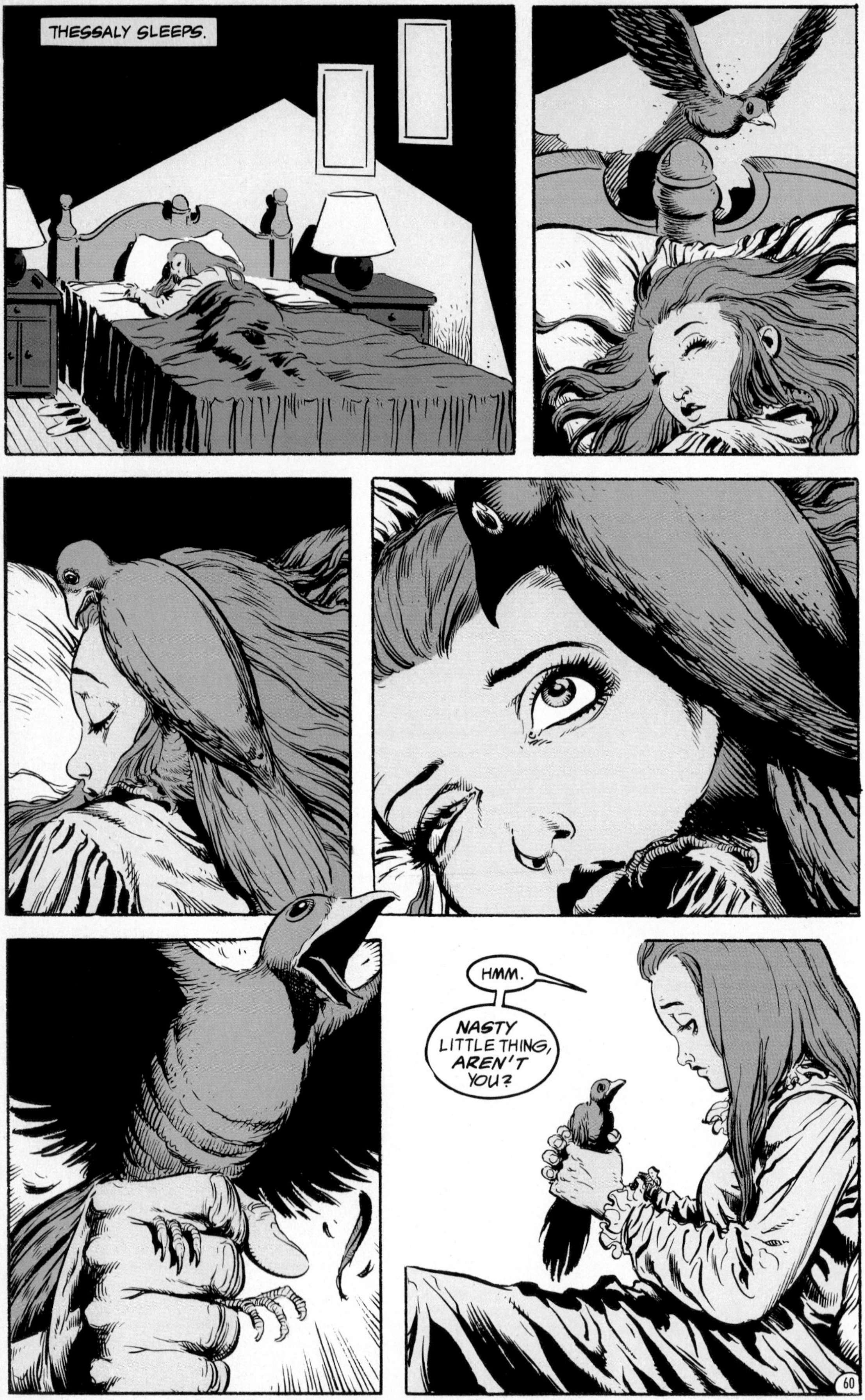
THESSALY SLEEPS.
HMM.
NASTY LITTLE THING, AREN'T YOU?

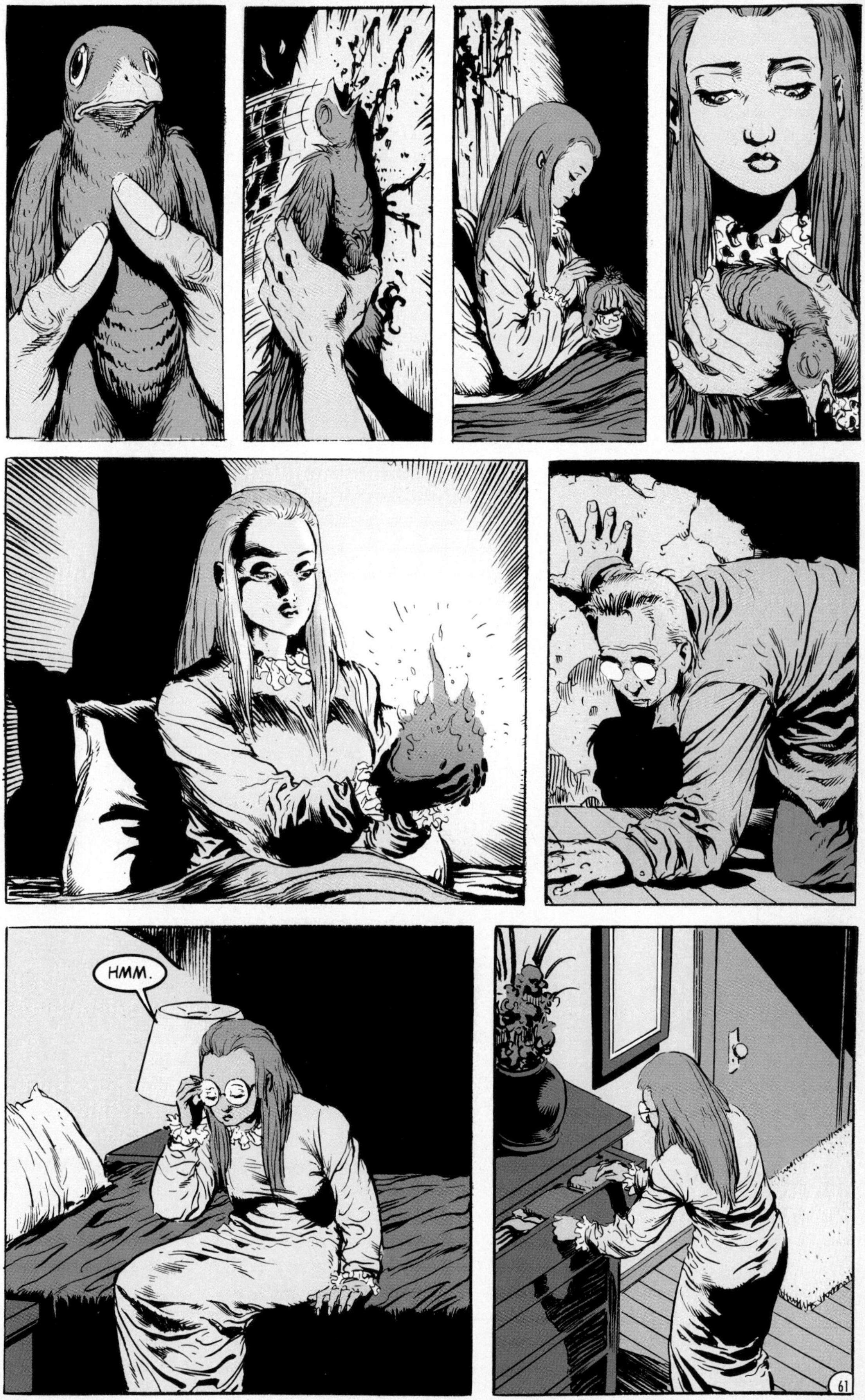
HMM.

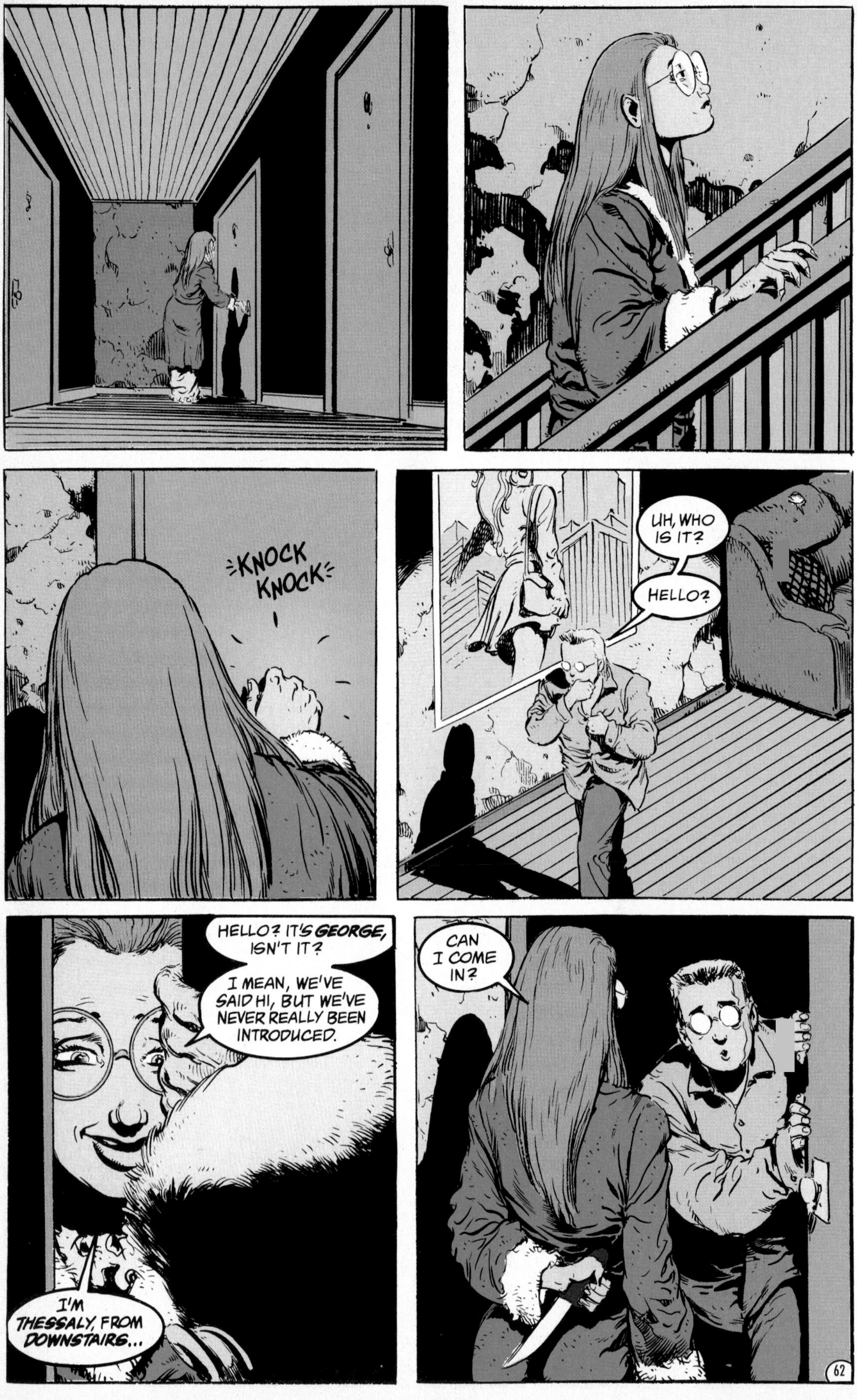

KNOCK KNOCK
UH, WHO IS IT?
HELLO?
HELLO? IT'S **GEORGE**, ISN'T IT?
I MEAN, WE'VE SAID HI, BUT WE'VE NEVER REALLY BEEN INTRODUCED.
I'M **THESSALY**, FROM **DOWNSTAIRS**...
CAN I COME IN?

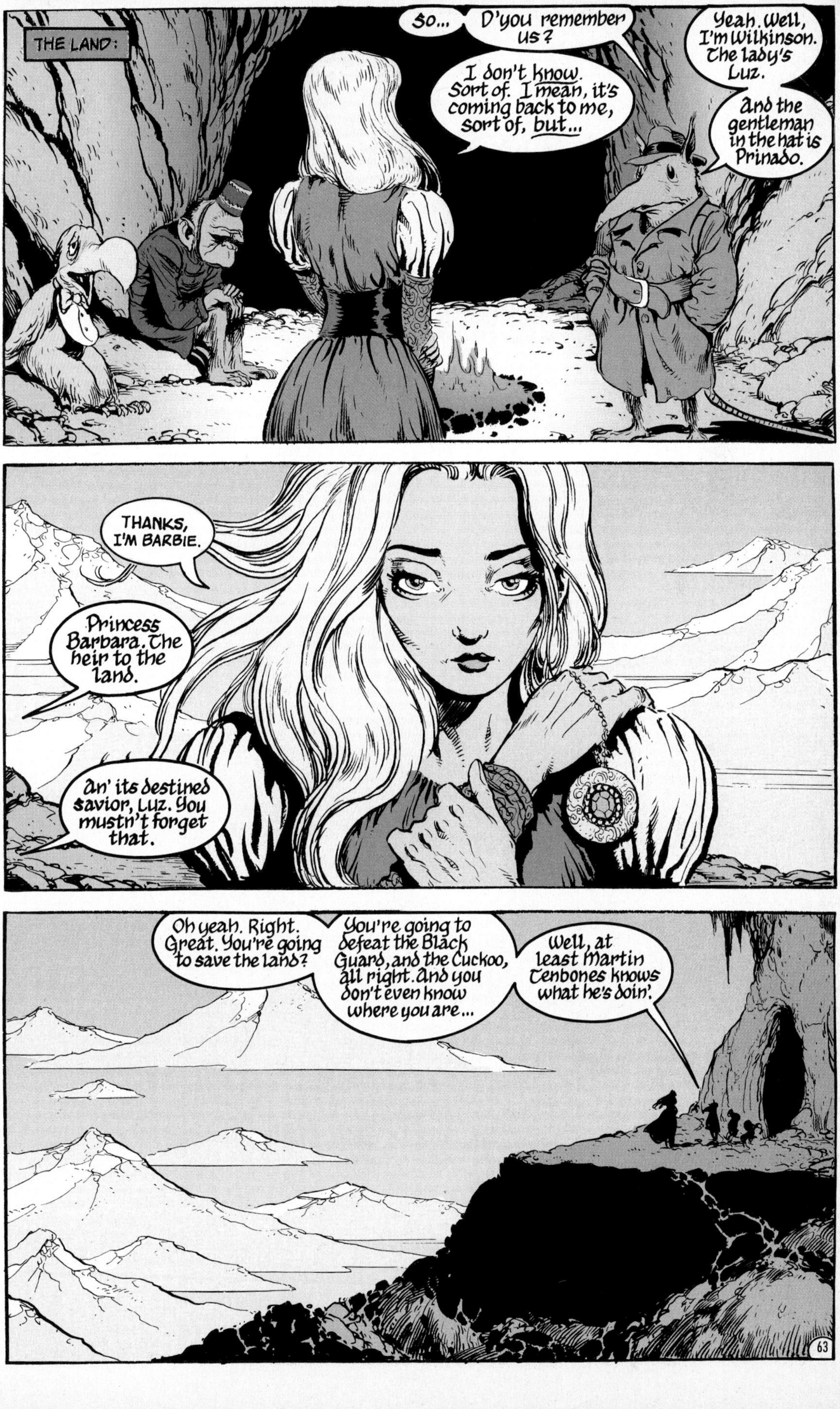

THE LAND:
So...
D'you remember us?
I don't know. Sort of. I mean, it's coming back to me, sort of, but...
Yeah. Well, I'm Wilkinson. The lady's Luz.
And the gentleman in the hat is Prinado.
THANKS, I'M BARBIE.
Princess Barbara. The heir to the land.
An' its destined savior, Luz. You mustn't forget that.
Oh yeah. Right. Great. You're going to save the land?
You're going to defeat the Black Guard, and the Cuckoo, all right. And you don't even know where you are...
Well, at least Martin Tenbones knows what he's doin'.

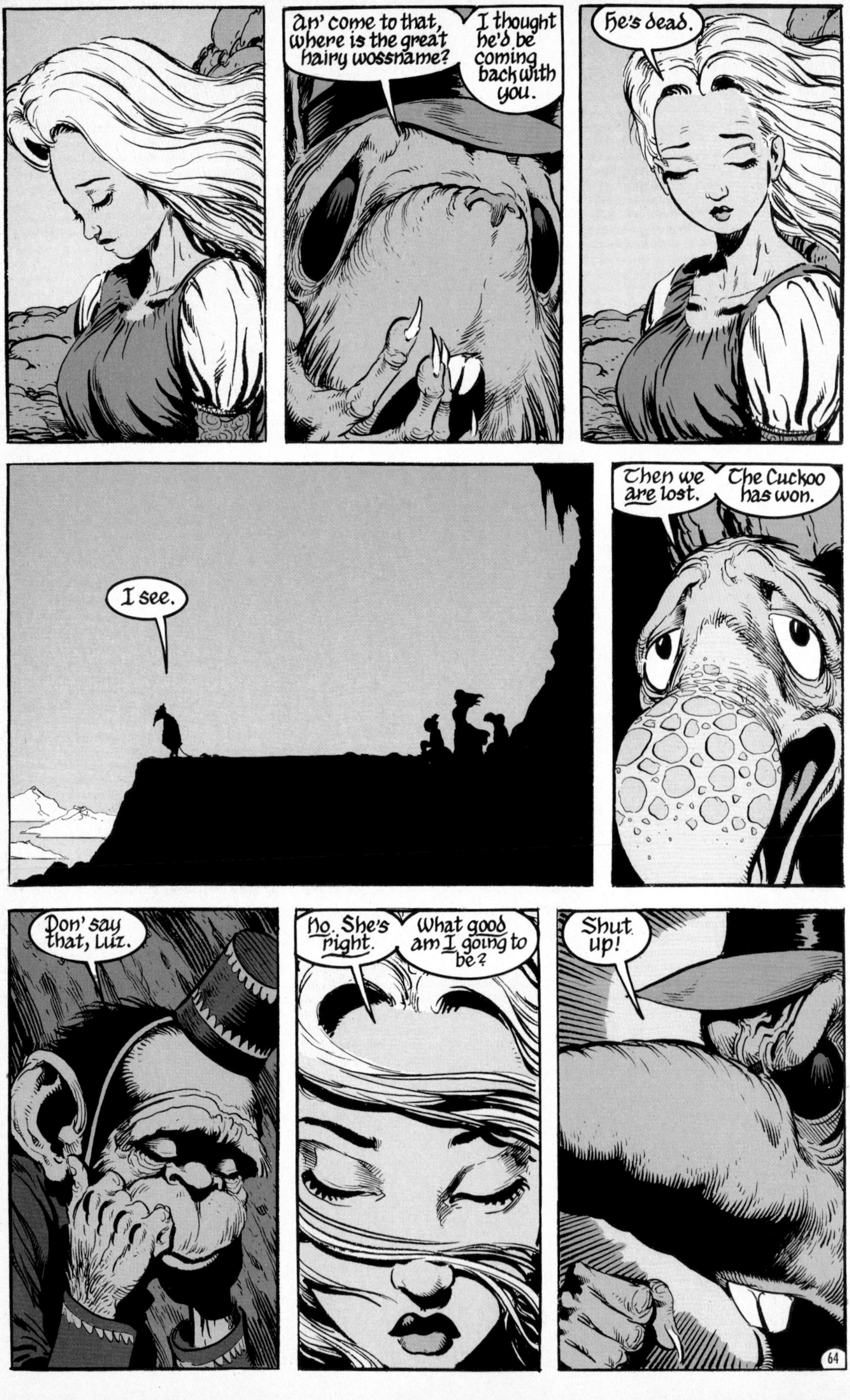
An' come to that, where is the great hairy wossname?
I thought he'd be coming back with you.
He's dead.
I see.
Then we are lost.
The Cuckoo has won.
Don' say that, Luz.
No. She's right.
What good am I going to be?
Shut up!

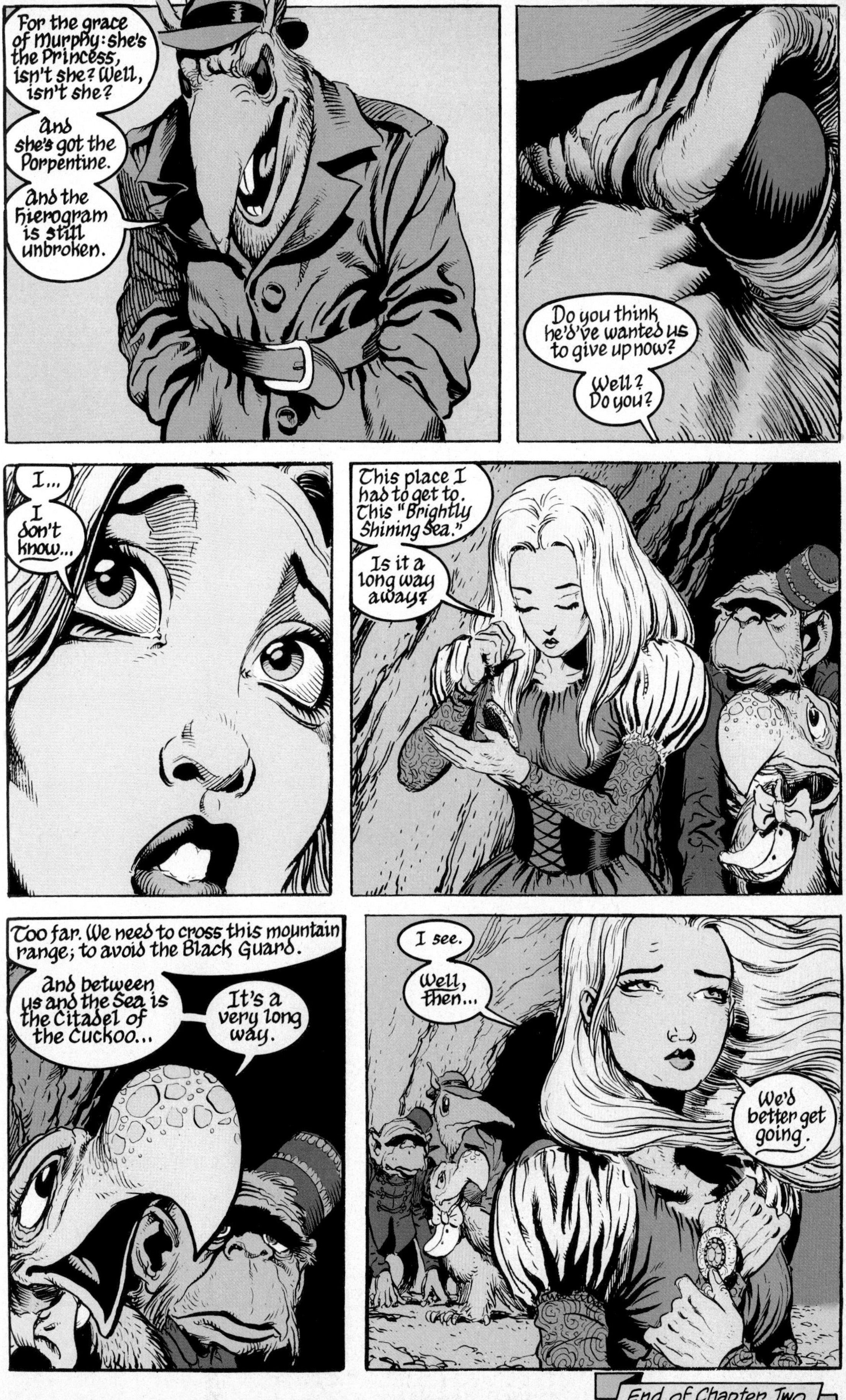
For the grace of Murphy: she's the Princess, isn't she? Well, isn't she?
And she's got the Porpentine.
And the Hierogram is still unbroken.
Do you think he'd've wanted us to give up now?
Well? Do you?
I... I don't know...
This place I had to get to. This "Brightly Shining Sea."
Is it a long way away?
Too far. We need to cross this mountain range; to avoid the Black Guard.
And between us and the Sea is the Citadel of the Cuckoo...
It's a very long way.
I see.
Well, then...
We'd better get going.
End of Chapter Two.

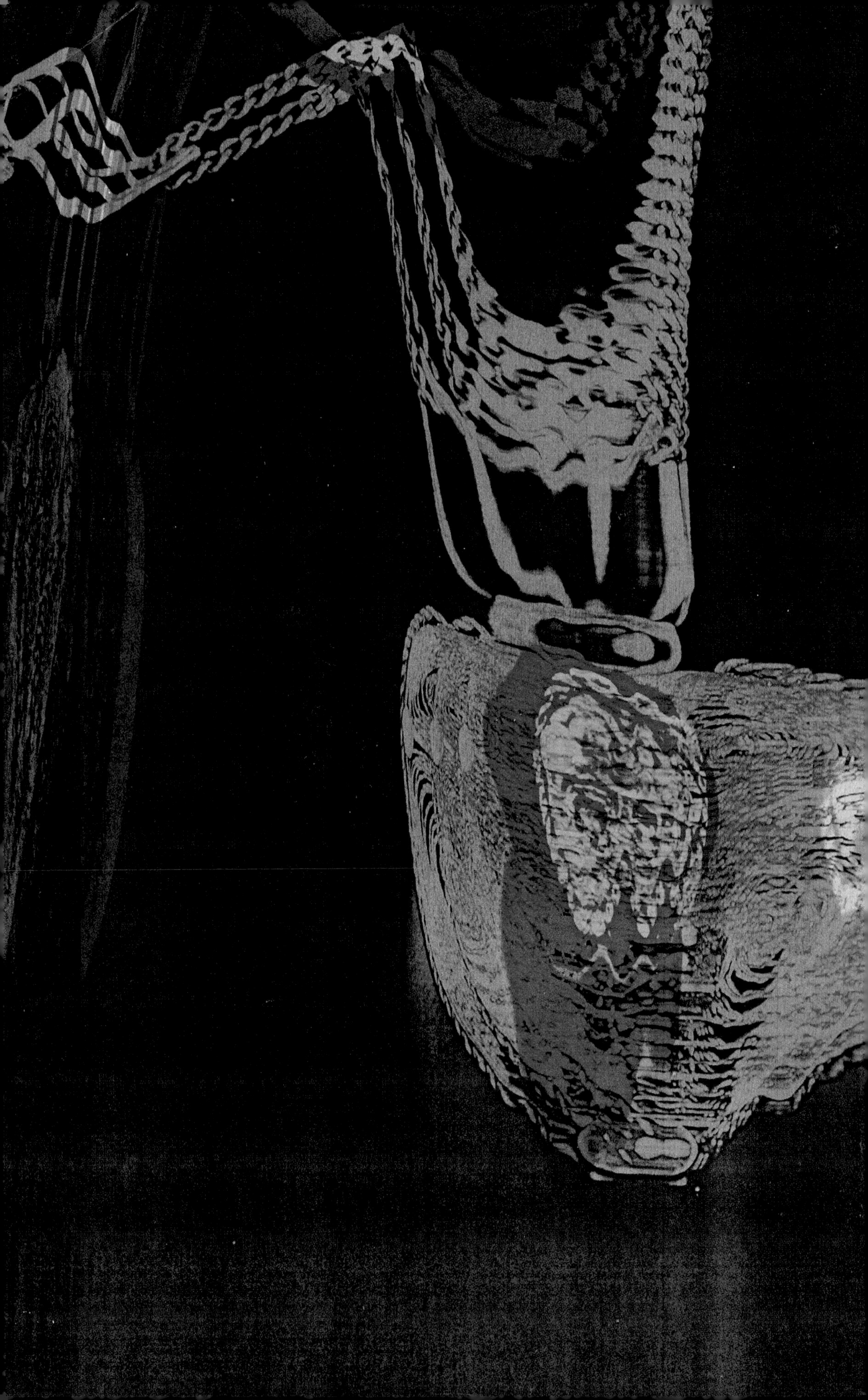

a game of you

chapter three

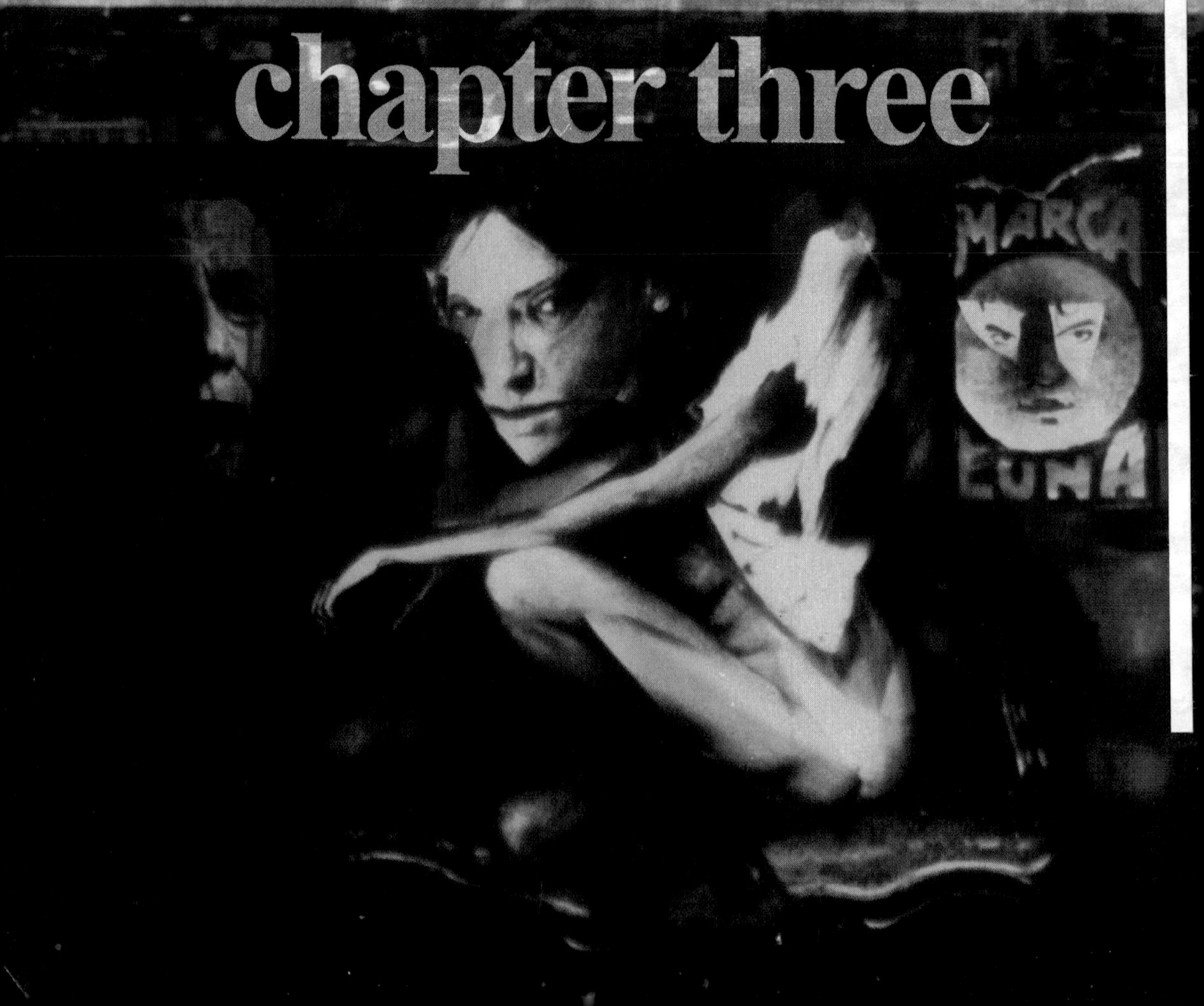
MARCA
LUNA

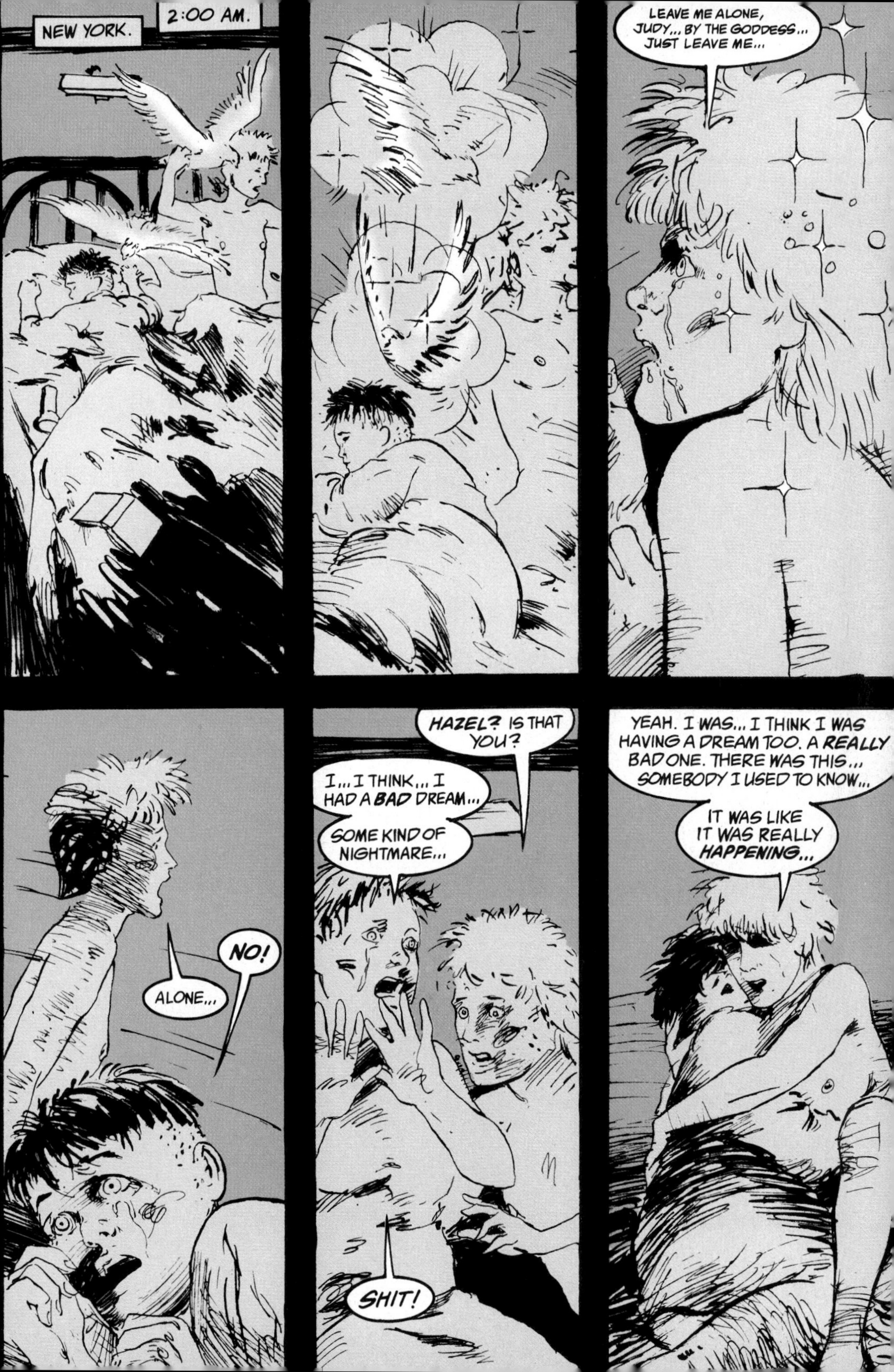
NEW YORK.
2:00 AM.
LEAVE ME ALONE, JUDY... BY THE GODDESS... JUST LEAVE ME...
ALONE...
NO!
HAZEL? IS THAT YOU?
I... I THINK... I HAD A BAD DREAM...
SOME KIND OF NIGHTMARE...
SHIT!
YEAH. I WAS... I THINK I WAS HAVING A DREAM TOO. A REALLY BAD ONE. THERE WAS THIS... SOMEBODY I USED TO KNOW...
IT WAS LIKE IT WAS REALLY HAPPENING...

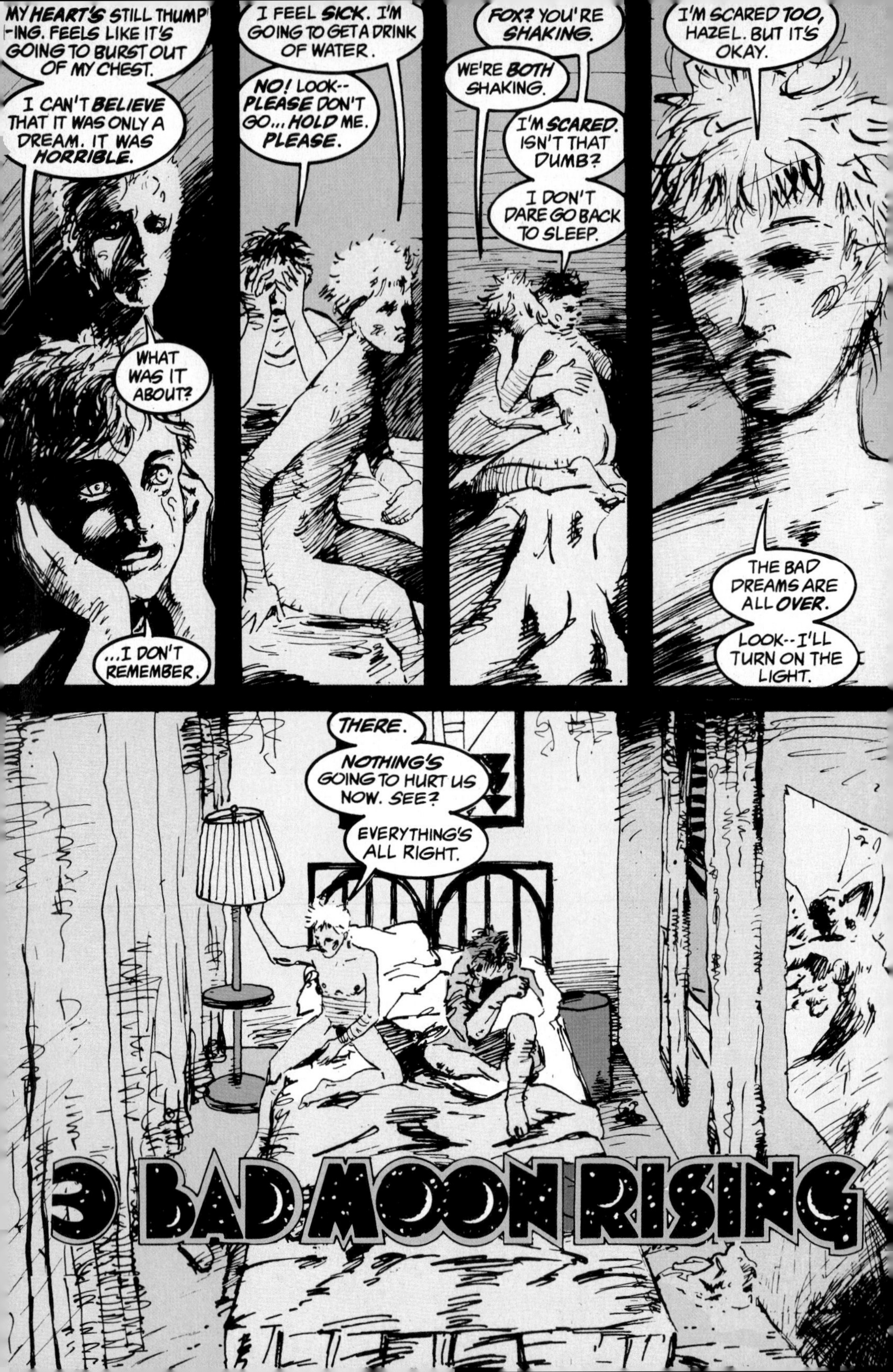
MY HEART'S STILL THUMPING. FEELS LIKE IT'S GOING TO BURST OUT OF MY CHEST.
I CAN'T BELIEVE THAT IT WAS ONLY A DREAM. IT WAS HORRIBLE.
WHAT WAS IT ABOUT?
...I DON'T REMEMBER.
I FEEL SICK. I'M GOING TO GET A DRINK OF WATER.
NO! LOOK-- PLEASE DON'T GO... HOLD ME. PLEASE.
FOX? YOU'RE SHAKING.
WE'RE BOTH SHAKING.
I'M SCARED. ISN'T THAT DUMB?
I DON'T DARE GO BACK TO SLEEP.
I'M SCARED TOO, HAZEL. BUT IT'S OKAY.
THE BAD DREAMS ARE ALL OVER.
LOOK--I'LL TURN ON THE LIGHT.
THERE.
NOTHING'S GOING TO HURT US NOW. SEE?
EVERYTHING'S ALL RIGHT.
3 BAD MOON RISING

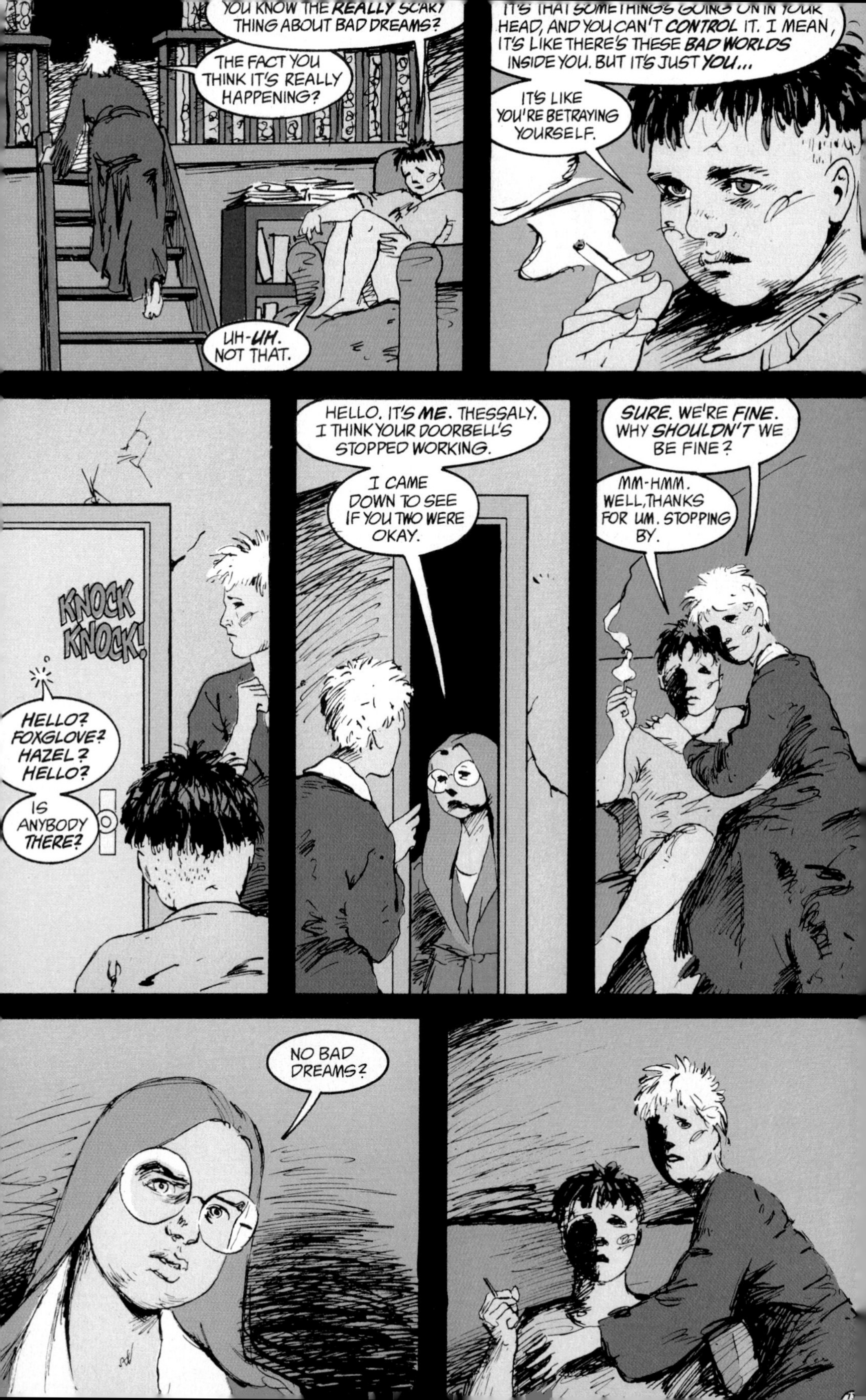
YOU KNOW THE REALLY SCARY THING ABOUT BAD DREAMS?
THE FACT YOU THINK IT'S REALLY HAPPENING?
UH-UH. NOT THAT.
IT'S THAT SOMETHING'S GOING ON IN YOUR HEAD, AND YOU CAN'T CONTROL IT. I MEAN, IT'S LIKE THERE'S THESE BAD WORLDS INSIDE YOU. BUT IT'S JUST YOU...
IT'S LIKE YOU'RE BETRAYING YOURSELF.
KNOCK KNOCK!
HELLO? FOXGLOVE? HAZEL? HELLO?
IS ANYBODY THERE?
HELLO. IT'S ME. THESSALY. I THINK YOUR DOORBELL'S STOPPED WORKING.
I CAME DOWN TO SEE IF YOU TWO WERE OKAY.
SURE. WE'RE FINE. WHY SHOULDN'T WE BE FINE?
MM-HMM. WELL, THANKS FOR UM. STOPPING BY.
NO BAD DREAMS?

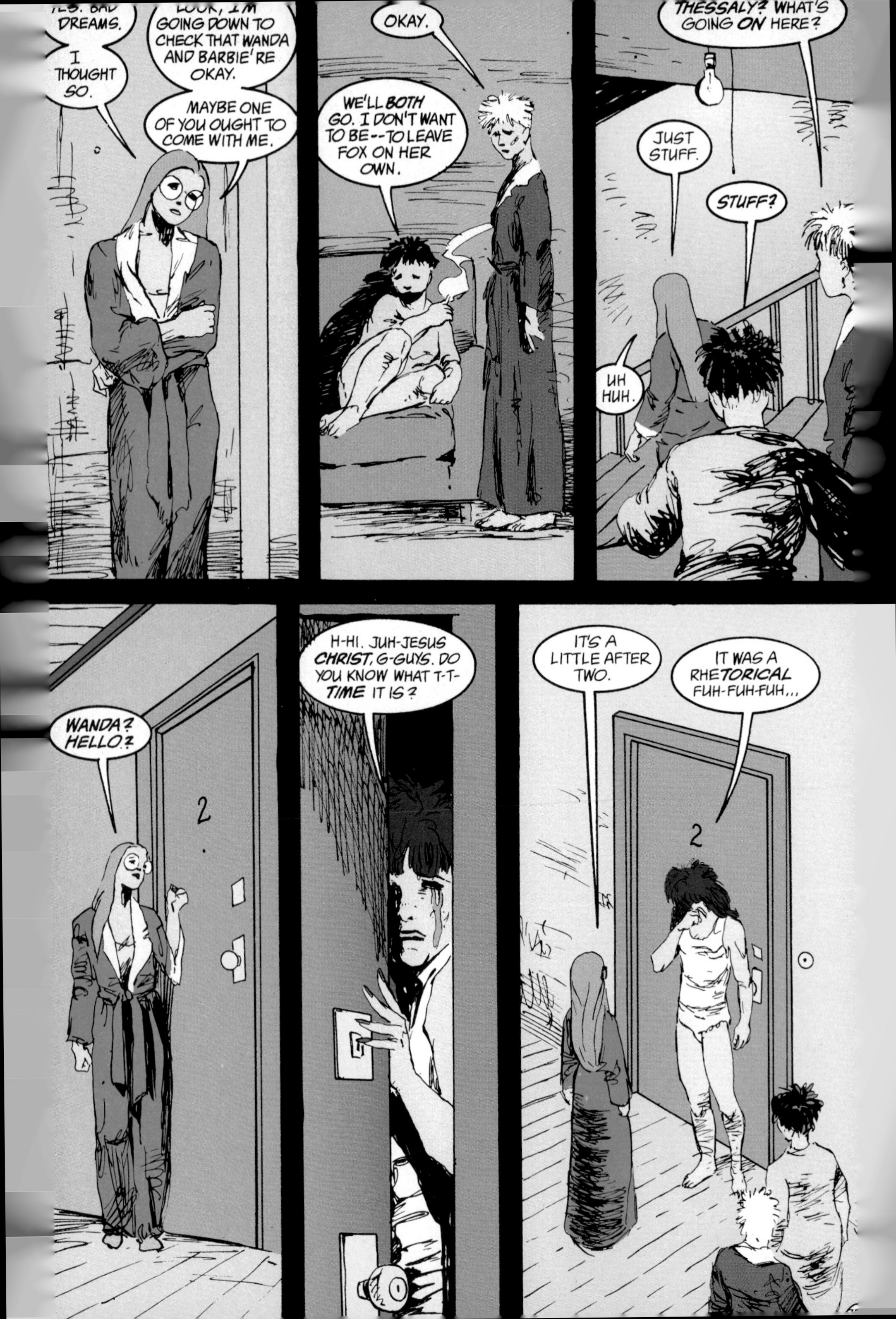

DREAMS.
I THOUGHT SO.
LOOK, I'M GOING DOWN TO CHECK THAT WANDA AND BARBIE'RE OKAY.
MAYBE ONE OF YOU OUGHT TO COME WITH ME.
OKAY.
WE'LL BOTH GO. I DON'T WANT TO BE--TO LEAVE FOX ON HER OWN.
THESSALY? WHAT'S GOING ON HERE?
JUST STUFF.
STUFF?
UH HUH.
WANDA? HELLO?
H-HI. JUH-JESUS CHRIST, G-GUYS. DO YOU KNOW WHAT T-T-TIME IT IS?
IT'S A LITTLE AFTER TWO.
IT WAS A RHETORICAL FUH-FUH-FUH...

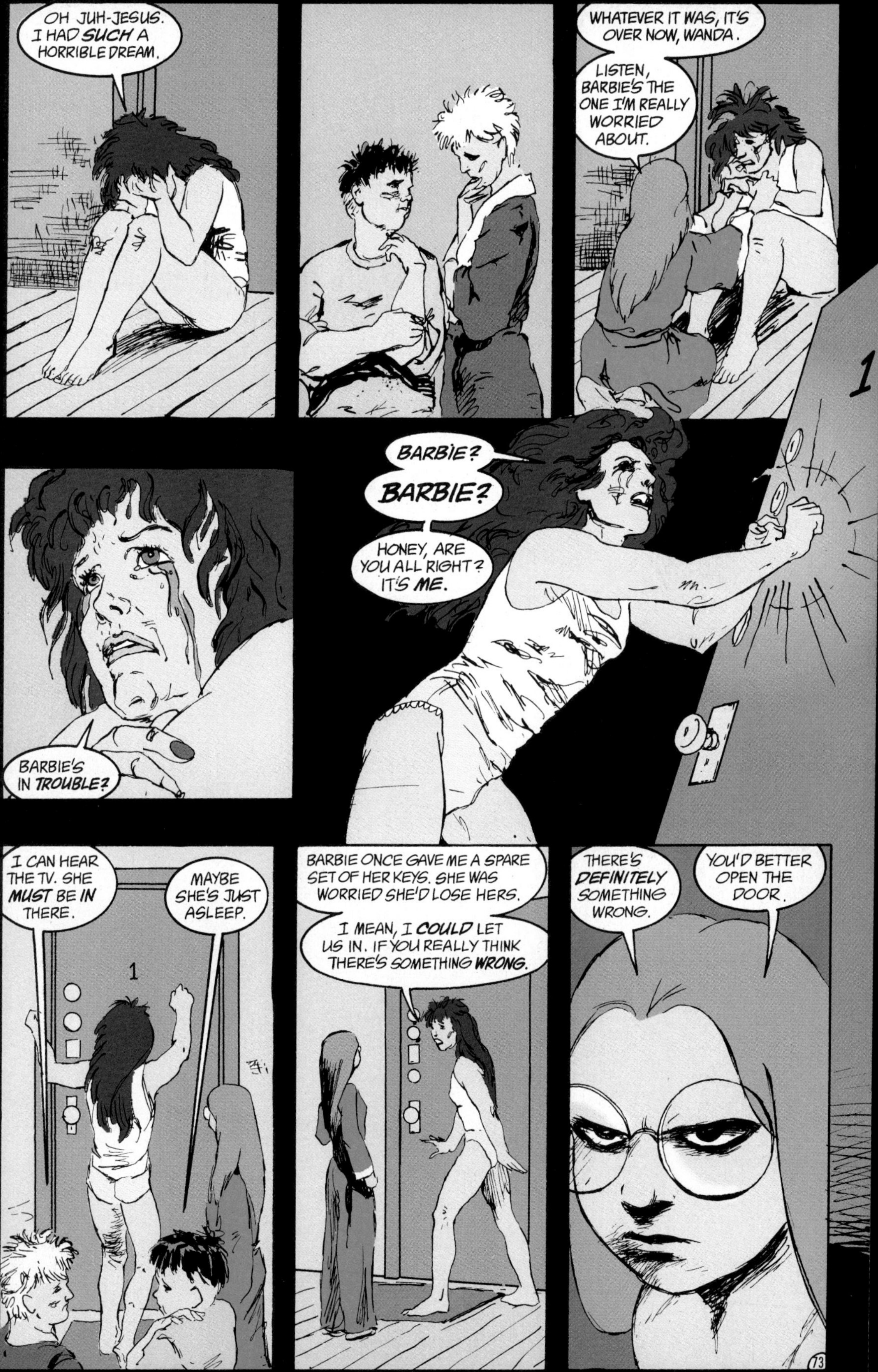
OH JUH-JESUS. I HAD SUCH A HORRIBLE DREAM.
WHATEVER IT WAS, IT'S OVER NOW, WANDA.
LISTEN, BARBIE'S THE ONE I'M REALLY WORRIED ABOUT.
BARBIE'S IN TROUBLE?
BARBIE?
BARBIE?
HONEY, ARE YOU ALL RIGHT? IT'S ME.
1
I CAN HEAR THE TV. SHE MUST BE IN THERE.
MAYBE SHE'S JUST ASLEEP.
1
BARBIE ONCE GAVE ME A SPARE SET OF HER KEYS. SHE WAS WORRIED SHE'D LOSE HERS.
I MEAN, I COULD LET US IN. IF YOU REALLY THINK THERE'S SOMETHING WRONG.
THERE'S DEFINITELY SOMETHING WRONG.
YOU'D BETTER OPEN THE DOOR.

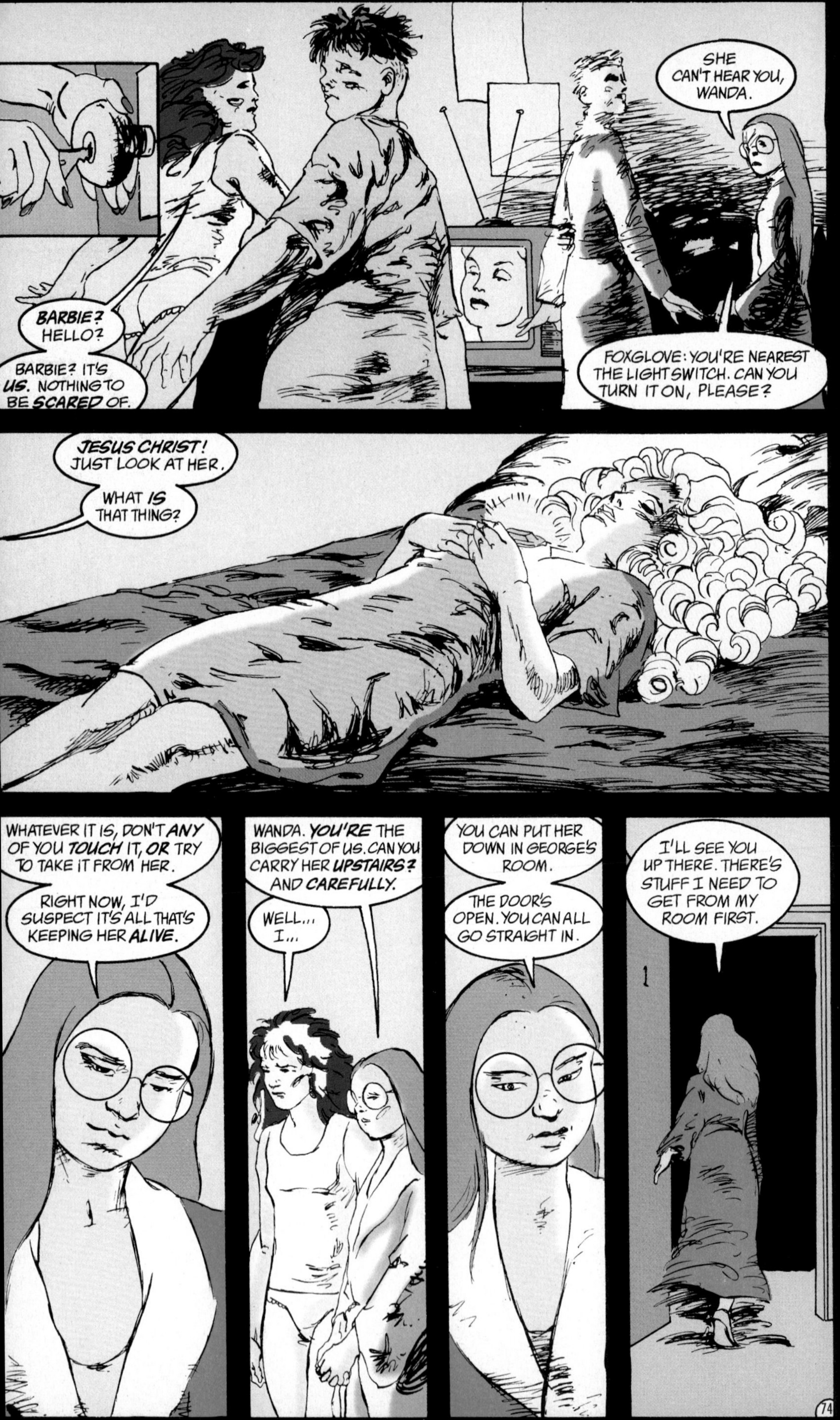
SHE CAN'T HEAR YOU, WANDA.
BARBIE? HELLO?
BARBIE? IT'S US. NOTHING TO BE SCARED OF.
FOXGLOVE: YOU'RE NEAREST THE LIGHT SWITCH. CAN YOU TURN IT ON, PLEASE?
JESUS CHRIST! JUST LOOK AT HER.
WHAT IS THAT THING?
WHATEVER IT IS, DON'T ANY OF YOU TOUCH IT, OR TRY TO TAKE IT FROM HER.
RIGHT NOW, I'D SUSPECT IT'S ALL THAT'S KEEPING HER ALIVE.
WANDA. YOU'RE THE BIGGEST OF US. CAN YOU CARRY HER UPSTAIRS? AND CAREFULLY.
WELL... I...
YOU CAN PUT HER DOWN IN GEORGE'S ROOM.
THE DOOR'S OPEN. YOU CAN ALL GO STRAIGHT IN.
I'LL SEE YOU UP THERE. THERE'S STUFF I NEED TO GET FROM MY ROOM FIRST.

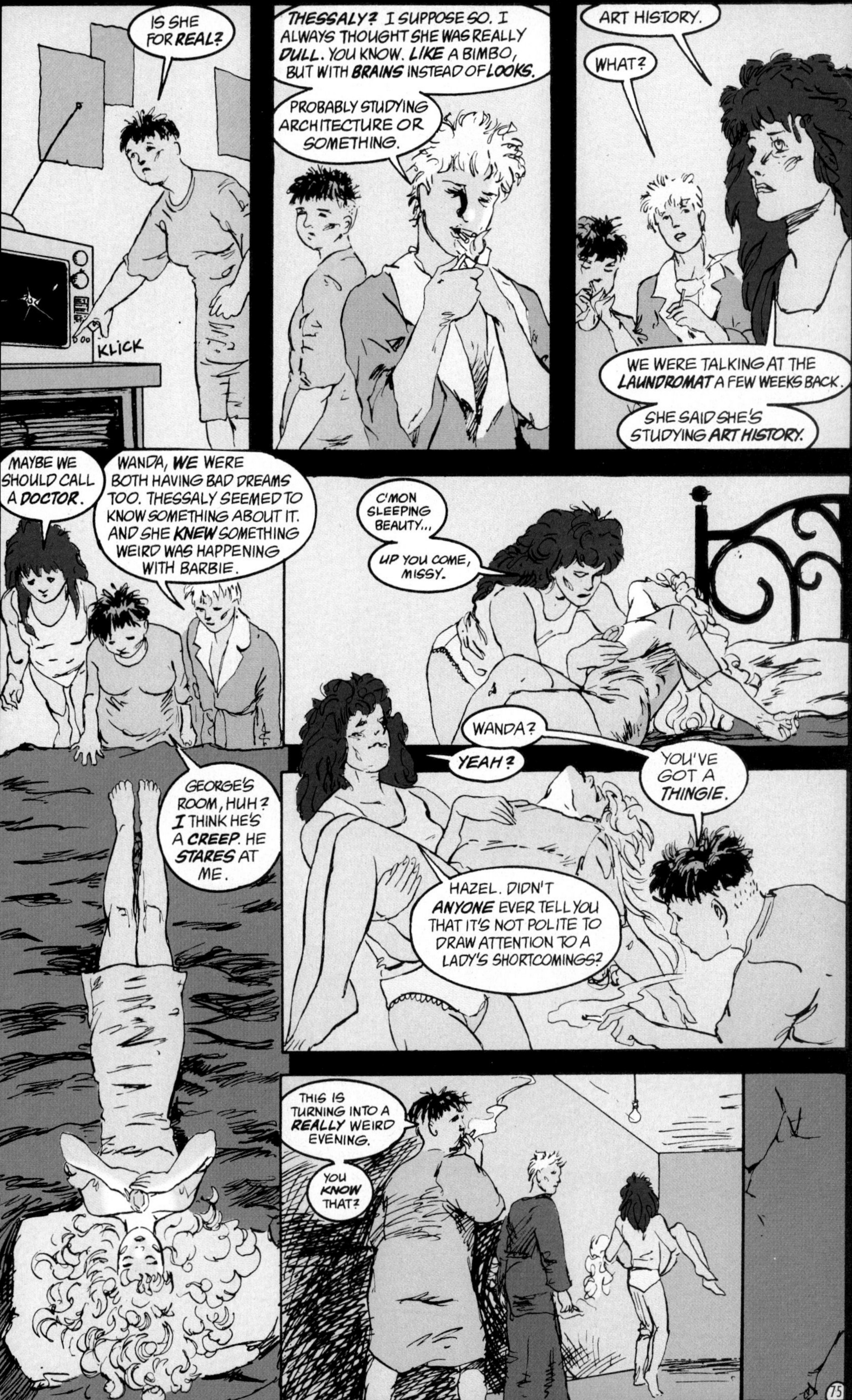

IS SHE FOR REAL?
KLICK
THESSALY? I SUPPOSE SO. I ALWAYS THOUGHT SHE WAS REALLY DULL. YOU KNOW. LIKE A BIMBO, BUT WITH BRAINS INSTEAD OF LOOKS.
PROBABLY STUDYING ARCHITECTURE OR SOMETHING.
ART HISTORY.
WHAT?
WE WERE TALKING AT THE LAUNDROMAT A FEW WEEKS BACK.
SHE SAID SHE'S STUDYING ART HISTORY.
MAYBE WE SHOULD CALL A DOCTOR.
WANDA, WE WERE BOTH HAVING BAD DREAMS TOO. THESSALY SEEMED TO KNOW SOMETHING ABOUT IT. AND SHE KNEW SOMETHING WEIRD WAS HAPPENING WITH BARBIE.
C'MON SLEEPING BEAUTY...
UP YOU COME, MISSY.
GEORGE'S ROOM, HUH? I THINK HE'S A CREEP. HE STARES AT ME.
WANDA?
YEAH?
YOU'VE GOT A THINGIE.
HAZEL. DIDN'T ANYONE EVER TELL YOU THAT IT'S NOT POLITE TO DRAW ATTENTION TO A LADY'S SHORTCOMINGS?
THIS IS TURNING INTO A REALLY WEIRD EVENING.
YOU KNOW THAT?

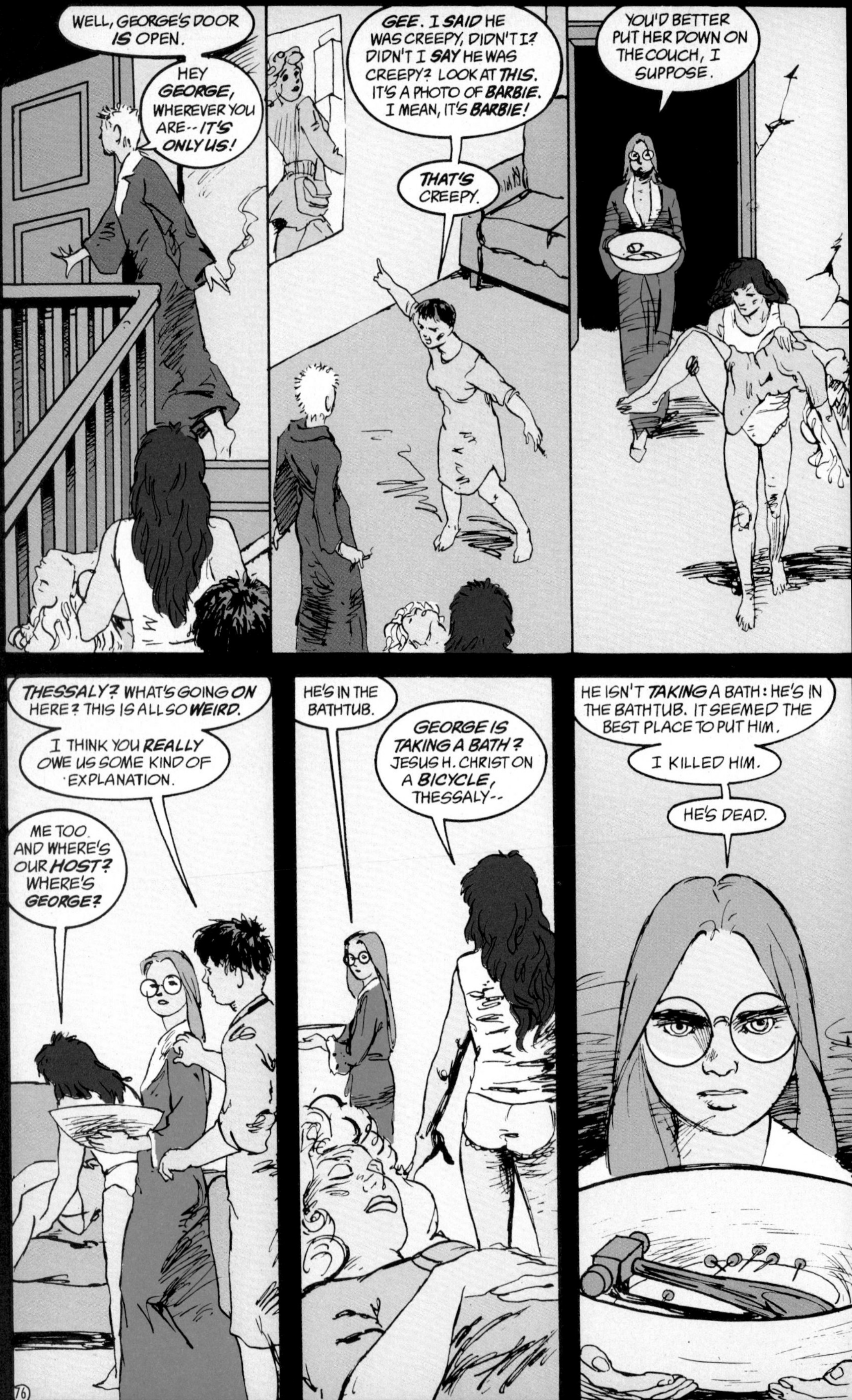

WELL, GEORGE'S DOOR IS OPEN.
HEY GEORGE, WHEREVER YOU ARE--IT'S ONLY US!
GEE. I SAID HE WAS CREEPY, DIDN'T I? DIDN'T I SAY HE WAS CREEPY? LOOK AT THIS. IT'S A PHOTO OF BARBIE. I MEAN, IT'S BARBIE!
THAT'S CREEPY.
YOU'D BETTER PUT HER DOWN ON THE COUCH, I SUPPOSE.
THESSALY? WHAT'S GOING ON HERE? THIS IS ALL SO WEIRD.
I THINK YOU REALLY OWE US SOME KIND OF EXPLANATION.
ME TOO. AND WHERE'S OUR HOST? WHERE'S GEORGE?
HE'S IN THE BATHTUB.
GEORGE IS TAKING A BATH? JESUS H. CHRIST ON A BICYCLE, THESSALY--
HE ISN'T TAKING A BATH: HE'S IN THE BATHTUB. IT SEEMED THE BEST PLACE TO PUT HIM.
I KILLED HIM.
HE'S DEAD.

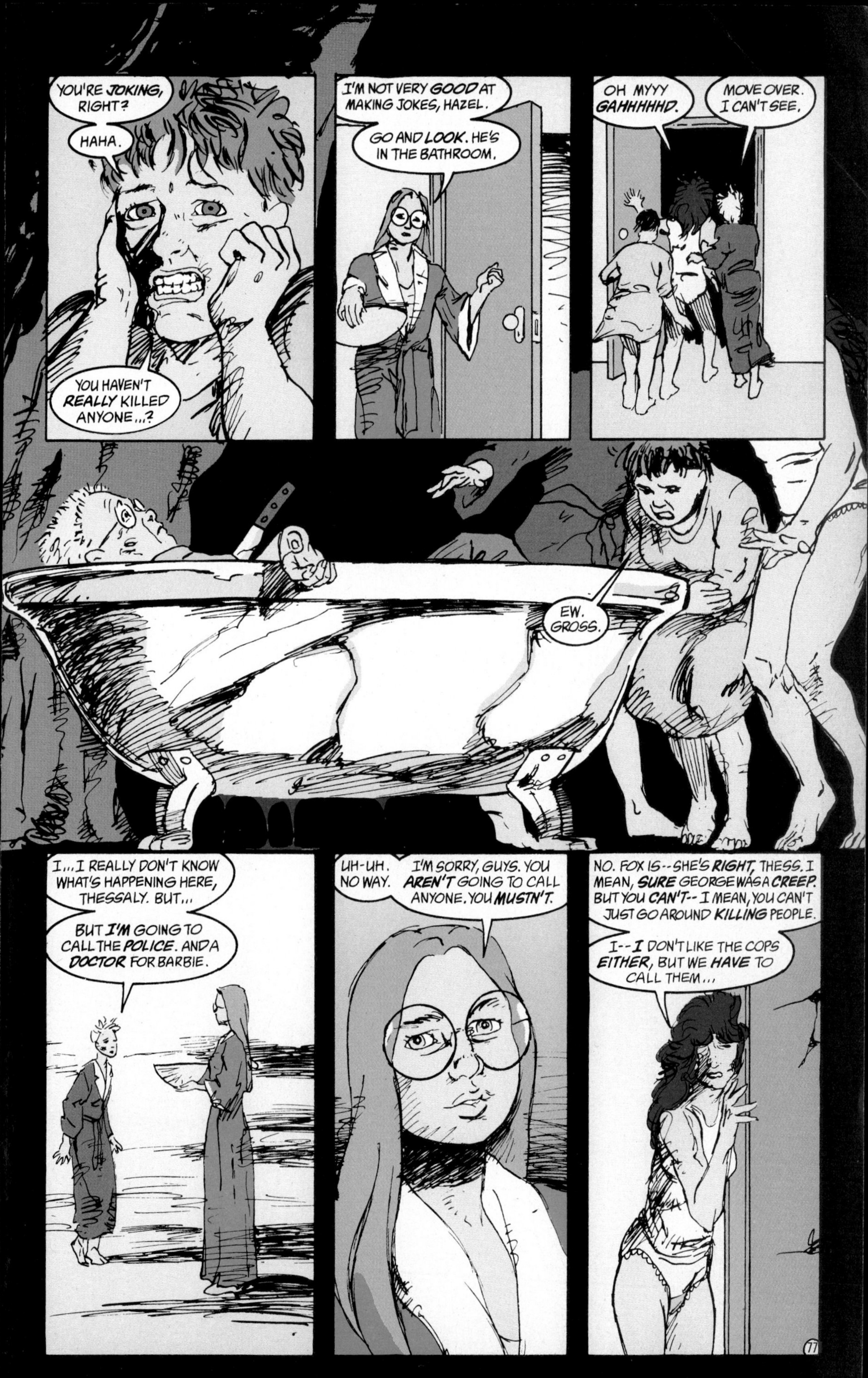

YOU'RE JOKING, RIGHT?
HAHA.
YOU HAVEN'T REALLY KILLED ANYONE...?
I'M NOT VERY GOOD AT MAKING JOKES, HAZEL.
GO AND LOOK. HE'S IN THE BATHROOM.
OH MYYY GAHHHHHD.
MOVE OVER. I CAN'T SEE.
EW. GROSS.
I...I REALLY DON'T KNOW WHAT'S HAPPENING HERE, THESSALY. BUT...
BUT I'M GOING TO CALL THE POLICE. AND A DOCTOR FOR BARBIE.
UH-UH. NO WAY.
I'M SORRY, GUYS. YOU AREN'T GOING TO CALL ANYONE. YOU MUSTN'T.
NO. FOX IS--SHE'S RIGHT, THESS. I MEAN, SURE GEORGE WAS A CREEP. BUT YOU CAN'T-- I MEAN, YOU CAN'T JUST GO AROUND KILLING PEOPLE.
I--I DON'T LIKE THE COPS EITHER, BUT WE HAVE TO CALL THEM...

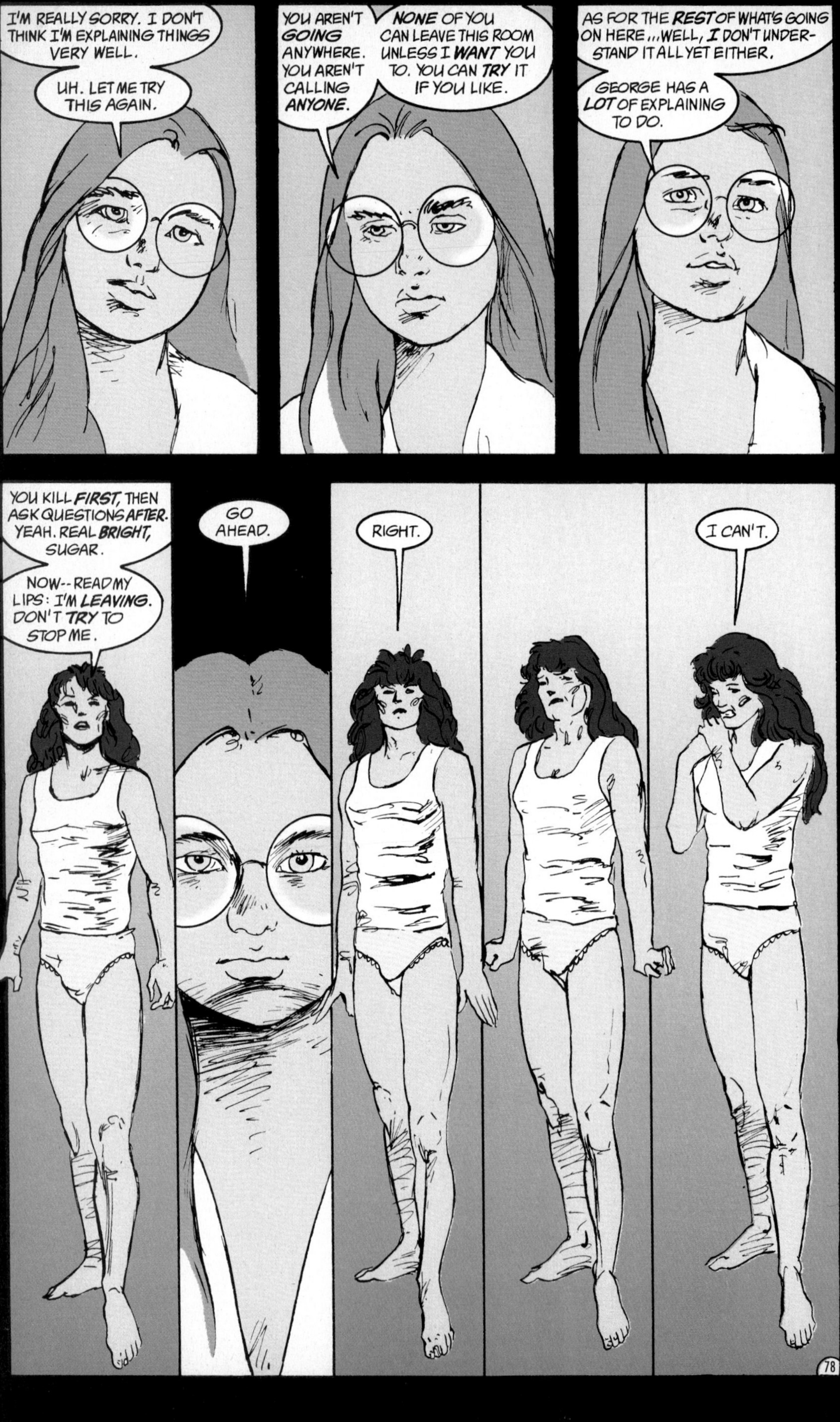
I'M REALLY SORRY. I DON'T THINK I'M EXPLAINING THINGS VERY WELL.
UH. LET ME TRY THIS AGAIN.
YOU AREN'T GOING ANYWHERE. YOU AREN'T CALLING ANYONE.
NONE OF YOU CAN LEAVE THIS ROOM UNLESS I WANT YOU TO. YOU CAN TRY IT IF YOU LIKE.
AS FOR THE REST OF WHAT'S GOING ON HERE,,,WELL, I DON'T UNDERSTAND IT ALL YET EITHER.
GEORGE HAS A LOT OF EXPLAINING TO DO.
YOU KILL FIRST, THEN ASK QUESTIONS AFTER. YEAH. REAL BRIGHT, SUGAR.
NOW--READ MY LIPS: I'M LEAVING. DON'T TRY TO STOP ME.
GO AHEAD.
RIGHT.
I CAN'T.

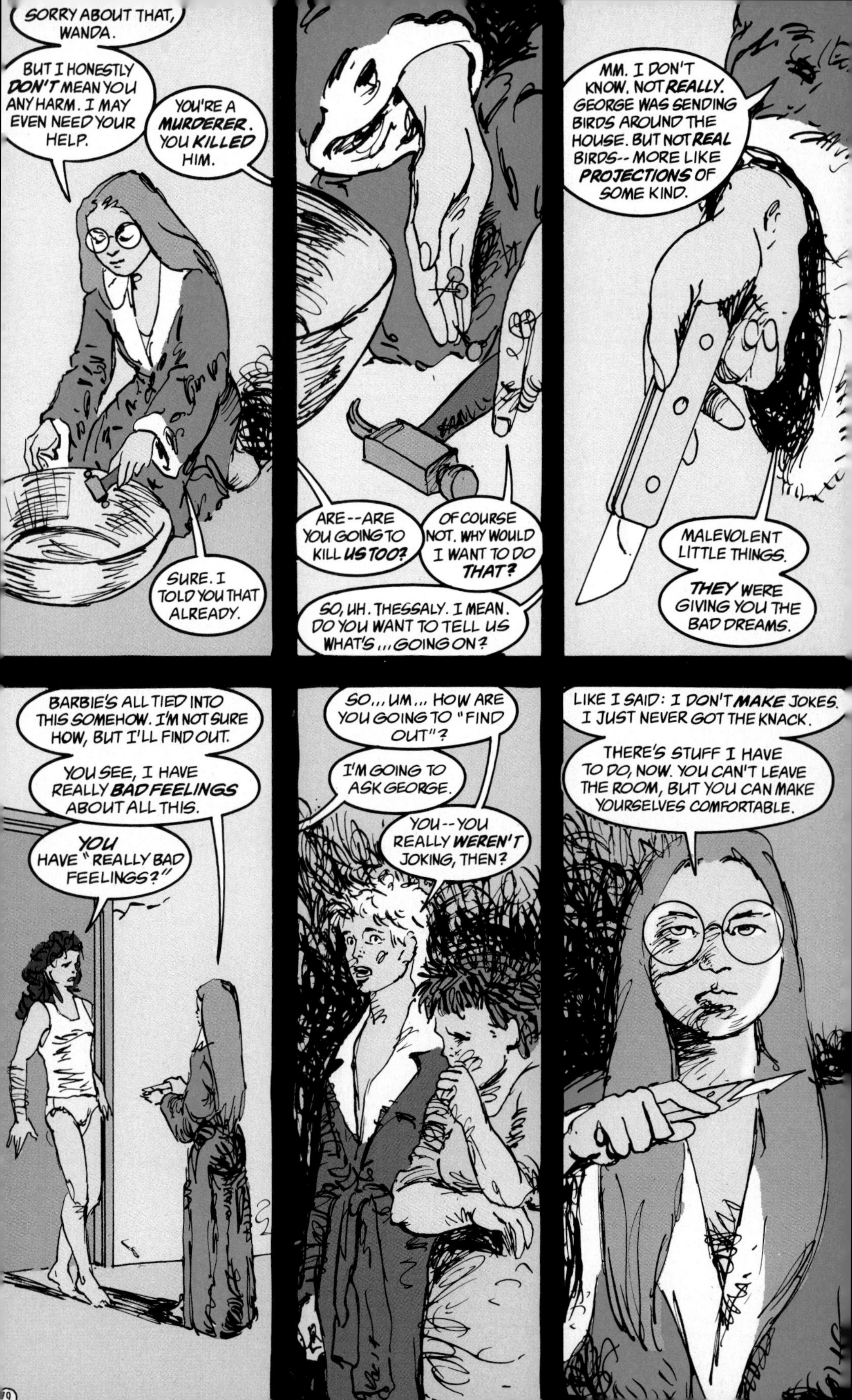
SORRY ABOUT THAT, WANDA.
BUT I HONESTLY DON'T MEAN YOU ANY HARM. I MAY EVEN NEED YOUR HELP.
YOU'RE A MURDERER. YOU KILLED HIM.
SURE. I TOLD YOU THAT ALREADY.
ARE--ARE YOU GOING TO KILL US TOO?
OF COURSE NOT. WHY WOULD I WANT TO DO THAT?
SO, UH. THESSALY. I MEAN. DO YOU WANT TO TELL US WHAT'S,,, GOING ON?
MM. I DON'T KNOW. NOT REALLY. GEORGE WAS SENDING BIRDS AROUND THE HOUSE. BUT NOT REAL BIRDS-- MORE LIKE PROJECTIONS OF SOME KIND.
MALEVOLENT LITTLE THINGS.
THEY WERE GIVING YOU THE BAD DREAMS.
BARBIE'S ALL TIED INTO THIS SOMEHOW. I'M NOT SURE HOW, BUT I'LL FIND OUT.
YOU SEE, I HAVE REALLY BAD FEELINGS ABOUT ALL THIS.
YOU HAVE "REALLY BAD FEELINGS?"
SO,,, UM,,, HOW ARE YOU GOING TO "FIND OUT"?
I'M GOING TO ASK GEORGE.
YOU--YOU REALLY WEREN'T JOKING, THEN?
LIKE I SAID: I DON'T MAKE JOKES. I JUST NEVER GOT THE KNACK.
THERE'S STUFF I HAVE TO DO, NOW. YOU CAN'T LEAVE THE ROOM, BUT YOU CAN MAKE YOURSELVES COMFORTABLE.

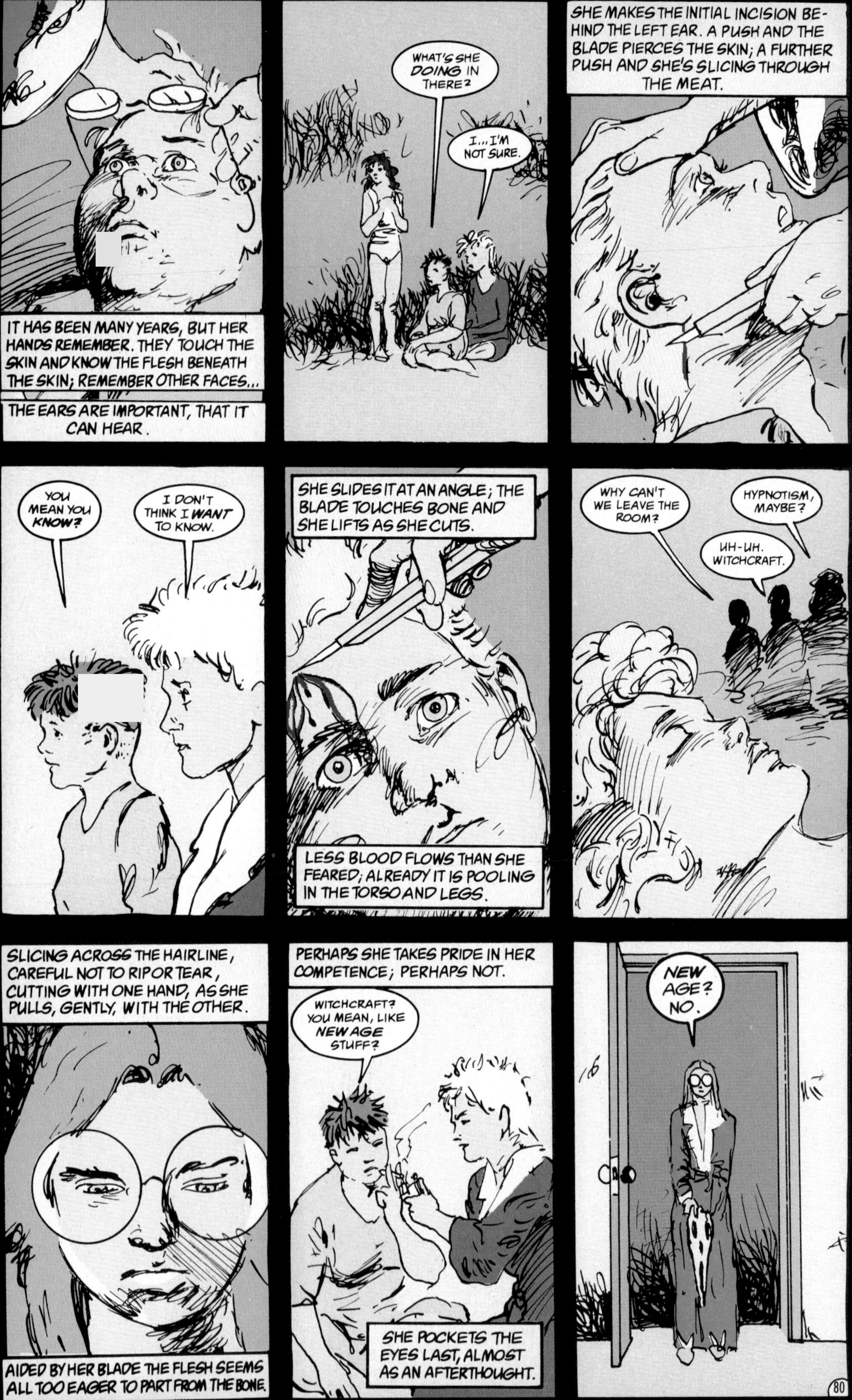

IT HAS BEEN MANY YEARS, BUT HER HANDS REMEMBER. THEY TOUCH THE SKIN AND KNOW THE FLESH BENEATH THE SKIN; REMEMBER OTHER FACES...
THE EARS ARE IMPORTANT, THAT IT CAN HEAR.
WHAT'S SHE DOING IN THERE?
I...I'M NOT SURE.
SHE MAKES THE INITIAL INCISION BEHIND THE LEFT EAR. A PUSH AND THE BLADE PIERCES THE SKIN; A FURTHER PUSH AND SHE'S SLICING THROUGH THE MEAT.
YOU MEAN YOU KNOW?
I DON'T THINK I WANT TO KNOW.
SHE SLIDES IT AT AN ANGLE; THE BLADE TOUCHES BONE AND SHE LIFTS AS SHE CUTS.
LESS BLOOD FLOWS THAN SHE FEARED; ALREADY IT IS POOLING IN THE TORSO AND LEGS.
WHY CAN'T WE LEAVE THE ROOM?
HYPNOTISM, MAYBE?
UH-UH. WITCHCRAFT.
SLICING ACROSS THE HAIRLINE, CAREFUL NOT TO RIP OR TEAR, CUTTING WITH ONE HAND, AS SHE PULLS, GENTLY, WITH THE OTHER.
AIDED BY HER BLADE THE FLESH SEEMS ALL TOO EAGER TO PART FROM THE BONE.
PERHAPS SHE TAKES PRIDE IN HER COMPETENCE; PERHAPS NOT.
WITCHCRAFT? YOU MEAN, LIKE NEW AGE STUFF?
SHE POCKETS THE EYES LAST, ALMOST AS AN AFTERTHOUGHT.
NEW AGE? NO.

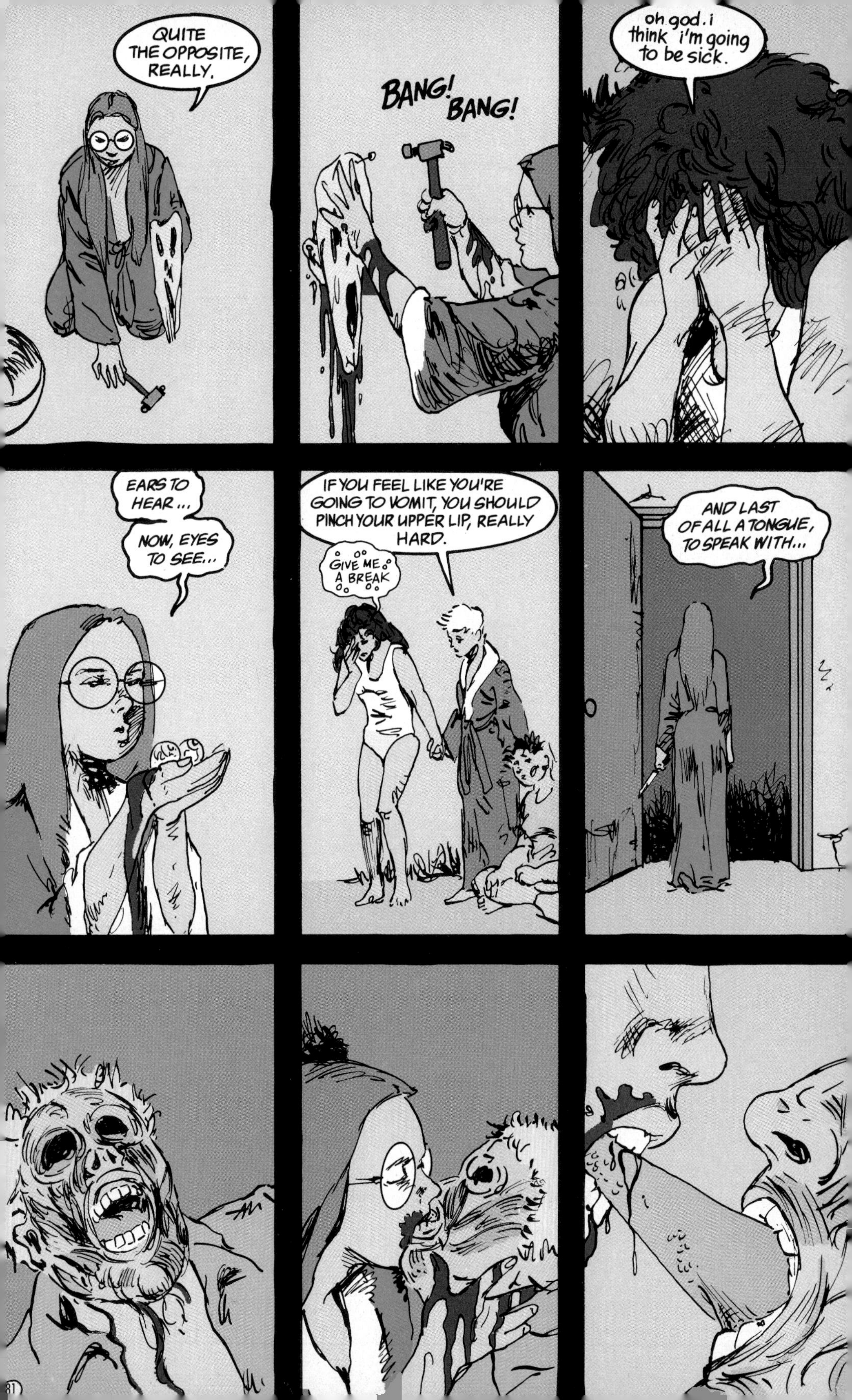
QUITE THE OPPOSITE, REALLY.
BANG! BANG!
oh god. i think i'm going to be sick.
EARS TO HEAR...
NOW, EYES TO SEE...
IF YOU FEEL LIKE YOU'RE GOING TO VOMIT, YOU SHOULD PINCH YOUR UPPER LIP, REALLY HARD.
GIVE ME A BREAK
AND LAST OF ALL A TONGUE, TO SPEAK WITH...

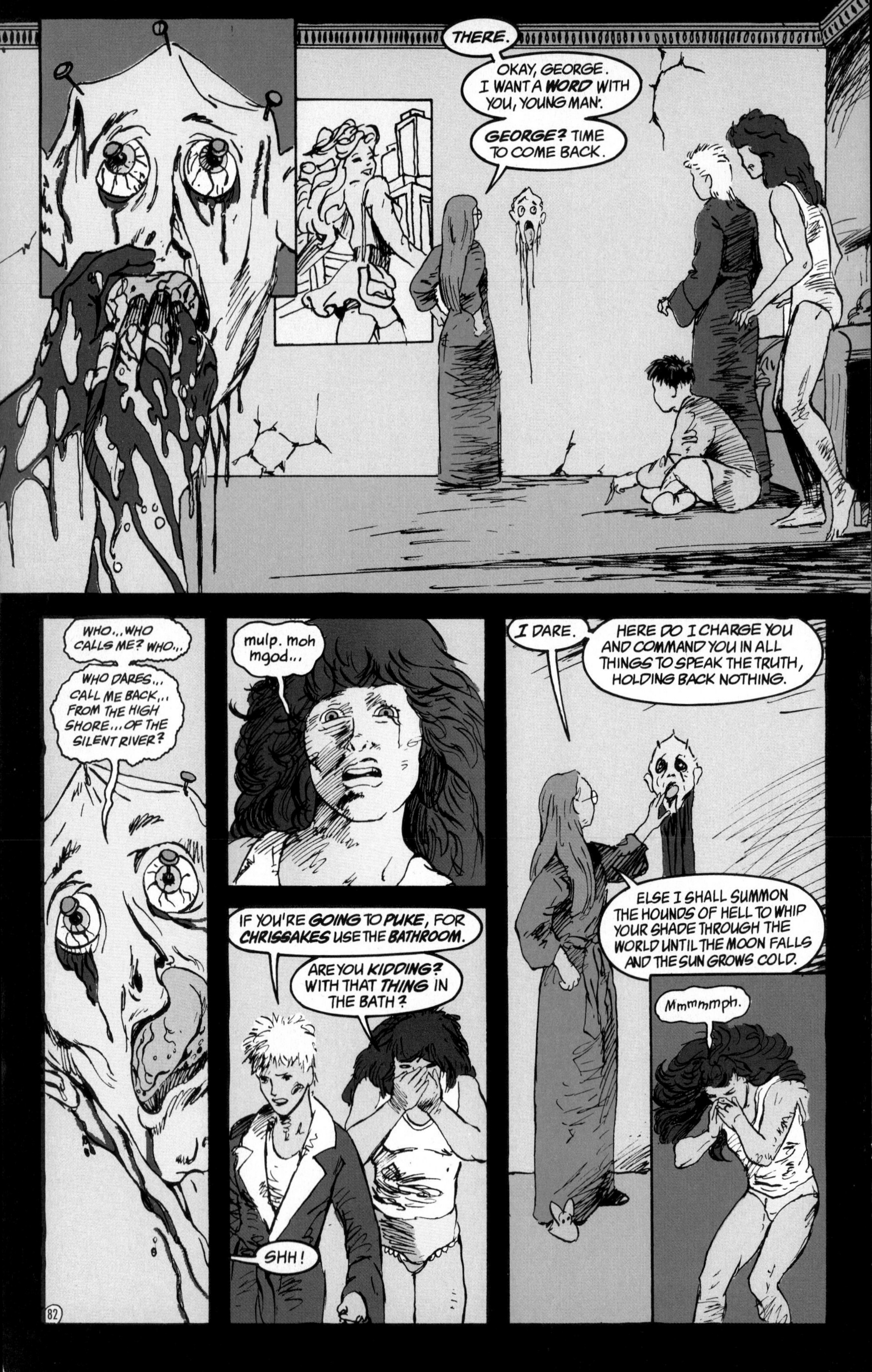
THERE.
OKAY, GEORGE. I WANT A WORD WITH YOU, YOUNG MAN.
GEORGE? TIME TO COME BACK.
WHO...WHO CALLS ME? WHO...
WHO DARES... CALL ME BACK... FROM THE HIGH SHORE...OF THE SILENT RIVER?
mulp. moh mgod...
IF YOU'RE GOING TO PUKE, FOR CHRISSAKES USE THE BATHROOM.
ARE YOU KIDDING? WITH THAT THING IN THE BATH?
SHH!
I DARE.
HERE DO I CHARGE YOU AND COMMAND YOU IN ALL THINGS TO SPEAK THE TRUTH, HOLDING BACK NOTHING.
ELSE I SHALL SUMMON THE HOUNDS OF HELL TO WHIP YOUR SHADE THROUGH THE WORLD UNTIL THE MOON FALLS AND THE SUN GROWS COLD.
Mmmmmph.

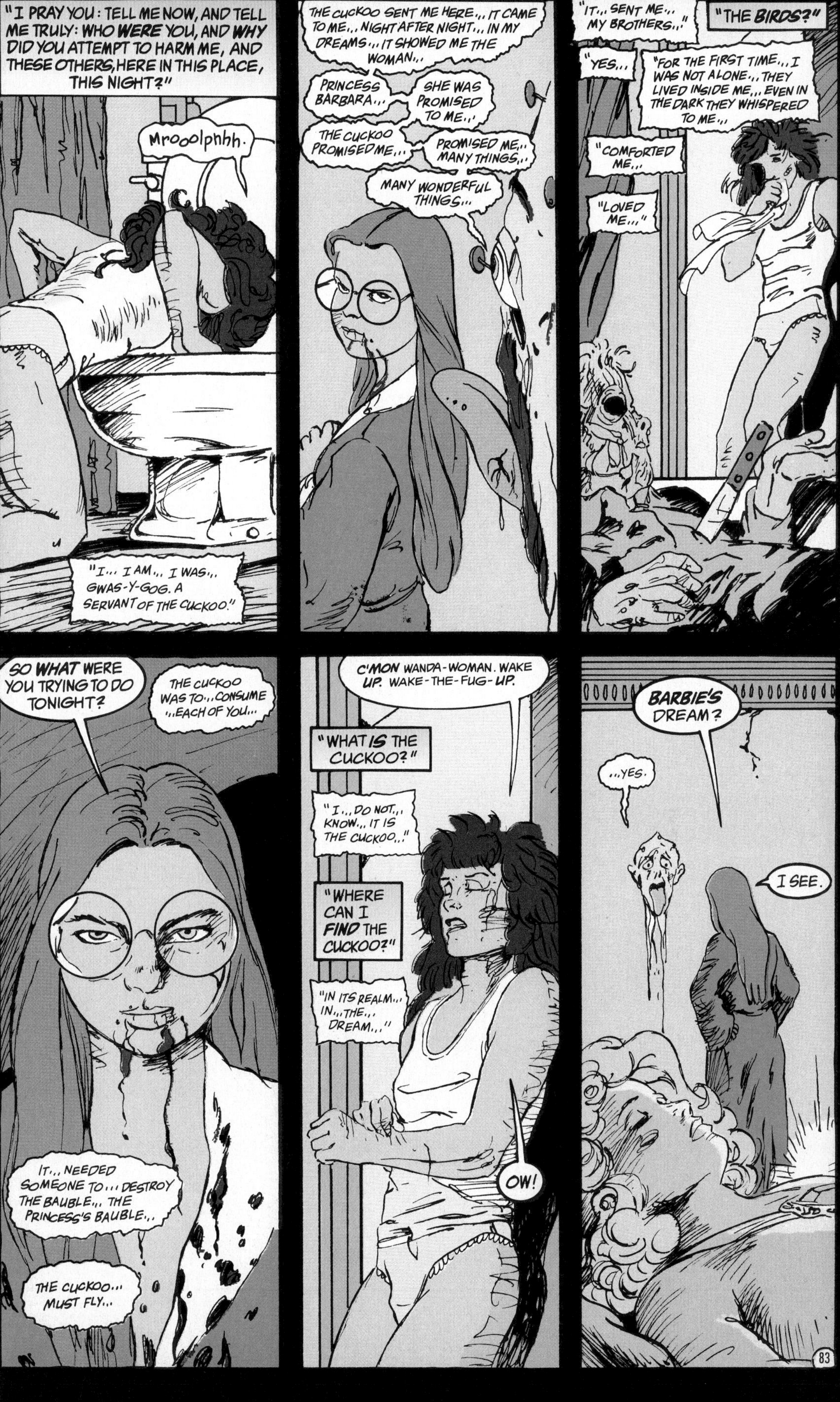
"I PRAY YOU: TELL ME NOW, AND TELL ME TRULY: WHO WERE YOU, AND WHY DID YOU ATTEMPT TO HARM ME, AND THESE OTHERS, HERE IN THIS PLACE, THIS NIGHT?"
Mroooolphhh.
"I... I AM... I WAS... GWAS-Y-GOG. A SERVANT OF THE CUCKOO."
THE CUCKOO SENT ME HERE... IT CAME TO ME... NIGHT AFTER NIGHT... IN MY DREAMS... IT SHOWED ME THE WOMAN...
PRINCESS BARBARA...
SHE WAS PROMISED TO ME...
THE CUCKOO PROMISED ME...
PROMISED ME... MANY THINGS...
MANY WONDERFUL THINGS...
"IT... SENT ME... MY BROTHERS..."
"THE BIRDS?"
"YES...
"FOR THE FIRST TIME... I WAS NOT ALONE... THEY LIVED INSIDE ME... EVEN IN THE DARK THEY WHISPERED TO ME...
"COMFORTED ME...
"LOVED ME..."
SO WHAT WERE YOU TRYING TO DO TONIGHT?
THE CUCKOO WAS TO... CONSUME ...EACH OF YOU...
IT... NEEDED SOMEONE TO... DESTROY THE BAUBLE... THE PRINCESS'S BAUBLE...
THE CUCKOO... MUST FLY...
C'MON WANDA-WOMAN. WAKE UP. WAKE-THE-FUG-UP.
"WHAT IS THE CUCKOO?"
"I... DO NOT... KNOW... IT IS THE CUCKOO..."
"WHERE CAN I FIND THE CUCKOO?"
"IN ITS REALM... IN... THE... DREAM..."
OW!
BARBIE'S DREAM?
...YES.
I SEE.

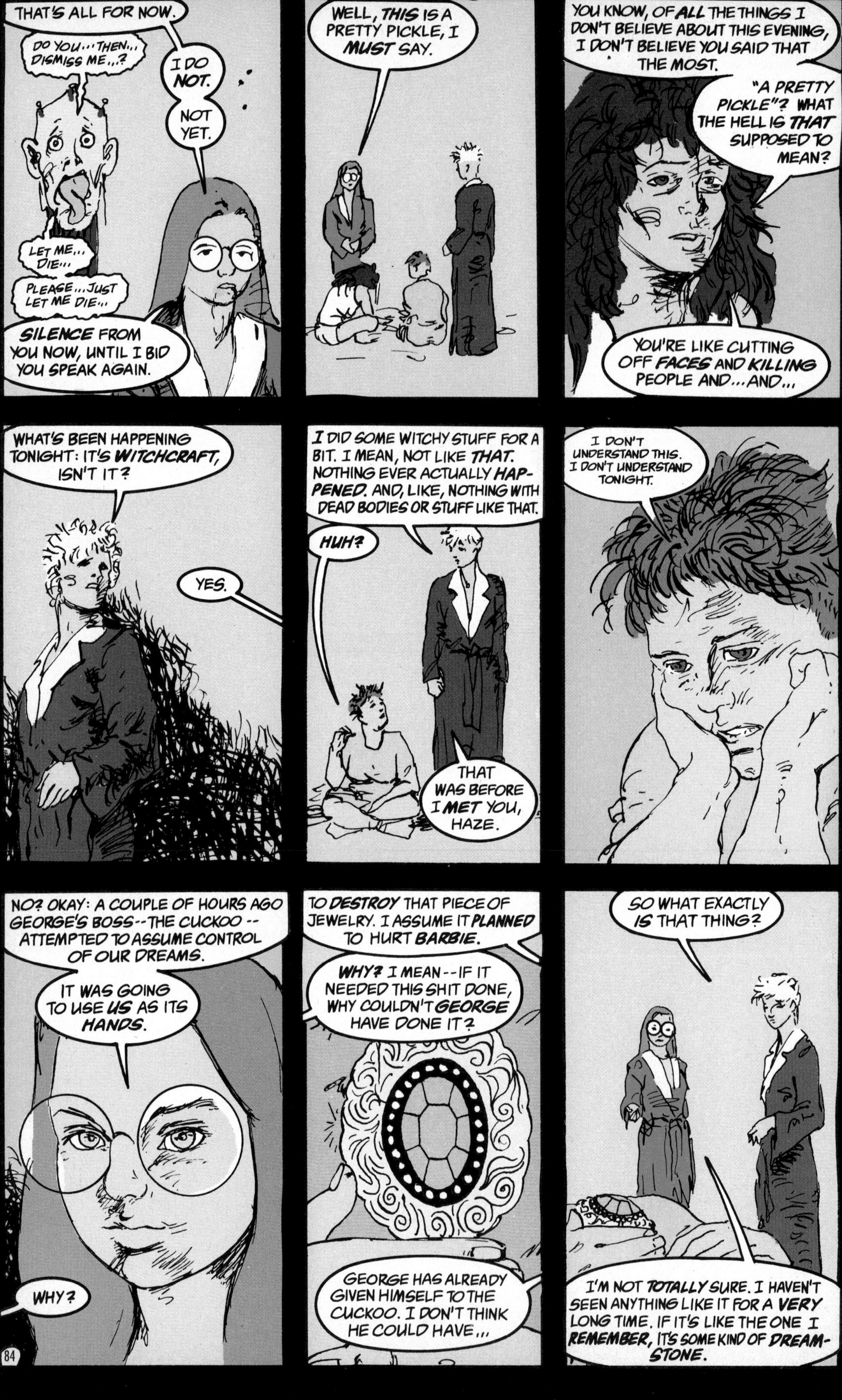
THAT'S ALL FOR NOW.
DO YOU... THEN... DISMISS ME...?
I DO NOT.
NOT YET.
LET ME... DIE...
PLEASE... JUST LET ME DIE...
SILENCE FROM YOU NOW, UNTIL I BID YOU SPEAK AGAIN.
WELL, THIS IS A PRETTY PICKLE, I MUST SAY.
YOU KNOW, OF ALL THE THINGS I DON'T BELIEVE ABOUT THIS EVENING, I DON'T BELIEVE YOU SAID THAT THE MOST.
"A PRETTY PICKLE"? WHAT THE HELL IS THAT SUPPOSED TO MEAN?
YOU'RE LIKE CUTTING OFF FACES AND KILLING PEOPLE AND... AND...
WHAT'S BEEN HAPPENING TONIGHT: IT'S WITCHCRAFT, ISN'T IT?
YES.
I DID SOME WITCHY STUFF FOR A BIT. I MEAN, NOT LIKE THAT. NOTHING EVER ACTUALLY HAP-PENED. AND, LIKE, NOTHING WITH DEAD BODIES OR STUFF LIKE THAT.
HUH?
THAT WAS BEFORE I MET YOU, HAZE.
I DON'T UNDERSTAND THIS. I DON'T UNDERSTAND TONIGHT.
NO? OKAY: A COUPLE OF HOURS AGO GEORGE'S BOSS--THE CUCKOO--ATTEMPTED TO ASSUME CONTROL OF OUR DREAMS.
IT WAS GOING TO USE US AS ITS HANDS.
WHY?
TO DESTROY THAT PIECE OF JEWELRY. I ASSUME IT PLANNED TO HURT BARBIE.
WHY? I MEAN--IF IT NEEDED THIS SHIT DONE, WHY COULDN'T GEORGE HAVE DONE IT?
GEORGE HAS ALREADY GIVEN HIMSELF TO THE CUCKOO. I DON'T THINK HE COULD HAVE...
SO WHAT EXACTLY IS THAT THING?
I'M NOT TOTALLY SURE. I HAVEN'T SEEN ANYTHING LIKE IT FOR A VERY LONG TIME. IF IT'S LIKE THE ONE I REMEMBER, IT'S SOME KIND OF DREAM-STONE.

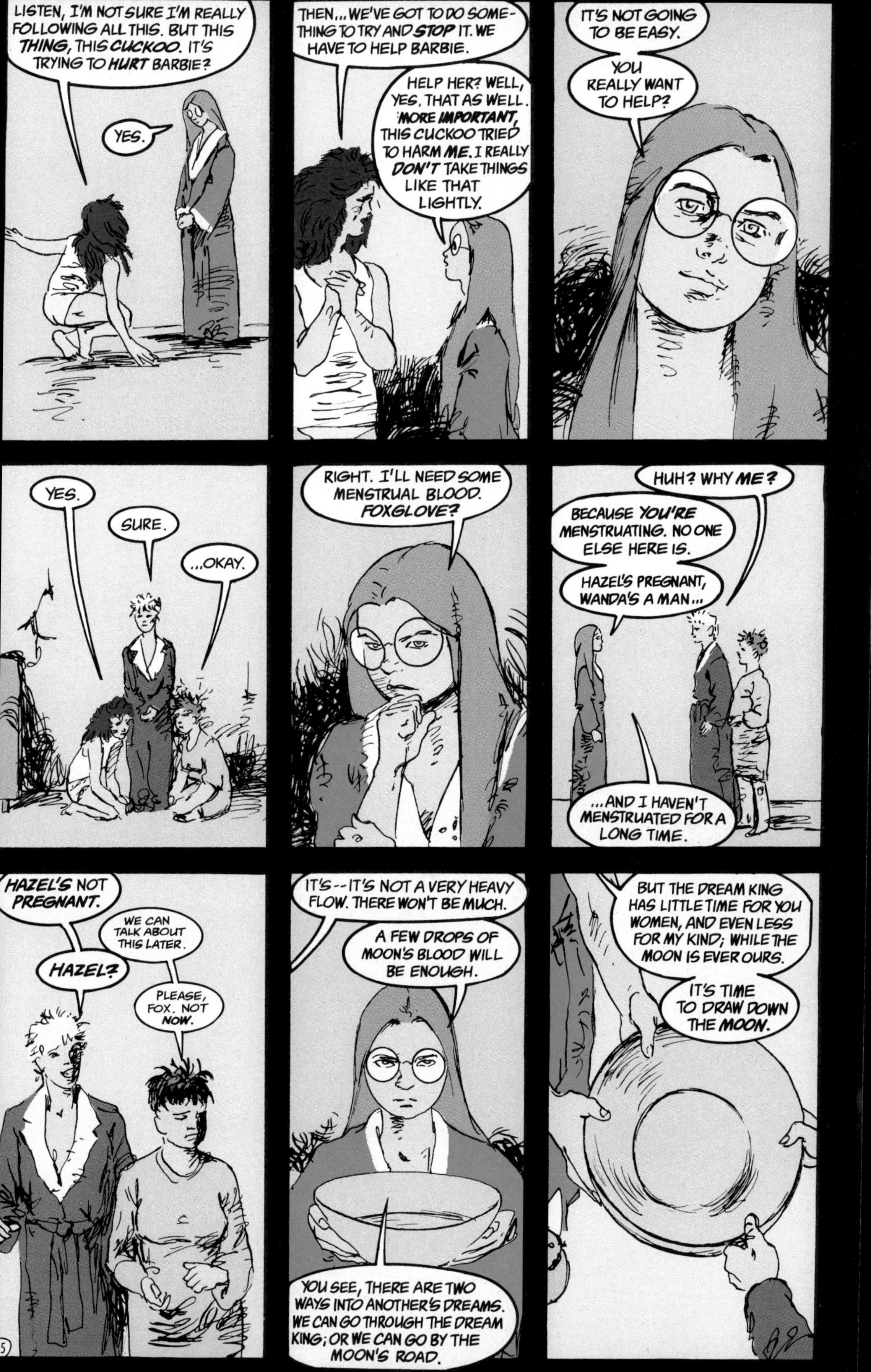
LISTEN, I'M NOT SURE I'M REALLY FOLLOWING ALL THIS. BUT THIS THING, THIS CUCKOO. IT'S TRYING TO HURT BARBIE?
YES.
THEN... WE'VE GOT TO DO SOMETHING TO TRY AND STOP IT. WE HAVE TO HELP BARBIE.
HELP HER? WELL, YES. THAT AS WELL. MORE IMPORTANT, THIS CUCKOO TRIED TO HARM ME. I REALLY DON'T TAKE THINGS LIKE THAT LIGHTLY.
IT'S NOT GOING TO BE EASY.
YOU REALLY WANT TO HELP?
YES.
SURE.
...OKAY.
RIGHT. I'LL NEED SOME MENSTRUAL BLOOD. FOXGLOVE?
HUH? WHY ME?
BECAUSE YOU'RE MENSTRUATING. NO ONE ELSE HERE IS.
HAZEL'S PREGNANT, WANDA'S A MAN...
...AND I HAVEN'T MENSTRUATED FOR A LONG TIME.
HAZEL'S NOT PREGNANT.
HAZEL?
WE CAN TALK ABOUT THIS LATER.
PLEASE, FOX. NOT NOW.
IT'S--IT'S NOT A VERY HEAVY FLOW. THERE WON'T BE MUCH.
A FEW DROPS OF MOON'S BLOOD WILL BE ENOUGH.
YOU SEE, THERE ARE TWO WAYS INTO ANOTHER'S DREAMS. WE CAN GO THROUGH THE DREAM KING; OR WE CAN GO BY THE MOON'S ROAD.
BUT THE DREAM KING HAS LITTLE TIME FOR YOU WOMEN, AND EVEN LESS FOR MY KIND; WHILE THE MOON IS EVER OURS.
IT'S TIME TO DRAW DOWN THE MOON.

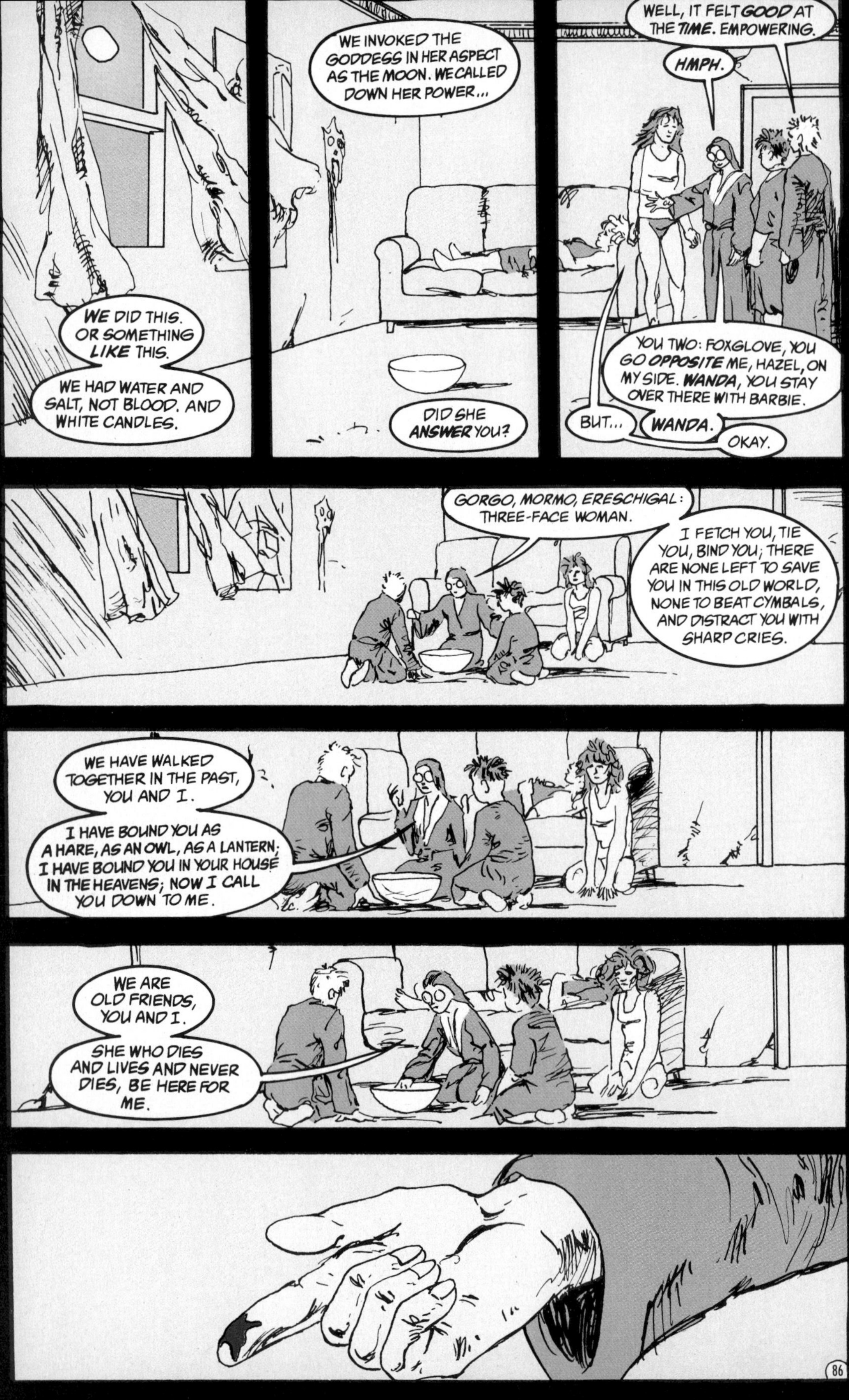
WE DID THIS. OR SOMETHING LIKE THIS.
WE HAD WATER AND SALT, NOT BLOOD. AND WHITE CANDLES.
WE INVOKED THE GODDESS IN HER ASPECT AS THE MOON. WE CALLED DOWN HER POWER...
DID SHE ANSWER YOU?
WELL, IT FELT GOOD AT THE TIME. EMPOWERING.
HMPH.
YOU TWO: FOXGLOVE, YOU GO OPPOSITE ME, HAZEL, ON MY SIDE. WANDA, YOU STAY OVER THERE WITH BARBIE.
BUT...
WANDA.
OKAY.
GORGO, MORMO, ERESCHIGAL: THREE-FACE WOMAN.
I FETCH YOU, TIE YOU, BIND YOU; THERE ARE NONE LEFT TO SAVE YOU IN THIS OLD WORLD, NONE TO BEAT CYMBALS, AND DISTRACT YOU WITH SHARP CRIES.
WE HAVE WALKED TOGETHER IN THE PAST, YOU AND I.
I HAVE BOUND YOU AS A HARE, AS AN OWL, AS A LANTERN; I HAVE BOUND YOU IN YOUR HOUSE IN THE HEAVENS; NOW I CALL YOU DOWN TO ME.
WE ARE OLD FRIENDS, YOU AND I.
SHE WHO DIES AND LIVES AND NEVER DIES, BE HERE FOR ME.

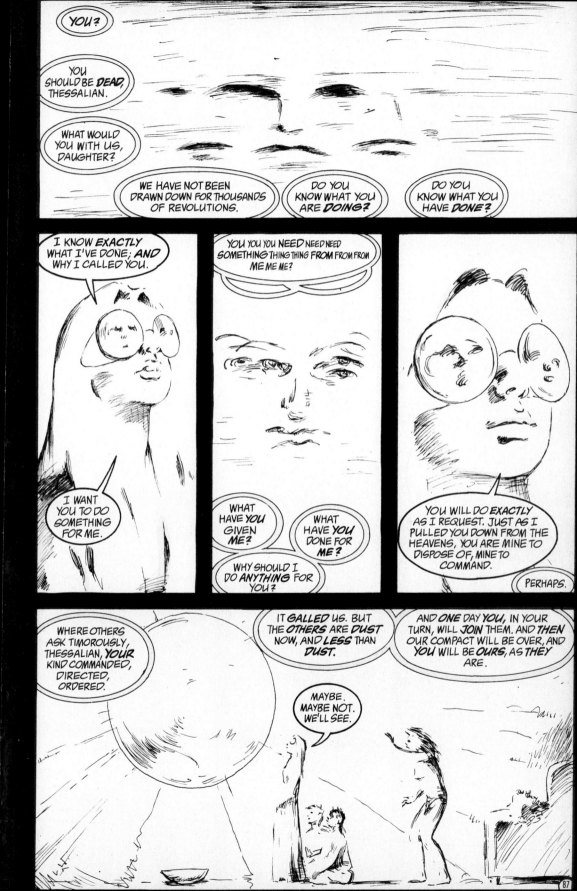

YOU?

YOU SHOULD BE **DEAD**, THESSALIAN.

WHAT WOULD YOU WITH US, DAUGHTER?

WE HAVE NOT BEEN DRAWN DOWN FOR THOUSANDS OF REVOLUTIONS.

DO YOU KNOW WHAT YOU ARE **DOING**?

DO YOU KNOW WHAT YOU HAVE **DONE**?

I KNOW **EXACTLY** WHAT I'VE DONE; **AND** WHY I CALLED YOU.

I WANT YOU TO DO SOMETHING FOR ME.

YOU YOU YOU **NEED** NEED NEED SOMETHING THING THING **FROM** FROM FROM ME ME ME?

WHAT HAVE **YOU** GIVEN **ME**?

WHAT HAVE **YOU** DONE FOR **ME**?

WHY SHOULD I DO **ANYTHING** FOR YOU?

YOU WILL DO **EXACTLY** AS I REQUEST. JUST AS I PULLED YOU DOWN FROM THE HEAVENS, YOU ARE MINE TO DISPOSE OF, MINE TO COMMAND.

PERHAPS.

WHERE OTHERS ASK TIMOROUSLY, THESSALIAN, **YOUR** KIND COMMANDED, DIRECTED, ORDERED.

IT **GALLED** US. BUT THE **OTHERS** ARE **DUST** NOW, AND **LESS** THAN **DUST**.

AND **ONE** DAY **YOU**, IN YOUR TURN, WILL **JOIN** THEM. AND **THEN** OUR COMPACT WILL BE OVER, AND **YOU** WILL BE **OURS**, AS **THEY** ARE.

MAYBE. MAYBE NOT. WE'LL SEE.

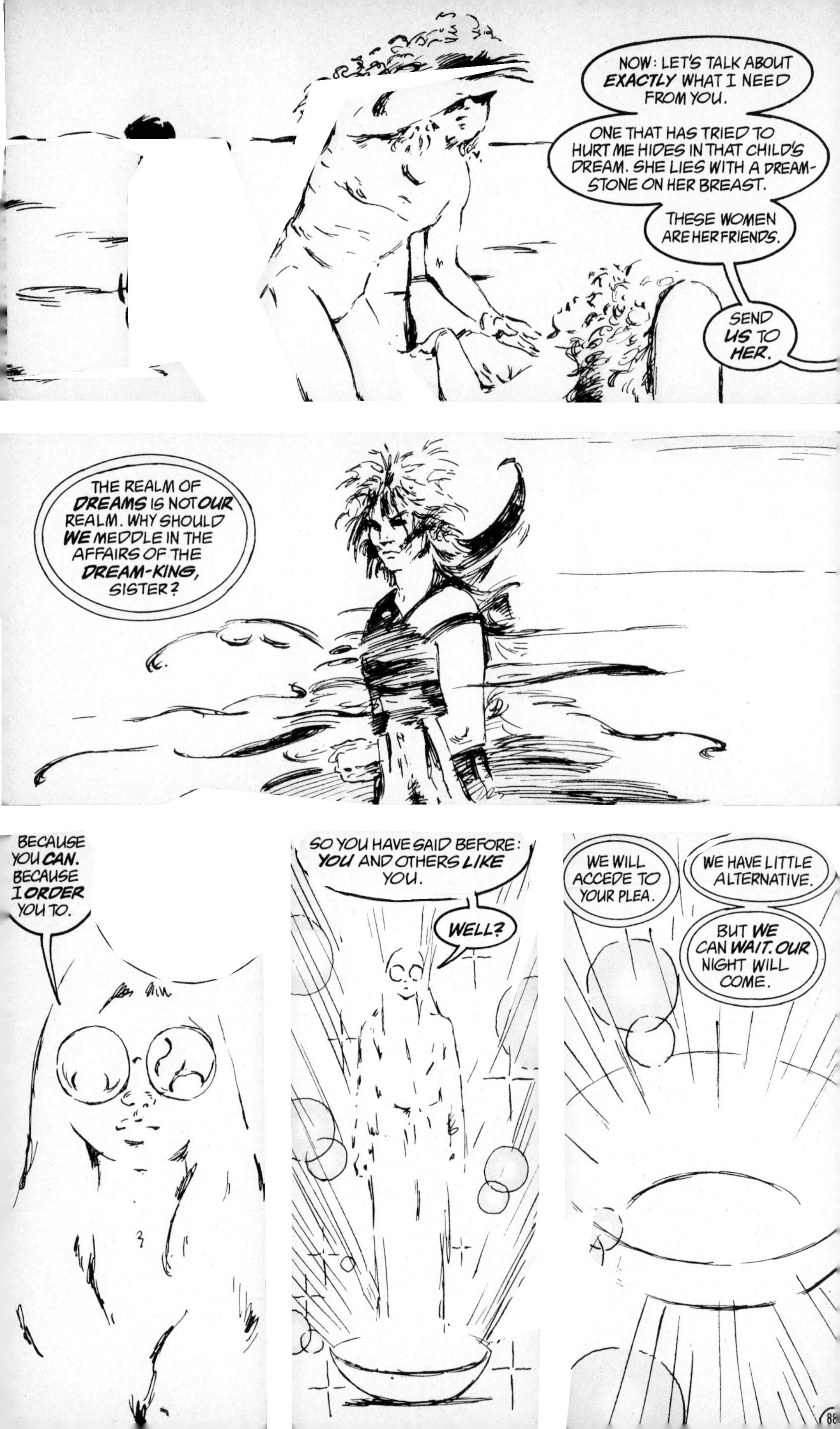
NOW: LET'S TALK ABOUT EXACTLY WHAT I NEED FROM YOU.
ONE THAT HAS TRIED TO HURT ME HIDES IN THAT CHILD'S DREAM. SHE LIES WITH A DREAM-STONE ON HER BREAST.
THESE WOMEN ARE HER FRIENDS.
SEND US TO HER.
THE REALM OF DREAMS IS NOT OUR REALM. WHY SHOULD WE MEDDLE IN THE AFFAIRS OF THE DREAM-KING, SISTER?
BECAUSE YOU CAN. BECAUSE I ORDER YOU TO.
SO YOU HAVE SAID BEFORE: YOU AND OTHERS LIKE YOU.
WELL?
WE WILL ACCEDE TO YOUR PLEA.
WE HAVE LITTLE ALTERNATIVE.
BUT WE CAN WAIT. OUR NIGHT WILL COME.

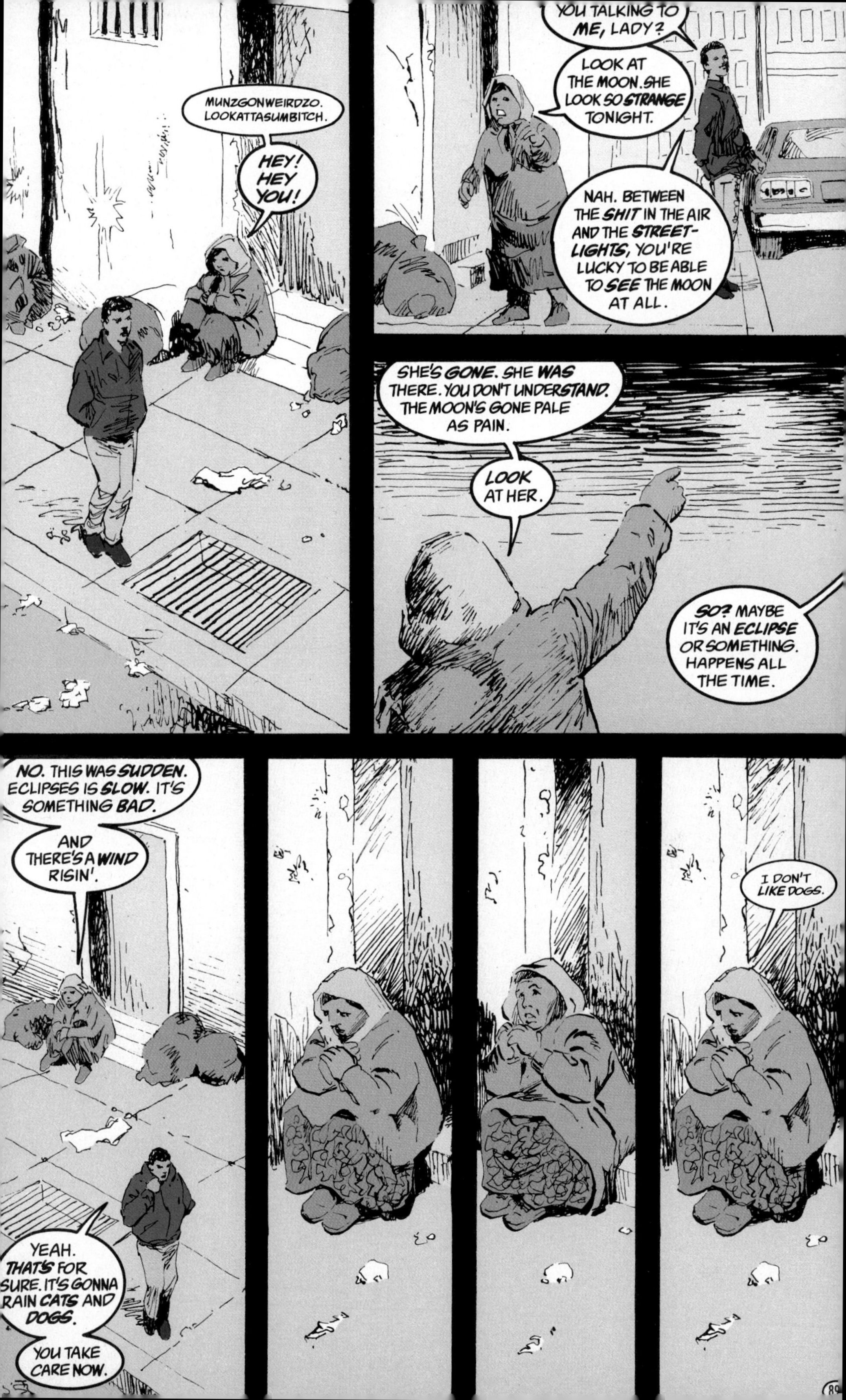
MUNZGONWEIRDZO. LOOKATTASUMBITCH.
HEY! HEY YOU!
YOU TALKING TO ME, LADY?
LOOK AT THE MOON. SHE LOOK SO STRANGE TONIGHT.
NAH. BETWEEN THE SHIT IN THE AIR AND THE STREET-LIGHTS, YOU'RE LUCKY TO BE ABLE TO SEE THE MOON AT ALL.
SHE'S GONE. SHE WAS THERE. YOU DON'T UNDERSTAND. THE MOON'S GONE PALE AS PAIN.
LOOK AT HER.
SO? MAYBE IT'S AN ECLIPSE OR SOMETHING. HAPPENS ALL THE TIME.
NO. THIS WAS SUDDEN. ECLIPSES IS SLOW. IT'S SOMETHING BAD.
AND THERE'S A WIND RISIN'.
YEAH. THAT'S FOR SURE. IT'S GONNA RAIN CATS AND DOGS.
YOU TAKE CARE NOW.
I DON'T LIKE DOGS.

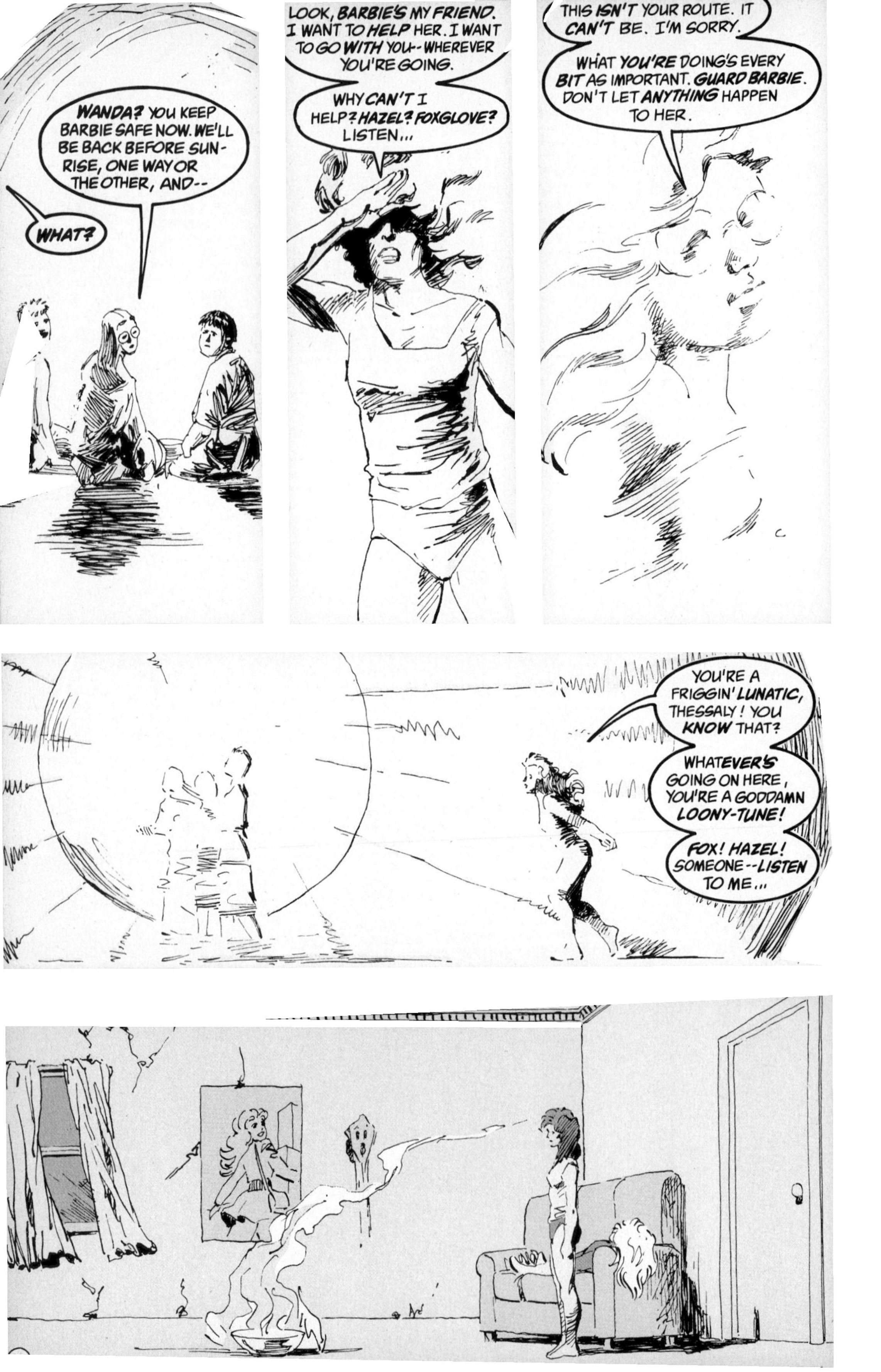
WANDA? YOU KEEP BARBIE SAFE NOW. WE'LL BE BACK BEFORE SUNRISE, ONE WAY OR THE OTHER, AND--
WHAT?
LOOK, BARBIE'S MY FRIEND. I WANT TO HELP HER. I WANT TO GO WITH YOU--WHEREVER YOU'RE GOING.
WHY CAN'T I HELP? HAZEL? FOXGLOVE? LISTEN...
THIS ISN'T YOUR ROUTE. IT CAN'T BE. I'M SORRY.
WHAT YOU'RE DOING'S EVERY BIT AS IMPORTANT. GUARD BARBIE. DON'T LET ANYTHING HAPPEN TO HER.
YOU'RE A FRIGGIN' LUNATIC, THESSALY! YOU KNOW THAT?
WHATEVER'S GOING ON HERE, YOU'RE A GODDAMN LOONY-TUNE!
FOX! HAZEL! SOMEONE--LISTEN TO ME...

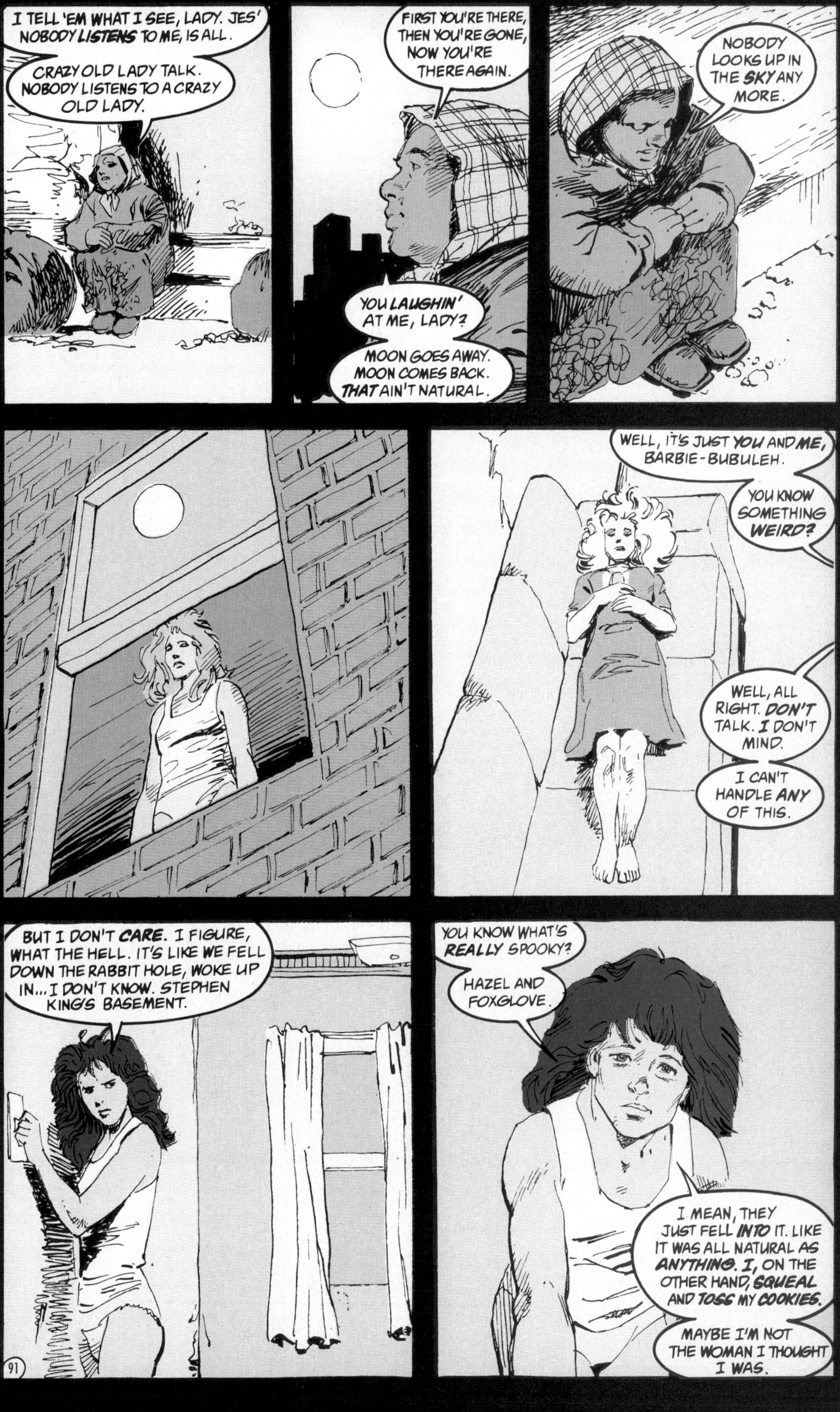
I TELL 'EM WHAT I SEE, LADY. JES' NOBODY LISTENS TO ME, IS ALL.
CRAZY OLD LADY TALK. NOBODY LISTENS TO A CRAZY OLD LADY.
FIRST YOU'RE THERE, THEN YOU'RE GONE, NOW YOU'RE THERE AGAIN.
YOU LAUGHIN' AT ME, LADY?
MOON GOES AWAY. MOON COMES BACK. THAT AIN'T NATURAL.
NOBODY LOOKS UP IN THE SKY ANY MORE.
WELL, IT'S JUST YOU AND ME, BARBIE-BUBULEH.
YOU KNOW SOMETHING WEIRD?
WELL, ALL RIGHT. DON'T TALK. I DON'T MIND.
I CAN'T HANDLE ANY OF THIS.
BUT I DON'T CARE. I FIGURE, WHAT THE HELL. IT'S LIKE WE FELL DOWN THE RABBIT HOLE, WOKE UP IN... I DON'T KNOW. STEPHEN KING'S BASEMENT.
YOU KNOW WHAT'S REALLY SPOOKY?
HAZEL AND FOXGLOVE.
I MEAN, THEY JUST FELL INTO IT. LIKE IT WAS ALL NATURAL AS ANYTHING. I, ON THE OTHER HAND, SQUEAL AND TOSS MY COOKIES.
MAYBE I'M NOT THE WOMAN I THOUGHT I WAS.

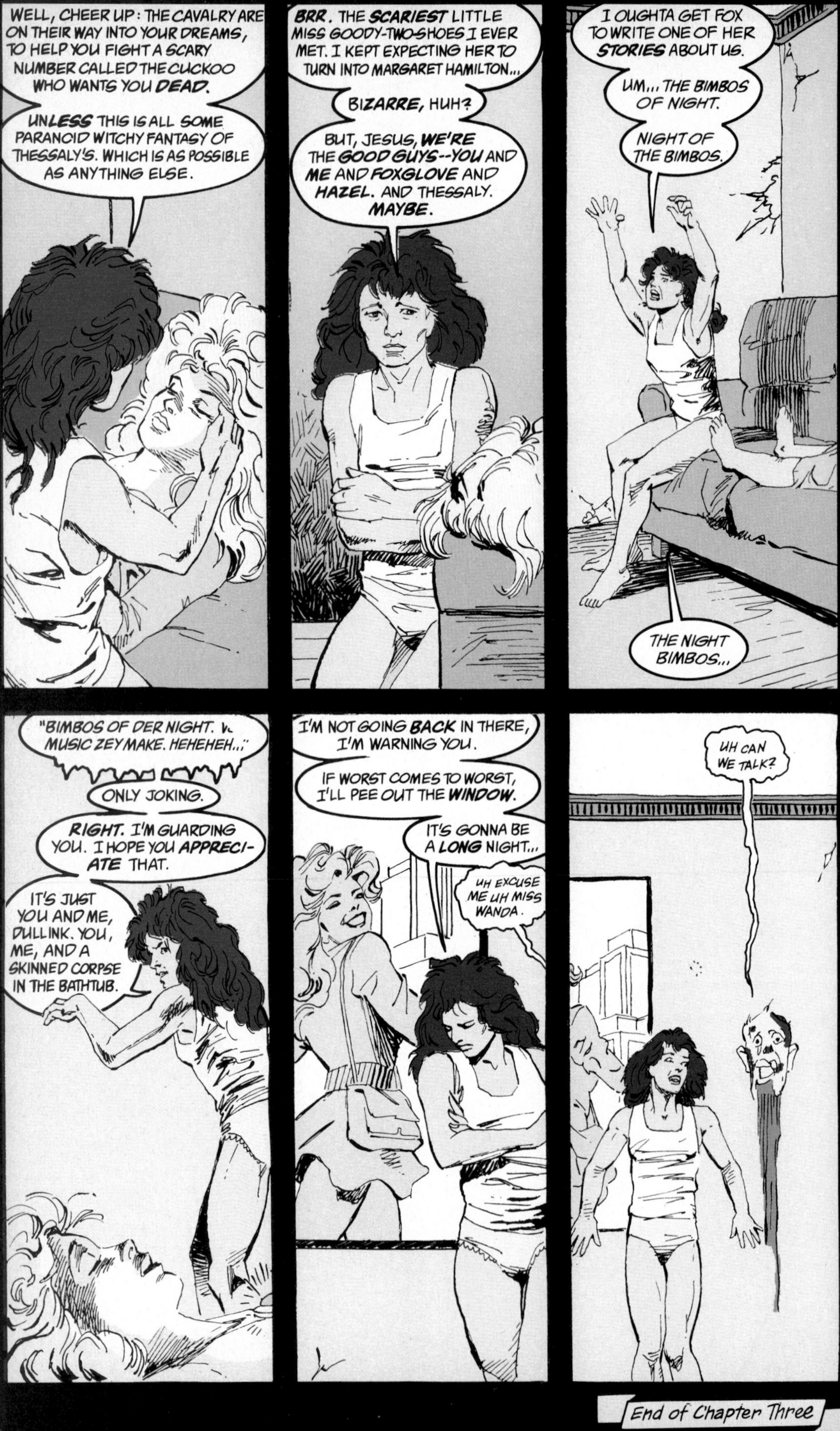
WELL, CHEER UP: THE CAVALRY ARE ON THEIR WAY INTO YOUR DREAMS, TO HELP YOU FIGHT A SCARY NUMBER CALLED THE CUCKOO WHO WANTS YOU DEAD.
UNLESS THIS IS ALL SOME PARANOID WITCHY FANTASY OF THESSALY'S. WHICH IS AS POSSIBLE AS ANYTHING ELSE.
BRR. THE SCARIEST LITTLE MISS GOODY-TWO-SHOES I EVER MET. I KEPT EXPECTING HER TO TURN INTO MARGARET HAMILTON...
BIZARRE, HUH?
BUT, JESUS, WE'RE THE GOOD GUYS--YOU AND ME AND FOXGLOVE AND HAZEL. AND THESSALY. MAYBE.
I OUGHTA GET FOX TO WRITE ONE OF HER STORIES ABOUT US.
UM... THE BIMBOS OF NIGHT.
NIGHT OF THE BIMBOS.
THE NIGHT BIMBOS...
"BIMBOS OF DER NIGHT. WHAT MUSIC ZEY MAKE. HEHEHEH..."
ONLY JOKING.
RIGHT. I'M GUARDING YOU. I HOPE YOU APPRECIATE THAT.
IT'S JUST YOU AND ME, DULLINK. YOU, ME, AND A SKINNED CORPSE IN THE BATHTUB.
I'M NOT GOING BACK IN THERE, I'M WARNING YOU.
IF WORST COMES TO WORST, I'LL PEE OUT THE WINDOW.
IT'S GONNA BE A LONG NIGHT...
UH EXCUSE ME UH MISS WANDA.
UH CAN WE TALK?

End of Chapter Three

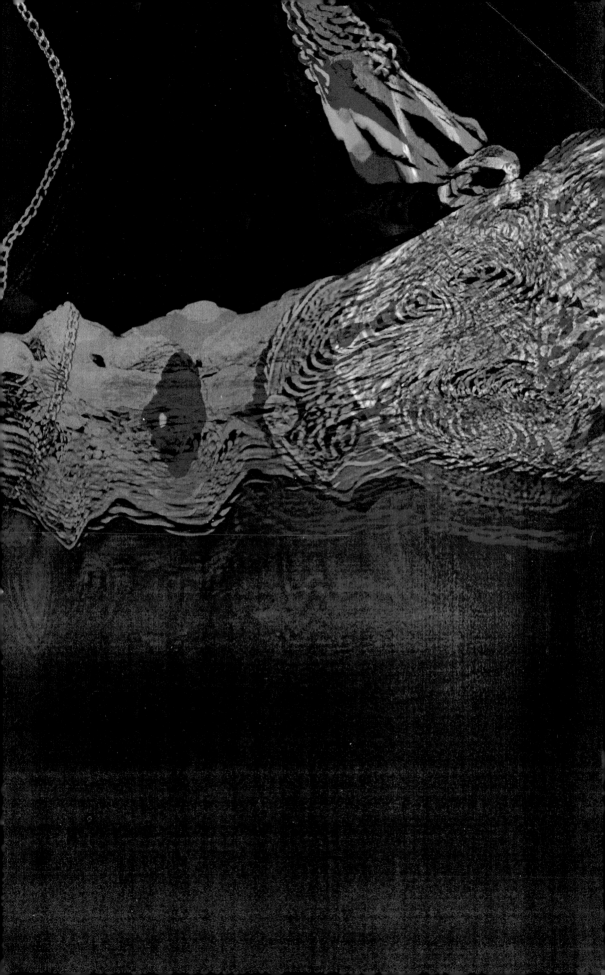

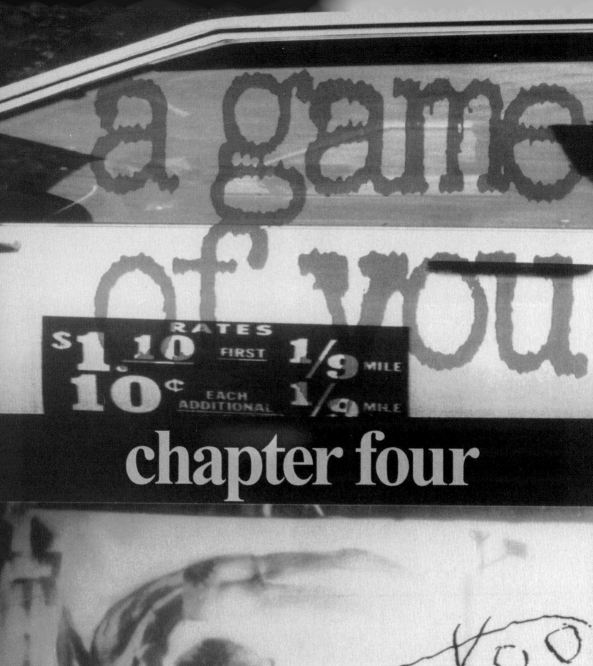

a game of you

RATES $1.10 FIRST 1/9 MILE
10¢ EACH ADDITIONAL 1/9 MILE

chapter four

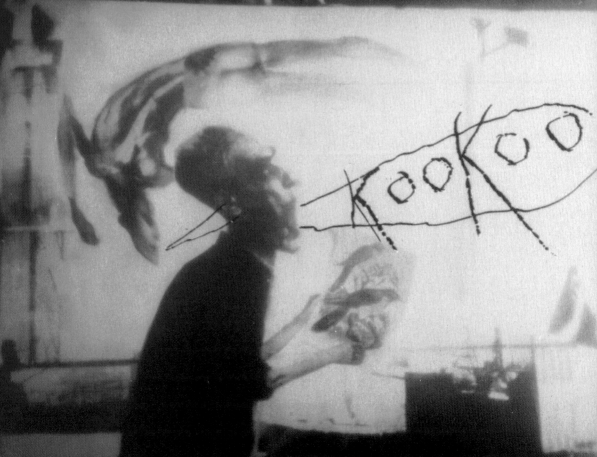

KOO KOO

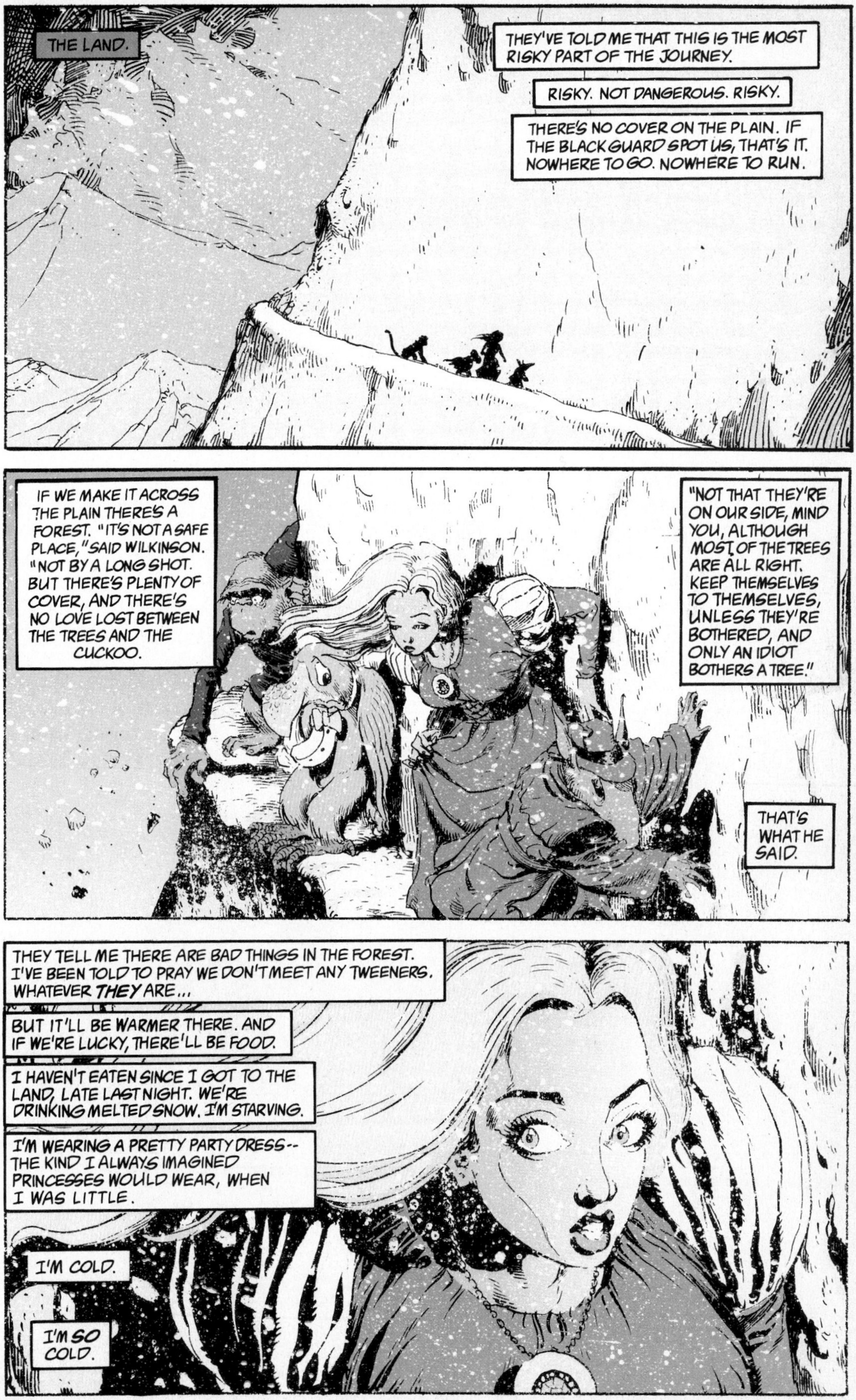
THE LAND.
THEY'VE TOLD ME THAT THIS IS THE MOST RISKY PART OF THE JOURNEY.
RISKY. NOT DANGEROUS. RISKY.
THERE'S NO COVER ON THE PLAIN. IF THE BLACK GUARD SPOT US, THAT'S IT. NOWHERE TO GO. NOWHERE TO RUN.
IF WE MAKE IT ACROSS THE PLAIN THERE'S A FOREST. "IT'S NOT A SAFE PLACE," SAID WILKINSON. "NOT BY A LONG SHOT. BUT THERE'S PLENTY OF COVER, AND THERE'S NO LOVE LOST BETWEEN THE TREES AND THE CUCKOO.
"NOT THAT THEY'RE ON OUR SIDE, MIND YOU, ALTHOUGH MOST OF THE TREES ARE ALL RIGHT. KEEP THEMSELVES TO THEMSELVES, UNLESS THEY'RE BOTHERED, AND ONLY AN IDIOT BOTHERS A TREE."
THAT'S WHAT HE SAID.
THEY TELL ME THERE ARE BAD THINGS IN THE FOREST. I'VE BEEN TOLD TO PRAY WE DON'T MEET ANY TWEENERS. WHATEVER *THEY* ARE...
BUT IT'LL BE WARMER THERE. AND IF WE'RE LUCKY, THERE'LL BE FOOD.
I HAVEN'T EATEN SINCE I GOT TO THE LAND, LATE LAST NIGHT. WE'RE DRINKING MELTED SNOW. I'M STARVING.
I'M WEARING A PRETTY PARTY DRESS-- THE KIND I ALWAYS IMAGINED PRINCESSES WOULD WEAR, WHEN I WAS LITTLE.
I'M COLD.
I'M *SO* COLD.

IT'S A LONG WAY TO TIPPERARY, IT'S A LONG WAY TO GO IT'S A LONG WAY TO TIPPERARY AN' THE SWEETEST GIRL I KNOW-OW-OW-OW...
Quiet, Wilkinson. You want to tell everyone we're here?
I was singing *quietly*. To keep our spirits up.
The wind'll carry voices away.
Wilkinson.
Okay, okay. No singing.
THERE'S SOMETHING OVER THERE, IN THE SNOW, ***LOOK***.
Something to eat, with any luck.
I can't see too well.
Iss too far away.
96

4: BEGINNING TO SEE THE LIGHT

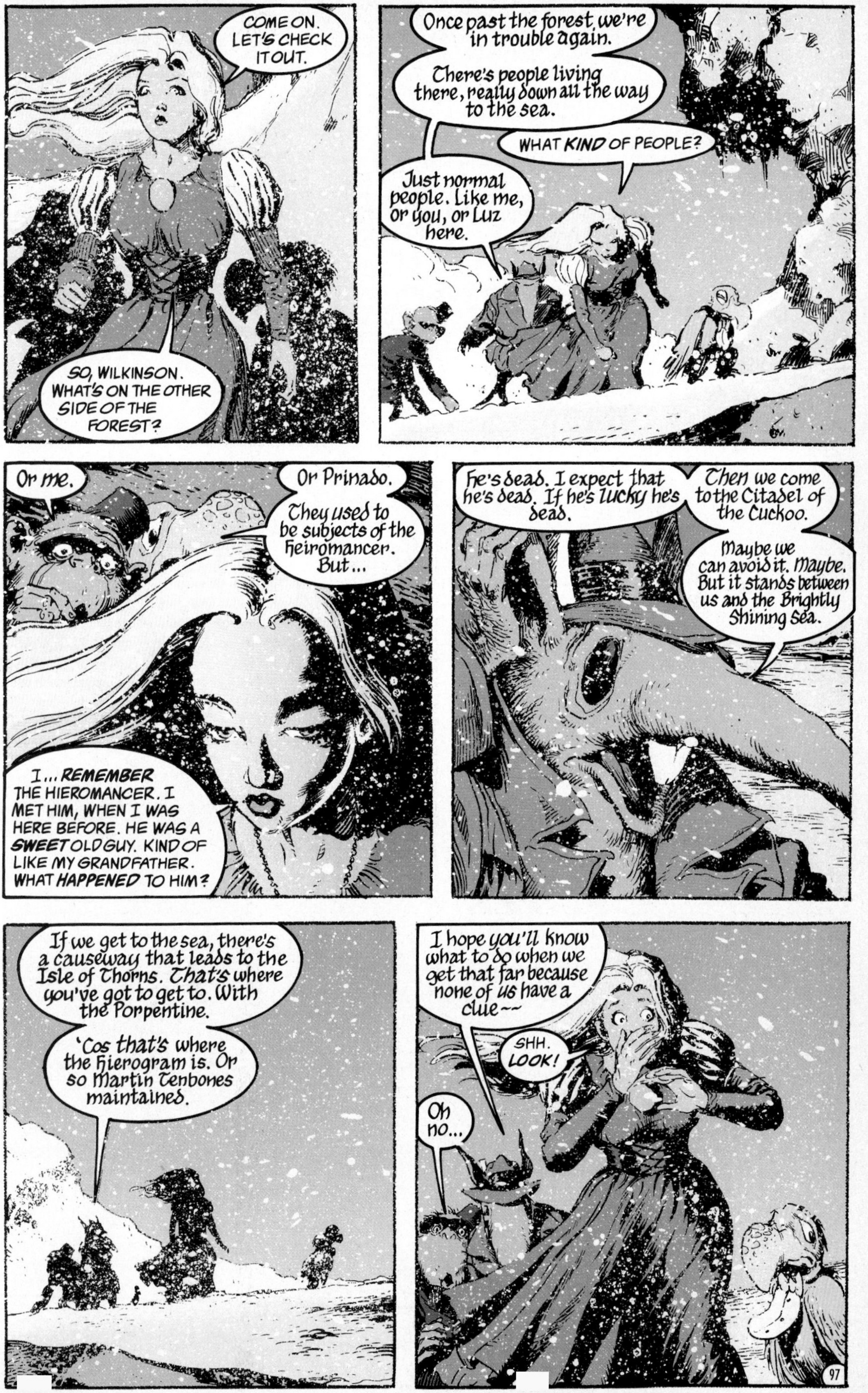
COME ON. LET'S CHECK IT OUT.
SO, WILKINSON. WHAT'S ON THE OTHER SIDE OF THE FOREST?
Once past the forest, we're in trouble again.
There's people living there, really down all the way to the sea.
WHAT KIND OF PEOPLE?
Just normal people. Like me, or you, or Luz here.
Or me.
Or Prinado.
They used to be subjects of the Heiromancer. But...
I... REMEMBER THE HIEROMANCER. I MET HIM, WHEN I WAS HERE BEFORE. HE WAS A SWEET OLD GUY. KIND OF LIKE MY GRANDFATHER. WHAT HAPPENED TO HIM?
He's dead. I expect that he's dead. If he's lucky he's dead.
Then we come to the Citadel of the Cuckoo.
Maybe we can avoid it. Maybe. But it stands between us and the Brightly Shining Sea.
If we get to the sea, there's a causeway that leads to the Isle of Thorns. That's where you've got to get to. With the Porpentine.
'Cos that's where the Hierogram is. Or so Martin Tenbones maintained.
I hope you'll know what to do when we get that far because none of us have a clue~~
SHH. LOOK!
Oh no...

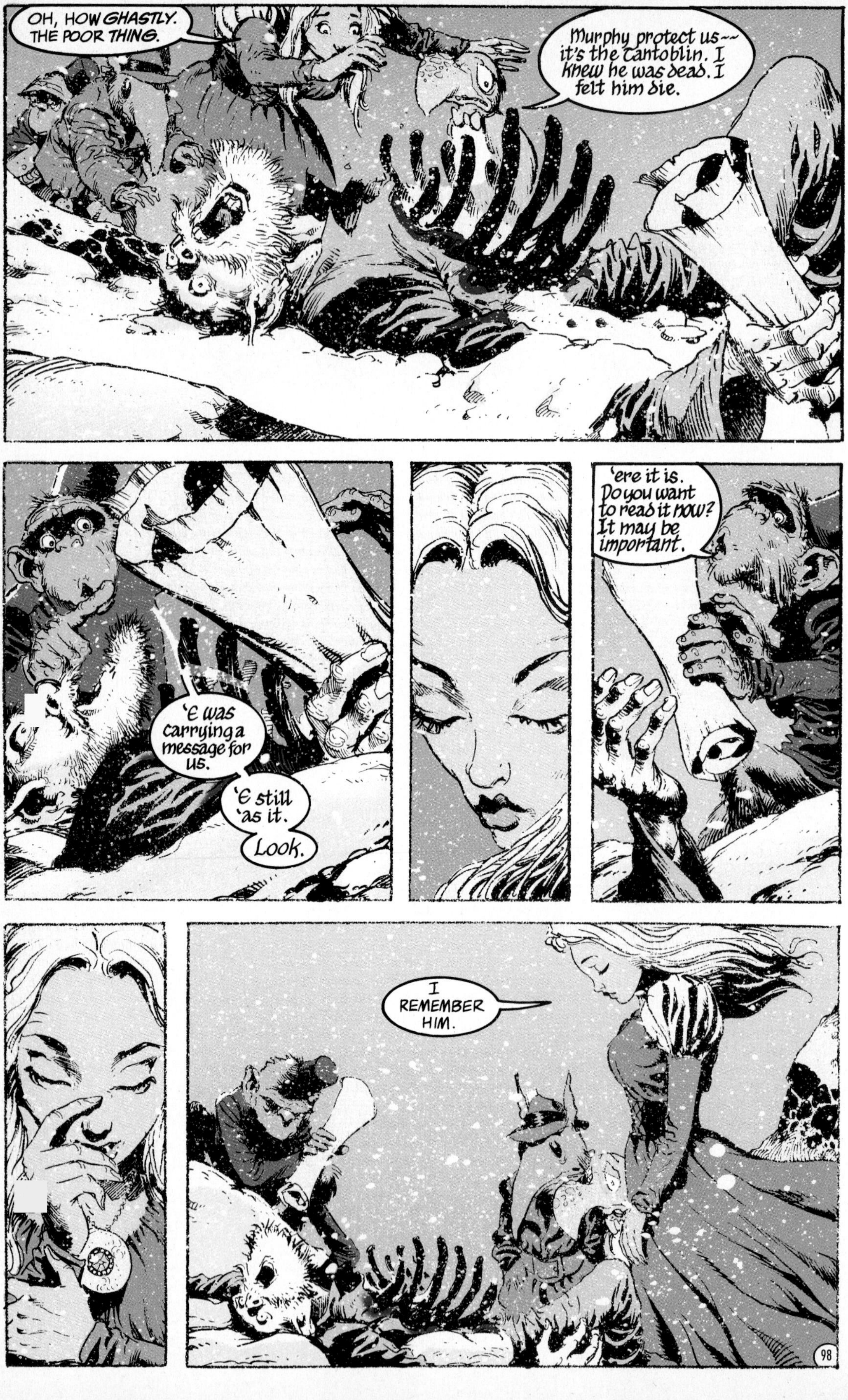

OH, HOW GHASTLY. THE POOR THING.
Murphy protect us-- it's the Cantoblin. I knew he was dead. I felt him die.
'E was carrying a message for us.
'E still 'as it.
Look.
'ere it is. Do you want to read it now? It may be important.
I REMEMBER HIM.

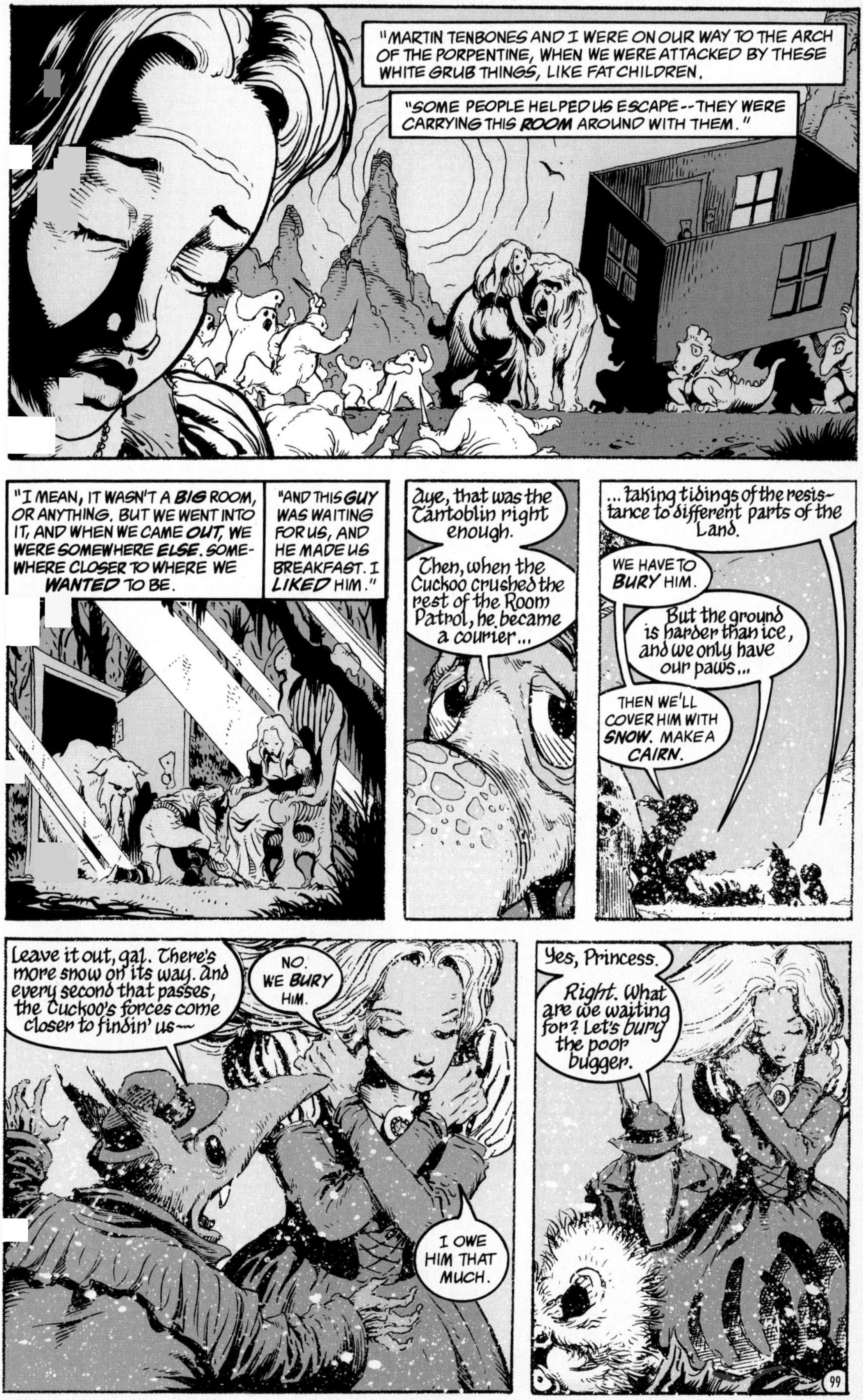
"MARTIN TENBONES AND I WERE ON OUR WAY TO THE ARCH OF THE PORPENTINE, WHEN WE WERE ATTACKED BY THESE WHITE GRUB THINGS, LIKE FAT CHILDREN.
"SOME PEOPLE HELPED US ESCAPE--THEY WERE CARRYING THIS ROOM AROUND WITH THEM."
"I MEAN, IT WASN'T A BIG ROOM, OR ANYTHING. BUT WE WENT INTO IT, AND WHEN WE CAME OUT, WE WERE SOMEWHERE ELSE. SOMEWHERE CLOSER TO WHERE WE WANTED TO BE.
"AND THIS GUY WAS WAITING FOR US, AND HE MADE US BREAKFAST. I LIKED HIM."
Aye, that was the Tantoblin right enough.
Then, when the Cuckoo crushed the rest of the Room Patrol, he became a courier...
...taking tidings of the resistance to different parts of the Land.
WE HAVE TO BURY HIM.
But the ground is harder than ice, and we only have our paws...
THEN WE'LL COVER HIM WITH SNOW. MAKE A CAIRN.
Leave it out, gal. There's more snow on its way. And every second that passes, the Cuckoo's forces come closer to findin' us--
NO. WE BURY HIM.
I OWE HIM THAT MUCH.
Yes, Princess.
Right. What are we waiting for? Let's bury the poor bugger.

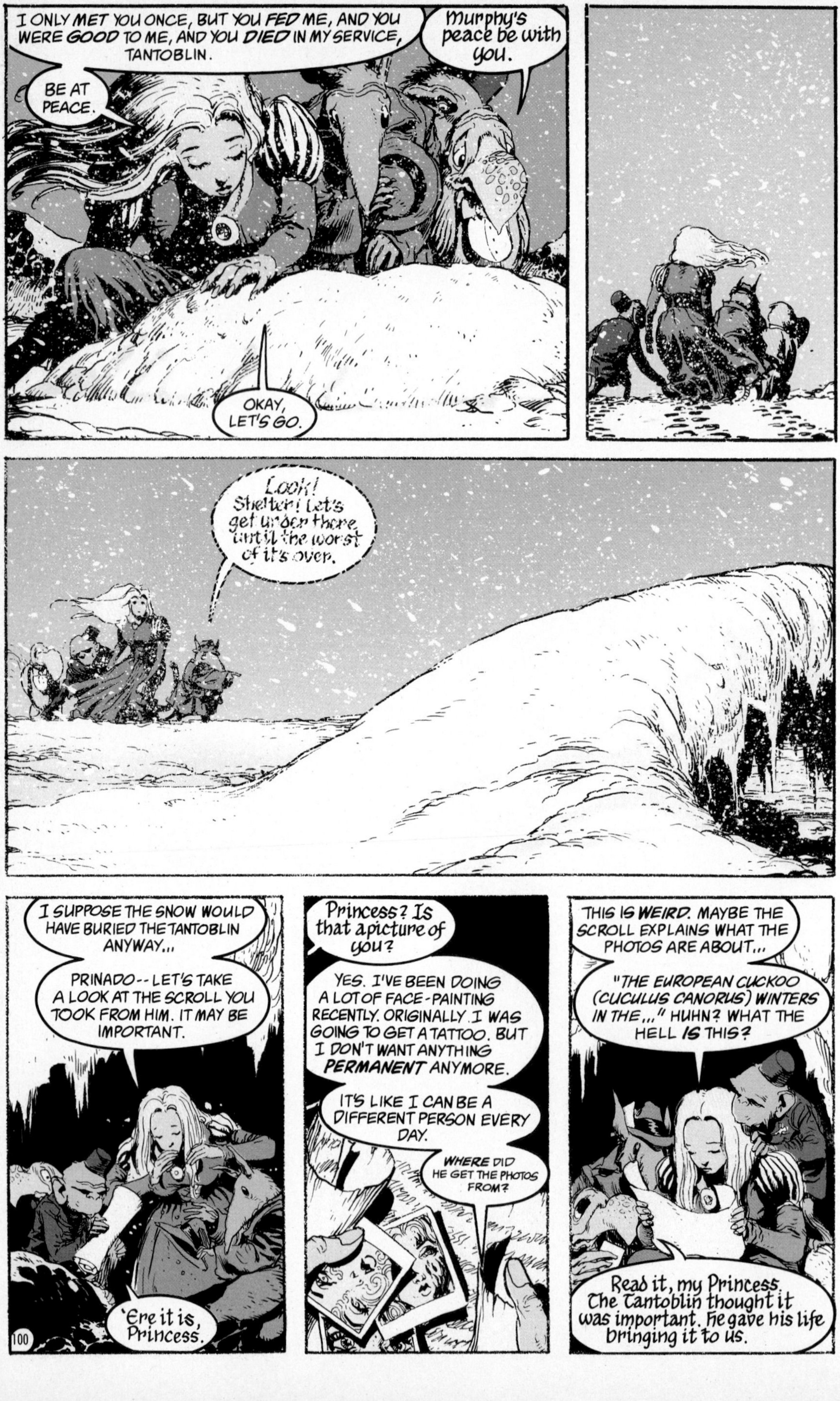

I ONLY MET YOU ONCE, BUT YOU FED ME, AND YOU WERE GOOD TO ME, AND YOU DIED IN MY SERVICE, TANTOBLIN.
BE AT PEACE.
Murphy's peace be with you.
OKAY, LET'S GO.
Look! Shelter! Let's get under there until the worst of it's over.
I SUPPOSE THE SNOW WOULD HAVE BURIED THE TANTOBLIN ANYWAY...
PRINADO-- LET'S TAKE A LOOK AT THE SCROLL YOU TOOK FROM HIM. IT MAY BE IMPORTANT.
'Ere it is, Princess.
Princess? Is that a picture of you?
YES. I'VE BEEN DOING A LOT OF FACE-PAINTING RECENTLY. ORIGINALLY I WAS GOING TO GET A TATTOO. BUT I DON'T WANT ANYTHING PERMANENT ANYMORE.
IT'S LIKE I CAN BE A DIFFERENT PERSON EVERY DAY.
WHERE DID HE GET THE PHOTOS FROM?
THIS IS WEIRD. MAYBE THE SCROLL EXPLAINS WHAT THE PHOTOS ARE ABOUT...
"THE EUROPEAN CUCKOO (CUCULUS CANORUS) WINTERS IN THE..." HUHN? WHAT THE HELL IS THIS?
Read it, my Princess. The Tantoblin thought it was important. He gave his life bringing it to us.

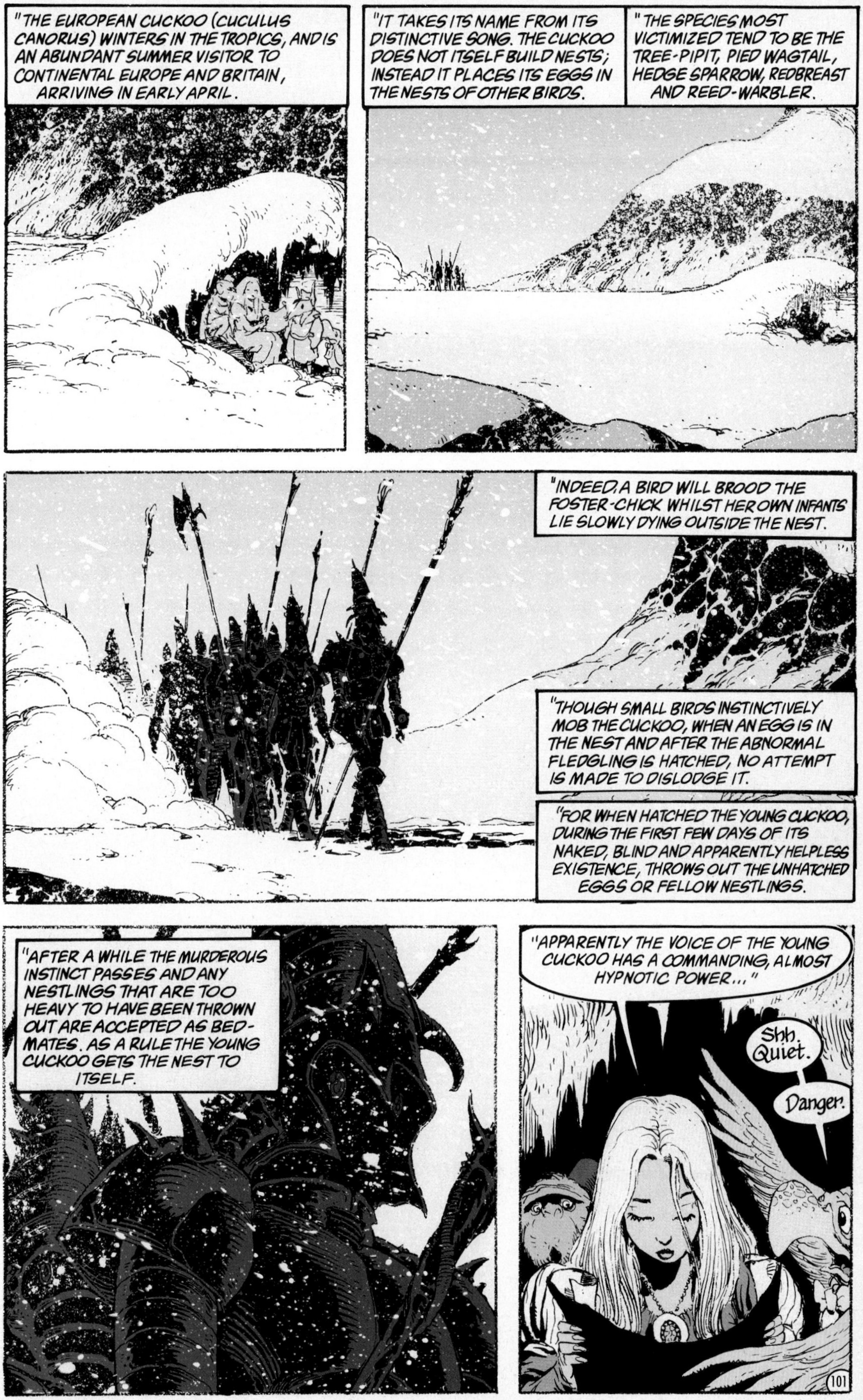
"THE EUROPEAN CUCKOO (CUCULUS CANORUS) WINTERS IN THE TROPICS, AND IS AN ABUNDANT SUMMER VISITOR TO CONTINENTAL EUROPE AND BRITAIN, ARRIVING IN EARLY APRIL.
"IT TAKES ITS NAME FROM ITS DISTINCTIVE SONG. THE CUCKOO DOES NOT ITSELF BUILD NESTS; INSTEAD IT PLACES ITS EGGS IN THE NESTS OF OTHER BIRDS.
"THE SPECIES MOST VICTIMIZED TEND TO BE THE TREE-PIPIT, PIED WAGTAIL, HEDGE SPARROW, REDBREAST AND REED-WARBLER.
"INDEED, A BIRD WILL BROOD THE FOSTER-CHICK WHILST HER OWN INFANTS LIE SLOWLY DYING OUTSIDE THE NEST.
"THOUGH SMALL BIRDS INSTINCTIVELY MOB THE CUCKOO, WHEN AN EGG IS IN THE NEST AND AFTER THE ABNORMAL FLEDGLING IS HATCHED, NO ATTEMPT IS MADE TO DISLODGE IT.
"FOR WHEN HATCHED THE YOUNG CUCKOO, DURING THE FIRST FEW DAYS OF ITS NAKED, BLIND AND APPARENTLY HELPLESS EXISTENCE, THROWS OUT THE UNHATCHED EGGS OR FELLOW NESTLINGS.
"AFTER A WHILE THE MURDEROUS INSTINCT PASSES AND ANY NESTLINGS THAT ARE TOO HEAVY TO HAVE BEEN THROWN OUT ARE ACCEPTED AS BED-MATES. AS A RULE THE YOUNG CUCKOO GETS THE NEST TO ITSELF.
"APPARENTLY THE VOICE OF THE YOUNG CUCKOO HAS A COMMANDING, ALMOST HYPNOTIC POWER..."
Shh. Quiet.
Danger.
101

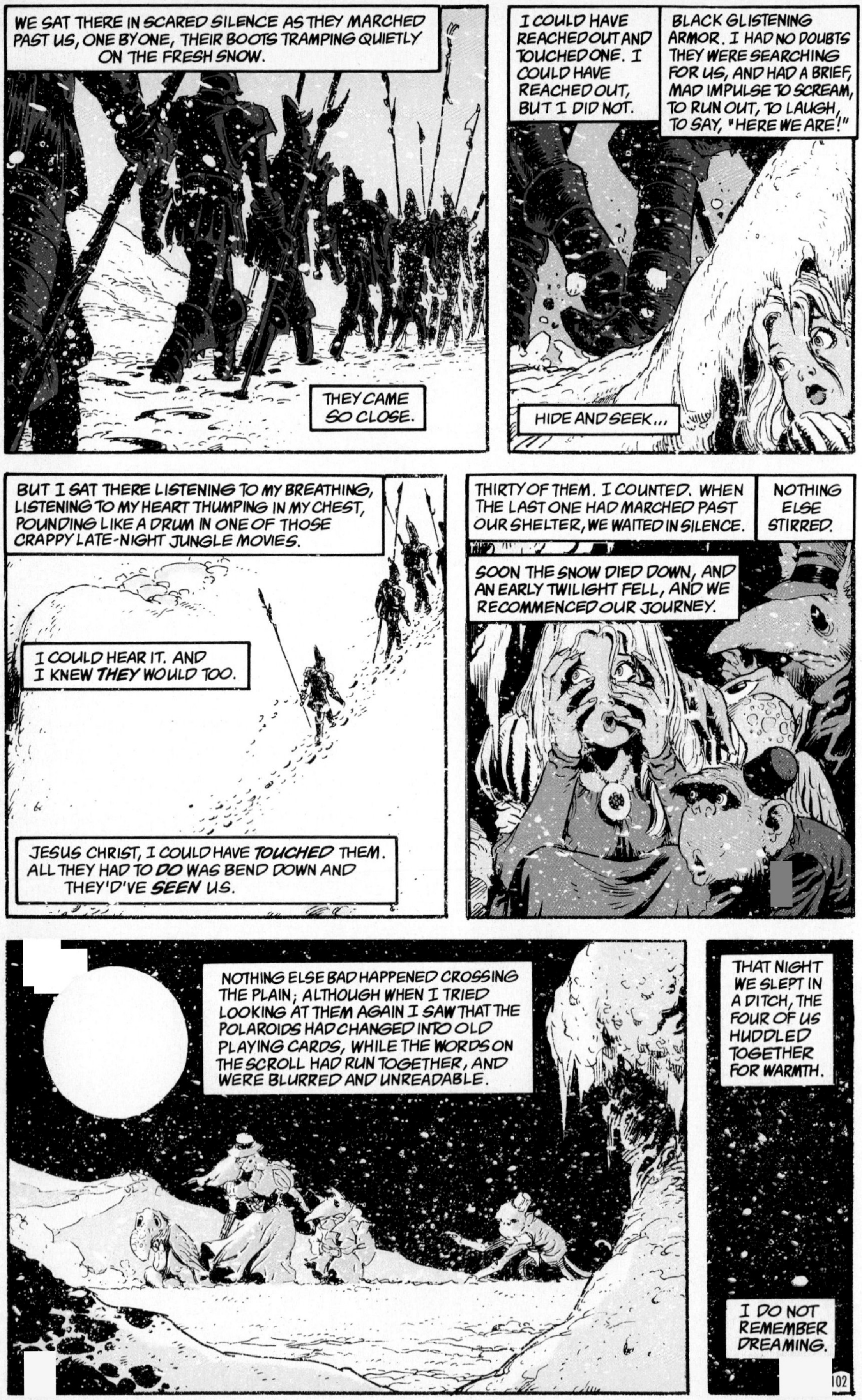
WE SAT THERE IN SCARED SILENCE AS THEY MARCHED PAST US, ONE BY ONE, THEIR BOOTS TRAMPING QUIETLY ON THE FRESH SNOW.
THEY CAME SO CLOSE.
I COULD HAVE REACHED OUT AND TOUCHED ONE. I COULD HAVE REACHED OUT, BUT I DID NOT.
BLACK GLISTENING ARMOR. I HAD NO DOUBTS THEY WERE SEARCHING FOR US, AND HAD A BRIEF, MAD IMPULSE TO SCREAM, TO RUN OUT, TO LAUGH, TO SAY, "HERE WE ARE!"
HIDE AND SEEK...
BUT I SAT THERE LISTENING TO MY BREATHING, LISTENING TO MY HEART THUMPING IN MY CHEST, POUNDING LIKE A DRUM IN ONE OF THOSE CRAPPY LATE-NIGHT JUNGLE MOVIES.
I COULD HEAR IT. AND I KNEW THEY WOULD TOO.
JESUS CHRIST, I COULD HAVE TOUCHED THEM. ALL THEY HAD TO DO WAS BEND DOWN AND THEY'D'VE SEEN US.
THIRTY OF THEM. I COUNTED. WHEN THE LAST ONE HAD MARCHED PAST OUR SHELTER, WE WAITED IN SILENCE.
NOTHING ELSE STIRRED.
SOON THE SNOW DIED DOWN, AND AN EARLY TWILIGHT FELL, AND WE RECOMMENCED OUR JOURNEY.
NOTHING ELSE BAD HAPPENED CROSSING THE PLAIN; ALTHOUGH WHEN I TRIED LOOKING AT THEM AGAIN I SAW THAT THE POLAROIDS HAD CHANGED INTO OLD PLAYING CARDS, WHILE THE WORDS ON THE SCROLL HAD RUN TOGETHER, AND WERE BLURRED AND UNREADABLE.
THAT NIGHT WE SLEPT IN A DITCH, THE FOUR OF US HUDDLED TOGETHER FOR WARMTH.
I DO NOT REMEMBER DREAMING.

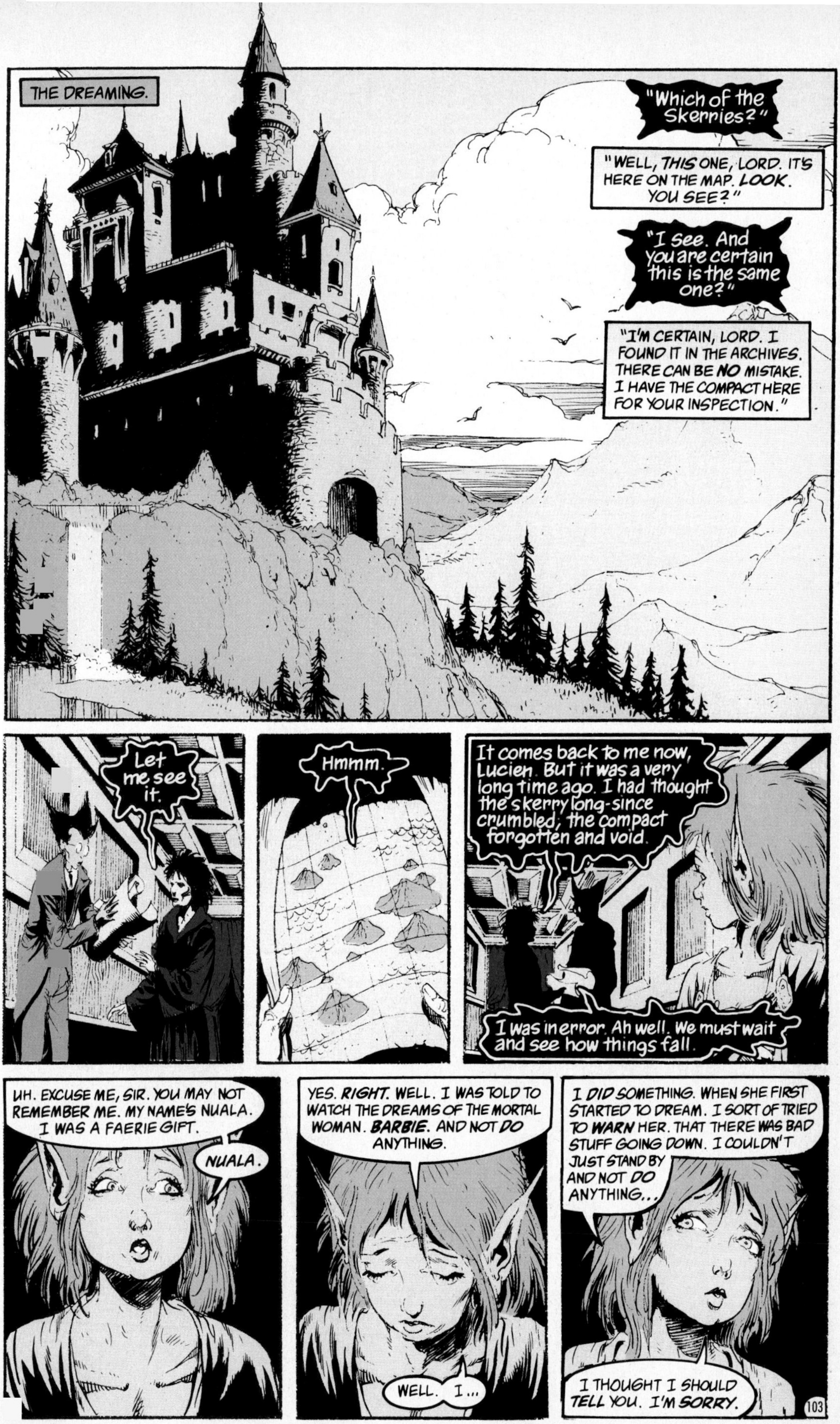
THE DREAMING.
"Which of the Skerries?"
"WELL, THIS ONE, LORD. IT'S HERE ON THE MAP. LOOK. YOU SEE?"
"I see. And you are certain this is the same one?"
"I'M CERTAIN, LORD. I FOUND IT IN THE ARCHIVES. THERE CAN BE NO MISTAKE. I HAVE THE COMPACT HERE FOR YOUR INSPECTION."
Let me see it.
Hmmm.
It comes back to me now, Lucien. But it was a very long time ago. I had thought the skerry long-since crumbled, the compact forgotten and void.
I was in error. Ah well. We must wait and see how things fall.
UH. EXCUSE ME, SIR. YOU MAY NOT REMEMBER ME. MY NAME'S NUALA. I WAS A FAERIE GIFT.
NUALA.
YES. RIGHT. WELL. I WAS TOLD TO WATCH THE DREAMS OF THE MORTAL WOMAN. BARBIE. AND NOT DO ANYTHING.
WELL. I...
I DID SOMETHING. WHEN SHE FIRST STARTED TO DREAM. I SORT OF TRIED TO WARN HER. THAT THERE WAS BAD STUFF GOING DOWN. I COULDN'T JUST STAND BY AND NOT DO ANYTHING...
I THOUGHT I SHOULD TELL YOU. I'M SORRY.

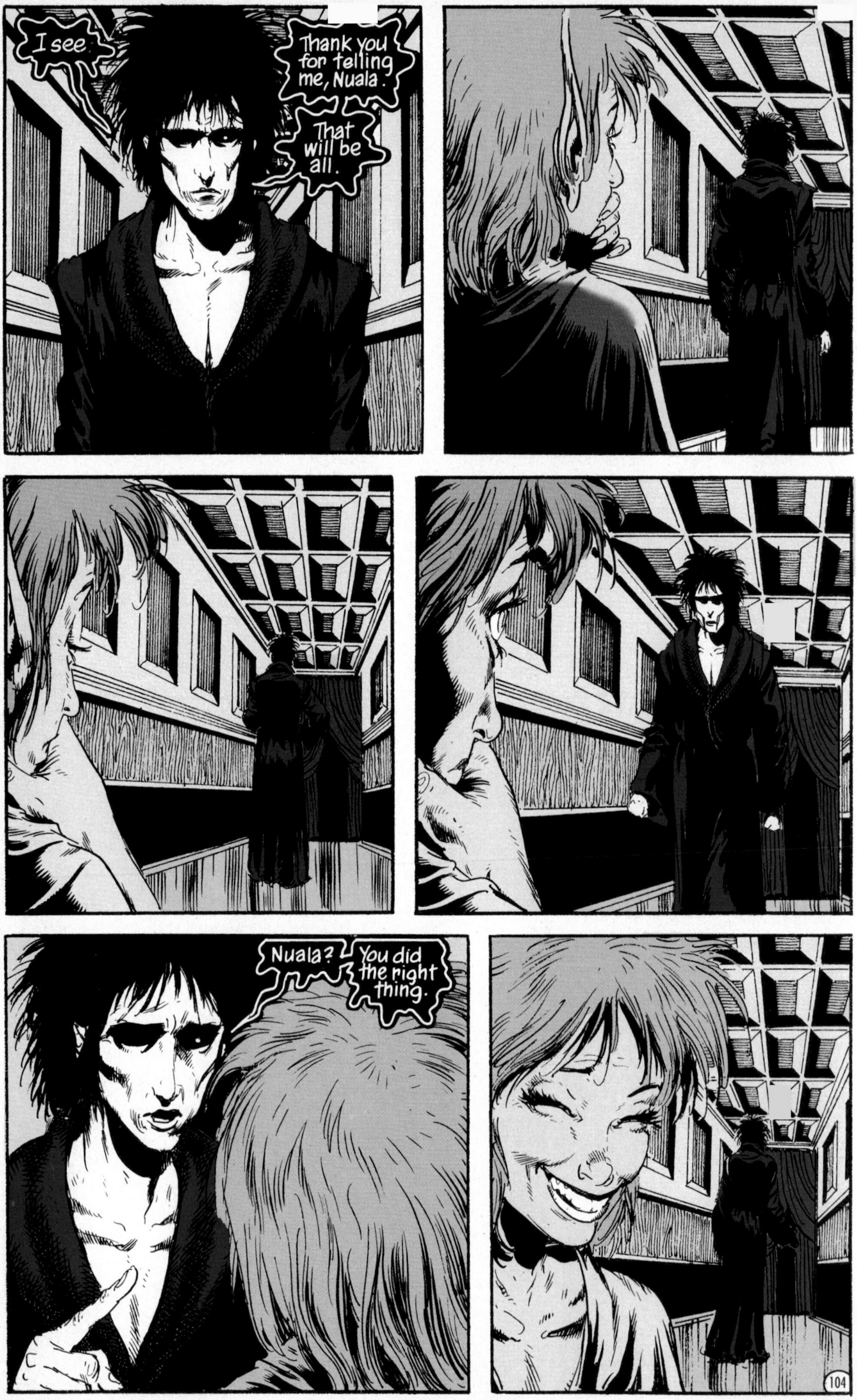
I see.
Thank you for telling me, Nuala.
That will be all.
Nuala?
You did the right thing.
104

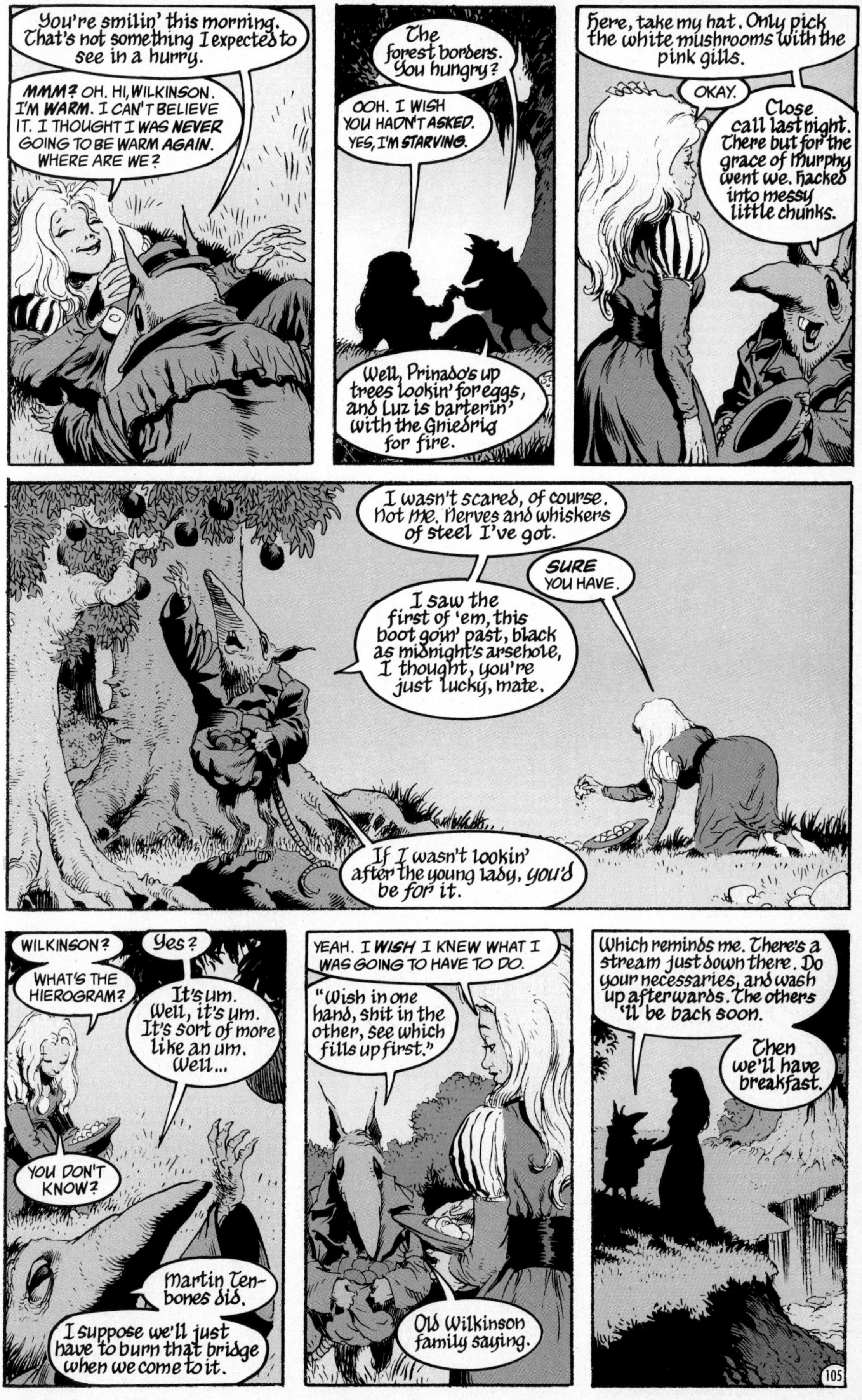
You're smilin' this morning. That's not something I expected to see in a hurry.
MMM? OH. HI, WILKINSON. I'M WARM. I CAN'T BELIEVE IT. I THOUGHT I WAS NEVER GOING TO BE WARM AGAIN. WHERE ARE WE?
The forest borders. You hungry?
OOH. I WISH YOU HADN'T ASKED. YES, I'M STARVING.
Well, Prinado's up trees lookin' for eggs, and Luz is barterin' with the Gniedrig for fire.
Here, take my hat. Only pick the white mushrooms with the pink gills.
OKAY.
Close call last night. There but for the grace of Murphy went we. Hacked into messy little chunks.
I wasn't scared, of course. Not me. Nerves and whiskers of steel I've got.
SURE YOU HAVE.
I saw the first of 'em, this boot goin' past, black as midnight's arsehole, I thought, you're just lucky, mate.
If I wasn't lookin' after the young lady, you'd be for it.
WILKINSON?
Yes?
WHAT'S THE HIEROGRAM?
It's um. Well, it's um. It's sort of more like an um. Well...
YOU DON'T KNOW?
Martin Tenbones did.
I suppose we'll just have to burn that bridge when we come to it.
YEAH. I WISH I KNEW WHAT I WAS GOING TO HAVE TO DO.
"Wish in one hand, shit in the other, see which fills up first."
Old Wilkinson family saying.
Which reminds me. There's a stream just down there. Do your necessaries, and wash up afterwards. The others 'll be back soon.
Then we'll have breakfast.

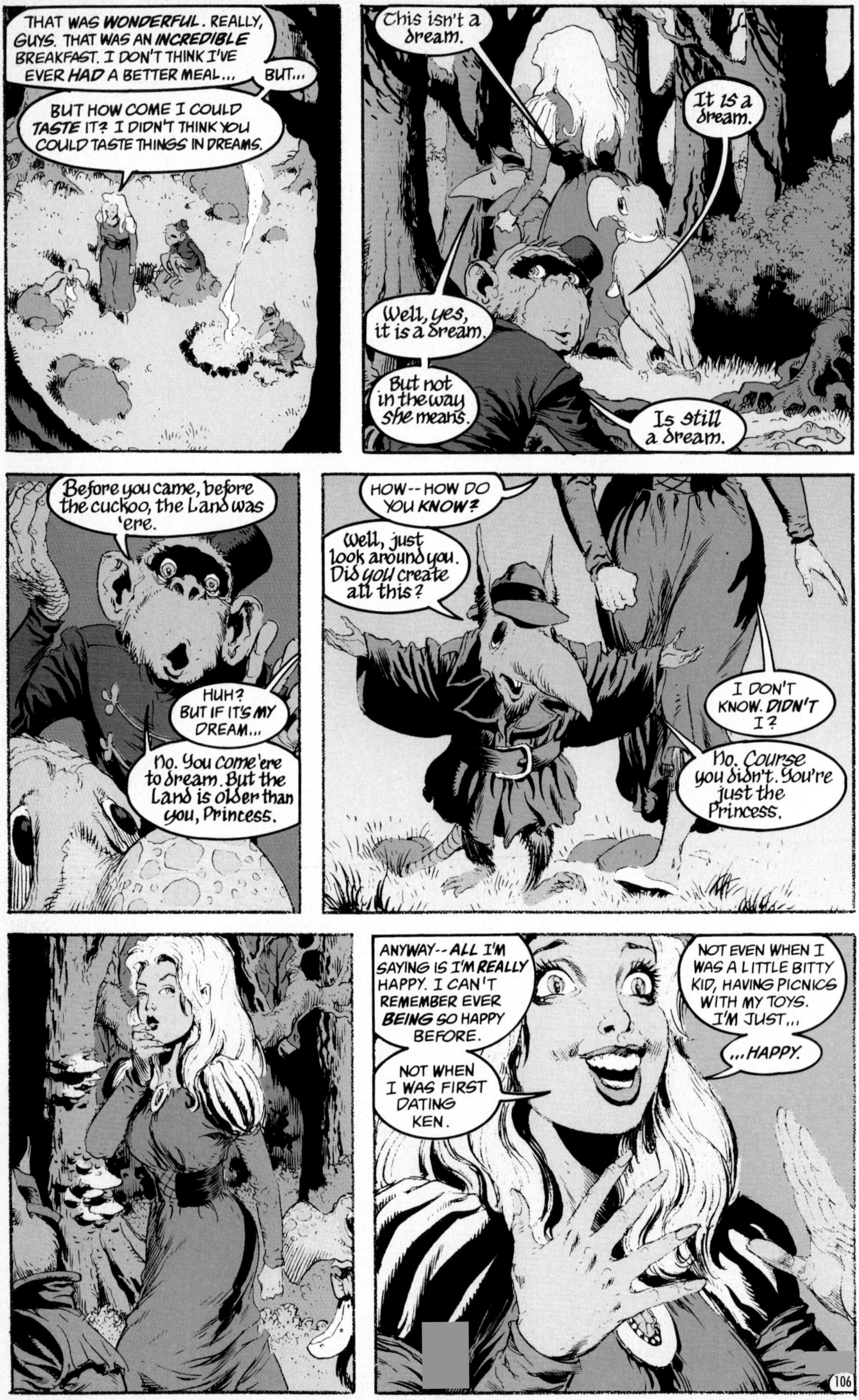
THAT WAS WONDERFUL. REALLY, GUYS. THAT WAS AN INCREDIBLE BREAKFAST. I DON'T THINK I'VE EVER HAD A BETTER MEAL...
BUT...
BUT HOW COME I COULD TASTE IT? I DIDN'T THINK YOU COULD TASTE THINGS IN DREAMS.
This isn't a dream.
It is a dream.
Well, yes, it is a dream.
But not in the way she means.
Is still a dream.
Before you came, before the cuckoo, the Land was 'ere.
HUH? BUT IF IT'S MY DREAM...
No. You come 'ere to dream. But the Land is older than you, Princess.
HOW--HOW DO YOU KNOW?
Well, just look around you. Did you create all this?
I DON'T KNOW. DIDN'T I?
No. Course you didn't. You're just the Princess.
ANYWAY--ALL I'M SAYING IS I'M REALLY HAPPY. I CAN'T REMEMBER EVER BEING SO HAPPY BEFORE.
NOT WHEN I WAS FIRST DATING KEN.
NOT EVEN WHEN I WAS A LITTLE BITTY KID, HAVING PICNICS WITH MY TOYS. I'M JUST...
...HAPPY.

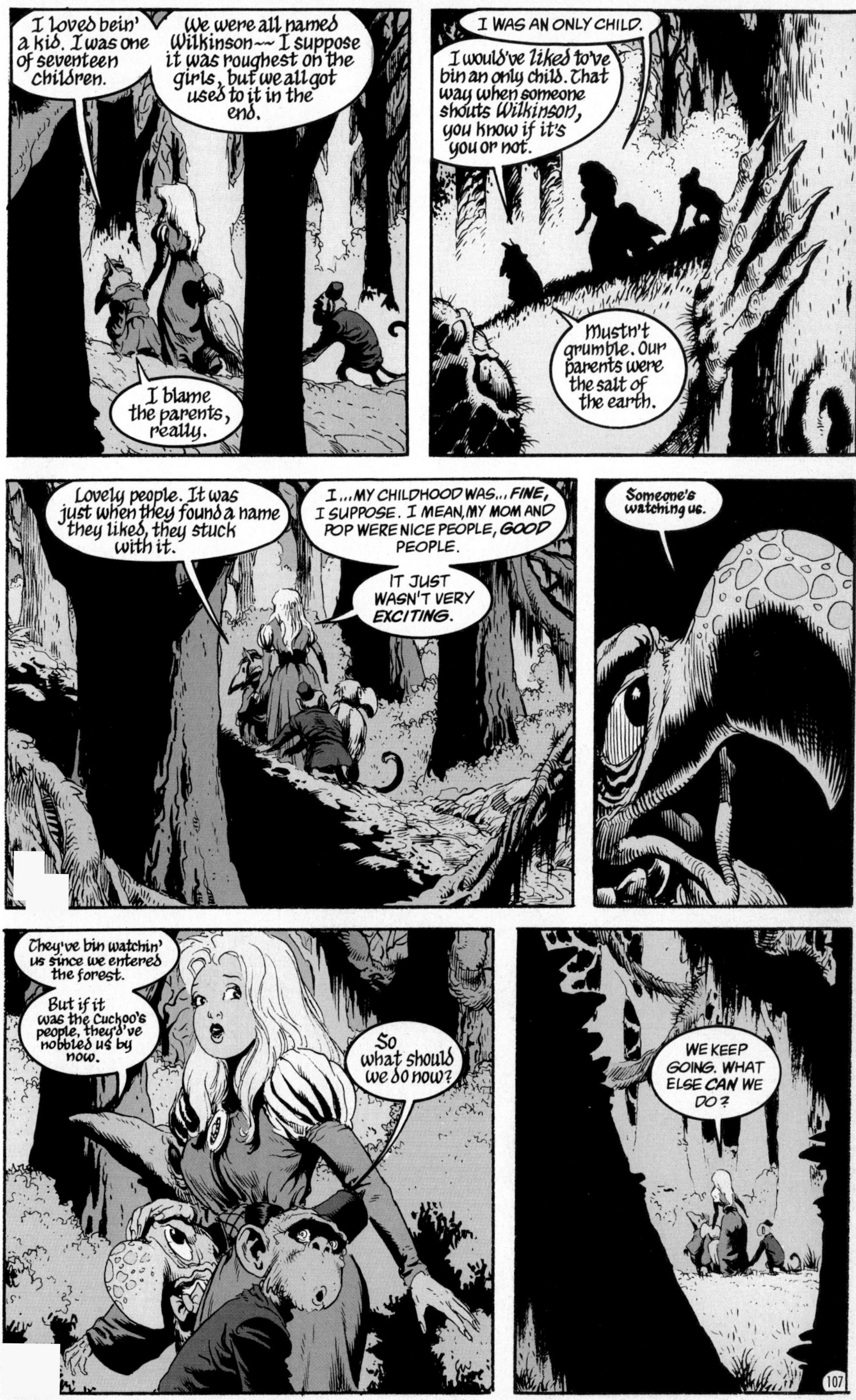
I loved bein' a kid. I was one of seventeen children.
We were all named Wilkinson-- I suppose it was roughest on the girls, but we all got used to it in the end.
I blame the parents, really.
I WAS AN ONLY CHILD.
I would've liked to've bin an only child. That way when someone shouts Wilkinson, you know if it's you or not.
Mustn't grumble. Our parents were the salt of the earth.
Lovely people. It was just when they found a name they liked, they stuck with it.
I... MY CHILDHOOD WAS... FINE, I SUPPOSE. I MEAN, MY MOM AND POP WERE NICE PEOPLE, GOOD PEOPLE.
IT JUST WASN'T VERY EXCITING.
Someone's watching us.
They've bin watchin' us since we entered the forest.
But if it was the Cuckoo's people, they'd've nobbled us by now.
So what should we do now?
WE KEEP GOING. WHAT ELSE CAN WE DO?

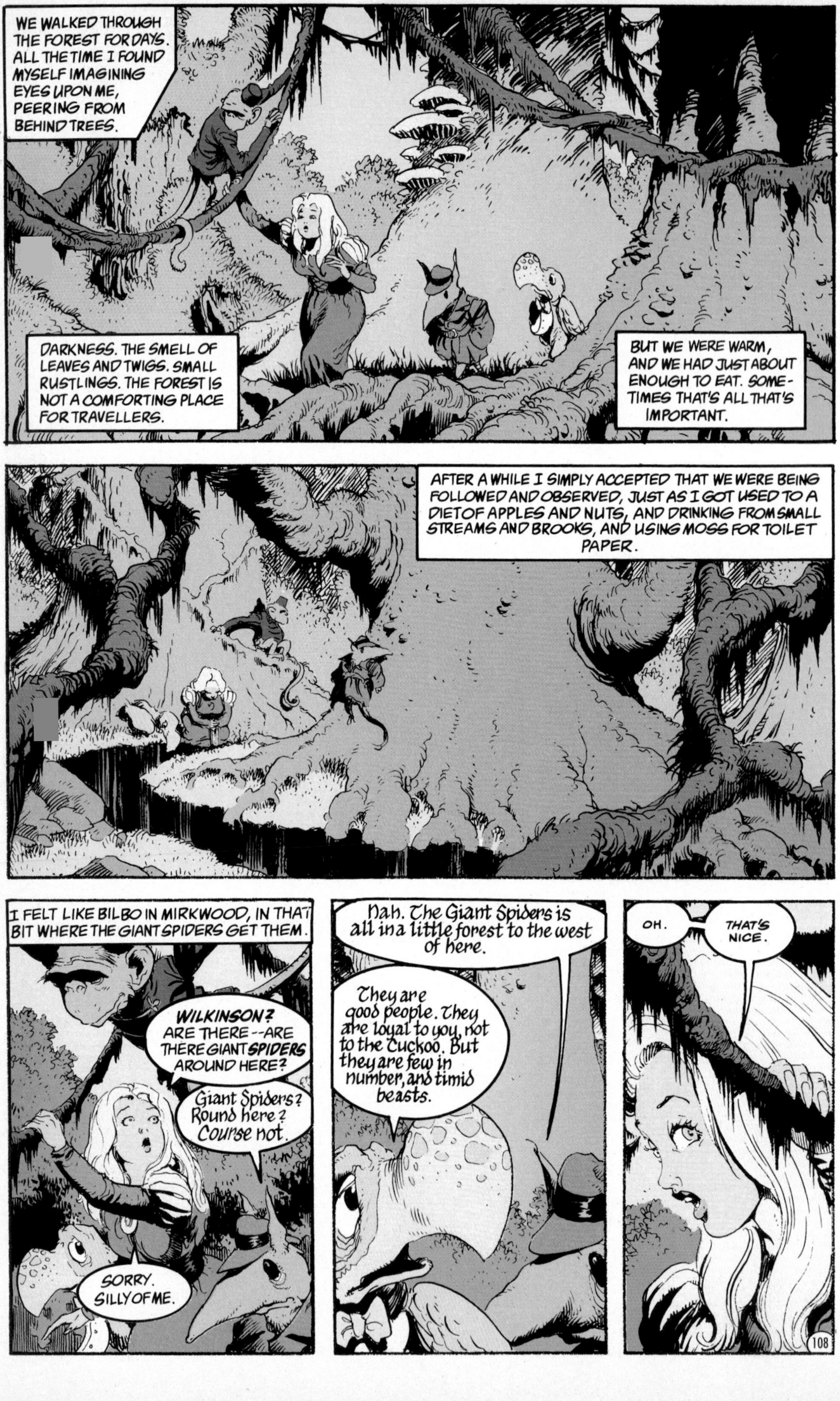
WE WALKED THROUGH THE FOREST FOR DAYS. ALL THE TIME I FOUND MYSELF IMAGINING EYES UPON ME, PEERING FROM BEHIND TREES.
DARKNESS. THE SMELL OF LEAVES AND TWIGS. SMALL RUSTLINGS. THE FOREST IS NOT A COMFORTING PLACE FOR TRAVELLERS.
BUT WE WERE WARM, AND WE HAD JUST ABOUT ENOUGH TO EAT. SOMETIMES THAT'S ALL THAT'S IMPORTANT.
AFTER A WHILE I SIMPLY ACCEPTED THAT WE WERE BEING FOLLOWED AND OBSERVED, JUST AS I GOT USED TO A DIET OF APPLES AND NUTS, AND DRINKING FROM SMALL STREAMS AND BROOKS, AND USING MOSS FOR TOILET PAPER.
I FELT LIKE BILBO IN MIRKWOOD, IN THAT BIT WHERE THE GIANT SPIDERS GET THEM.
WILKINSON? ARE THERE--ARE THERE GIANT SPIDERS AROUND HERE?
Giant Spiders? Round here? Course not.
SORRY. SILLY OF ME.
Nah. The Giant Spiders is all in a little forest to the west of here.
They are good people. They are loyal to you, not to the Cuckoo. But they are few in number, and timid beasts.
OH.
THAT'S NICE.

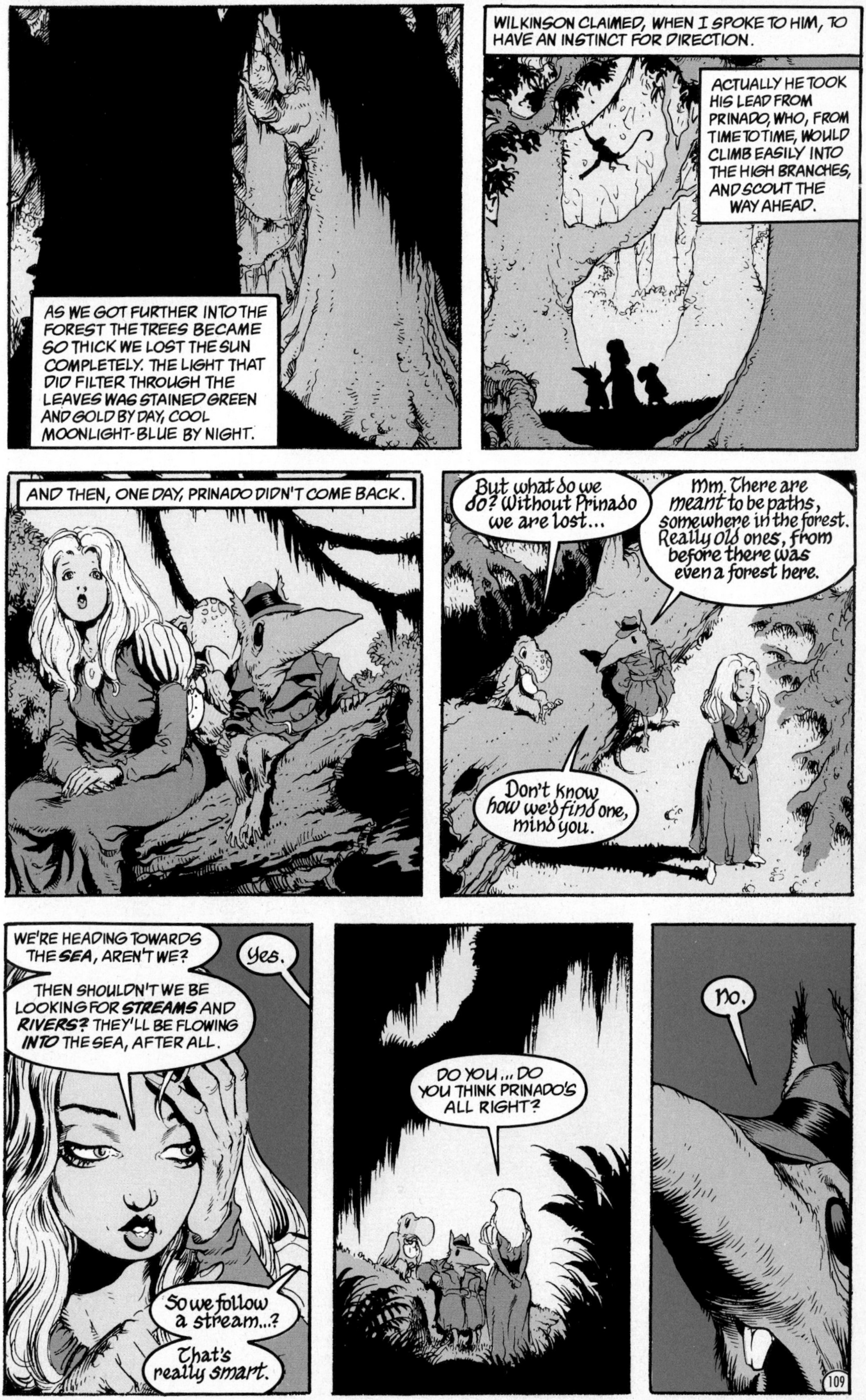
AS WE GOT FURTHER INTO THE FOREST THE TREES BECAME SO THICK WE LOST THE SUN COMPLETELY. THE LIGHT THAT DID FILTER THROUGH THE LEAVES WAS STAINED GREEN AND GOLD BY DAY, COOL MOONLIGHT-BLUE BY NIGHT.
WILKINSON CLAIMED, WHEN I SPOKE TO HIM, TO HAVE AN INSTINCT FOR DIRECTION.
ACTUALLY HE TOOK HIS LEAD FROM PRINADO, WHO, FROM TIME TO TIME, WOULD CLIMB EASILY INTO THE HIGH BRANCHES, AND SCOUT THE WAY AHEAD.
AND THEN, ONE DAY, PRINADO DIDN'T COME BACK.
But what do we do? Without Prinado we are lost...
Mm. There are *meant* to be paths, somewhere in the forest. Really old ones, from before there was even a forest here.
Don't know how we'd find one, mind you.
WE'RE HEADING TOWARDS THE *SEA*, AREN'T WE?
Yes.
THEN SHOULDN'T WE BE LOOKING FOR *STREAMS* AND *RIVERS*? THEY'LL BE FLOWING *INTO* THE SEA, AFTER ALL.
So we follow a stream...?
That's really *smart*.
DO YOU... DO YOU THINK PRINADO'S ALL RIGHT?
No.

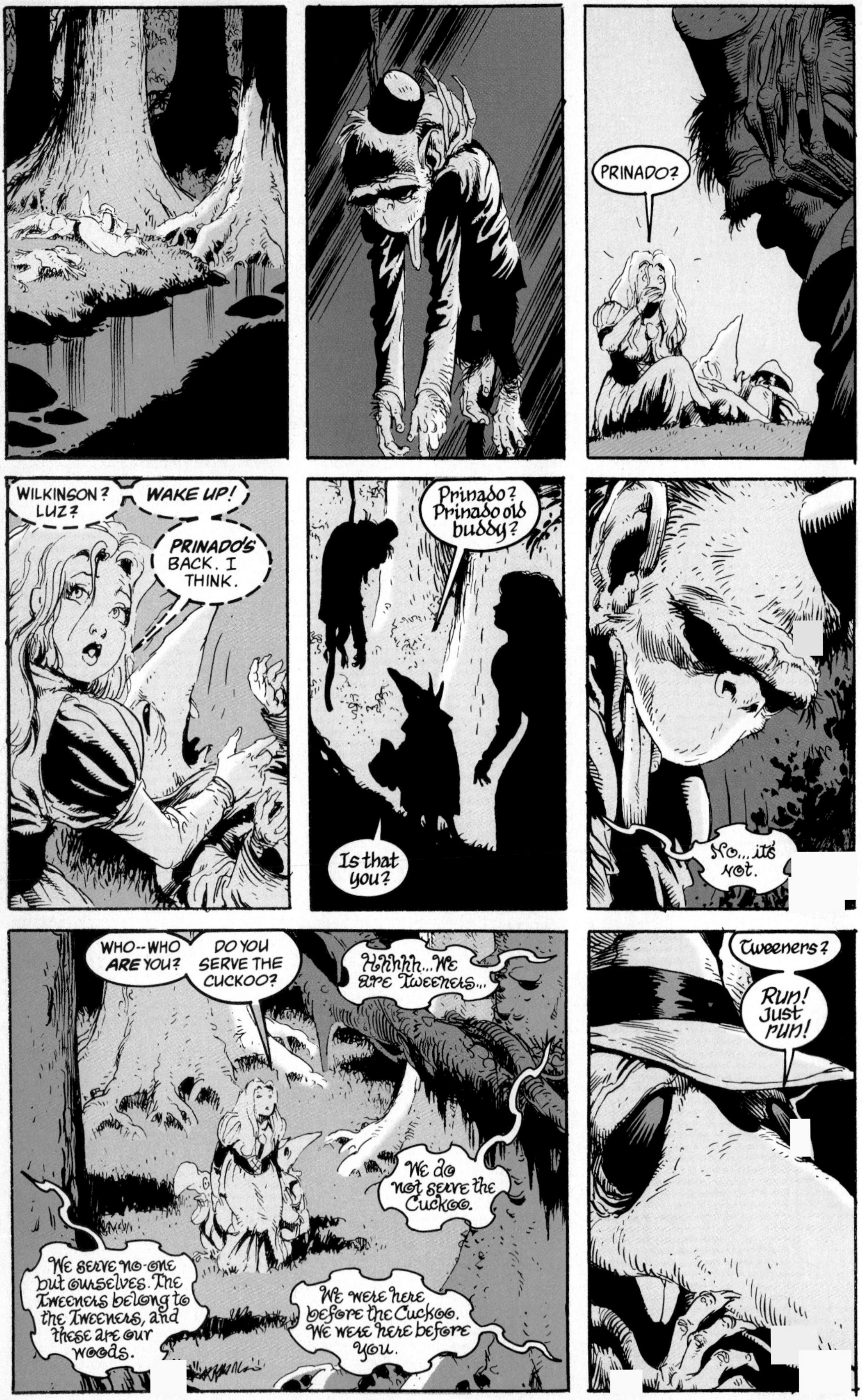
PRINADO?
WILKINSON? LUZ?
WAKE UP!
PRINADO'S BACK. I THINK.
Prinado? Prinado old buddy?
Is that you?
No... it's not.
WHO--WHO ARE YOU?
DO YOU SERVE THE CUCKOO?
Hhhhh... We are Tweeners...
We do not serve the Cuckoo.
We serve no-one but ourselves. The Tweeners belong to the Tweeners, and these are our woods.
We were here before the Cuckoo. We were here before you.
Tweeners?
Run! Just run!

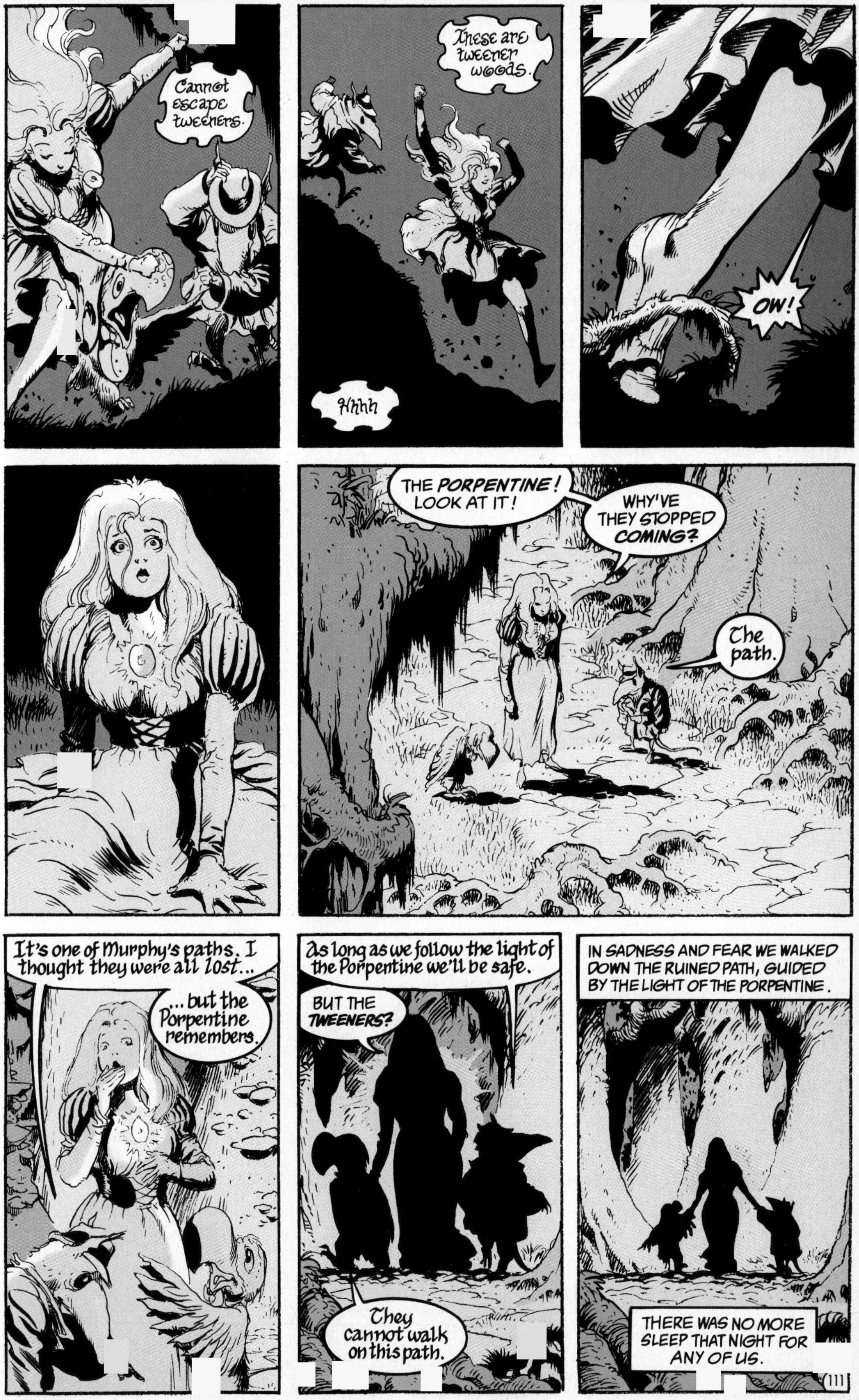

Cannot escape tweeners.
These are tweener woods.
Hhhh
OW!
THE PORPENTINE! LOOK AT IT!
WHY'VE THEY STOPPED COMING?
The path.
It's one of Murphy's paths. I thought they were all lost...
...but the Porpentine remembers.
As long as we follow the light of the Porpentine we'll be safe.
BUT THE TWEENERS?
They cannot walk on this path.
IN SADNESS AND FEAR WE WALKED DOWN THE RUINED PATH, GUIDED BY THE LIGHT OF THE PORPENTINE.
THERE WAS NO MORE SLEEP THAT NIGHT FOR ANY OF US.

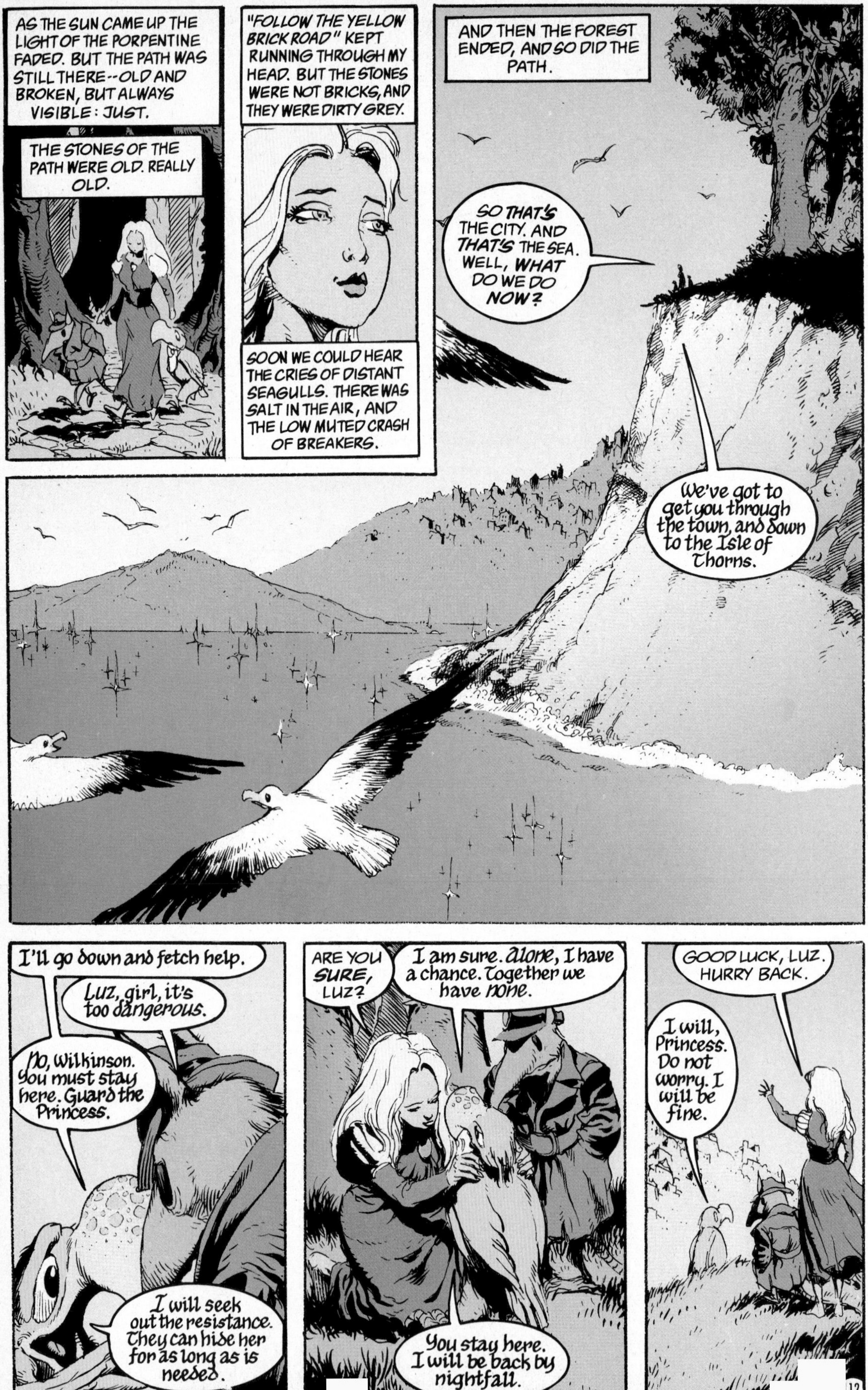
AS THE SUN CAME UP THE LIGHT OF THE PORPENTINE FADED. BUT THE PATH WAS STILL THERE--OLD AND BROKEN, BUT ALWAYS VISIBLE: JUST.
THE STONES OF THE PATH WERE OLD. REALLY OLD.
"FOLLOW THE YELLOW BRICK ROAD" KEPT RUNNING THROUGH MY HEAD. BUT THE STONES WERE NOT BRICKS, AND THEY WERE DIRTY GREY.
SOON WE COULD HEAR THE CRIES OF DISTANT SEAGULLS. THERE WAS SALT IN THE AIR, AND THE LOW MUTED CRASH OF BREAKERS.
AND THEN THE FOREST ENDED, AND SO DID THE PATH.
SO THAT'S THE CITY. AND THAT'S THE SEA. WELL, WHAT DO WE DO NOW?
We've got to get you through the town, and down to the Isle of Thorns.
I'll go down and fetch help.
Luz, girl, it's too dangerous.
No, Wilkinson. You must stay here. Guard the Princess.
I will seek out the resistance. They can hide her for as long as is needed.
ARE YOU SURE, LUZ?
I am sure. Alone, I have a chance. Together we have none.
You stay here. I will be back by nightfall.
GOOD LUCK, LUZ. HURRY BACK.
I will, Princess. Do not worry. I will be fine.

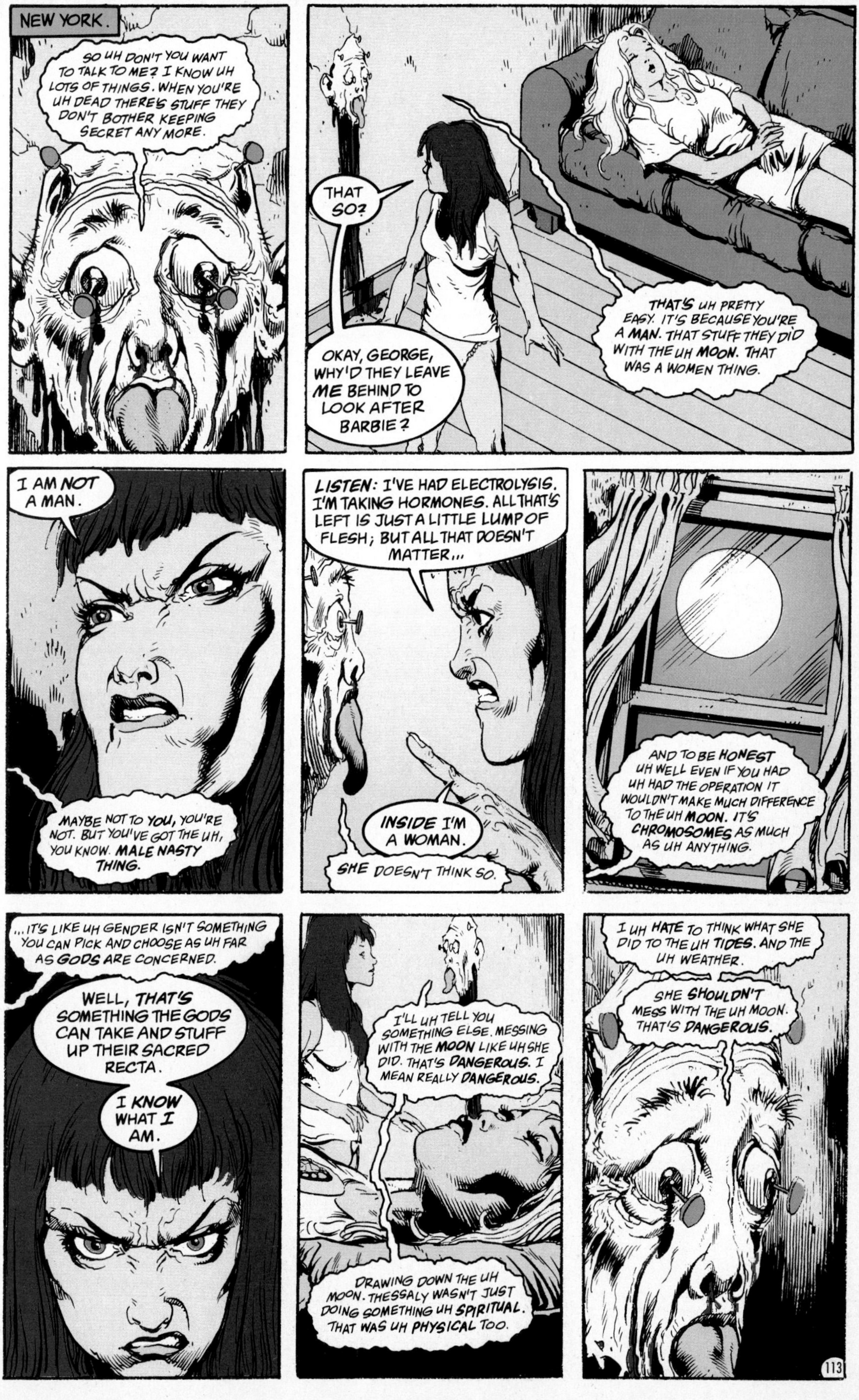
NEW YORK.
SO UH DON'T YOU WANT TO TALK TO ME? I KNOW UH LOTS OF THINGS. WHEN YOU'RE UH DEAD THERE'S STUFF THEY DON'T BOTHER KEEPING SECRET ANY MORE.
THAT SO?
OKAY, GEORGE, WHY'D THEY LEAVE ME BEHIND TO LOOK AFTER BARBIE?
THAT'S UH PRETTY EASY. IT'S BECAUSE YOU'RE A MAN. THAT STUFF THEY DID WITH THE UH MOON. THAT WAS A WOMEN THING.
I AM NOT A MAN.
MAYBE NOT TO YOU, YOU'RE NOT. BUT YOU'VE GOT THE UH, YOU KNOW. MALE NASTY THING.
LISTEN: I'VE HAD ELECTROLYSIS. I'M TAKING HORMONES. ALL THAT'S LEFT IS JUST A LITTLE LUMP OF FLESH; BUT ALL THAT DOESN'T MATTER...
INSIDE I'M A WOMAN.
SHE DOESN'T THINK SO.
AND TO BE HONEST UH WELL EVEN IF YOU HAD UH HAD THE OPERATION IT WOULDN'T MAKE MUCH DIFFERENCE TO THE UH MOON. IT'S CHROMOSOMES AS MUCH AS UH ANYTHING.
...IT'S LIKE UH GENDER ISN'T SOMETHING YOU CAN PICK AND CHOOSE AS UH FAR AS GODS ARE CONCERNED.
WELL, THAT'S SOMETHING THE GODS CAN TAKE AND STUFF UP THEIR SACRED RECTA.
I KNOW WHAT I AM.
I'LL UH TELL YOU SOMETHING ELSE. MESSING WITH THE MOON LIKE UH SHE DID. THAT'S DANGEROUS. I MEAN REALLY DANGEROUS.
DRAWING DOWN THE UH MOON. THESSALY WASN'T JUST DOING SOMETHING UH SPIRITUAL. THAT WAS UH PHYSICAL TOO.
I UH HATE TO THINK WHAT SHE DID TO THE UH TIDES. AND THE UH WEATHER.
SHE SHOULDN'T MESS WITH THE UH MOON. THAT'S DANGEROUS.

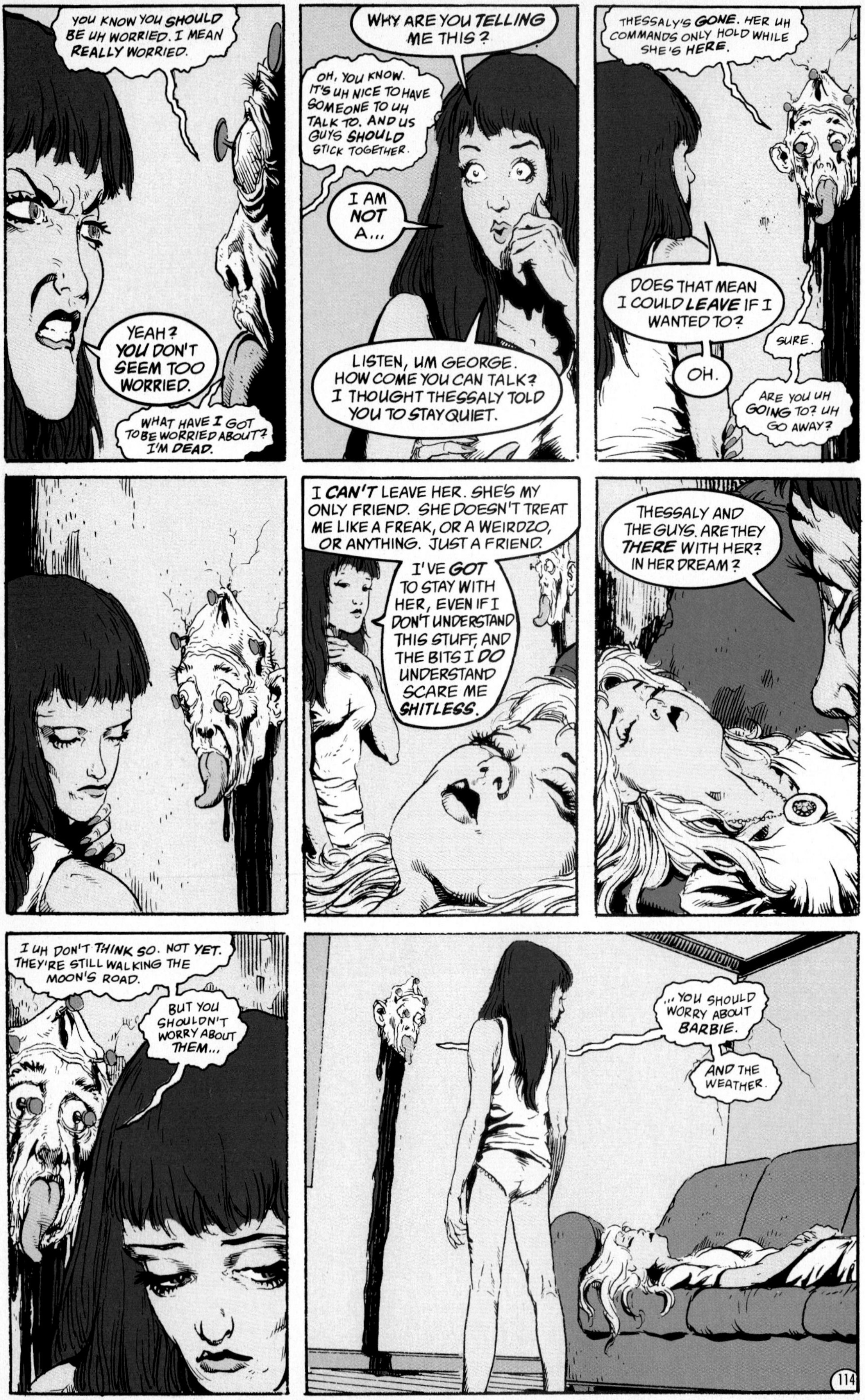

YOU KNOW YOU SHOULD BE UH WORRIED. I MEAN REALLY WORRIED.
YEAH? YOU DON'T SEEM TOO WORRIED.
WHAT HAVE I GOT TO BE WORRIED ABOUT? I'M DEAD.
WHY ARE YOU TELLING ME THIS?
OH, YOU KNOW. IT'S UH NICE TO HAVE SOMEONE TO UH TALK TO. AND US GUYS SHOULD STICK TOGETHER.
I AM NOT A...
LISTEN, UM GEORGE. HOW COME YOU CAN TALK? I THOUGHT THESSALY TOLD YOU TO STAY QUIET.
THESSALY'S GONE. HER UH COMMANDS ONLY HOLD WHILE SHE'S HERE.
DOES THAT MEAN I COULD LEAVE IF I WANTED TO?
SURE.
OH.
ARE YOU UH GOING TO? UH GO AWAY?
I CAN'T LEAVE HER. SHE'S MY ONLY FRIEND. SHE DOESN'T TREAT ME LIKE A FREAK, OR A WEIRDZO, OR ANYTHING. JUST A FRIEND.
I'VE GOT TO STAY WITH HER, EVEN IF I DON'T UNDERSTAND THIS STUFF, AND THE BITS I DO UNDERSTAND SCARE ME SHITLESS.
THESSALY AND THE GUYS. ARE THEY THERE WITH HER? IN HER DREAM?
I UH DON'T THINK SO. NOT YET. THEY'RE STILL WALKING THE MOON'S ROAD.
BUT YOU SHOULDN'T WORRY ABOUT THEM...
...YOU SHOULD WORRY ABOUT BARBIE.
AND THE WEATHER.

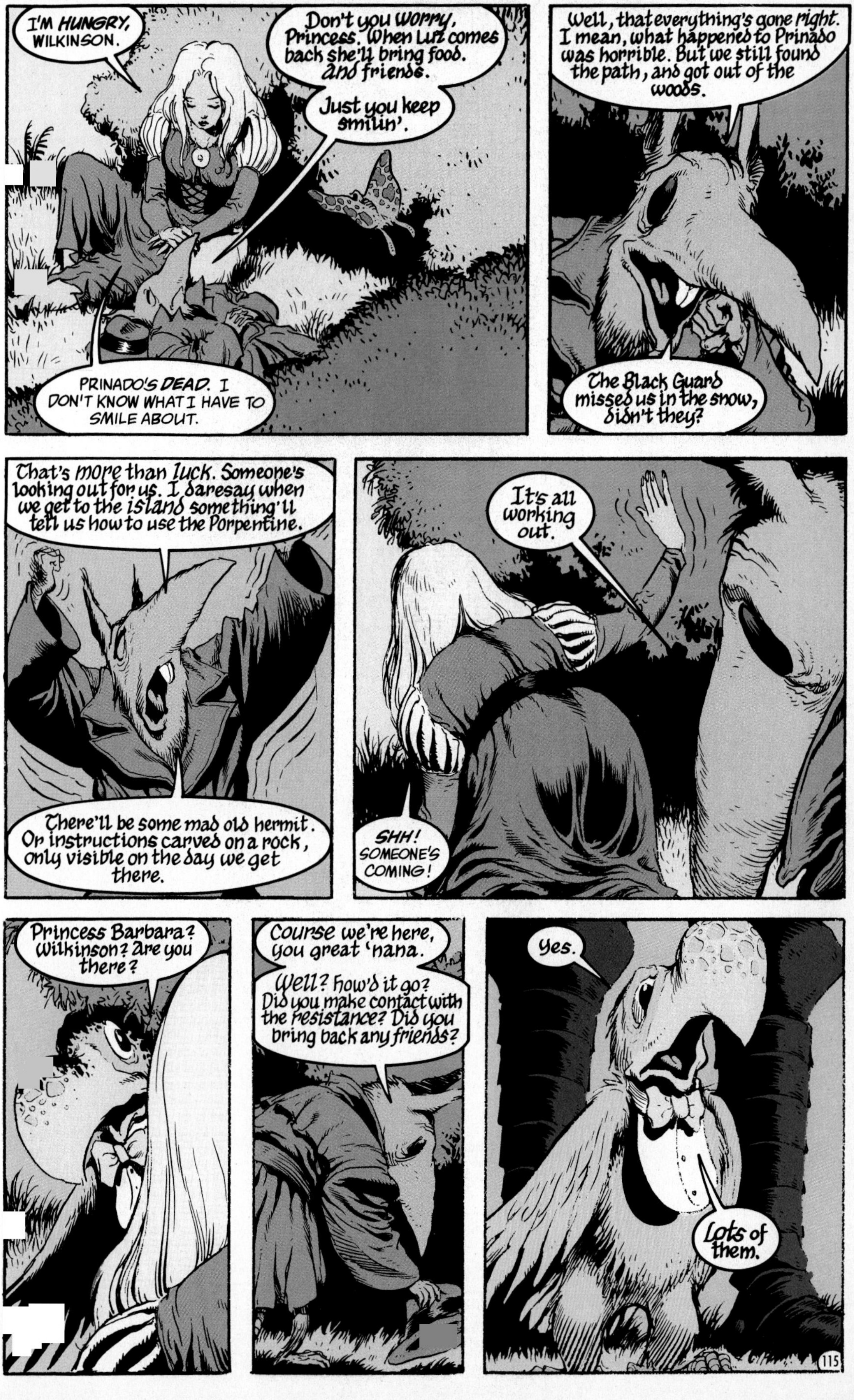
I'M HUNGRY, WILKINSON.
Don't you worry, Princess. When Luz comes back she'll bring food. And friends.
Just you keep smilin'.
PRINADO'S DEAD. I DON'T KNOW WHAT I HAVE TO SMILE ABOUT.
Well, that everything's gone right. I mean, what happened to Prinado was horrible. But we still found the path, and got out of the woods.
The Black Guard missed us in the snow, didn't they?
That's more than luck. Someone's looking out for us. I daresay when we get to the island something'll tell us how to use the Porpentine.
There'll be some mad old hermit. Or instructions carved on a rock, only visible on the day we get there.
It's all working out.
SHH! SOMEONE'S COMING!
Princess Barbara? Wilkinson? Are you there?
Course we're here, you great 'nana.
Well? How'd it go? Did you make contact with the resistance? Did you bring back any friends?
Yes.
Lots of them.

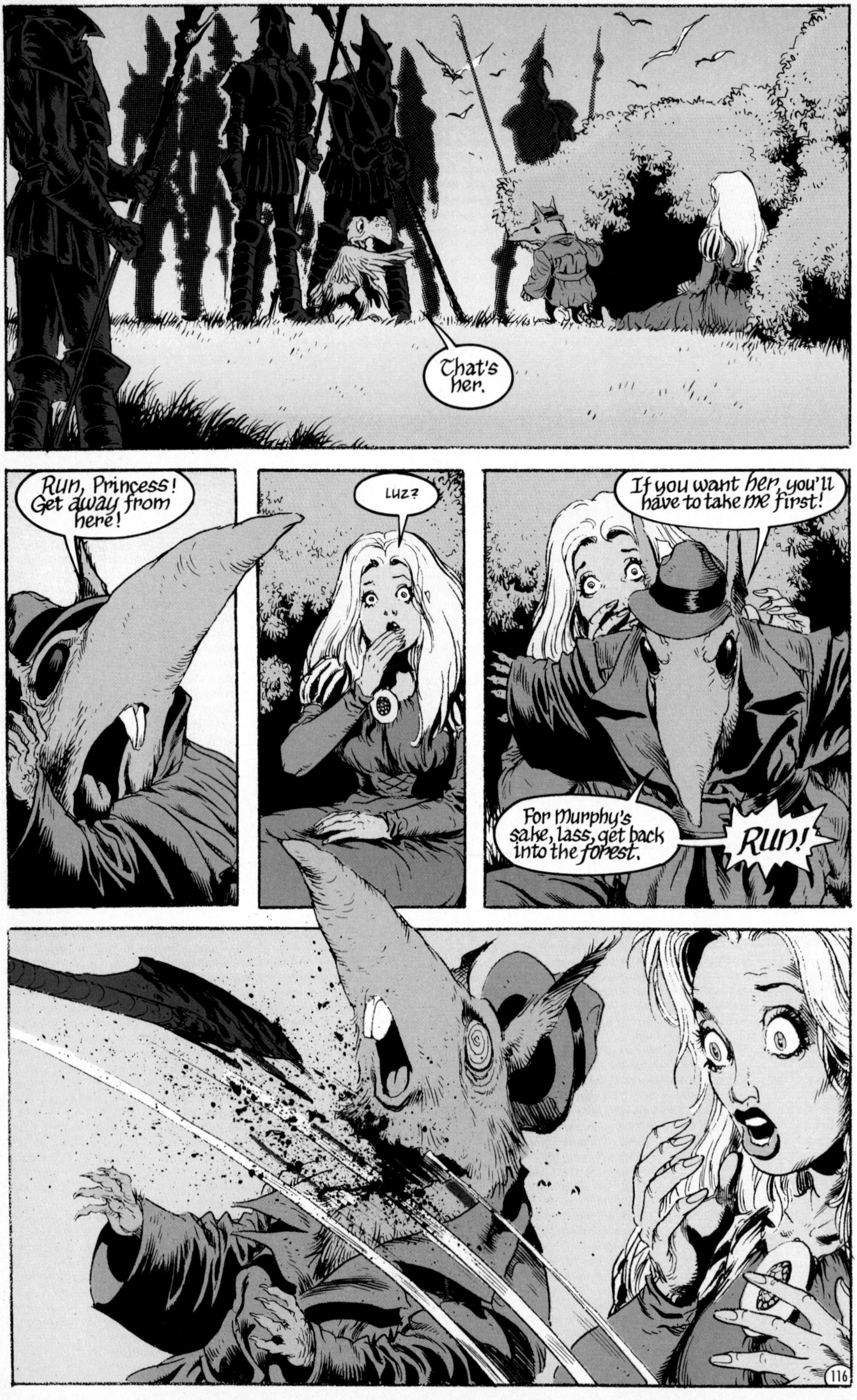

That's her.
Run, Princess! Get away from here!
LUZ?
If you want her, you'll have to take me first!
For Murphy's sake, lass, get back into the forest.
RUN!

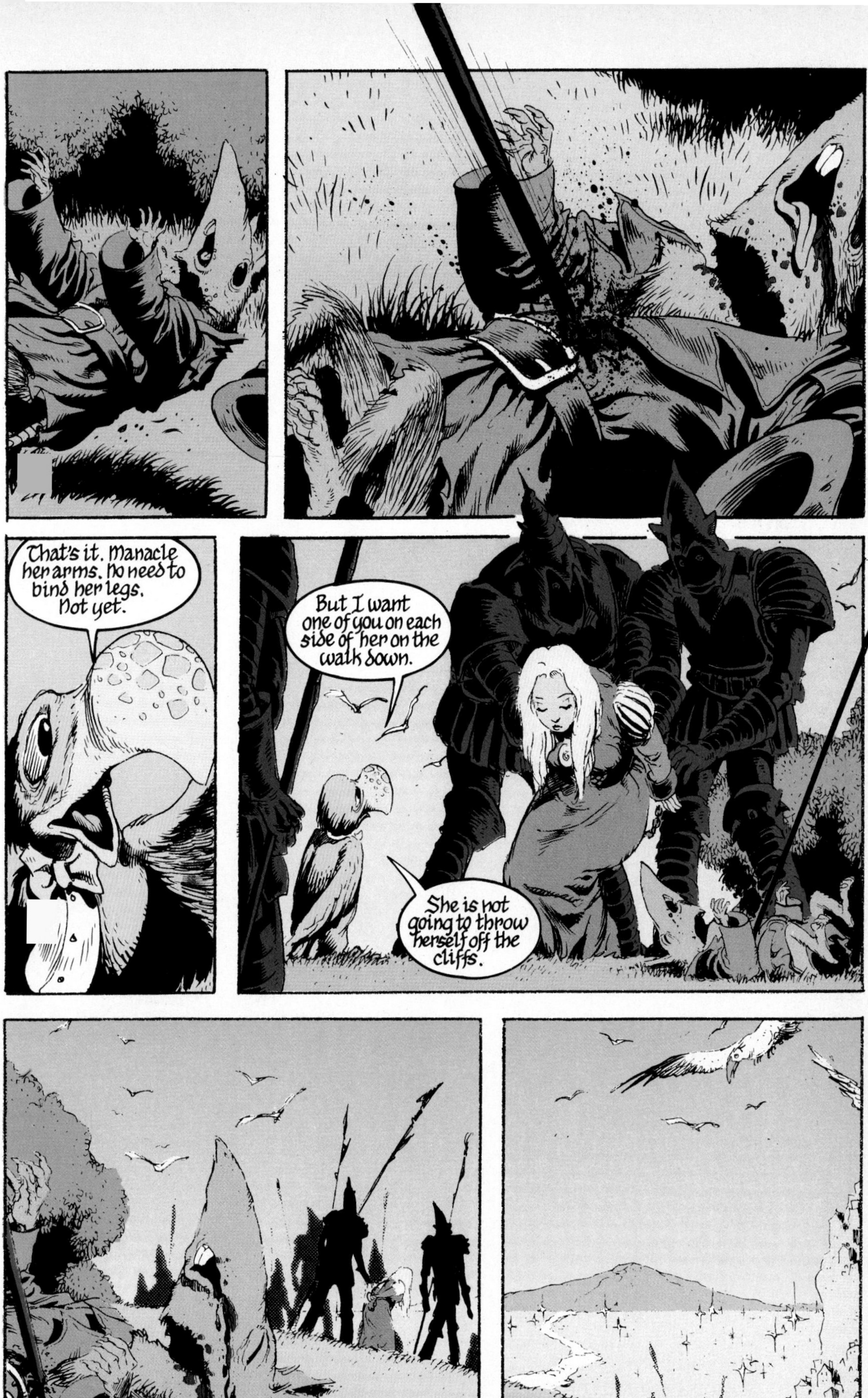
That's it. Manacle her arms. No need to bind her legs. Not yet.
But I want one of you on each side of her on the walk down.
She is not going to throw herself off the cliffs.

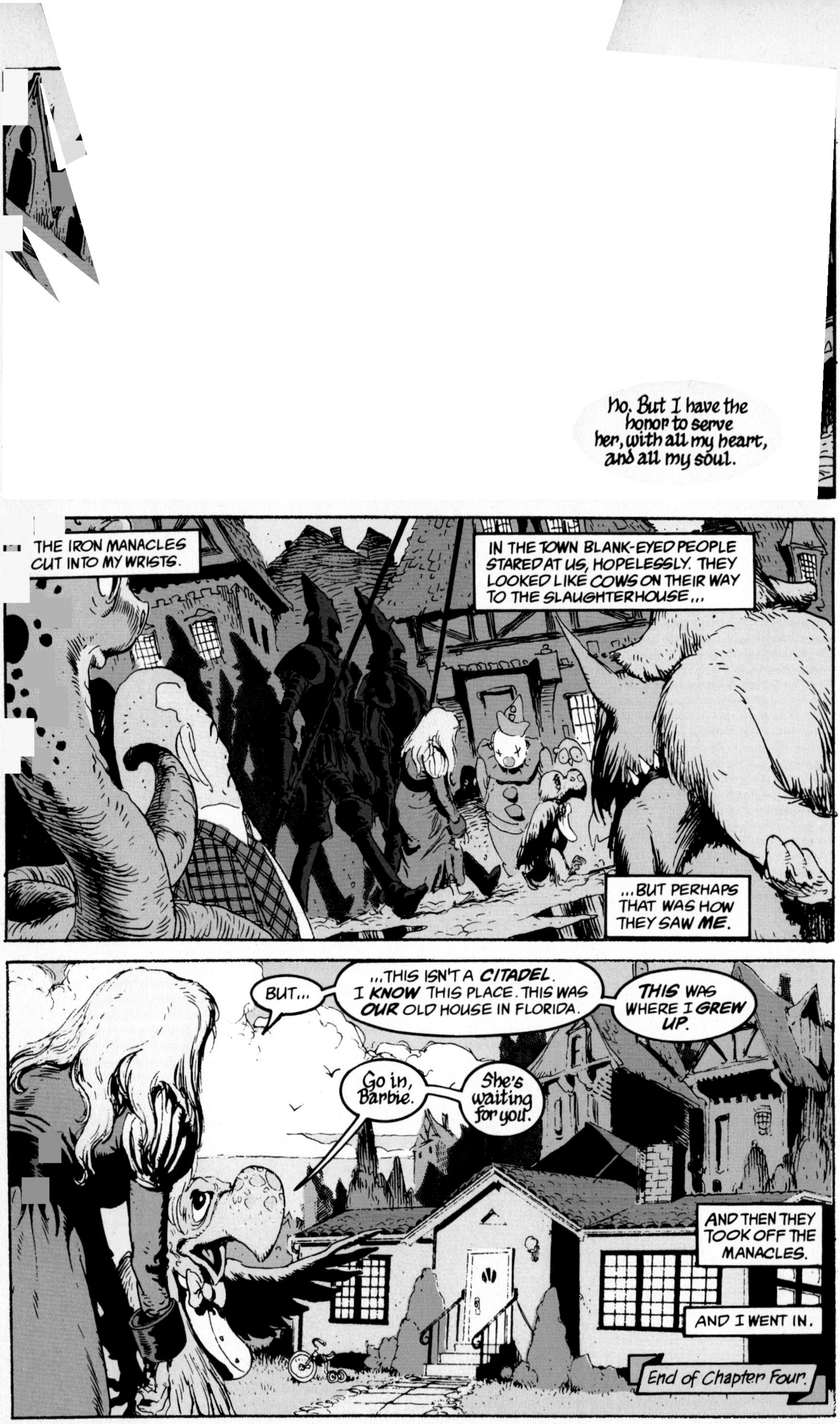
No. But I have the honor to serve her, with all my heart, and all my soul.
THE IRON MANACLES CUT INTO MY WRISTS.
IN THE TOWN BLANK-EYED PEOPLE STARED AT US, HOPELESSLY. THEY LOOKED LIKE COWS ON THEIR WAY TO THE SLAUGHTERHOUSE...
...BUT PERHAPS THAT WAS HOW THEY SAW ME.
BUT...
...THIS ISN'T A CITADEL. I KNOW THIS PLACE. THIS WAS OUR OLD HOUSE IN FLORIDA.
THIS WAS WHERE I GREW UP.
Go in, Barbie.
She's waiting for you.
AND THEN THEY TOOK OFF THE MANACLES.
AND I WENT IN.
End of Chapter Four.

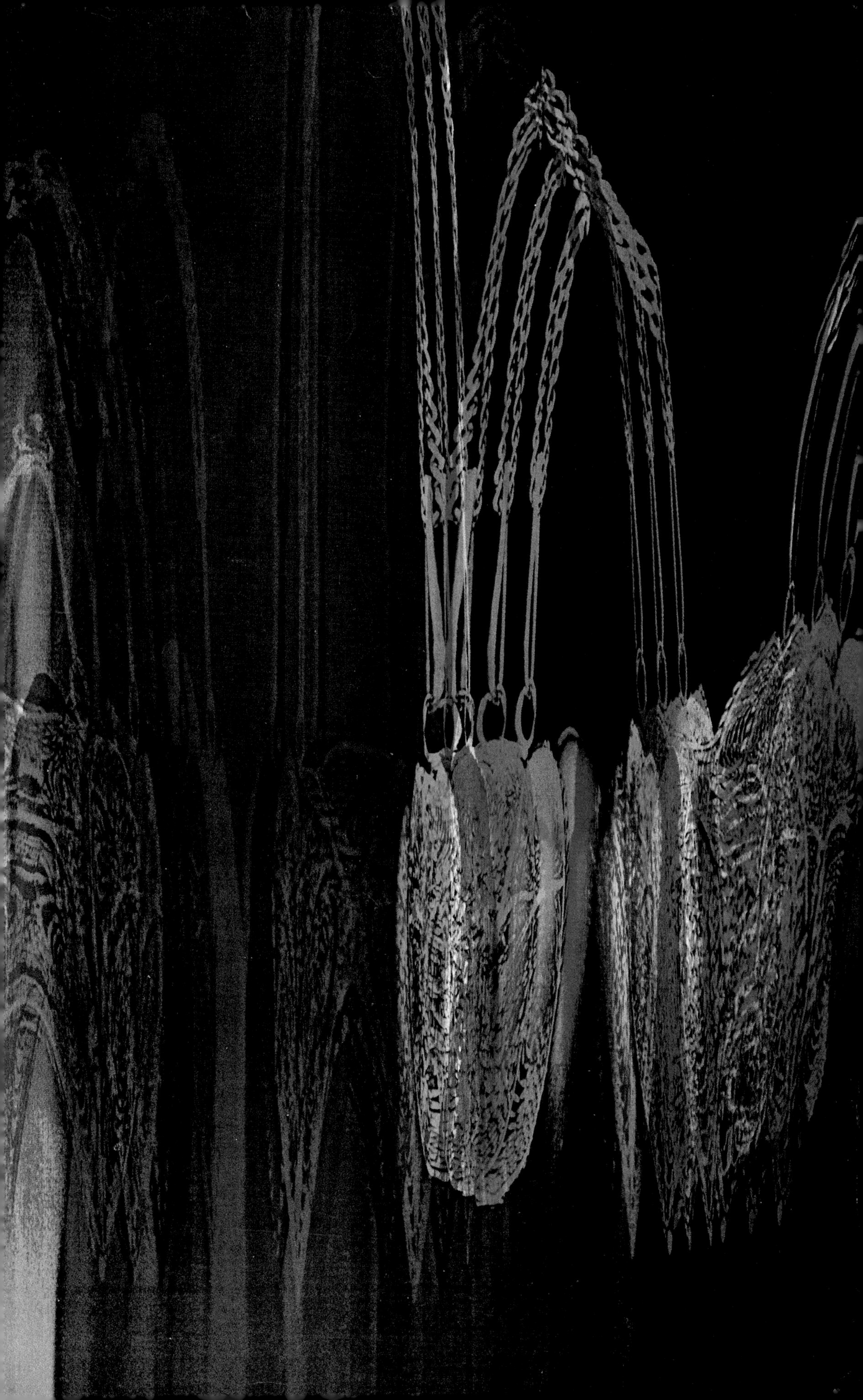

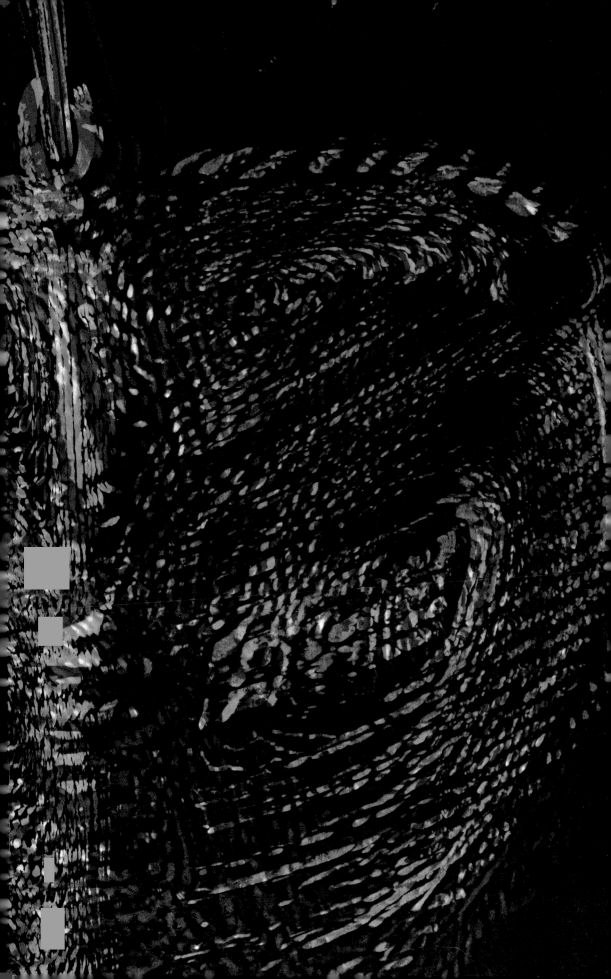

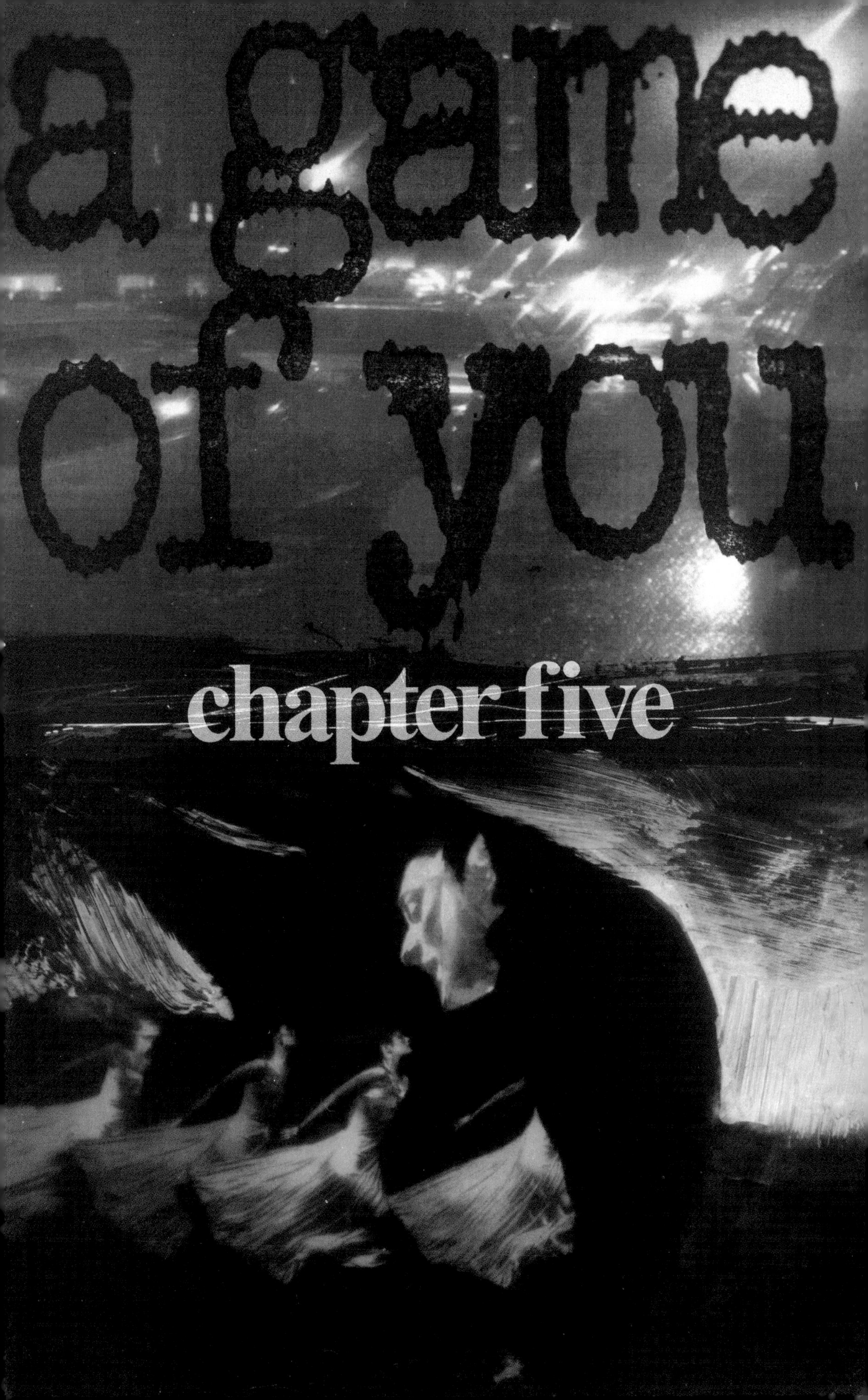
a game of you
chapter five

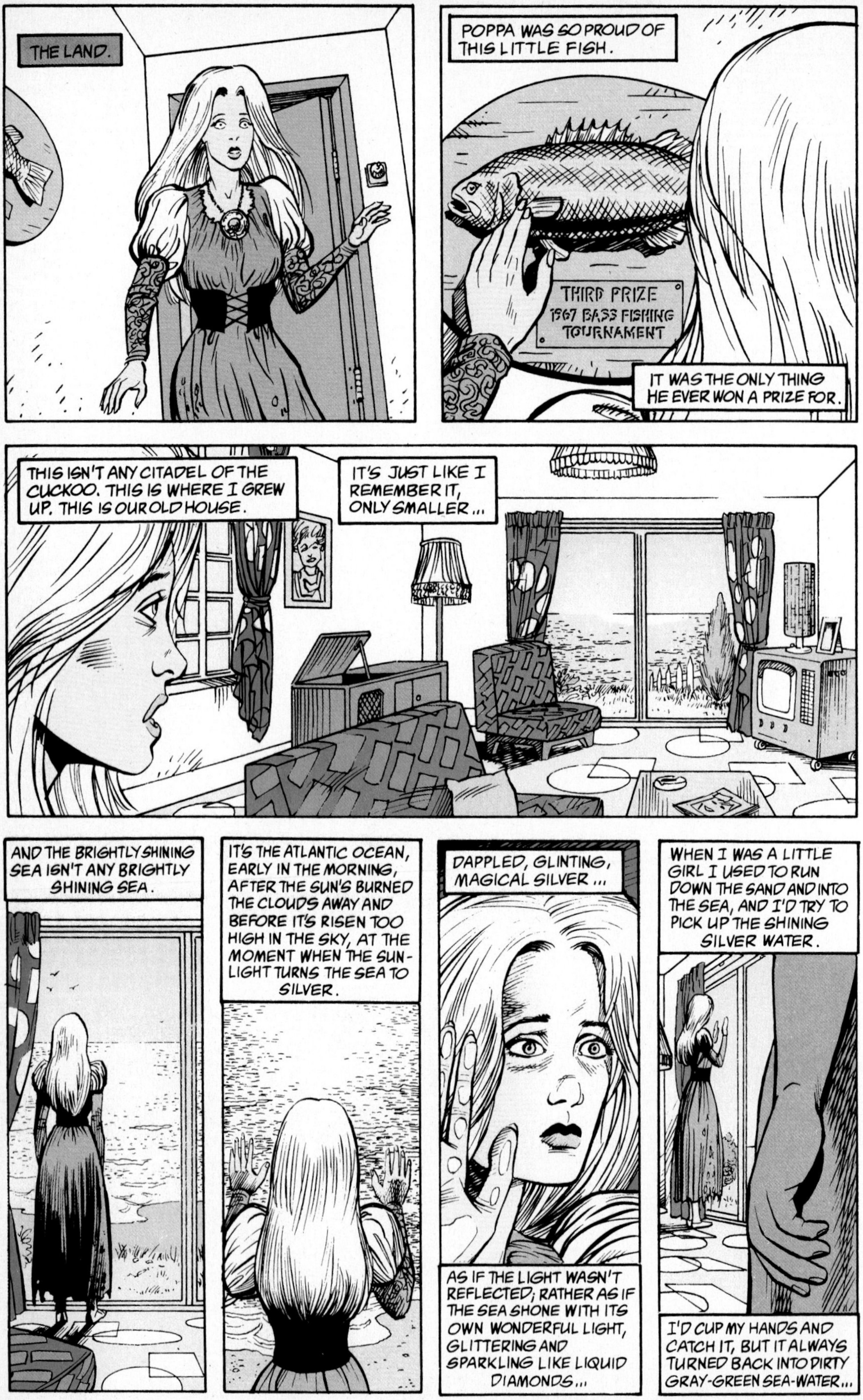
THE LAND.
POPPA WAS SO PROUD OF THIS LITTLE FISH.
THIRD PRIZE 1967 BASS FISHING TOURNAMENT
IT WAS THE ONLY THING HE EVER WON A PRIZE FOR.
THIS ISN'T ANY CITADEL OF THE CUCKOO. THIS IS WHERE I GREW UP. THIS IS OUR OLD HOUSE.
IT'S JUST LIKE I REMEMBER IT, ONLY SMALLER...
AND THE BRIGHTLY SHINING SEA ISN'T ANY BRIGHTLY SHINING SEA.
IT'S THE ATLANTIC OCEAN, EARLY IN THE MORNING, AFTER THE SUN'S BURNED THE CLOUDS AWAY AND BEFORE IT'S RISEN TOO HIGH IN THE SKY, AT THE MOMENT WHEN THE SUN-LIGHT TURNS THE SEA TO SILVER.
DAPPLED, GLINTING, MAGICAL SILVER...
AS IF THE LIGHT WASN'T REFLECTED; RATHER AS IF THE SEA SHONE WITH ITS OWN WONDERFUL LIGHT, GLITTERING AND SPARKLING LIKE LIQUID DIAMONDS...
WHEN I WAS A LITTLE GIRL I USED TO RUN DOWN THE SAND AND INTO THE SEA, AND I'D TRY TO PICK UP THE SHINING SILVER WATER.
I'D CUP MY HANDS AND CATCH IT, BUT IT ALWAYS TURNED BACK INTO DIRTY GRAY-GREEN SEA-WATER...

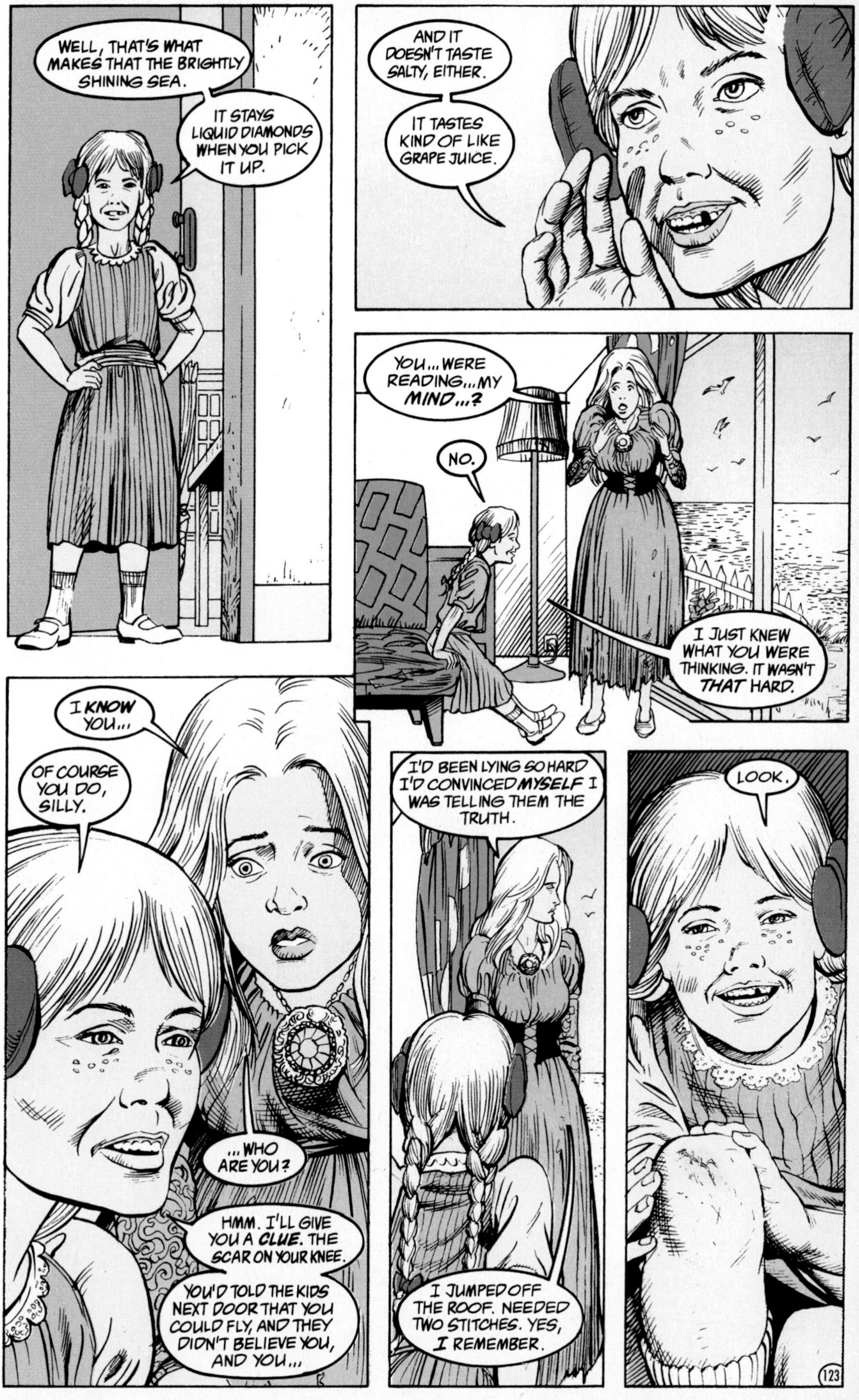
WELL, THAT'S WHAT MAKES THAT THE BRIGHTLY SHINING SEA.
IT STAYS LIQUID DIAMONDS WHEN YOU PICK IT UP.
AND IT DOESN'T TASTE SALTY, EITHER.
IT TASTES KIND OF LIKE GRAPE JUICE.
YOU... WERE READING... MY MIND...?
NO.
I JUST KNEW WHAT YOU WERE THINKING. IT WASN'T THAT HARD.
I KNOW YOU...
OF COURSE YOU DO, SILLY.
...WHO ARE YOU?
HMM. I'LL GIVE YOU A CLUE. THE SCAR ON YOUR KNEE.
YOU'D TOLD THE KIDS NEXT DOOR THAT YOU COULD FLY, AND THEY DIDN'T BELIEVE YOU, AND YOU...
I'D BEEN LYING SO HARD I'D CONVINCED MYSELF I WAS TELLING THEM THE TRUTH.
I JUMPED OFF THE ROOF. NEEDED TWO STITCHES. YES, I REMEMBER.
LOOK.

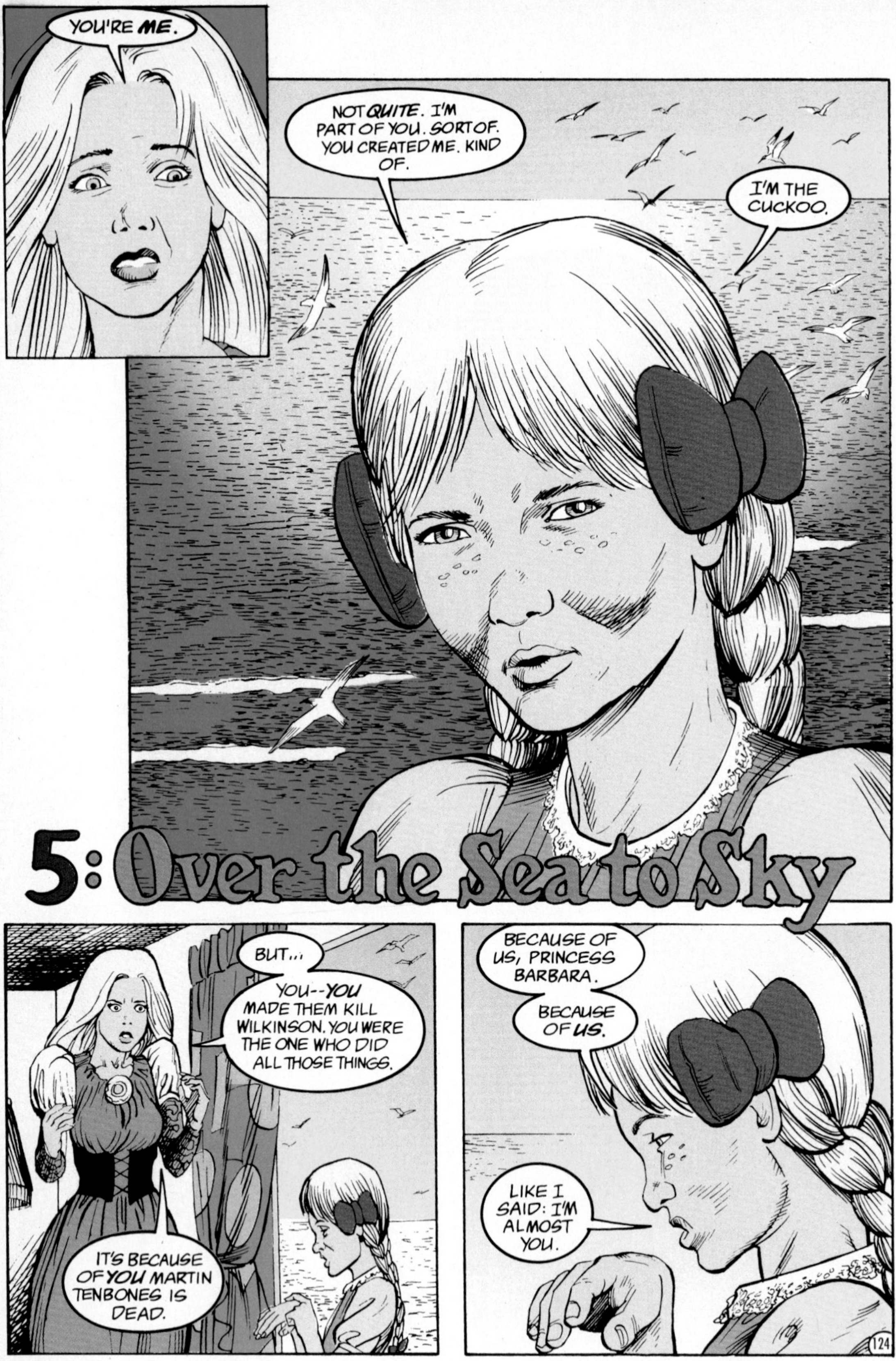
YOU'RE ME.
NOT QUITE. I'M PART OF YOU. SORT OF. YOU CREATED ME. KIND OF.
I'M THE CUCKOO.
5: Over the Sea to Sky
BUT...
YOU--YOU MADE THEM KILL WILKINSON. YOU WERE THE ONE WHO DID ALL THOSE THINGS.
IT'S BECAUSE OF YOU MARTIN TENBONES IS DEAD.
BECAUSE OF US, PRINCESS BARBARA.
BECAUSE OF US.
LIKE I SAID: I'M ALMOST YOU.

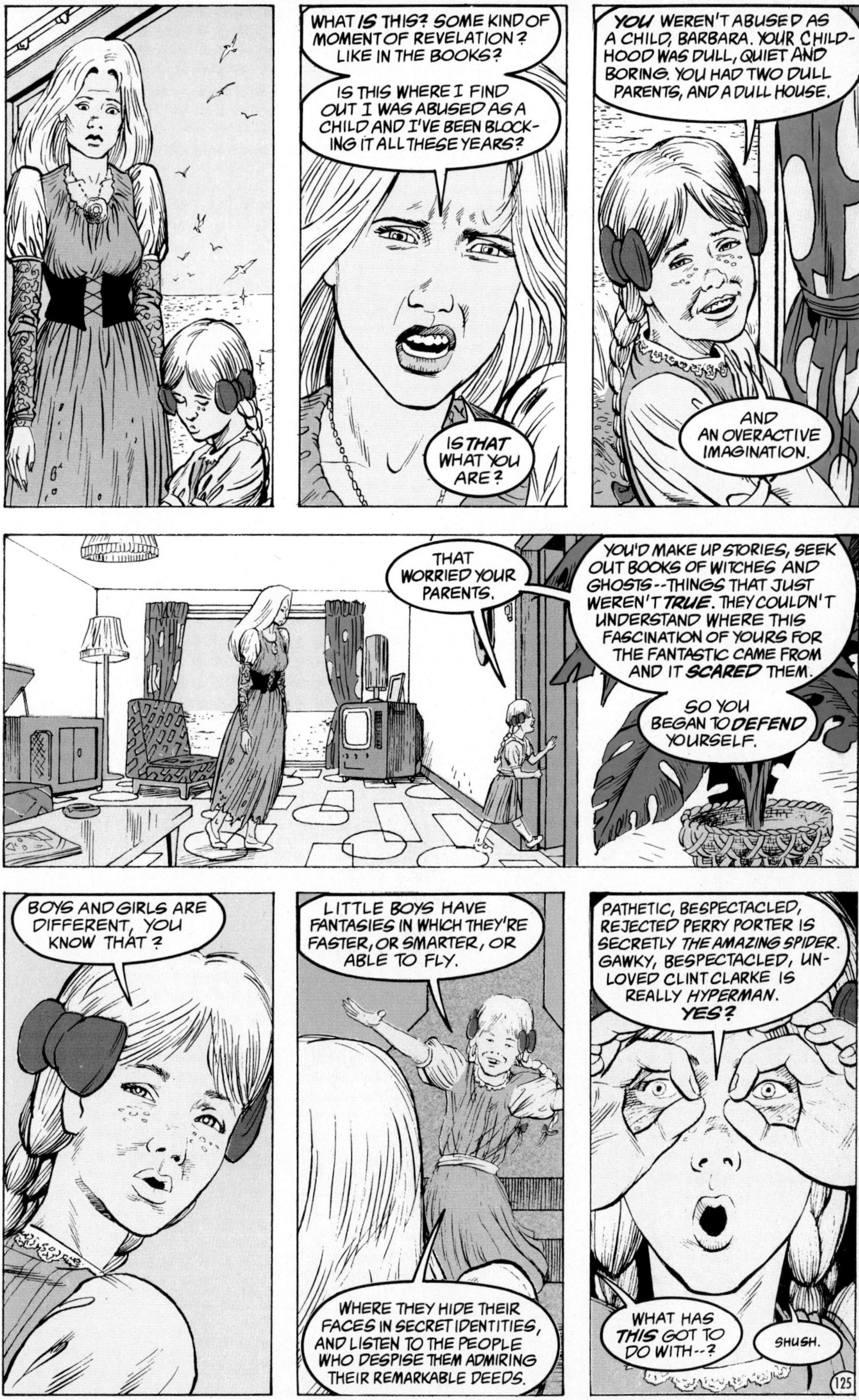

WHAT IS THIS? SOME KIND OF MOMENT OF REVELATION? LIKE IN THE BOOKS?
IS THIS WHERE I FIND OUT I WAS ABUSED AS A CHILD AND I'VE BEEN BLOCKING IT ALL THESE YEARS?
IS THAT WHAT YOU ARE?
YOU WEREN'T ABUSED AS A CHILD, BARBARA. YOUR CHILDHOOD WAS DULL, QUIET AND BORING. YOU HAD TWO DULL PARENTS, AND A DULL HOUSE.
AND AN OVERACTIVE IMAGINATION.
THAT WORRIED YOUR PARENTS.
YOU'D MAKE UP STORIES, SEEK OUT BOOKS OF WITCHES AND GHOSTS--THINGS THAT JUST WEREN'T TRUE. THEY COULDN'T UNDERSTAND WHERE THIS FASCINATION OF YOURS FOR THE FANTASTIC CAME FROM AND IT SCARED THEM.
SO YOU BEGAN TO DEFEND YOURSELF.
BOYS AND GIRLS ARE DIFFERENT, YOU KNOW THAT?
LITTLE BOYS HAVE FANTASIES IN WHICH THEY'RE FASTER, OR SMARTER, OR ABLE TO FLY.
WHERE THEY HIDE THEIR FACES IN SECRET IDENTITIES, AND LISTEN TO THE PEOPLE WHO DESPISE THEM ADMIRING THEIR REMARKABLE DEEDS.
PATHETIC, BESPECTACLED, REJECTED PERRY PORTER IS SECRETLY THE AMAZING SPIDER. GAWKY, BESPECTACLED, UNLOVED CLINT CLARKE IS REALLY HYPERMAN. YES?
WHAT HAS THIS GOT TO DO WITH--?
SHUSH.

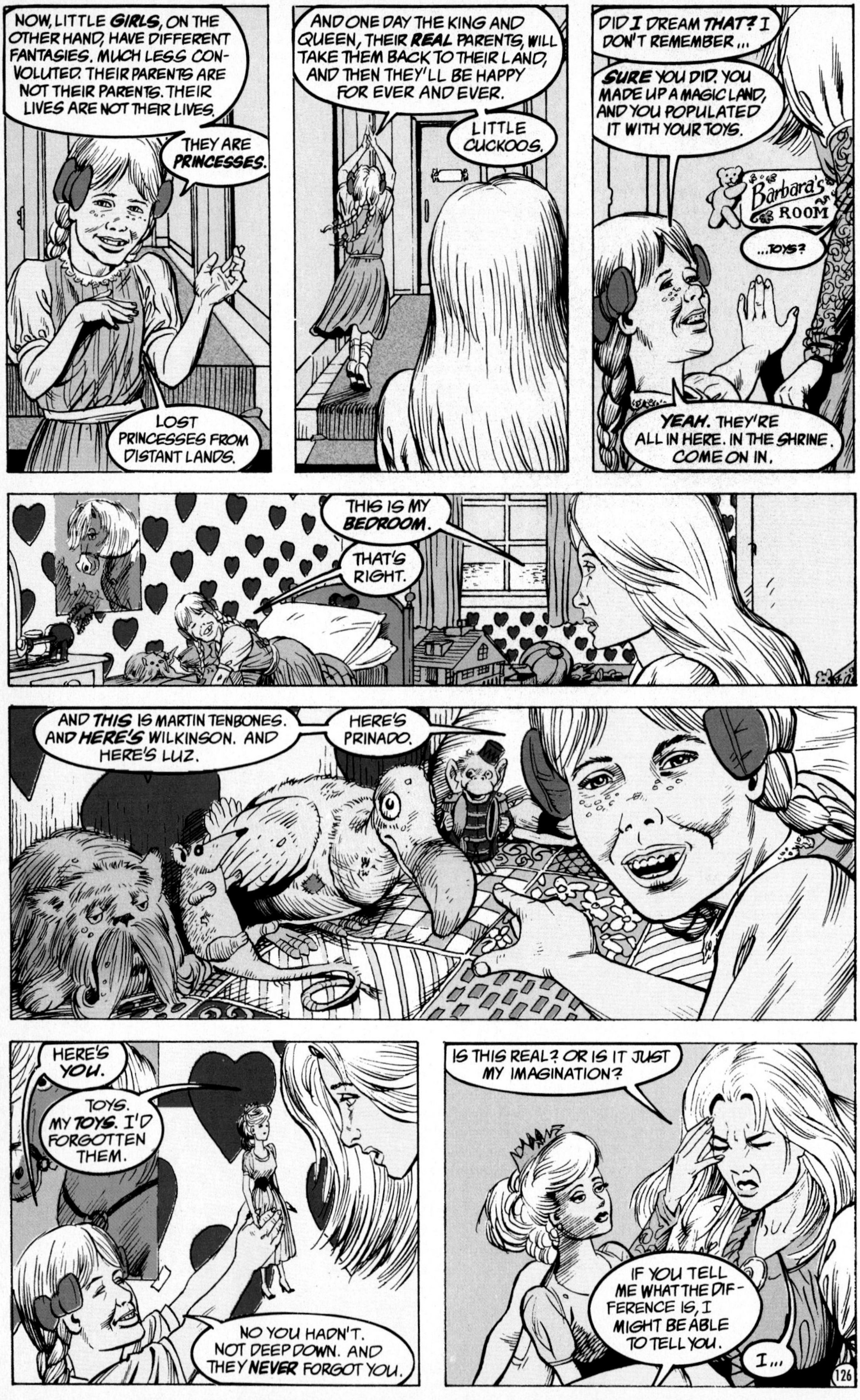
NOW, LITTLE GIRLS, ON THE OTHER HAND, HAVE DIFFERENT FANTASIES. MUCH LESS CONVOLUTED. THEIR PARENTS ARE NOT THEIR PARENTS. THEIR LIVES ARE NOT THEIR LIVES.
THEY ARE PRINCESSES.
LOST PRINCESSES FROM DISTANT LANDS.
AND ONE DAY THE KING AND QUEEN, THEIR REAL PARENTS, WILL TAKE THEM BACK TO THEIR LAND, AND THEN THEY'LL BE HAPPY FOR EVER AND EVER.
LITTLE CUCKOOS.
DID I DREAM THAT? I DON'T REMEMBER...
SURE YOU DID. YOU MADE UP A MAGIC LAND, AND YOU POPULATED IT WITH YOUR TOYS.
Barbara's ROOM
...TOYS?
YEAH. THEY'RE ALL IN HERE. IN THE SHRINE. COME ON IN.
THIS IS MY BEDROOM.
THAT'S RIGHT.
AND THIS IS MARTIN TENBONES. AND HERE'S WILKINSON. AND HERE'S LUZ.
HERE'S PRINADO.
HERE'S YOU.
TOYS. MY TOYS. I'D FORGOTTEN THEM.
NO YOU HADN'T. NOT DEEP DOWN. AND THEY NEVER FORGOT YOU.
IS THIS REAL? OR IS IT JUST MY IMAGINATION?
IF YOU TELL ME WHAT THE DIFFERENCE IS, I MIGHT BE ABLE TO TELL YOU.
I...

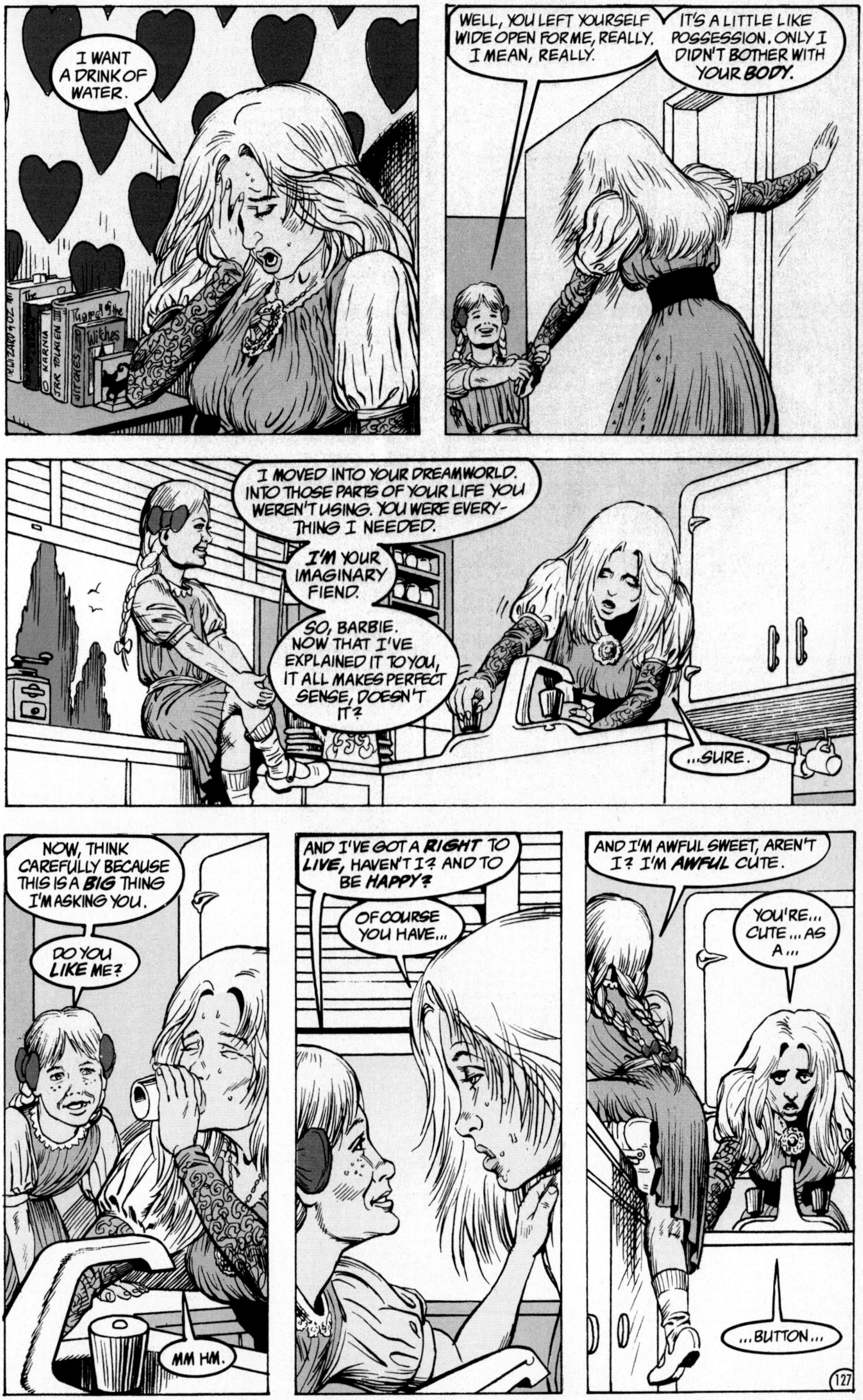
I WANT A DRINK OF WATER.
WELL, YOU LEFT YOURSELF WIDE OPEN FOR ME, REALLY. I MEAN, REALLY.
IT'S A LITTLE LIKE POSSESSION. ONLY I DIDN'T BOTHER WITH YOUR BODY.
I MOVED INTO YOUR DREAMWORLD. INTO THOSE PARTS OF YOUR LIFE YOU WEREN'T USING. YOU WERE EVERYTHING I NEEDED.
I'M YOUR IMAGINARY FIEND.
SO, BARBIE. NOW THAT I'VE EXPLAINED IT TO YOU, IT ALL MAKES PERFECT SENSE, DOESN'T IT?
...SURE.
NOW, THINK CAREFULLY BECAUSE THIS IS A BIG THING I'M ASKING YOU.
DO YOU LIKE ME?
MM HM.
AND I'VE GOT A RIGHT TO LIVE, HAVEN'T I? AND TO BE HAPPY?
OF COURSE YOU HAVE...
AND I'M AWFUL SWEET, AREN'T I? I'M AWFUL CUTE.
YOU'RE... CUTE... AS A...
...BUTTON...

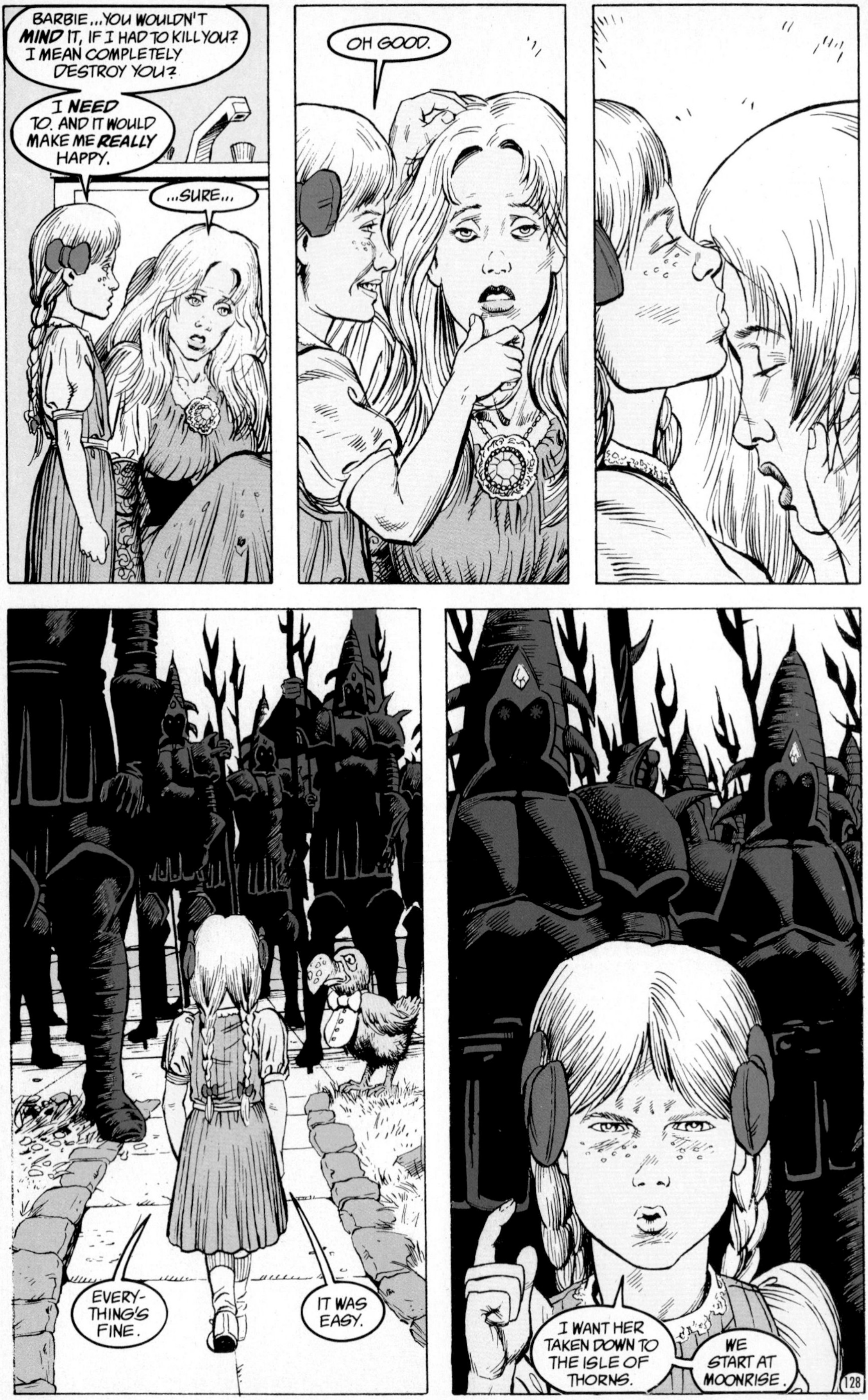
BARBIE...YOU WOULDN'T MIND IT, IF I HAD TO KILL YOU? I MEAN COMPLETELY DESTROY YOU?
I NEED TO. AND IT WOULD MAKE ME REALLY HAPPY.
...SURE...
OH GOOD.
EVERY-THING'S FINE.
IT WAS EASY.
I WANT HER TAKEN DOWN TO THE ISLE OF THORNS.
WE START AT MOONRISE.
128

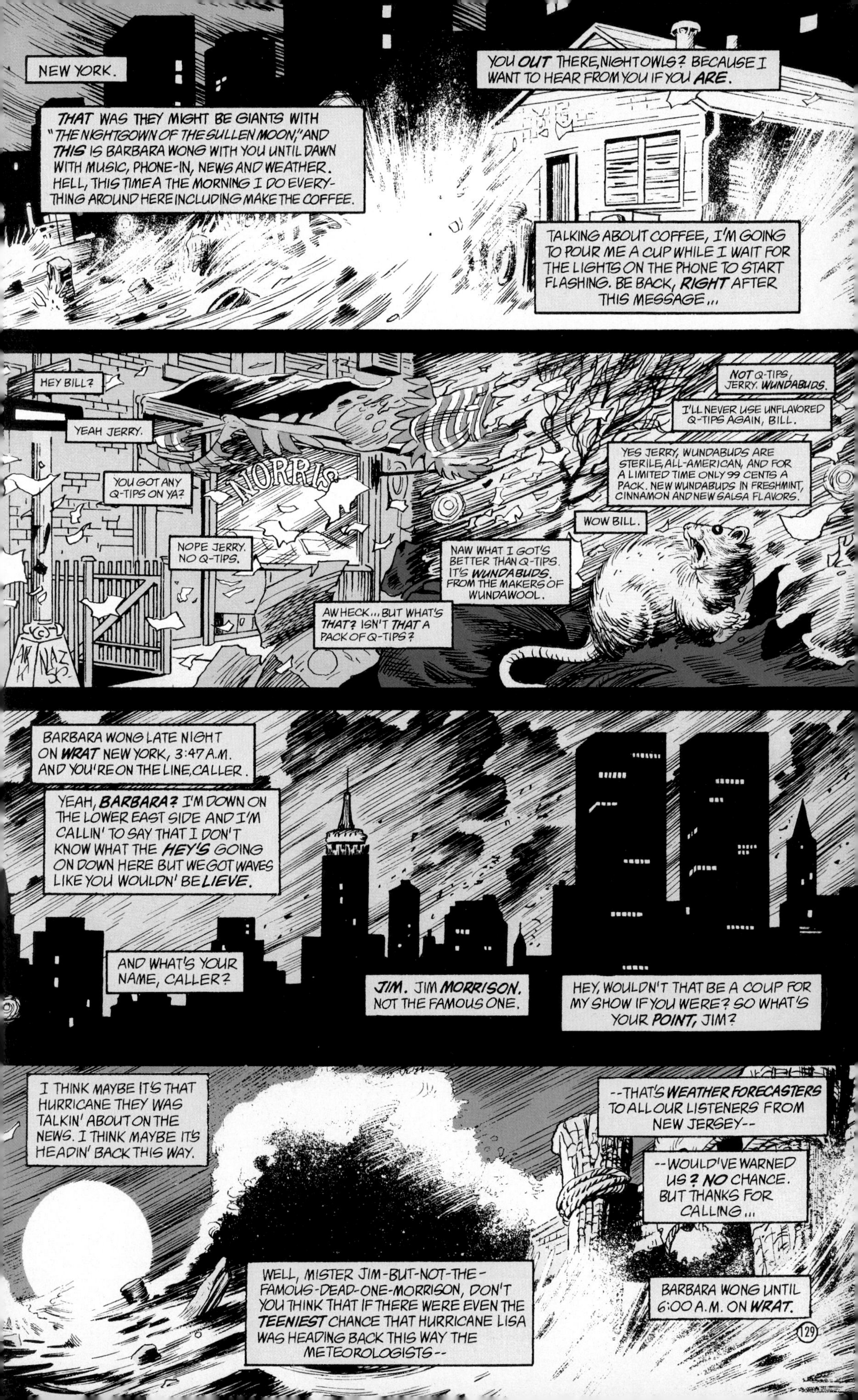
NEW YORK.
THAT WAS THEY MIGHT BE GIANTS WITH "THE NIGHTGOWN OF THE SULLEN MOON," AND THIS IS BARBARA WONG WITH YOU UNTIL DAWN WITH MUSIC, PHONE-IN, NEWS AND WEATHER. HELL, THIS TIME A THE MORNING I DO EVERYTHING AROUND HERE INCLUDING MAKE THE COFFEE.
YOU OUT THERE, NIGHT OWLS? BECAUSE I WANT TO HEAR FROM YOU IF YOU ARE.
TALKING ABOUT COFFEE, I'M GOING TO POUR ME A CUP WHILE I WAIT FOR THE LIGHTS ON THE PHONE TO START FLASHING. BE BACK, RIGHT AFTER THIS MESSAGE...
HEY BILL?
YEAH JERRY.
YOU GOT ANY Q-TIPS ON YA?
NOPE JERRY. NO Q-TIPS.
AW HECK... BUT WHAT'S THAT? ISN'T THAT A PACK OF Q-TIPS?
NAW WHAT I GOT'S BETTER THAN Q-TIPS. IT'S WUNDABUDS. FROM THE MAKERS OF WUNDAWOOL.
WOW BILL.
YES JERRY, WUNDABUDS ARE STERILE, ALL-AMERICAN, AND FOR A LIMITED TIME ONLY 99 CENTS A PACK. NEW WUNDABUDS IN FRESHMINT, CINNAMON AND NEW SALSA FLAVORS.
I'LL NEVER USE UNFLAVORED Q-TIPS AGAIN, BILL.
NOT Q-TIPS, JERRY. WUNDABUDS.
NORRIS
BARBARA WONG LATE NIGHT ON WRAT NEW YORK, 3:47 A.M. AND YOU'RE ON THE LINE, CALLER.
YEAH, BARBARA? I'M DOWN ON THE LOWER EAST SIDE AND I'M CALLIN' TO SAY THAT I DON'T KNOW WHAT THE HEY'S GOING ON DOWN HERE BUT WE GOT WAVES LIKE YOU WOULDN' BELIEVE.
AND WHAT'S YOUR NAME, CALLER?
JIM. JIM MORRISON. NOT THE FAMOUS ONE.
HEY, WOULDN'T THAT BE A COUP FOR MY SHOW IF YOU WERE? SO WHAT'S YOUR POINT, JIM?
I THINK MAYBE IT'S THAT HURRICANE THEY WAS TALKIN' ABOUT ON THE NEWS. I THINK MAYBE IT'S HEADIN' BACK THIS WAY.
WELL, MISTER JIM-BUT-NOT-THE-FAMOUS-DEAD-ONE-MORRISON, DON'T YOU THINK THAT IF THERE WERE EVEN THE TEENIEST CHANCE THAT HURRICANE LISA WAS HEADING BACK THIS WAY THE METEOROLOGISTS--
--THAT'S WEATHER FORECASTERS TO ALL OUR LISTENERS FROM NEW JERSEY--
--WOULD'VE WARNED US? NO CHANCE. BUT THANKS FOR CALLING...
BARBARA WONG UNTIL 6:00 A.M. ON WRAT.

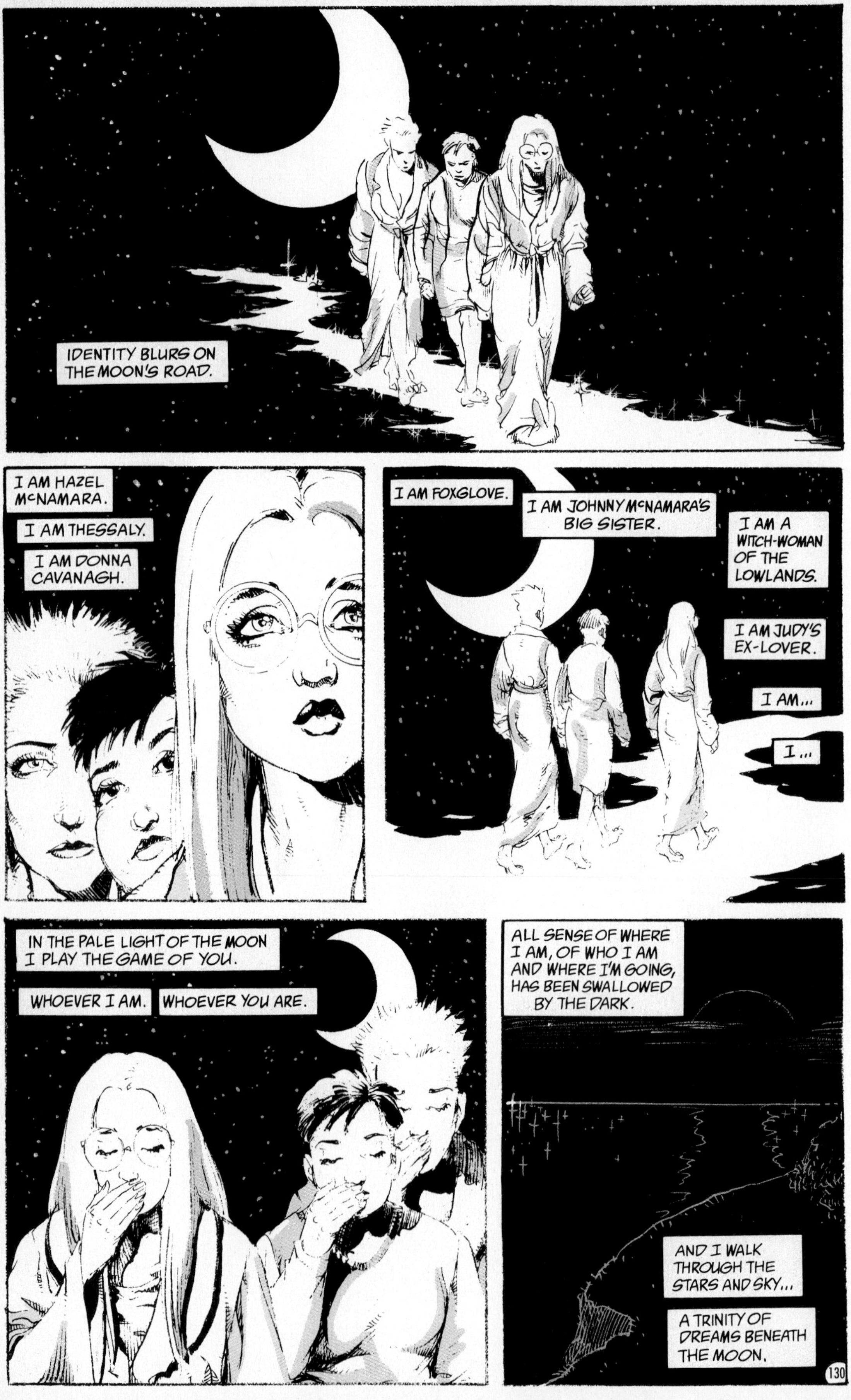
IDENTITY BLURS ON THE MOON'S ROAD.
I AM HAZEL McNAMARA.
I AM THESSALY.
I AM DONNA CAVANAGH.
I AM FOXGLOVE.
I AM JOHNNY McNAMARA'S BIG SISTER.
I AM A WITCH-WOMAN OF THE LOWLANDS.
I AM JUDY'S EX-LOVER.
I AM...
I...
IN THE PALE LIGHT OF THE MOON I PLAY THE GAME OF YOU.
WHOEVER I AM.
WHOEVER YOU ARE.
ALL SENSE OF WHERE I AM, OF WHO I AM AND WHERE I'M GOING, HAS BEEN SWALLOWED BY THE DARK.
AND I WALK THROUGH THE STARS AND SKY...
A TRINITY OF DREAMS BENEATH THE MOON.

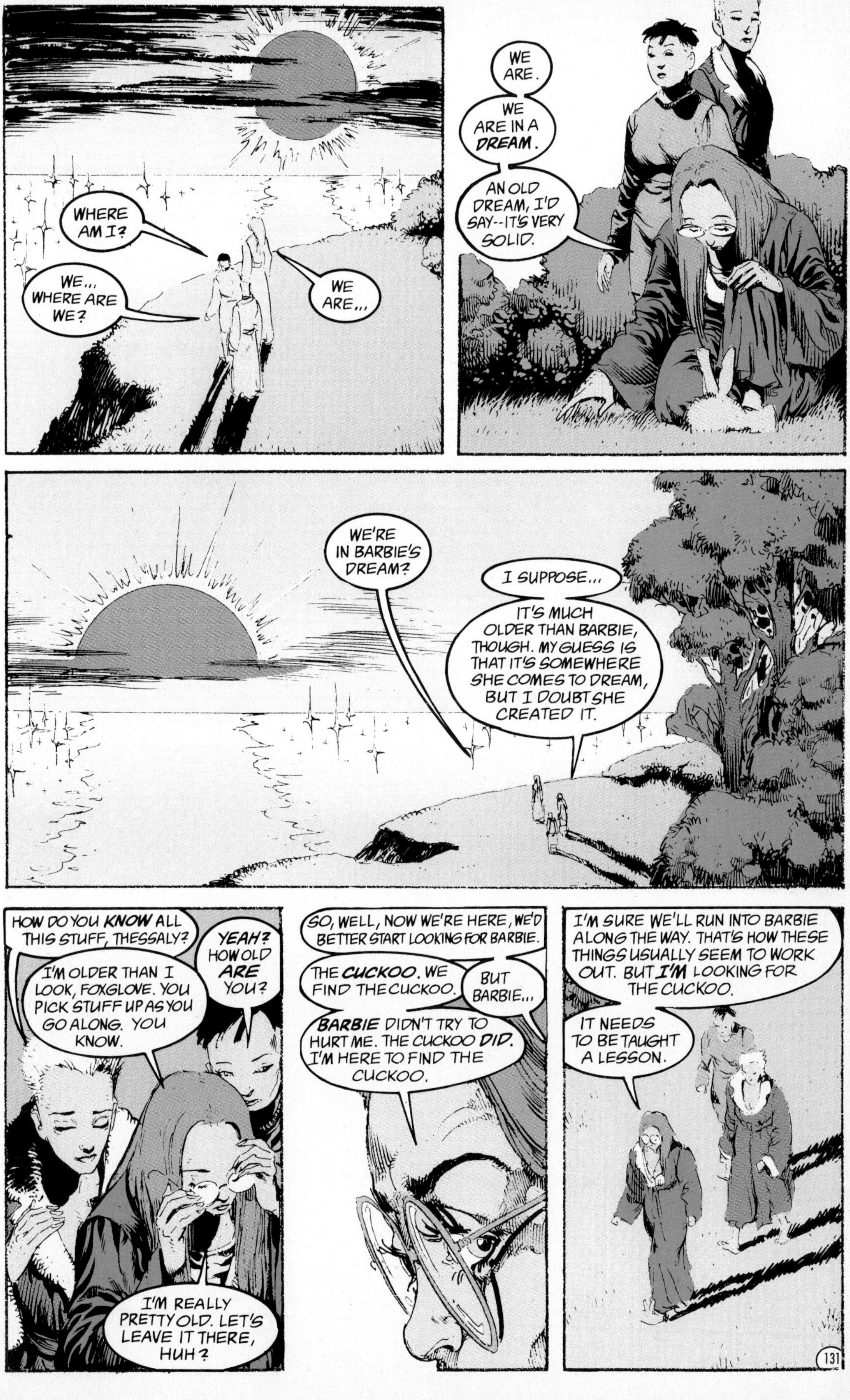
WHERE AM I?
WE... WHERE ARE WE?
WE ARE...
WE ARE.
WE ARE IN A DREAM.
AN OLD DREAM, I'D SAY--IT'S VERY SOLID.
WE'RE IN BARBIE'S DREAM?
I SUPPOSE...
IT'S MUCH OLDER THAN BARBIE, THOUGH. MY GUESS IS THAT IT'S SOMEWHERE SHE COMES TO DREAM, BUT I DOUBT SHE CREATED IT.
HOW DO YOU KNOW ALL THIS STUFF, THESSALY?
YEAH? HOW OLD ARE YOU?
I'M OLDER THAN I LOOK, FOXGLOVE. YOU PICK STUFF UP AS YOU GO ALONG. YOU KNOW.
I'M REALLY PRETTY OLD. LET'S LEAVE IT THERE, HUH?
SO, WELL, NOW WE'RE HERE, WE'D BETTER START LOOKING FOR BARBIE.
THE CUCKOO. WE FIND THE CUCKOO.
BUT BARBIE...
BARBIE DIDN'T TRY TO HURT ME. THE CUCKOO DID. I'M HERE TO FIND THE CUCKOO.
I'M SURE WE'LL RUN INTO BARBIE ALONG THE WAY. THAT'S HOW THESE THINGS USUALLY SEEM TO WORK OUT. BUT I'M LOOKING FOR THE CUCKOO.
IT NEEDS TO BE TAUGHT A LESSON.

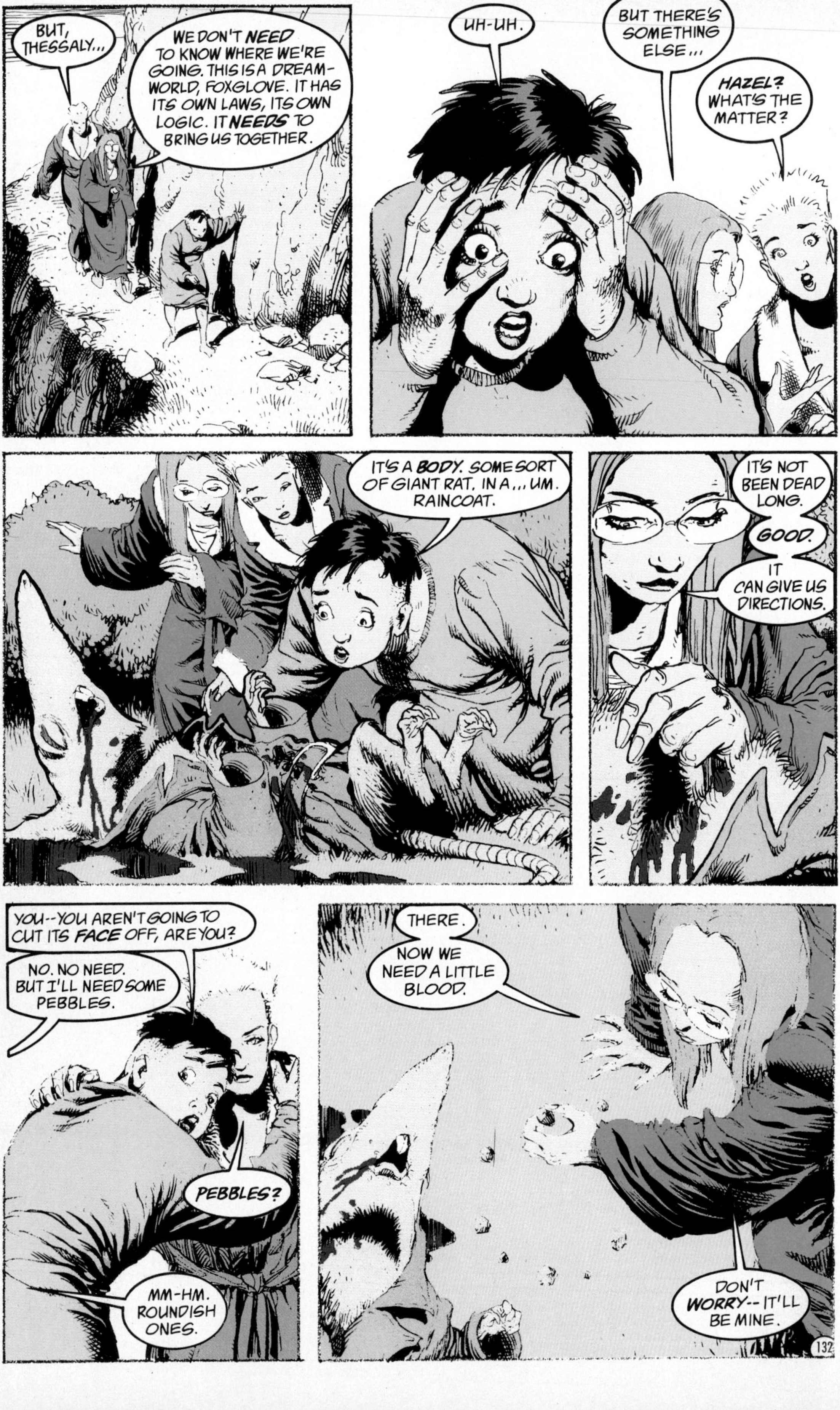
BUT, THESSALY...
WE DON'T NEED TO KNOW WHERE WE'RE GOING. THIS IS A DREAM-WORLD, FOXGLOVE. IT HAS ITS OWN LAWS, ITS OWN LOGIC. IT NEEDS TO BRING US TOGETHER.
UH-UH.
BUT THERE'S SOMETHING ELSE...
HAZEL? WHAT'S THE MATTER?
IT'S A BODY. SOME SORT OF GIANT RAT, IN A... UM. RAINCOAT.
IT'S NOT BEEN DEAD LONG.
GOOD.
IT CAN GIVE US DIRECTIONS.
YOU--YOU AREN'T GOING TO CUT ITS FACE OFF, ARE YOU?
NO. NO NEED. BUT I'LL NEED SOME PEBBLES.
PEBBLES?
MM-HM. ROUNDISH ONES.
THERE.
NOW WE NEED A LITTLE BLOOD.
DON'T WORRY-- IT'LL BE MINE.

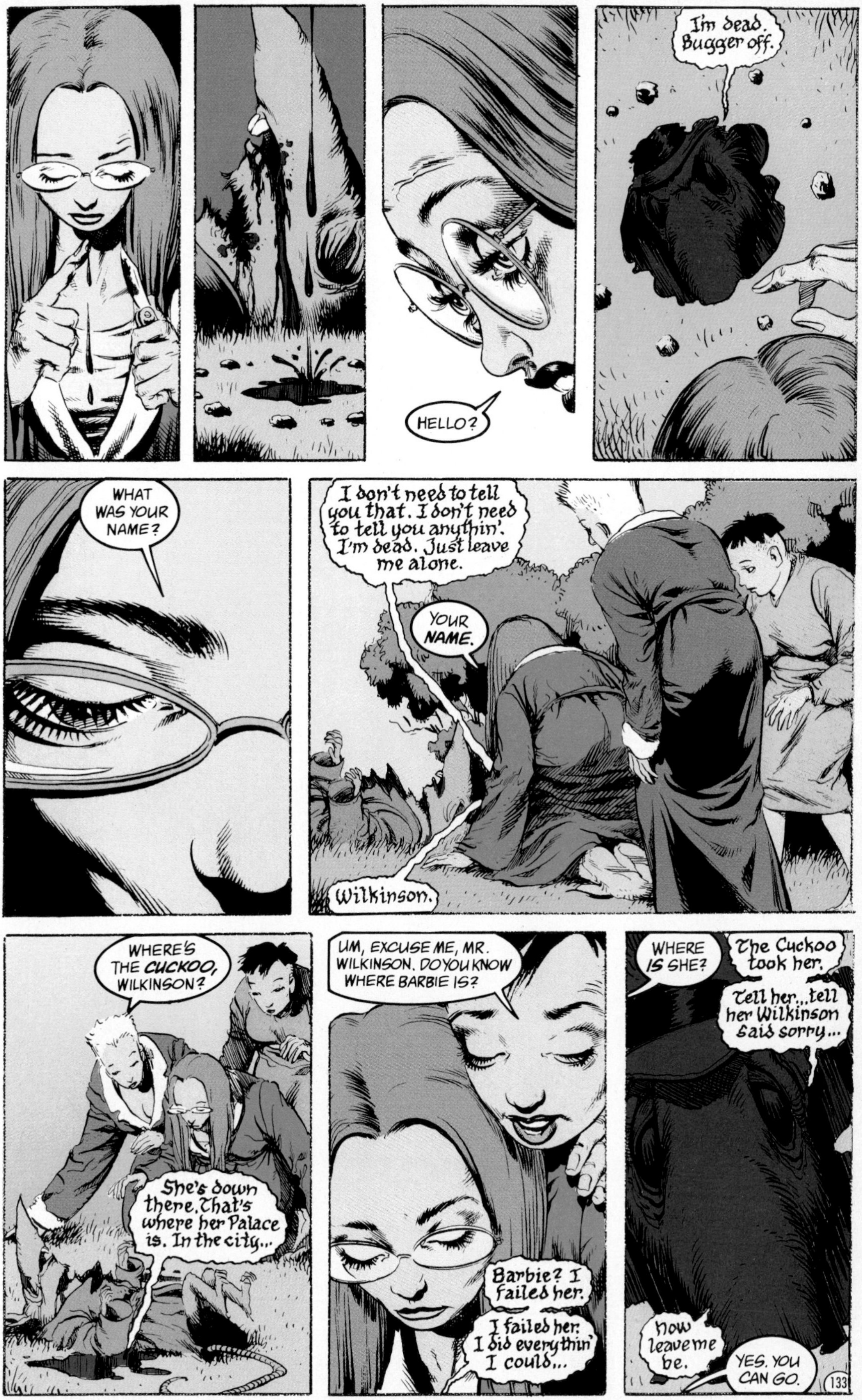

HELLO?
I'm dead. Bugger off.
WHAT WAS YOUR NAME?
I don't need to tell you that. I don't need to tell you anythin'. I'm dead. Just leave me alone.
YOUR NAME.
Wilkinson.
WHERE'S THE CUCKOO, WILKINSON?
She's down there. That's where her Palace is. In the city...
UM, EXCUSE ME, MR. WILKINSON. DO YOU KNOW WHERE BARBIE IS?
Barbie? I failed her.
I failed her. I did everythin' I could...
WHERE IS SHE?
The Cuckoo took her.
Tell her... tell her Wilkinson said sorry...
Now leave me be.
YES. YOU CAN GO.

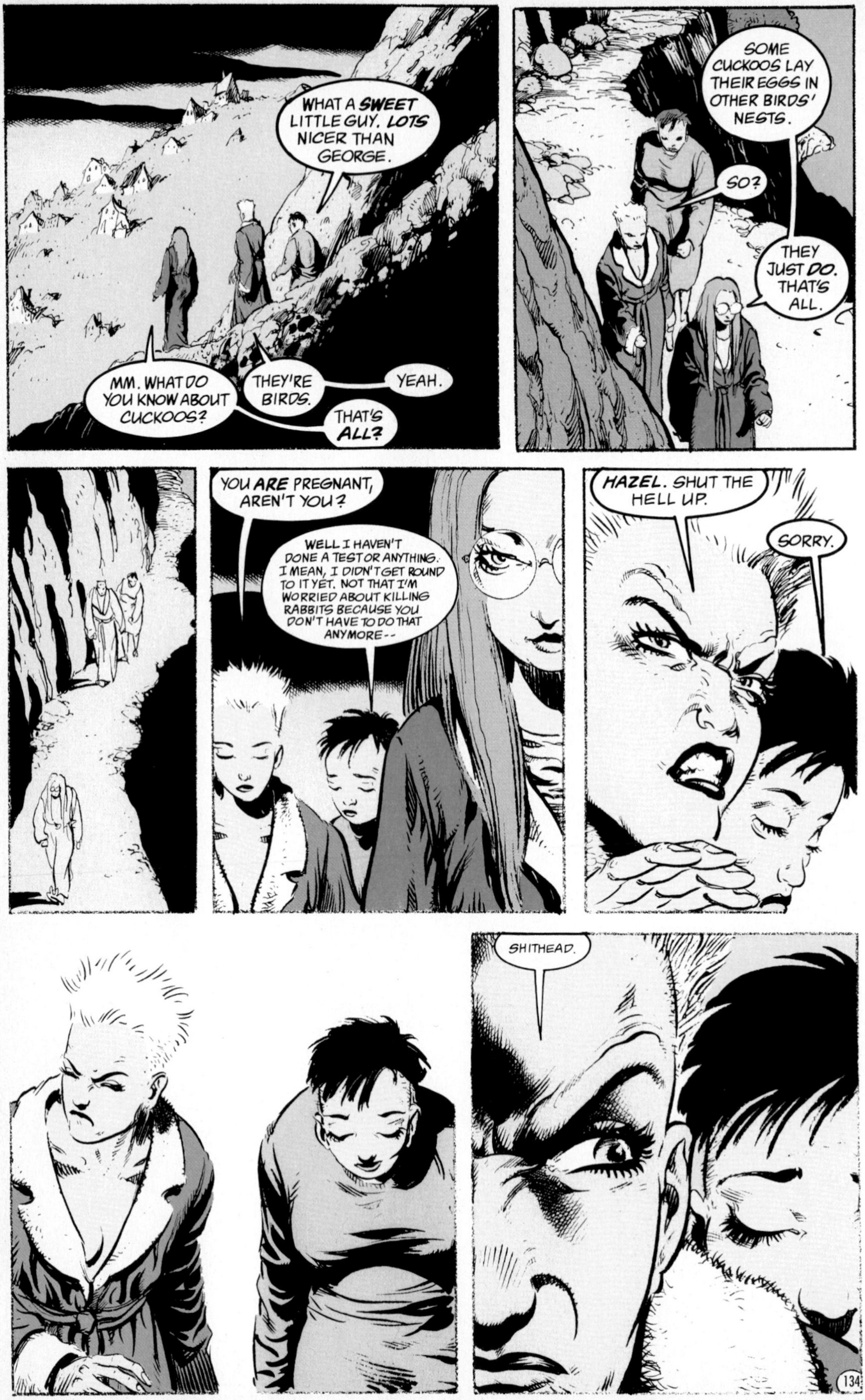

WHAT A SWEET LITTLE GUY. LOTS NICER THAN GEORGE.
MM. WHAT DO YOU KNOW ABOUT CUCKOOS?
THEY'RE BIRDS.
YEAH.
THAT'S ALL?
SOME CUCKOOS LAY THEIR EGGS IN OTHER BIRDS' NESTS.
SO?
THEY JUST DO. THAT'S ALL.
YOU ARE PREGNANT, AREN'T YOU?
WELL I HAVEN'T DONE A TEST OR ANYTHING. I MEAN, I DIDN'T GET ROUND TO IT YET. NOT THAT I'M WORRIED ABOUT KILLING RABBITS BECAUSE YOU DON'T HAVE TO DO THAT ANYMORE--
HAZEL. SHUT THE HELL UP.
SORRY.
SHITHEAD.

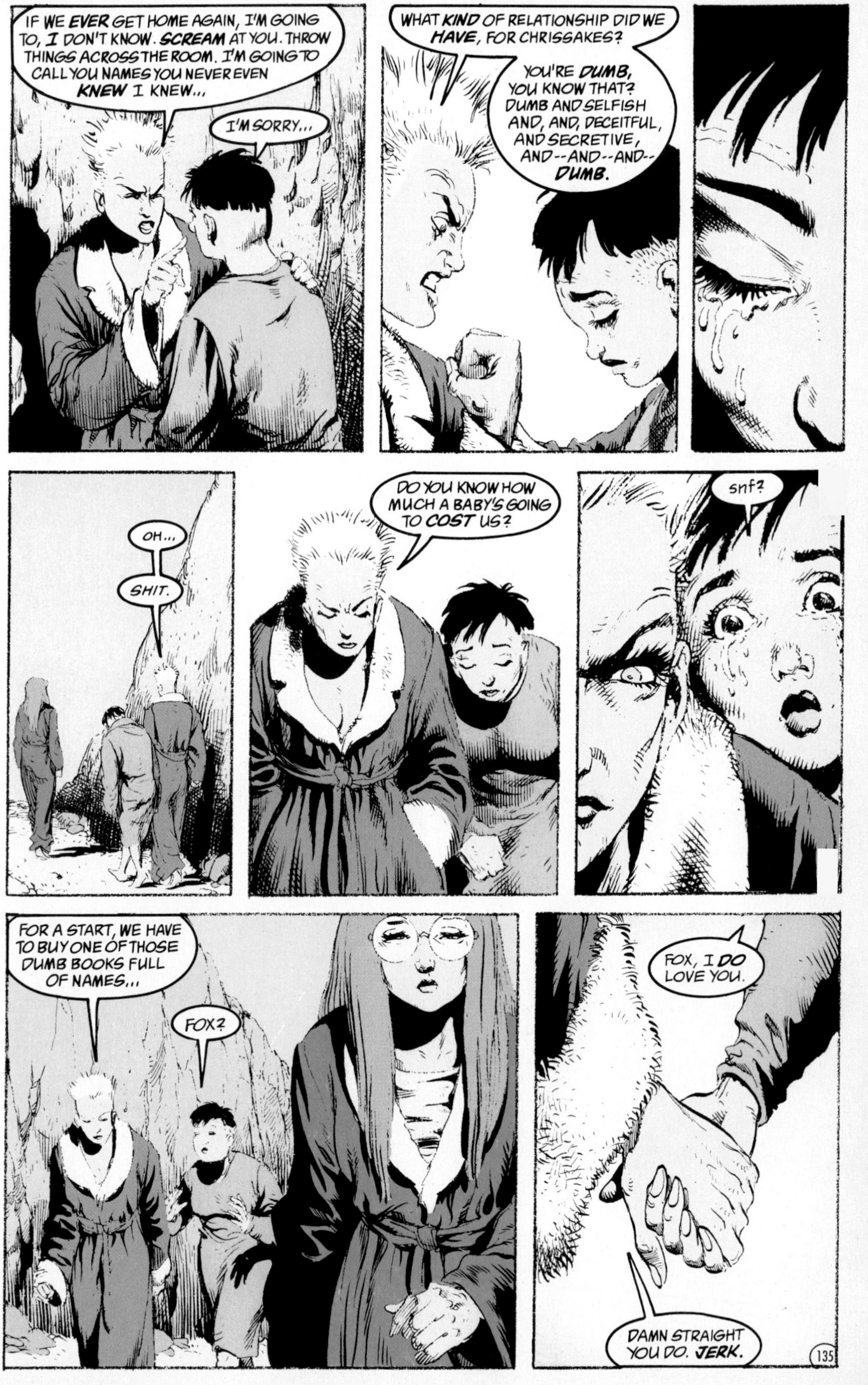
IF WE EVER GET HOME AGAIN, I'M GOING TO, I DON'T KNOW. SCREAM AT YOU. THROW THINGS ACROSS THE ROOM. I'M GOING TO CALL YOU NAMES YOU NEVER EVEN KNEW I KNEW...
I'M SORRY...
WHAT KIND OF RELATIONSHIP DID WE HAVE, FOR CHRISSAKES?
YOU'RE DUMB, YOU KNOW THAT? DUMB AND SELFISH AND, AND, DECEITFUL, AND SECRETIVE, AND--AND--AND-- DUMB.
OH...
SHIT.
DO YOU KNOW HOW MUCH A BABY'S GOING TO COST US?
snf?
FOR A START, WE HAVE TO BUY ONE OF THOSE DUMB BOOKS FULL OF NAMES...
FOX?
FOX, I DO LOVE YOU.
DAMN STRAIGHT YOU DO. JERK.

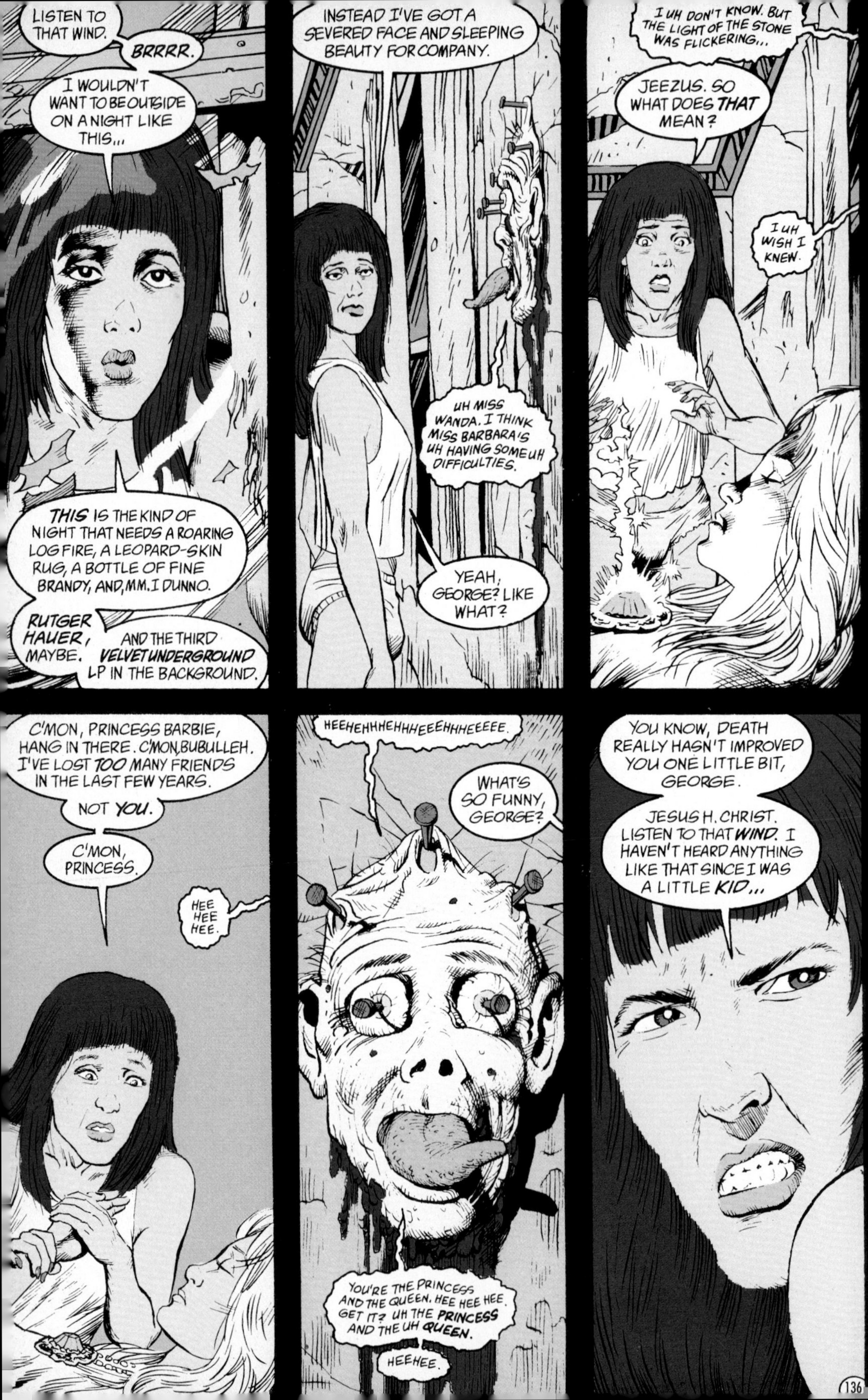

LISTEN TO THAT WIND.
BRRRR.
I WOULDN'T WANT TO BE OUTSIDE ON A NIGHT LIKE THIS...
THIS IS THE KIND OF NIGHT THAT NEEDS A ROARING LOG FIRE, A LEOPARD-SKIN RUG, A BOTTLE OF FINE BRANDY, AND, MM. I DUNNO.
RUTGER HAUER, MAYBE.
AND THE THIRD VELVET UNDERGROUND LP IN THE BACKGROUND.
INSTEAD I'VE GOT A SEVERED FACE AND SLEEPING BEAUTY FOR COMPANY.
UH MISS WANDA. I THINK MISS BARBARA'S UH HAVING SOME UH DIFFICULTIES.
YEAH, GEORGE? LIKE WHAT?
I UH DON'T KNOW. BUT THE LIGHT OF THE STONE WAS FLICKERING...
JEEZUS. SO WHAT DOES THAT MEAN?
I UH WISH I KNEW.
C'MON, PRINCESS BARBIE, HANG IN THERE. C'MON, BUBULLEH. I'VE LOST TOO MANY FRIENDS IN THE LAST FEW YEARS.
NOT YOU.
C'MON, PRINCESS.
HEE HEE HEE.
HEEHEHHHEHHHEEEHHHEEEEE.
WHAT'S SO FUNNY, GEORGE?
YOU'RE THE PRINCESS AND THE QUEEN. HEE HEE HEE. GET IT? UH THE PRINCESS AND THE UH QUEEN.
HEEHEE.
YOU KNOW, DEATH REALLY HASN'T IMPROVED YOU ONE LITTLE BIT, GEORGE.
JESUS H. CHRIST. LISTEN TO THAT WIND. I HAVEN'T HEARD ANYTHING LIKE THAT SINCE I WAS A LITTLE KID...

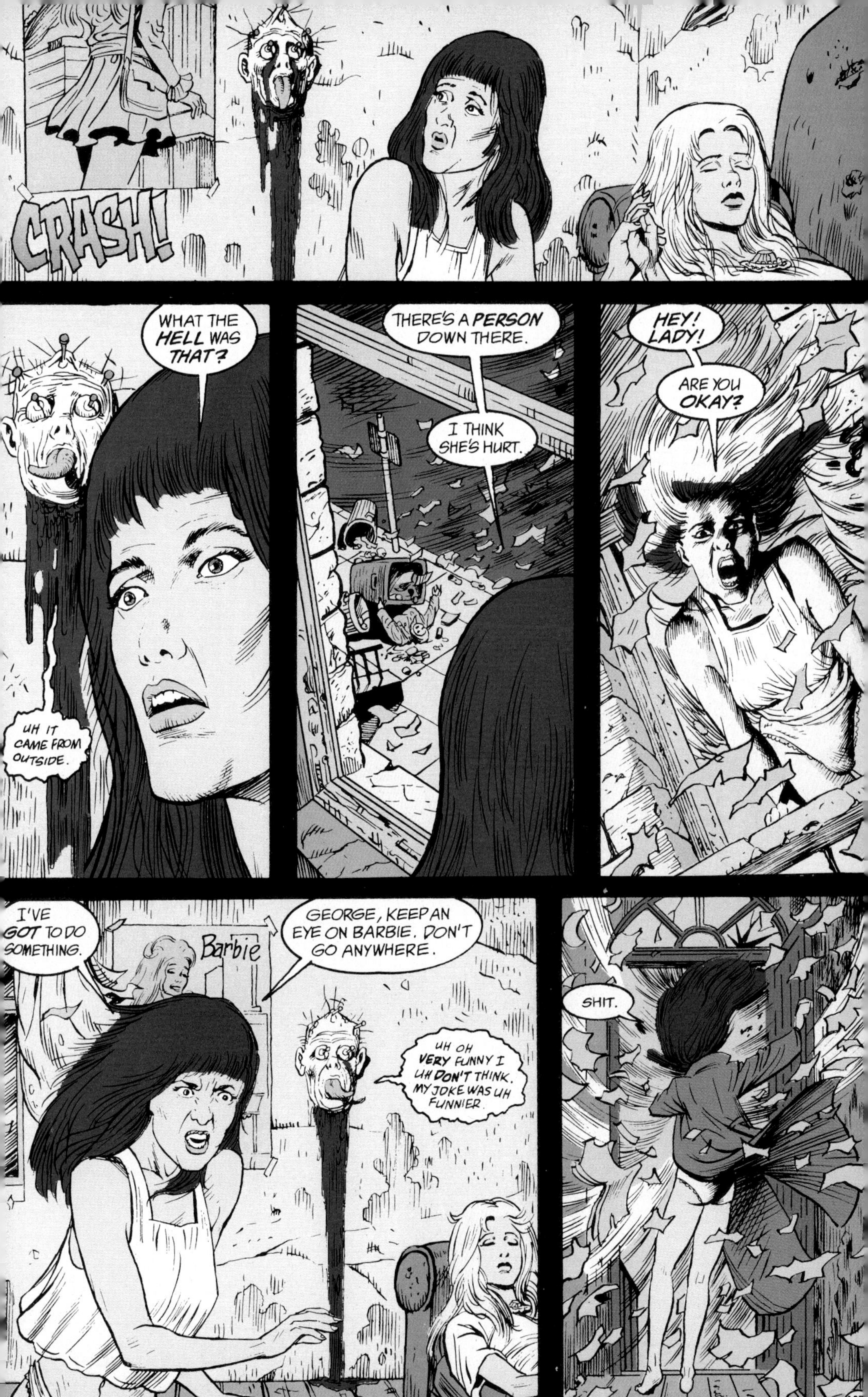
CRASH!
WHAT THE HELL WAS THAT?
UH IT CAME FROM OUTSIDE.
THERE'S A PERSON DOWN THERE.
I THINK SHE'S HURT.
HEY! LADY!
ARE YOU OKAY?
I'VE GOT TO DO SOMETHING.
Barbie
GEORGE, KEEP AN EYE ON BARBIE. DON'T GO ANYWHERE.
UH OH VERY FUNNY I UH DON'T THINK. MY JOKE WAS UH FUNNIER.
SHIT.

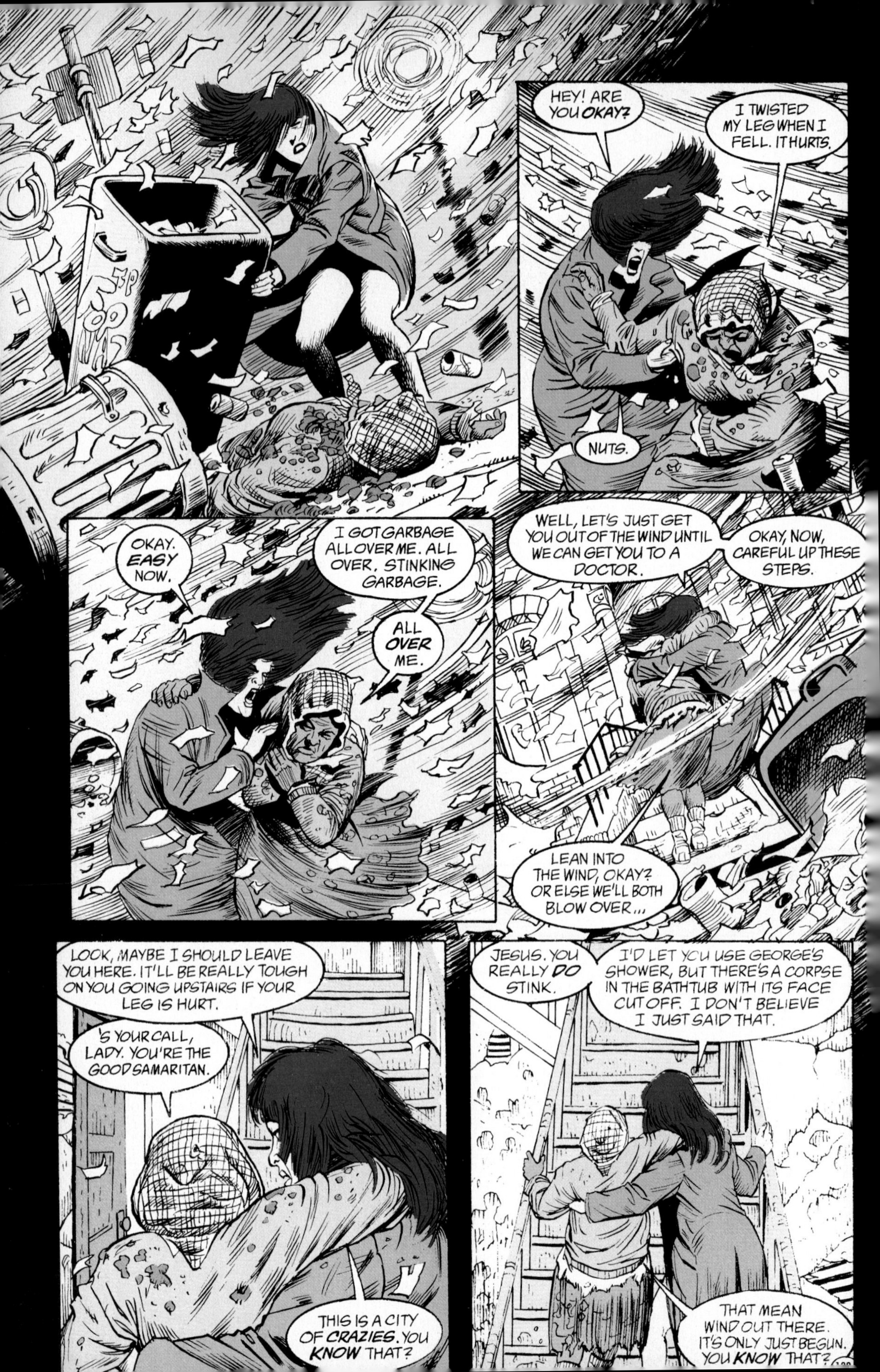
HEY! ARE YOU OKAY?
I TWISTED MY LEG WHEN I FELL. IT HURTS.
NUTS.
OKAY. EASY NOW.
I GOT GARBAGE ALL OVER ME. ALL OVER. STINKING GARBAGE.
ALL OVER ME.
WELL, LET'S JUST GET YOU OUT OF THE WIND UNTIL WE CAN GET YOU TO A DOCTOR.
OKAY, NOW, CAREFUL UP THESE STEPS.
LEAN INTO THE WIND, OKAY? OR ELSE WE'LL BOTH BLOW OVER...
LOOK, MAYBE I SHOULD LEAVE YOU HERE. IT'LL BE REALLY TOUGH ON YOU GOING UPSTAIRS IF YOUR LEG IS HURT.
'S YOUR CALL, LADY. YOU'RE THE GOOD SAMARITAN.
THIS IS A CITY OF CRAZIES. YOU KNOW THAT?
JESUS. YOU REALLY DO STINK.
I'D LET YOU USE GEORGE'S SHOWER, BUT THERE'S A CORPSE IN THE BATHTUB WITH ITS FACE CUT OFF. I DON'T BELIEVE I JUST SAID THAT.
THAT MEAN WIND OUT THERE. IT'S ONLY JUST BEGUN. YOU KNOW THAT?

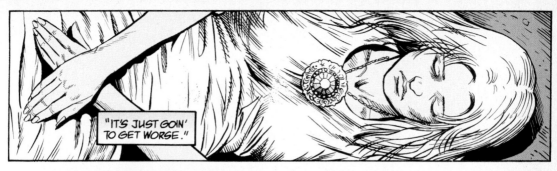

"IT'S JUST GOIN' TO GET WORSE."

"WELL, LUZ, NOT MUCH LONGER NOW."

"No, my lady."

"DOES THAT MAKE YOU HAPPY?"

"Very happy, my lady."

"BECAUSE YOU WANT TO PROTECT ME. YOU WANT TO HELP ME. YOU WANT TO MAKE ME HAPPY."

"Yes, lady."

IT'S TIME FOR ME TO FLY THE NEST. EVERYONE HAS TO GROW UP *SOME* TIME...

I'LL MISS THIS LAND. I REALLY *WILL*. IT'S A NICE PLACE.

WILL YOU, LUZ? THAT'S SWEET.

We'll miss you too, lady.

ESPECIALLY SINCE YOU'VE SPENT THE LAST HALF DOZEN YEARS PLOTTING MY DOWNFALL...

I was misguided, lady.

OF *COURSE* YOU WERE. AND IT JUST TOOK A LITTLE TALK TO SHOW YOU THE ERROR OF YOUR WAYS.

MMPH.

"INDEED A BIRD WILL BROOD THE FOSTER-CHICK WHILST HER OWN INFANTS LIE SLOWLY DYING OUTSIDE THE NEST..."

SHE *NEVER* UNDERSTOOD. SHE KEPT TRYING TO TELL HERSELF THE TRUTH, AND SHE *NEVER* LISTENED.

THEY DIVIDE THEMSELVES UP INTO SUCH COMPLEX PUZZLES, LITTLE BIRD...

SHE WAS THE PERFECT ENVIRONMENT TO GROW IN...

BUT WE *CANNOT* BE CHILDREN FOREVER. ALL GOOD THINGS MUST END...

139

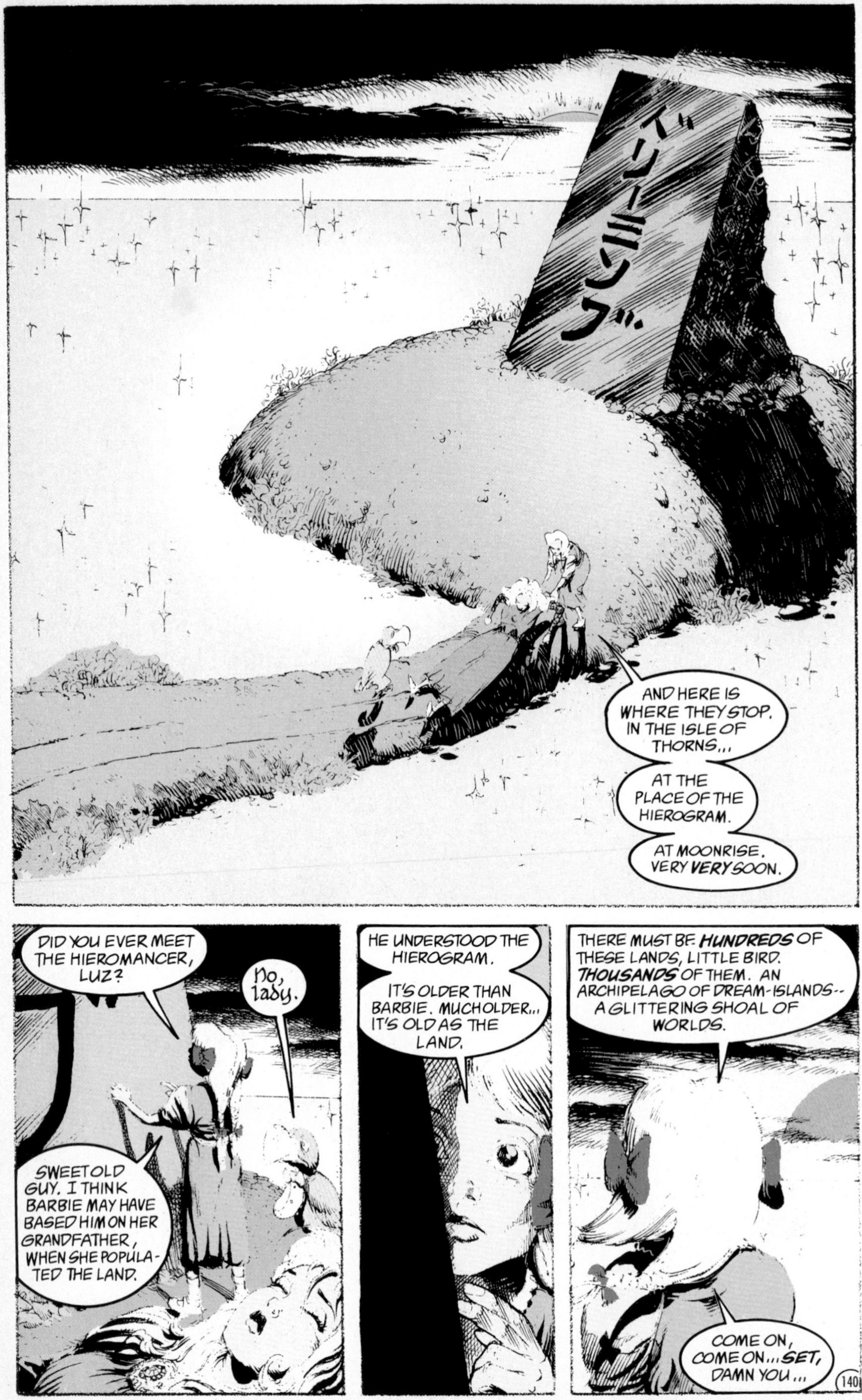

バリーミンブ
AND HERE IS WHERE THEY STOP. IN THE ISLE OF THORNS...
AT THE PLACE OF THE HIEROGRAM.
AT MOONRISE. VERY **VERY** SOON.
DID YOU EVER MEET THE HIEROMANCER, LUZ?
No, Lady.
SWEET OLD GUY. I THINK BARBIE MAY HAVE BASED HIM ON HER GRANDFATHER, WHEN SHE POPULATED THE LAND.
HE UNDERSTOOD THE HIEROGRAM.
IT'S OLDER THAN BARBIE. MUCH OLDER... IT'S OLD AS THE LAND.
THERE MUST BE **HUNDREDS** OF THESE LANDS, LITTLE BIRD. **THOUSANDS** OF THEM. AN ARCHIPELAGO OF DREAM-ISLANDS-- A GLITTERING SHOAL OF WORLDS.
COME ON, COME ON... **SET**, DAMN YOU...

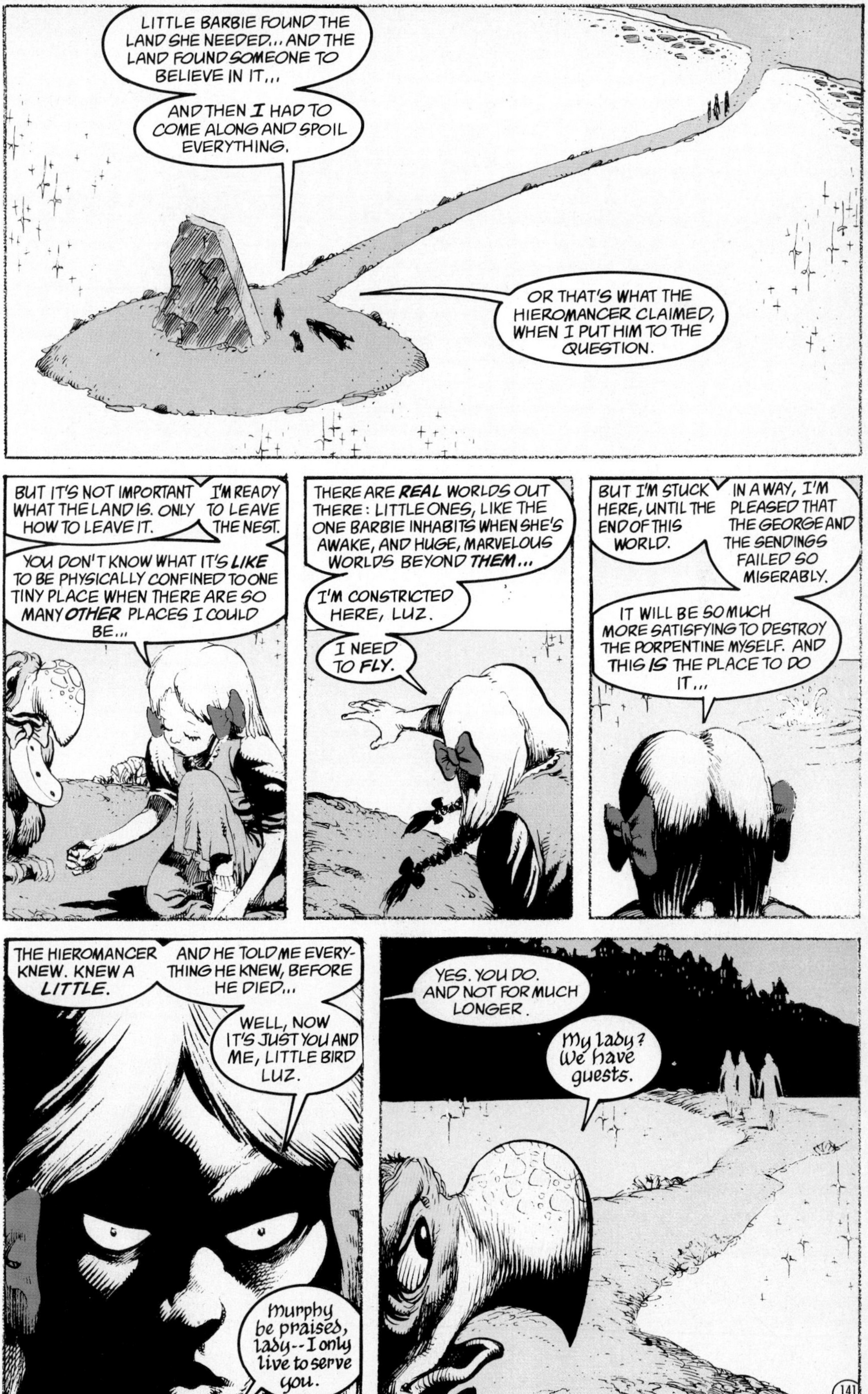

LITTLE BARBIE FOUND THE LAND SHE NEEDED... AND THE LAND FOUND SOMEONE TO BELIEVE IN IT...
AND THEN I HAD TO COME ALONG AND SPOIL EVERYTHING.
OR THAT'S WHAT THE HIEROMANCER CLAIMED, WHEN I PUT HIM TO THE QUESTION.
BUT IT'S NOT IMPORTANT WHAT THE LAND IS. ONLY HOW TO LEAVE IT.
I'M READY TO LEAVE THE NEST.
YOU DON'T KNOW WHAT IT'S LIKE TO BE PHYSICALLY CONFINED TO ONE TINY PLACE WHEN THERE ARE SO MANY OTHER PLACES I COULD BE...
THERE ARE REAL WORLDS OUT THERE: LITTLE ONES, LIKE THE ONE BARBIE INHABITS WHEN SHE'S AWAKE, AND HUGE, MARVELOUS WORLDS BEYOND THEM...
I'M CONSTRICTED HERE, LUZ.
I NEED TO FLY.
BUT I'M STUCK HERE, UNTIL THE END OF THIS WORLD.
IN A WAY, I'M PLEASED THAT THE GEORGE AND THE SENDINGS FAILED SO MISERABLY.
IT WILL BE SO MUCH MORE SATISFYING TO DESTROY THE PORPENTINE MYSELF. AND THIS IS THE PLACE TO DO IT...
THE HIEROMANCER KNEW. KNEW A LITTLE.
AND HE TOLD ME EVERYTHING HE KNEW, BEFORE HE DIED...
WELL, NOW IT'S JUST YOU AND ME, LITTLE BIRD LUZ.
Murphy be praised, lady--I only live to serve you.
YES. YOU DO. AND NOT FOR MUCH LONGER.
My lady? We have guests.

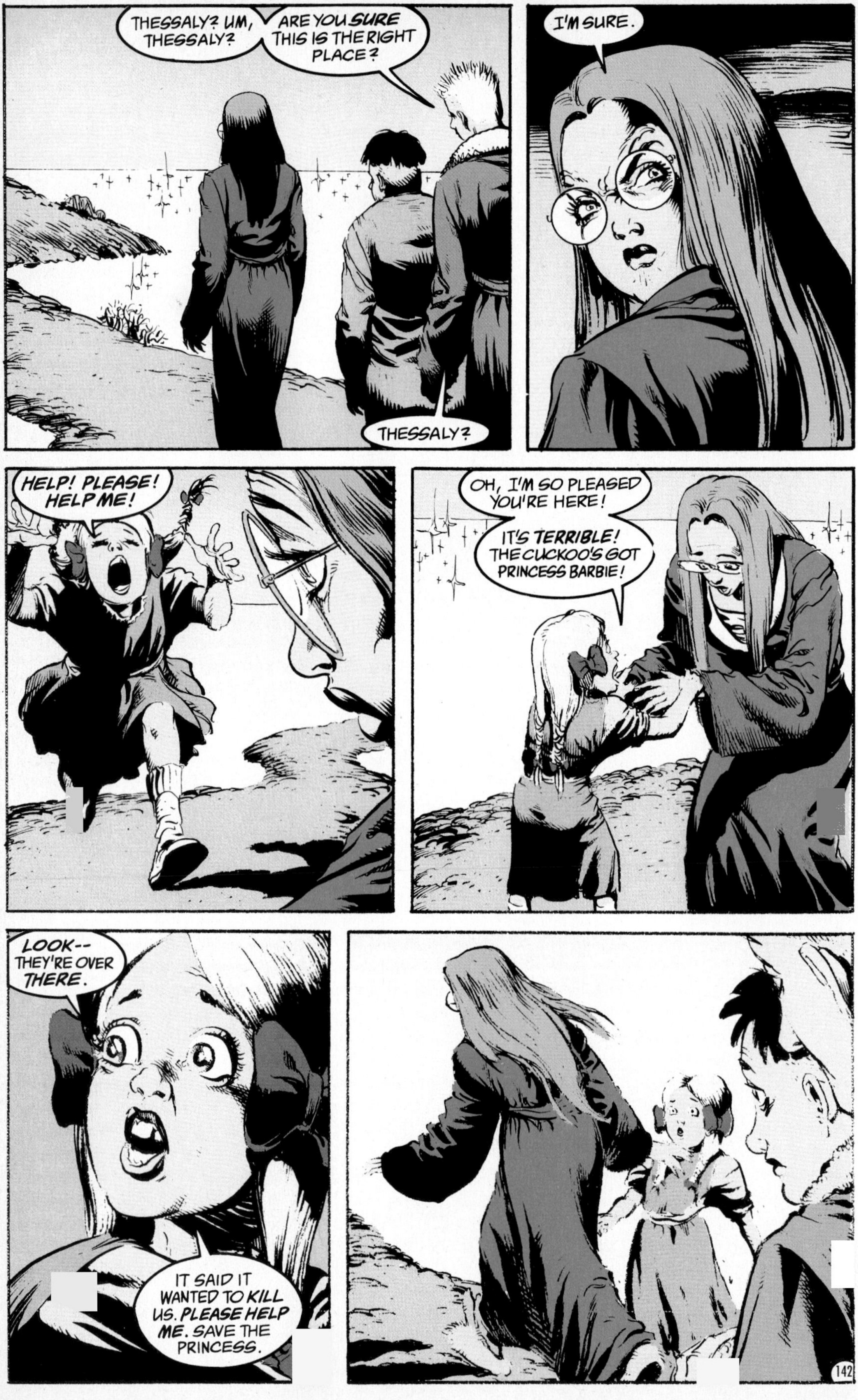
THESSALY? UM, THESSALY?
ARE YOU SURE THIS IS THE RIGHT PLACE?
THESSALY?
I'M SURE.
HELP! PLEASE! HELP ME!
OH, I'M SO PLEASED YOU'RE HERE!
IT'S TERRIBLE! THE CUCKOO'S GOT PRINCESS BARBIE!
LOOK-- THEY'RE OVER THERE.
IT SAID IT WANTED TO KILL US. PLEASE HELP ME. SAVE THE PRINCESS.

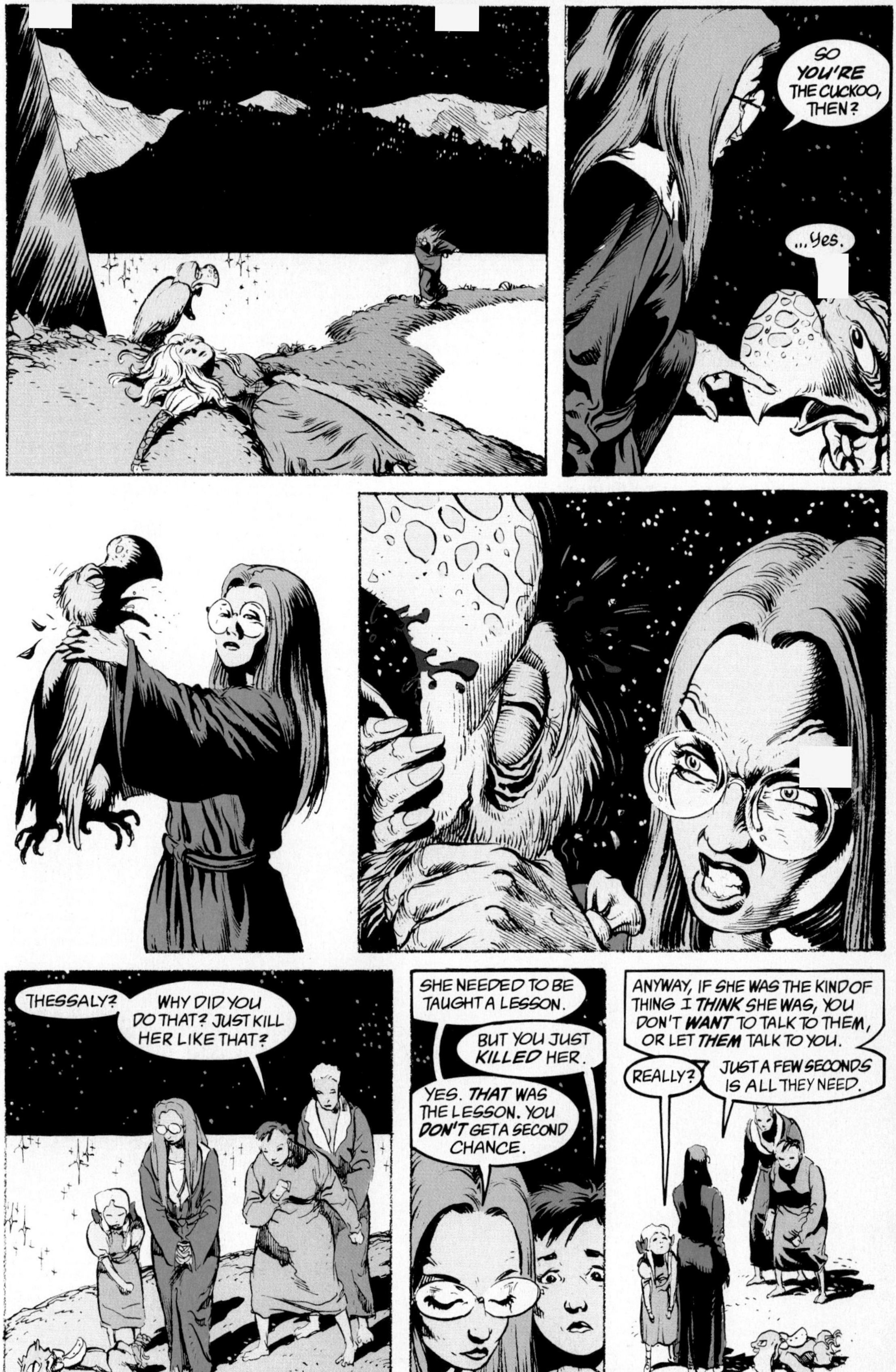
SO YOU'RE THE CUCKOO, THEN?
...Yes.
THESSALY?
WHY DID YOU DO THAT? JUST KILL HER LIKE THAT?
SHE NEEDED TO BE TAUGHT A LESSON.
BUT YOU JUST KILLED HER.
YES. THAT WAS THE LESSON. YOU DON'T GET A SECOND CHANCE.
ANYWAY, IF SHE WAS THE KIND OF THING I THINK SHE WAS, YOU DON'T WANT TO TALK TO THEM, OR LET THEM TALK TO YOU.
REALLY?
JUST A FEW SECONDS IS ALL THEY NEED.

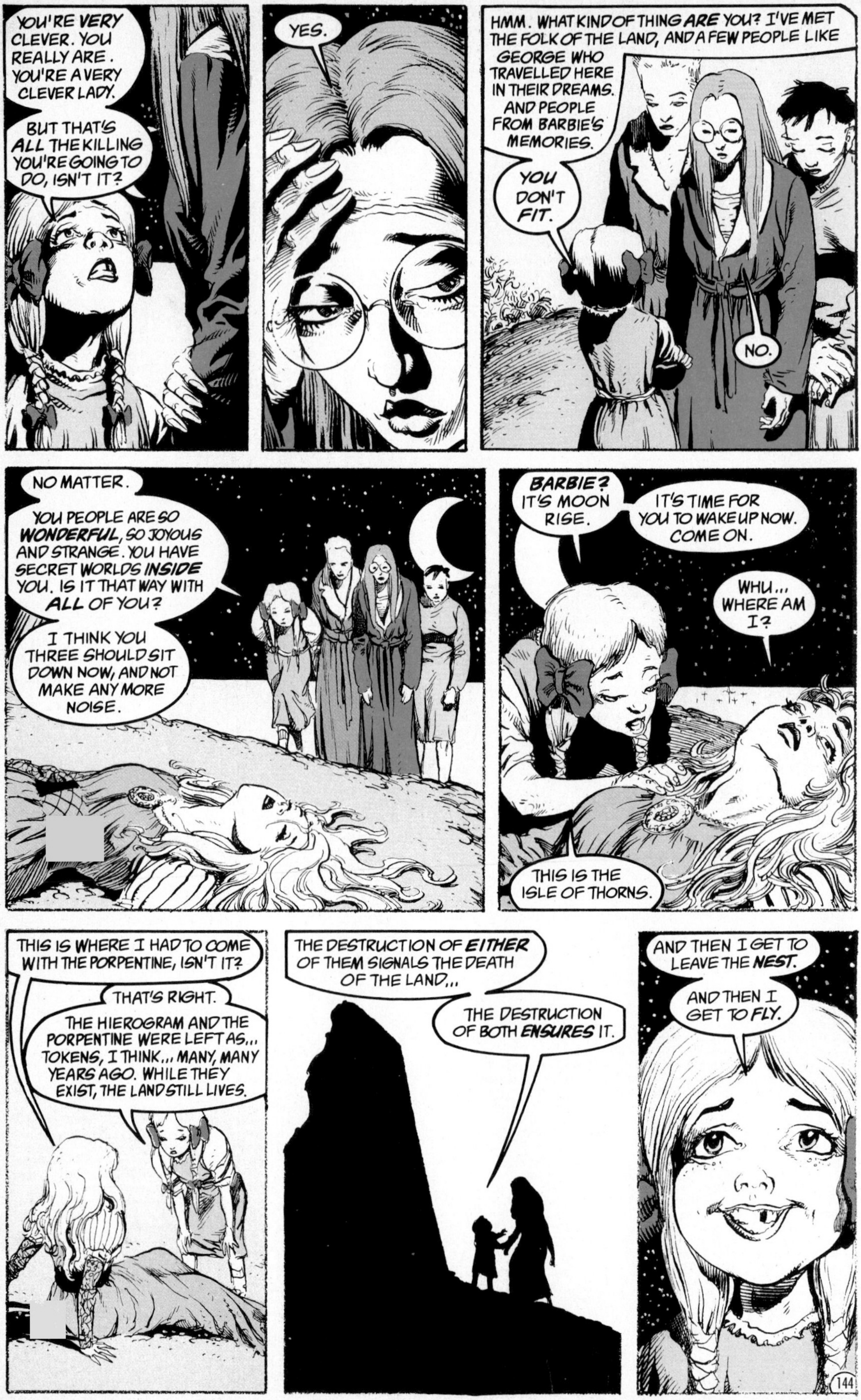

YOU'RE VERY CLEVER. YOU REALLY ARE. YOU'RE A VERY CLEVER LADY.
BUT THAT'S ALL THE KILLING YOU'RE GOING TO DO, ISN'T IT?
YES.
HMM. WHAT KIND OF THING ARE YOU? I'VE MET THE FOLK OF THE LAND, AND A FEW PEOPLE LIKE GEORGE WHO TRAVELLED HERE IN THEIR DREAMS. AND PEOPLE FROM BARBIE'S MEMORIES.
YOU DON'T FIT.
NO.
NO MATTER.
YOU PEOPLE ARE SO WONDERFUL, SO JOYOUS AND STRANGE. YOU HAVE SECRET WORLDS INSIDE YOU. IS IT THAT WAY WITH ALL OF YOU?
I THINK YOU THREE SHOULD SIT DOWN NOW, AND NOT MAKE ANY MORE NOISE.
BARBIE? IT'S MOON RISE.
IT'S TIME FOR YOU TO WAKE UP NOW. COME ON.
WHU... WHERE AM I?
THIS IS THE ISLE OF THORNS.
THIS IS WHERE I HAD TO COME WITH THE PORPENTINE, ISN'T IT?
THAT'S RIGHT.
THE HIEROGRAM AND THE PORPENTINE WERE LEFT AS... TOKENS, I THINK... MANY, MANY YEARS AGO. WHILE THEY EXIST, THE LAND STILL LIVES.
THE DESTRUCTION OF EITHER OF THEM SIGNALS THE DEATH OF THE LAND...
THE DESTRUCTION OF BOTH ENSURES IT.
AND THEN I GET TO LEAVE THE NEST.
AND THEN I GET TO FLY.

Panel 1: THIS IS *BAD* STUFF. *HOODOO* STUFF. *YOU* DO THIS STUFF?

NO.

THASS GOOD.

Panel 2: *THIS* IS GEORGE. THIS IS HIS APARTMENT. HE TALKS.

I DON' TALK TO NO DEAD PEOPLE. 'S BAD LUCK.

Panel 3: AND THIS IS BARBIE.

OH YEAH. *I* KNOW HER--SHE GAVE ME FIFTY CENTS ONNA SUBWAY THIS MORNING, BUT I DROPPED IT...

Panel 4: *JESUS!* YOU'RE THE I-DON'T-LIKE-DOGS LADY.

DON'T YOU GO TAKIN' THE LORD'S NAME IN VAIN. MY NAME'S MAISIE HILL, MAISIE TO MY FRIENDS.

Panel 5: I'M WANDA.

HMPH. SO WHAT'RE YOU? A GUY OR A GAL?

I'M... I WAS *BORN* A GUY. AND *NOW* I'M A GAL. ONLY I HAVEN'T GONE ALL THE WAY...

Panel 6: YEAH. MY GRANDSON, BILLY, WAS LIKE YOU. HE WAS A CUTE LITTLE THING. HE'D SASHAY AROUND SWEET AS ANYTHIN'. HE WAS SAVIN' UP FER THE OPERATION.

HIS MAW USED TO SAY HE WAS THE DAUGHTER SHE'D NEVER HAD.

Panel 7: I WISH *MY* MOM HAD SAID THAT. *SHE* SAID I WAS THE SPAWN OF THE DEVIL.

THASS *DUMB.* JUST BECAUSE SOME-ONE'S DIFFERENT DON'T MAKE 'EM *BAD.*

SO WHAT HAPPENED TO BILLY?

Panel 8: THEY FOUND HIM INNA MOTEL ROOM IN QUEENS, FIVE YEARS BACK. SOME-ONE HAD CRUSHED IN HIS HEAD WITH A MONKEY-WRENCH. DONE OTHER SHIT TO HIM, HE'D BEEN DEAD FOR LIKE A WEEK.

EVERYONE TOL' HIM NOT TO GO WITH STRANGERS.

THERE NEVER *WAS* ANY TELLIN' THAT BOY ANYTHIN'...

Panel 9: I'M SORRY.

YOU'RE SORRY? HOW'D YOU THINK *I* FELT?

SO *WHY* DON'T YOU LIKE *DOGS?*

...I JUS' DON'T. THASS ALL.

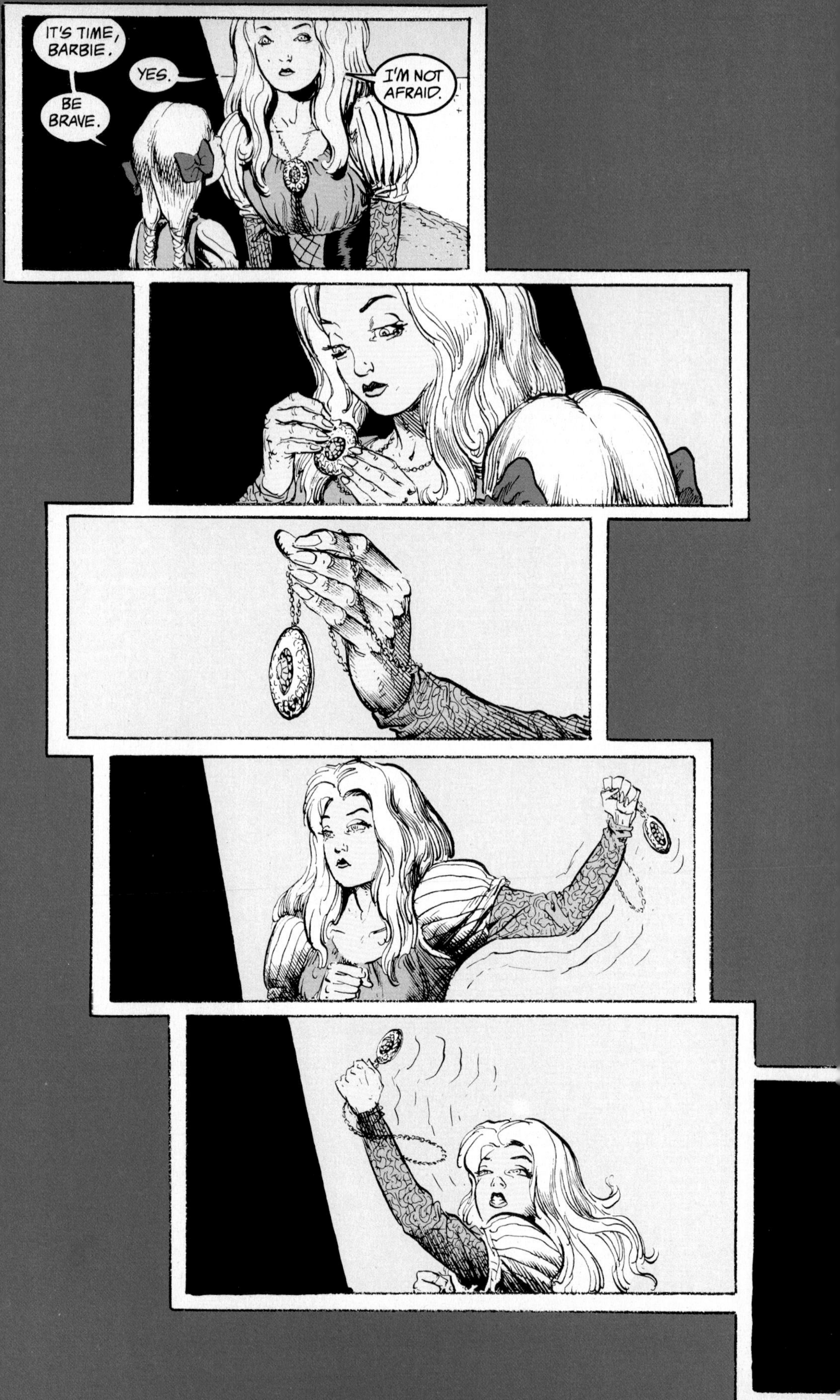
IT'S TIME, BARBIE.
BE BRAVE.
YES.
I'M NOT AFRAID.

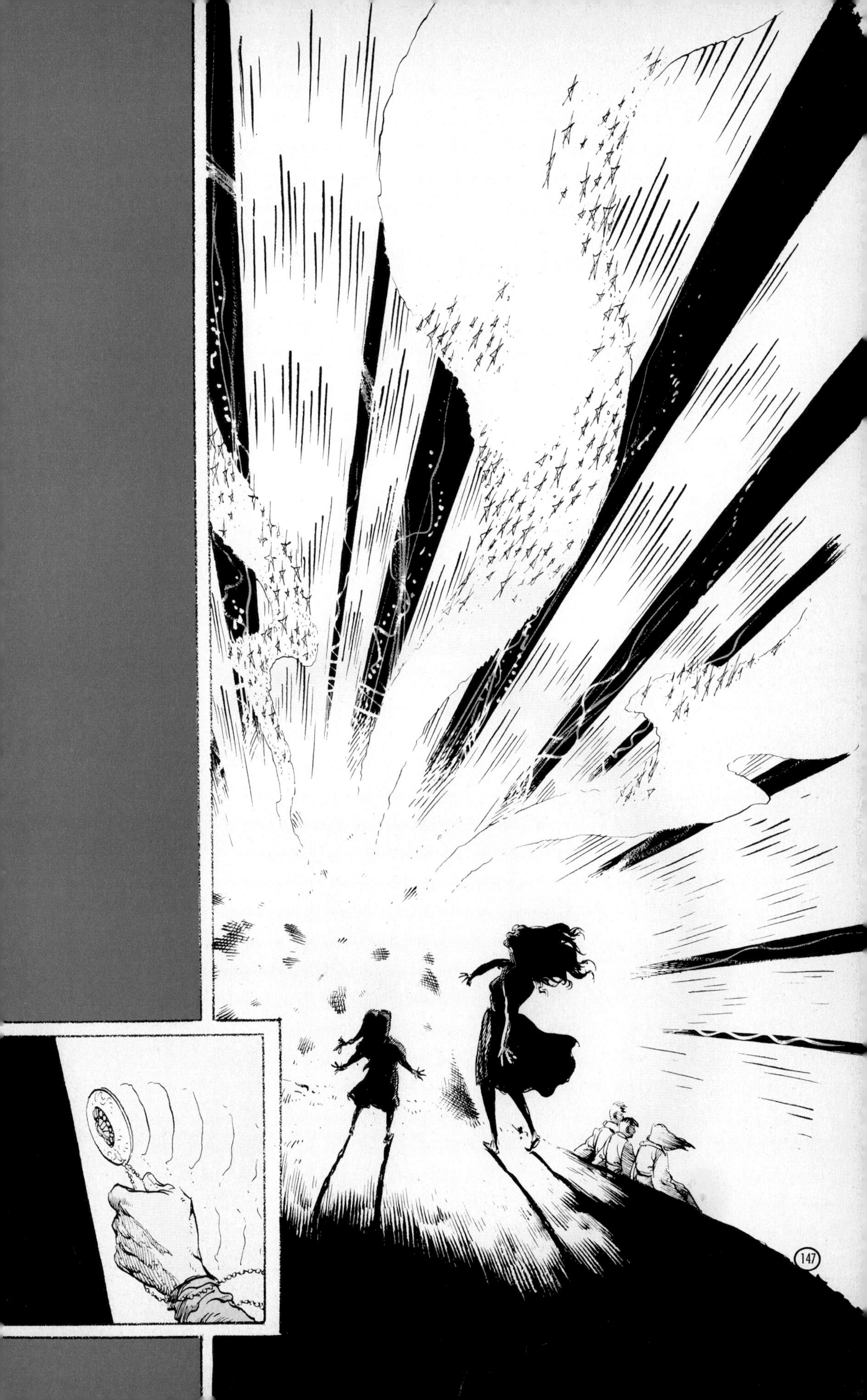

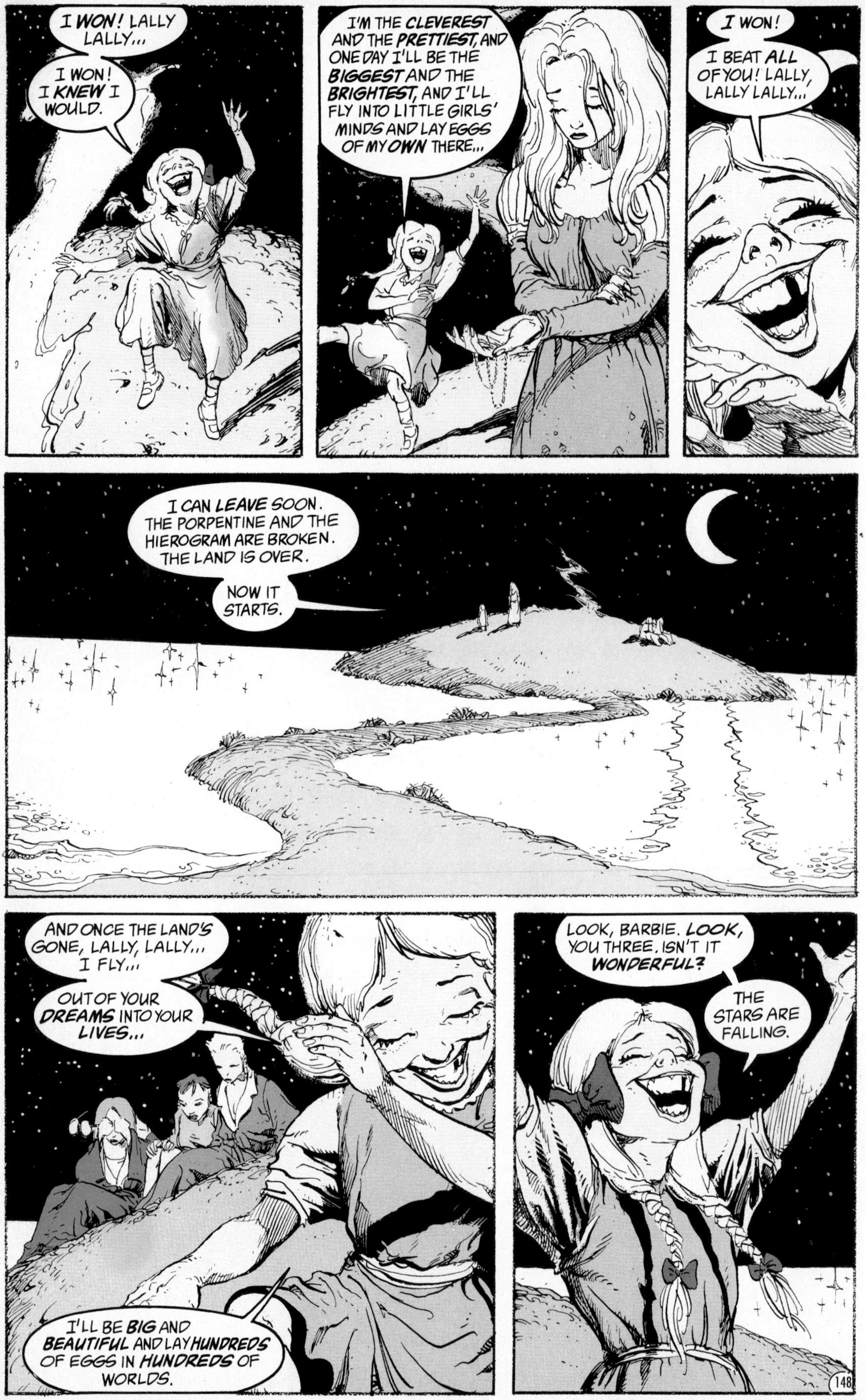
I WON! LALLY LALLY...
I WON! I KNEW I WOULD.
I'M THE CLEVEREST AND THE PRETTIEST, AND ONE DAY I'LL BE THE BIGGEST AND THE BRIGHTEST, AND I'LL FLY INTO LITTLE GIRLS' MINDS AND LAY EGGS OF MY OWN THERE...
I WON!
I BEAT ALL OF YOU! LALLY, LALLY LALLY...
I CAN LEAVE SOON. THE PORPENTINE AND THE HIEROGRAM ARE BROKEN. THE LAND IS OVER.
NOW IT STARTS.
AND ONCE THE LAND'S GONE, LALLY, LALLY... I FLY...
OUT OF YOUR DREAMS INTO YOUR LIVES...
I'LL BE BIG AND BEAUTIFUL AND LAY HUNDREDS OF EGGS IN HUNDREDS OF WORLDS.
LOOK, BARBIE. LOOK, YOU THREE. ISN'T IT WONDERFUL?
THE STARS ARE FALLING.

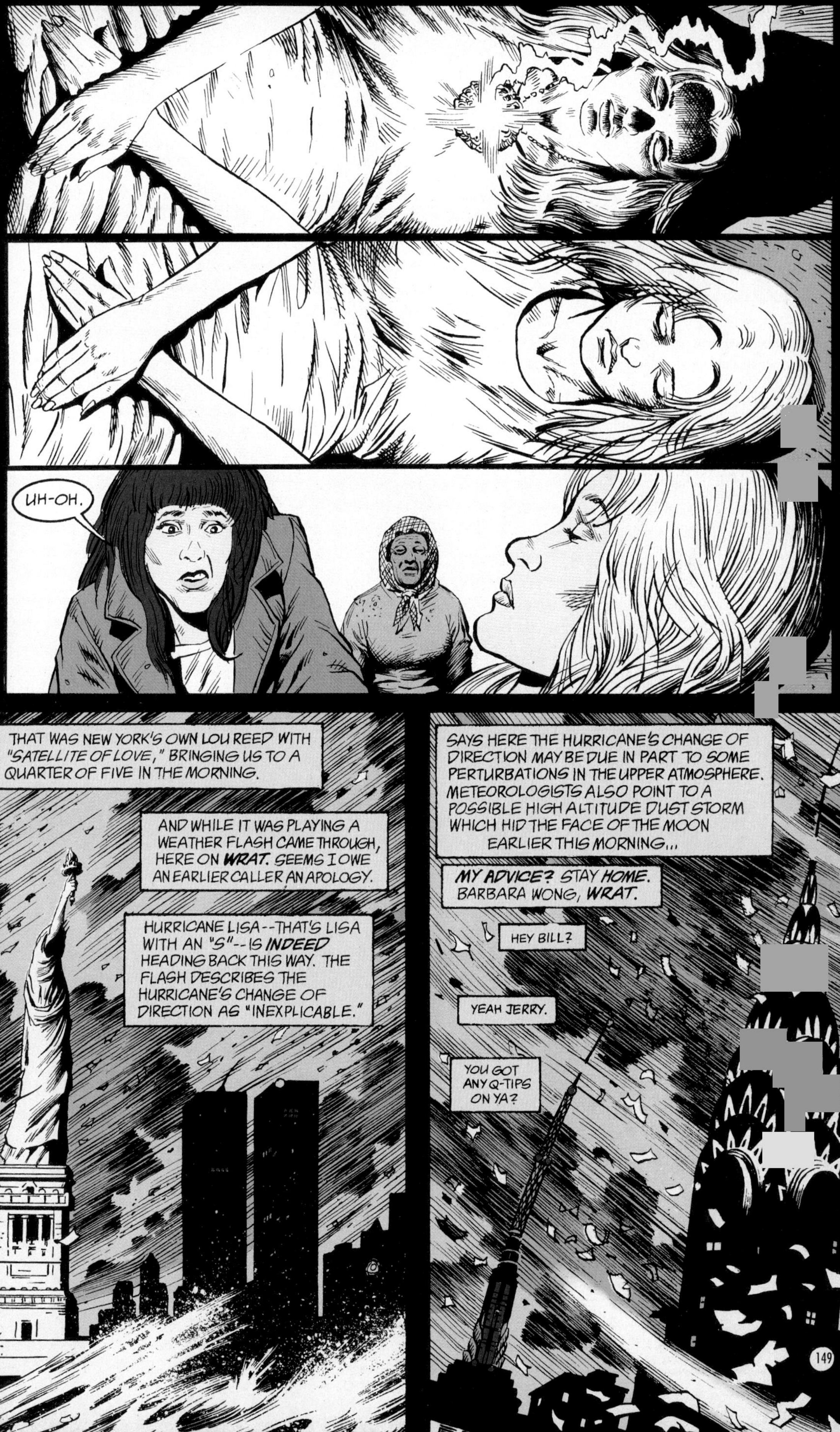
UH-OH.
THAT WAS NEW YORK'S OWN LOU REED WITH "SATELLITE OF LOVE," BRINGING US TO A QUARTER OF FIVE IN THE MORNING.
AND WHILE IT WAS PLAYING A WEATHER FLASH CAME THROUGH, HERE ON WRAT. SEEMS I OWE AN EARLIER CALLER AN APOLOGY.
HURRICANE LISA--THAT'S LISA WITH AN "S"--IS INDEED HEADING BACK THIS WAY. THE FLASH DESCRIBES THE HURRICANE'S CHANGE OF DIRECTION AS "INEXPLICABLE."
SAYS HERE THE HURRICANE'S CHANGE OF DIRECTION MAY BE DUE IN PART TO SOME PERTURBATIONS IN THE UPPER ATMOSPHERE. METEOROLOGISTS ALSO POINT TO A POSSIBLE HIGH ALTITUDE DUST STORM WHICH HID THE FACE OF THE MOON EARLIER THIS MORNING...
MY ADVICE? STAY HOME. BARBARA WONG, WRAT.
HEY BILL?
YEAH JERRY.
YOU GOT ANY Q-TIPS ON YA?

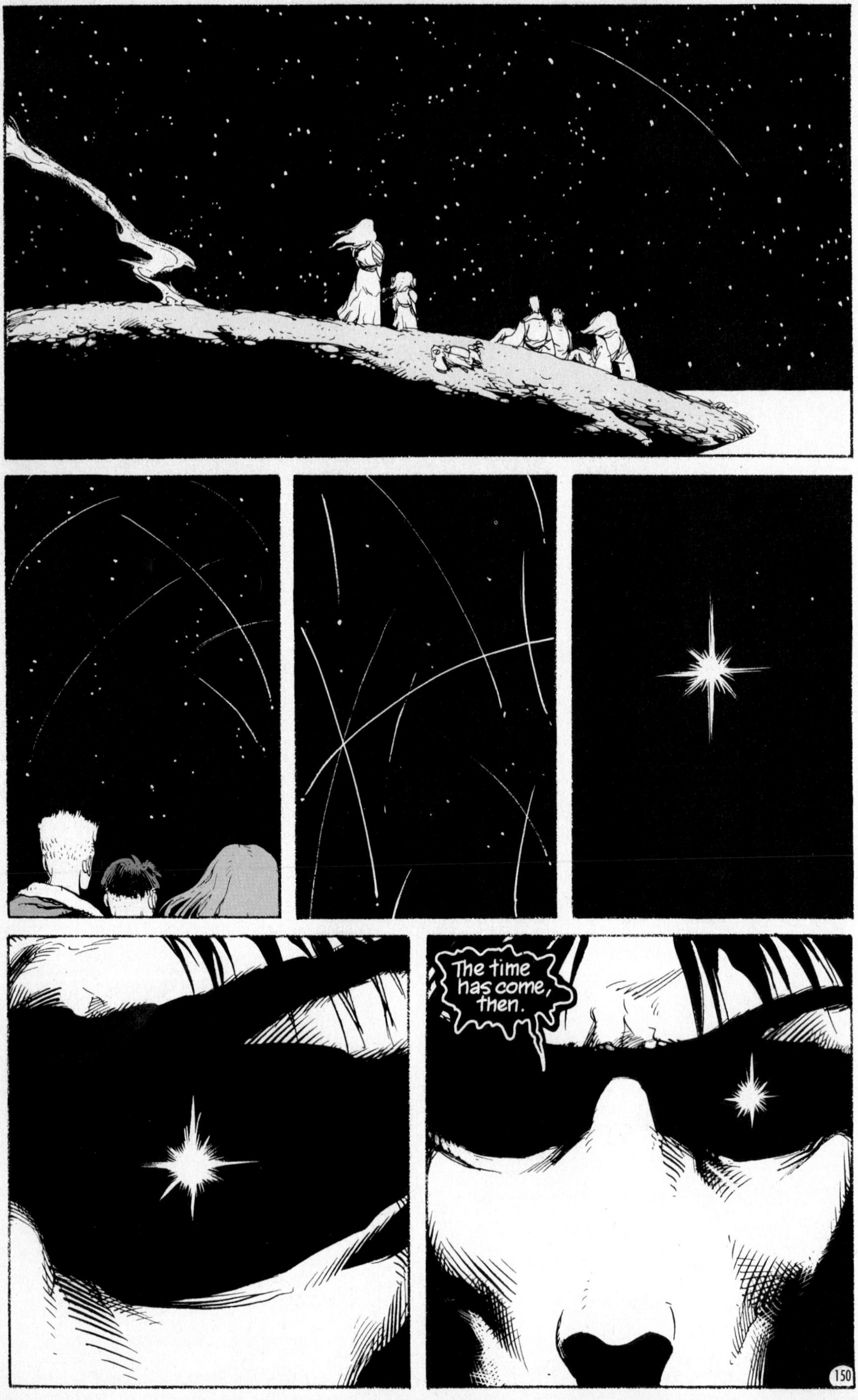
The time has come, then.

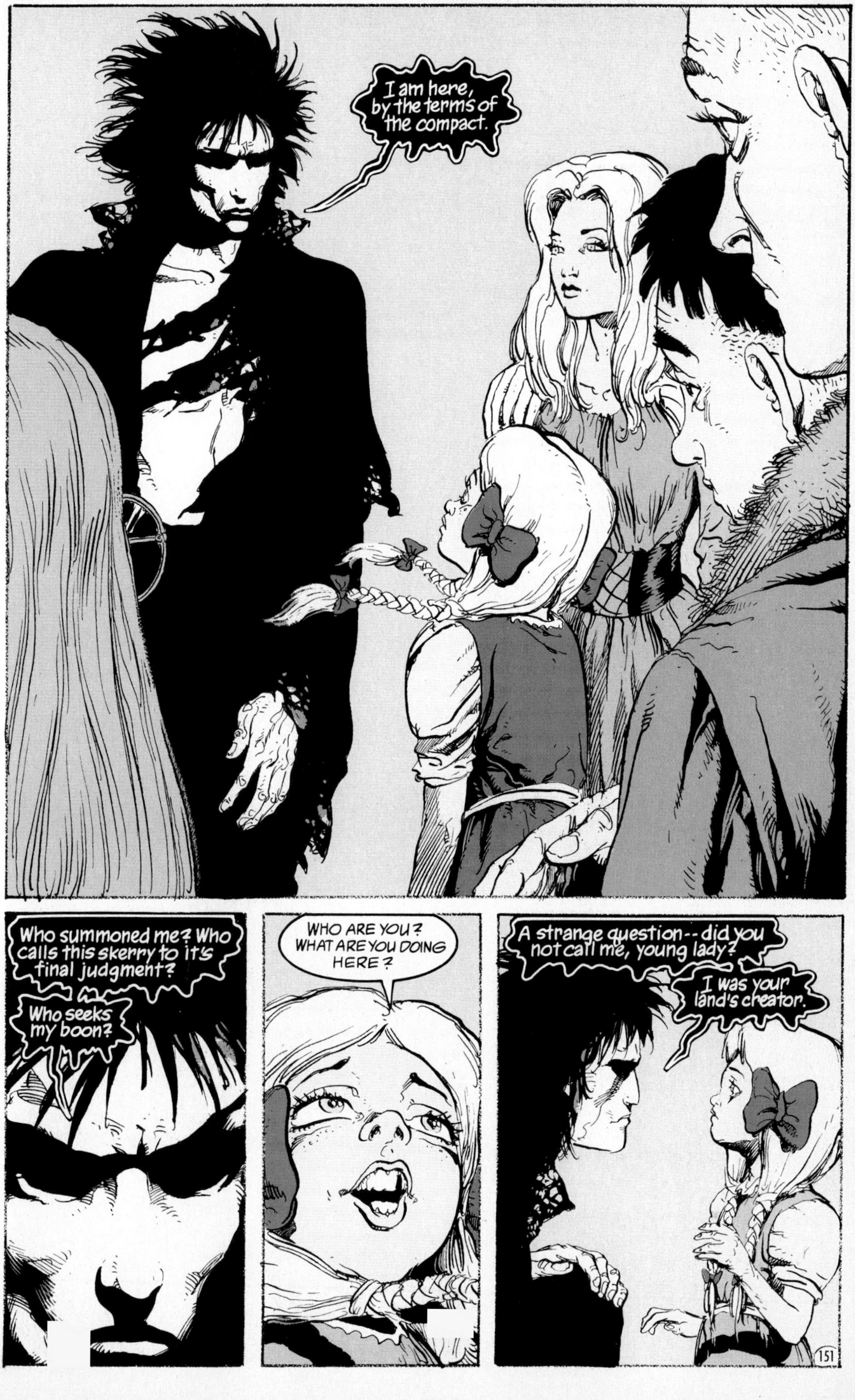
I am here, by the terms of the compact.
Who summoned me? Who calls this skerry to it's final judgment?
Who seeks my boon?
WHO ARE YOU? WHAT ARE YOU DOING HERE?
A strange question-- did you not call me, young lady?
I was your land's creator.

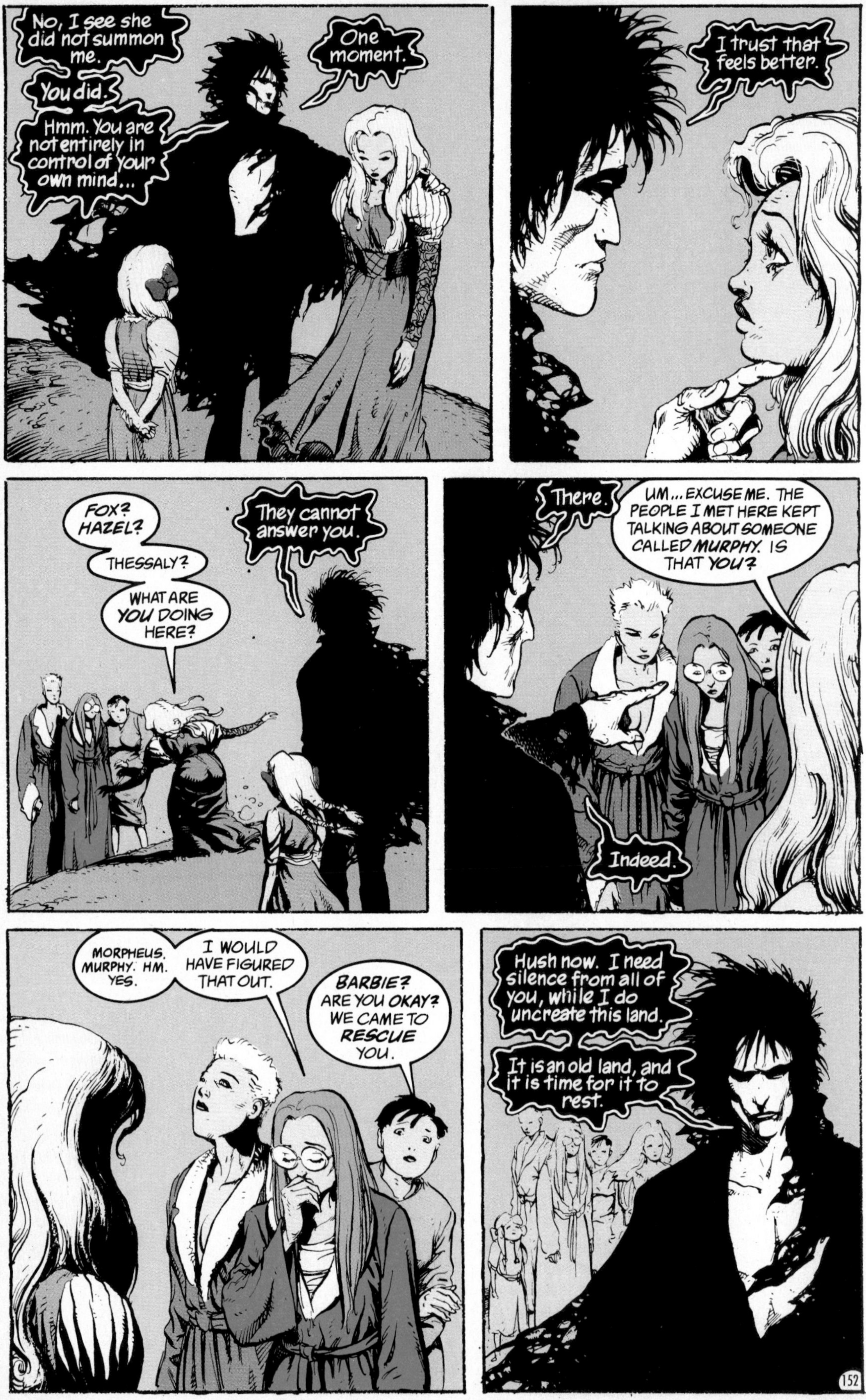
No, I see she did not summon me.
You did.
Hmm. You are not entirely in control of your own mind...
One moment.
I trust that feels better.
FOX? HAZEL?
THESSALY?
WHAT ARE YOU DOING HERE?
They cannot answer you.
There.
UM... EXCUSE ME. THE PEOPLE I MET HERE KEPT TALKING ABOUT SOMEONE CALLED MURPHY. IS THAT YOU?
Indeed.
MORPHEUS. MURPHY. HM. YES.
I WOULD HAVE FIGURED THAT OUT.
BARBIE? ARE YOU OKAY? WE CAME TO RESCUE YOU.
Hush now. I need silence from all of you, while I do uncreate this land.
It is an old land, and it is time for it to rest.
152

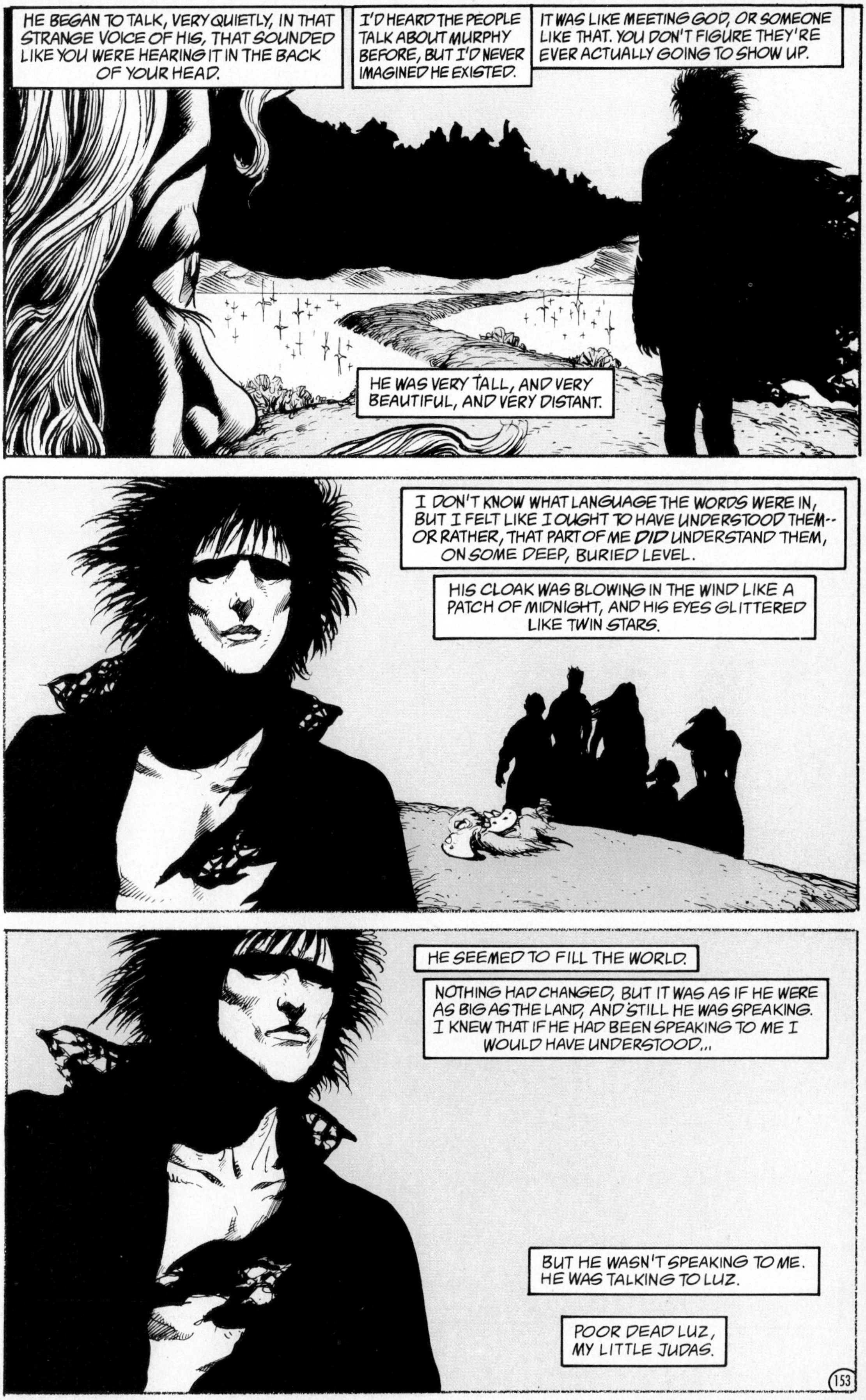
HE BEGAN TO TALK, VERY QUIETLY, IN THAT STRANGE VOICE OF HIS, THAT SOUNDED LIKE YOU WERE HEARING IT IN THE BACK OF YOUR HEAD.
I'D HEARD THE PEOPLE TALK ABOUT MURPHY BEFORE, BUT I'D NEVER IMAGINED HE EXISTED.
IT WAS LIKE MEETING GOD, OR SOMEONE LIKE THAT. YOU DON'T FIGURE THEY'RE EVER ACTUALLY GOING TO SHOW UP.
HE WAS VERY TALL, AND VERY BEAUTIFUL, AND VERY DISTANT.
I DON'T KNOW WHAT LANGUAGE THE WORDS WERE IN, BUT I FELT LIKE I OUGHT TO HAVE UNDERSTOOD THEM-- OR RATHER, THAT PART OF ME DID UNDERSTAND THEM, ON SOME DEEP, BURIED LEVEL.
HIS CLOAK WAS BLOWING IN THE WIND LIKE A PATCH OF MIDNIGHT, AND HIS EYES GLITTERED LIKE TWIN STARS.
HE SEEMED TO FILL THE WORLD.
NOTHING HAD CHANGED, BUT IT WAS AS IF HE WERE AS BIG AS THE LAND, AND STILL HE WAS SPEAKING. I KNEW THAT IF HE HAD BEEN SPEAKING TO ME I WOULD HAVE UNDERSTOOD...
BUT HE WASN'T SPEAKING TO ME. HE WAS TALKING TO LUZ.
POOR DEAD LUZ, MY LITTLE JUDAS.

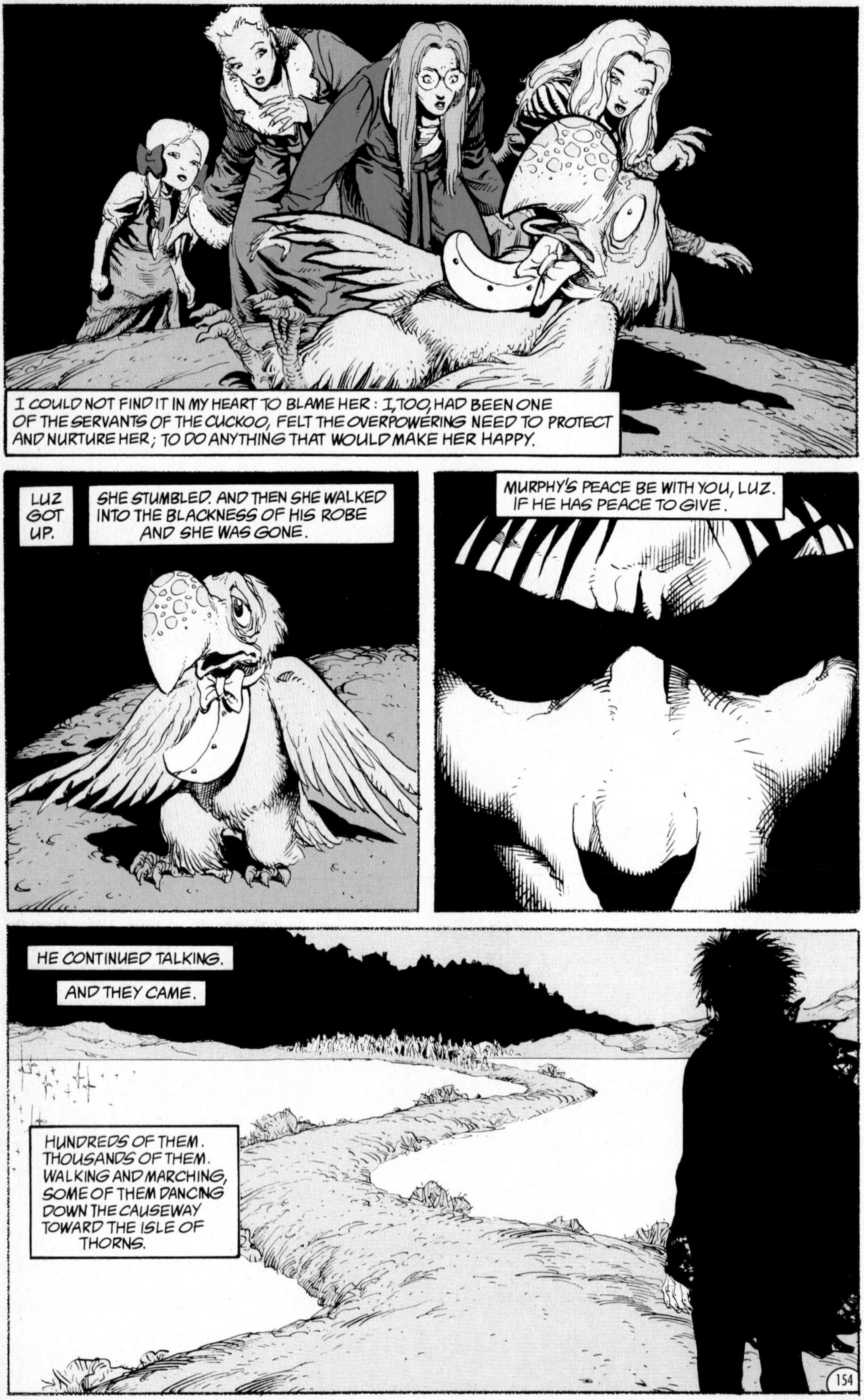
I COULD NOT FIND IT IN MY HEART TO BLAME HER: I, TOO, HAD BEEN ONE OF THE SERVANTS OF THE CUCKOO, FELT THE OVERPOWERING NEED TO PROTECT AND NURTURE HER; TO DO ANYTHING THAT WOULD MAKE HER HAPPY.
LUZ GOT UP.
SHE STUMBLED. AND THEN SHE WALKED INTO THE BLACKNESS OF HIS ROBE AND SHE WAS GONE.
MURPHY'S PEACE BE WITH YOU, LUZ. IF HE HAS PEACE TO GIVE.
HE CONTINUED TALKING.
AND THEY CAME.
HUNDREDS OF THEM. THOUSANDS OF THEM. WALKING AND MARCHING, SOME OF THEM DANCING DOWN THE CAUSEWAY TOWARD THE ISLE OF THORNS.

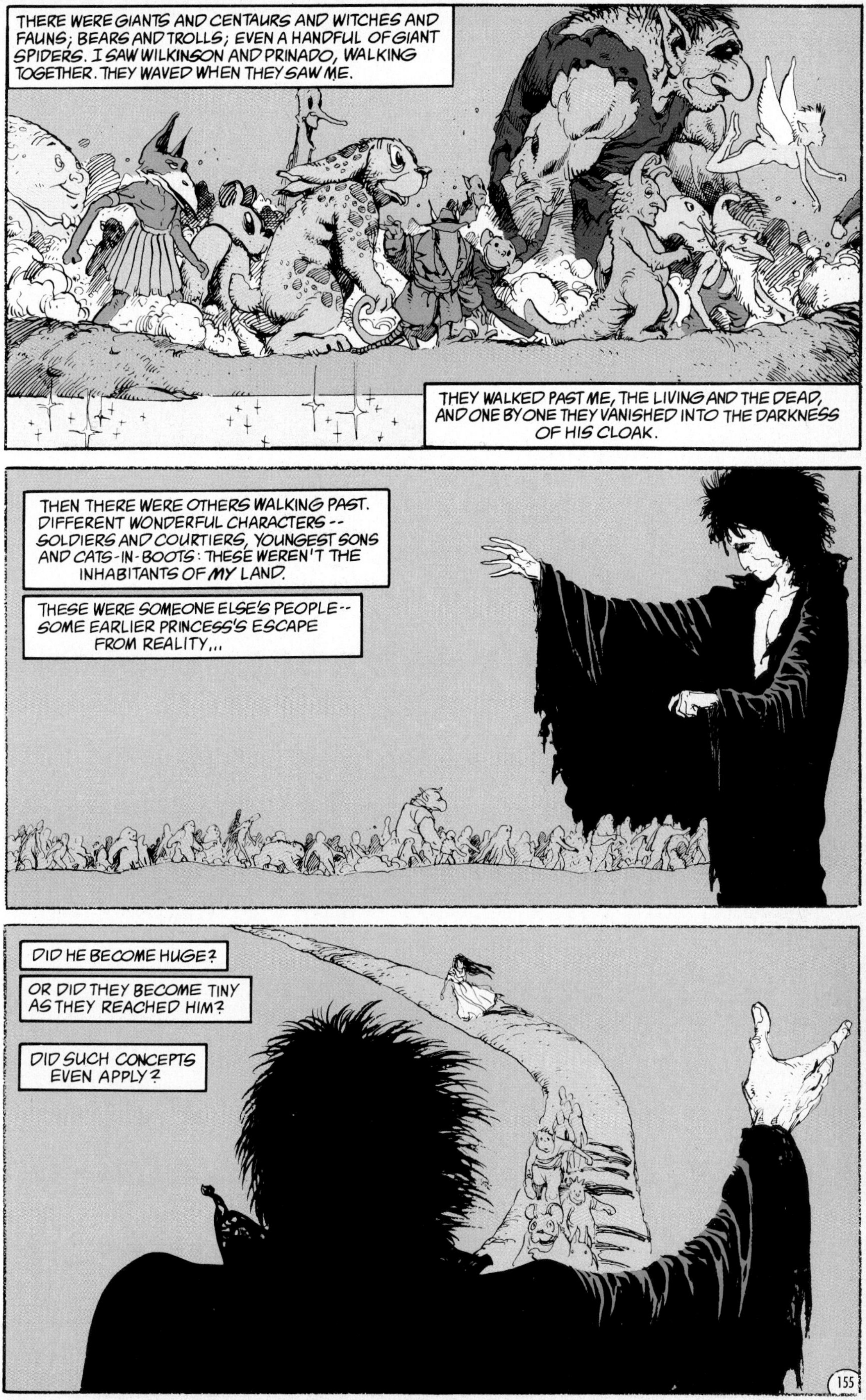
THERE WERE GIANTS AND CENTAURS AND WITCHES AND FAUNS; BEARS AND TROLLS; EVEN A HANDFUL OF GIANT SPIDERS. I SAW WILKINSON AND PRINADO, WALKING TOGETHER. THEY WAVED WHEN THEY SAW ME.
THEY WALKED PAST ME, THE LIVING AND THE DEAD, AND ONE BY ONE THEY VANISHED INTO THE DARKNESS OF HIS CLOAK.
THEN THERE WERE OTHERS WALKING PAST. DIFFERENT WONDERFUL CHARACTERS -- SOLDIERS AND COURTIERS, YOUNGEST SONS AND CATS-IN-BOOTS: THESE WEREN'T THE INHABITANTS OF MY LAND.
THESE WERE SOMEONE ELSE'S PEOPLE -- SOME EARLIER PRINCESS'S ESCAPE FROM REALITY...
DID HE BECOME HUGE?
OR DID THEY BECOME TINY AS THEY REACHED HIM?
DID SUCH CONCEPTS EVEN APPLY?

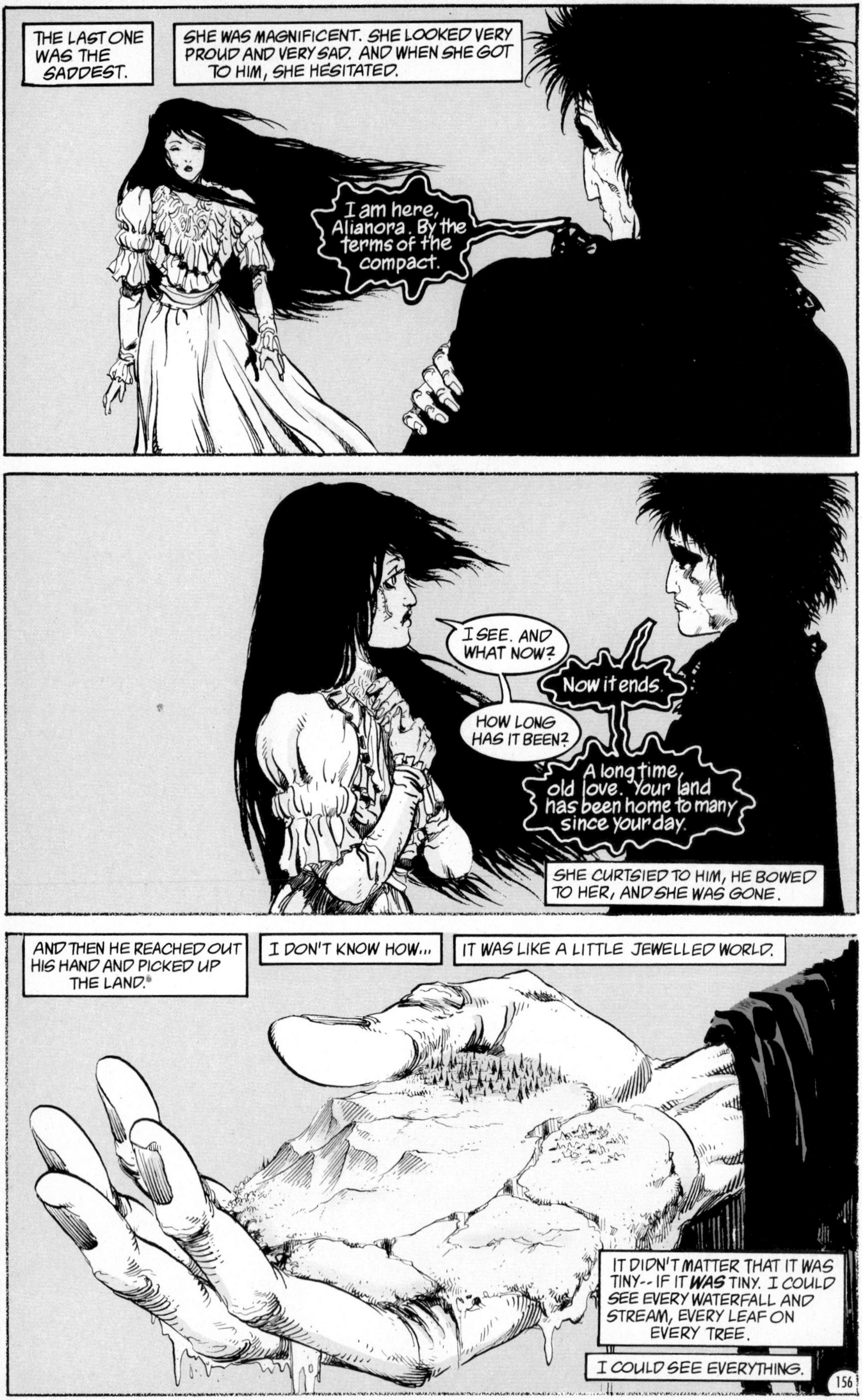
THE LAST ONE WAS THE SADDEST.
SHE WAS MAGNIFICENT. SHE LOOKED VERY PROUD AND VERY SAD. AND WHEN SHE GOT TO HIM, SHE HESITATED.
I am here, Alianora. By the terms of the compact.
I SEE. AND WHAT NOW?
Now it ends.
HOW LONG HAS IT BEEN?
A long time, old love. Your land has been home to many since your day.
SHE CURTSIED TO HIM, HE BOWED TO HER, AND SHE WAS GONE.
AND THEN HE REACHED OUT HIS HAND AND PICKED UP THE LAND.
I DON'T KNOW HOW...
IT WAS LIKE A LITTLE JEWELLED WORLD.
IT DIDN'T MATTER THAT IT WAS TINY-- IF IT *WAS* TINY. I COULD SEE EVERY WATERFALL AND STREAM, EVERY LEAF ON EVERY TREE.
I COULD SEE EVERYTHING.

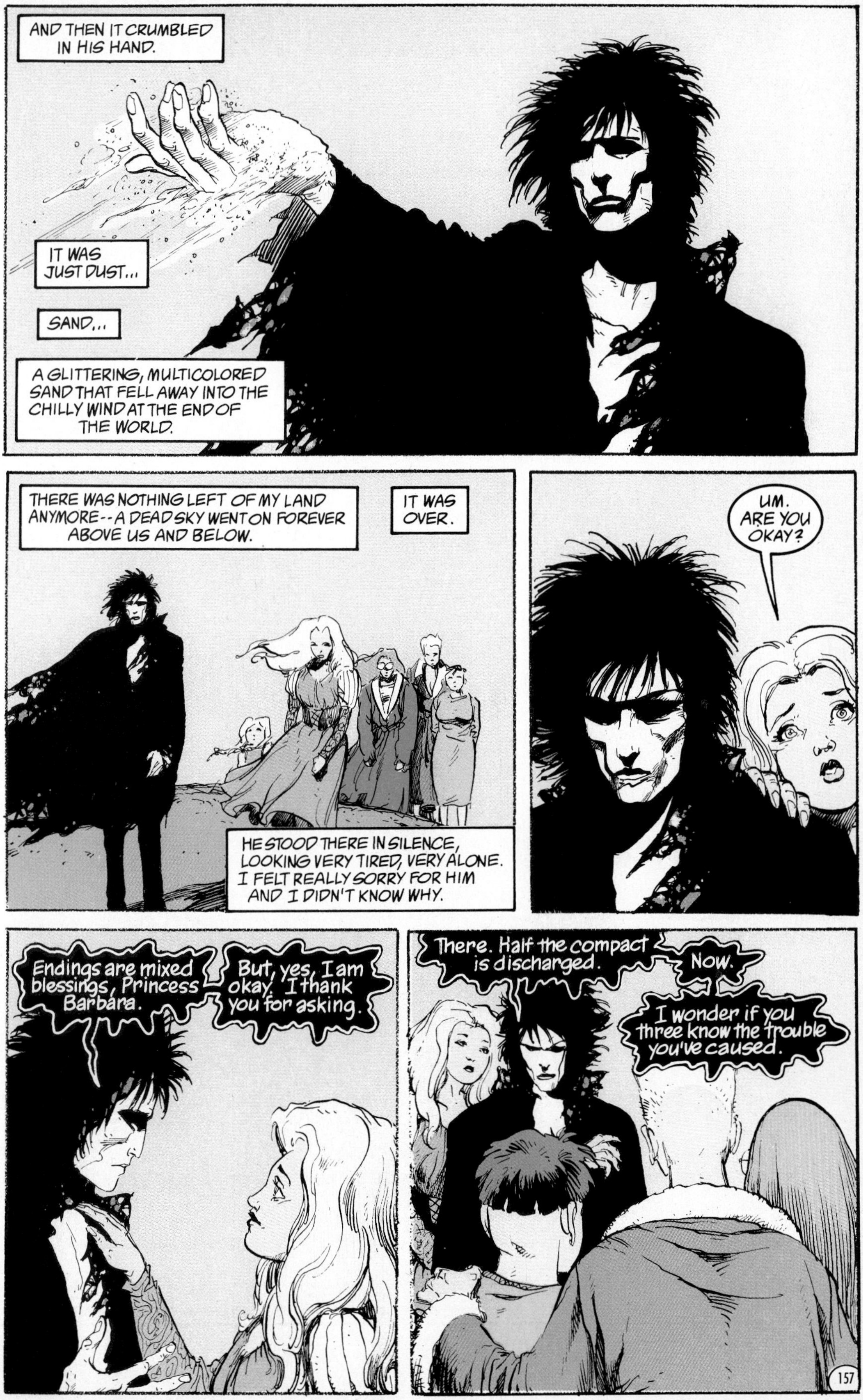
AND THEN IT CRUMBLED IN HIS HAND.
IT WAS JUST DUST...
SAND,...
A GLITTERING, MULTICOLORED SAND THAT FELL AWAY INTO THE CHILLY WIND AT THE END OF THE WORLD.
THERE WAS NOTHING LEFT OF MY LAND ANYMORE--A DEAD SKY WENT ON FOREVER ABOVE US AND BELOW.
IT WAS OVER.
HE STOOD THERE IN SILENCE, LOOKING VERY TIRED, VERY ALONE. I FELT REALLY SORRY FOR HIM AND I DIDN'T KNOW WHY.
UM. ARE YOU OKAY?
Endings are mixed blessings, Princess Barbara.
But, yes, I am okay. I thank you for asking.
There. Half the compact is discharged.
Now.
I wonder if you three know the trouble you've caused.

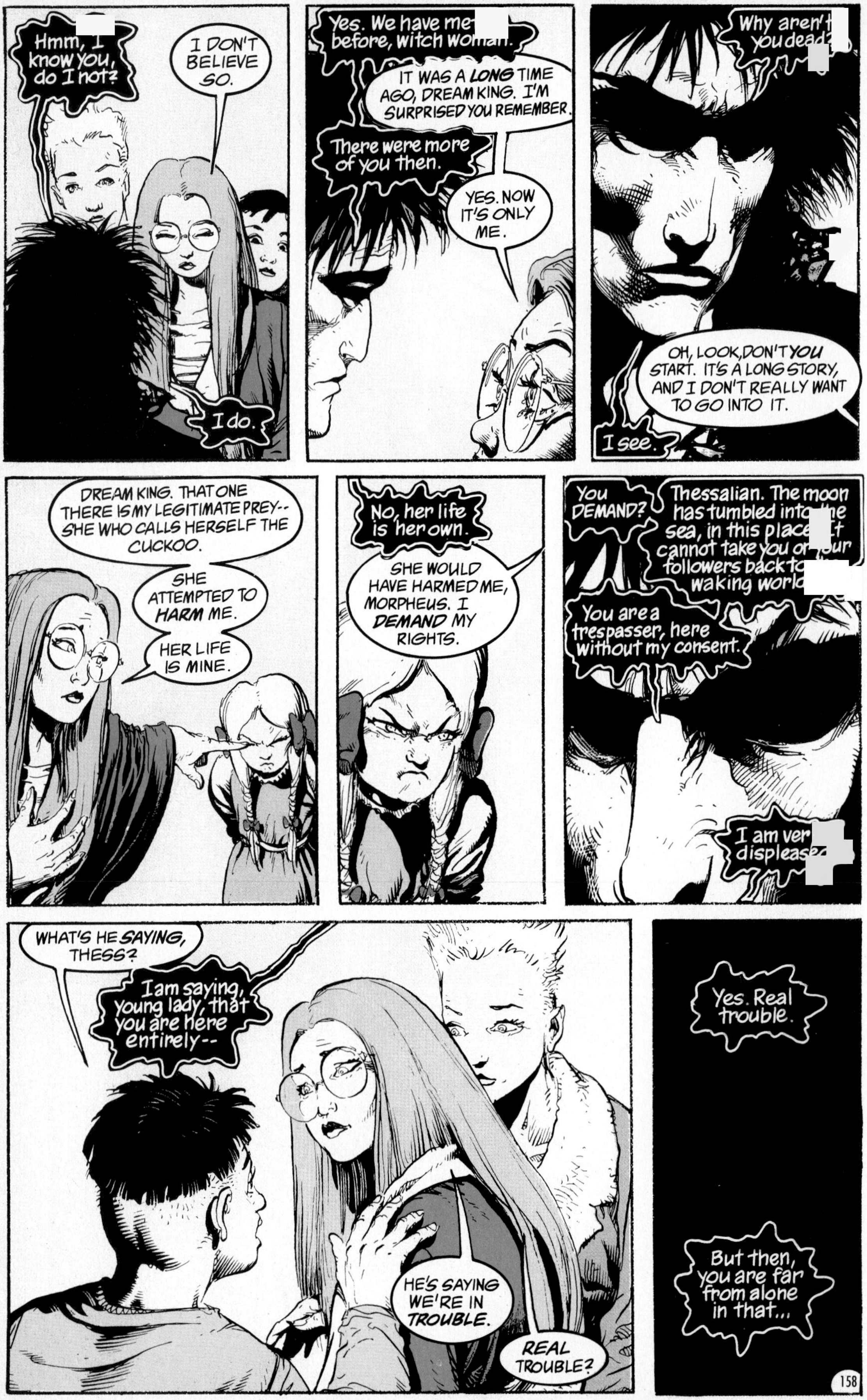
Hmm, I know you, do I not?
I DON'T BELIEVE SO.
I do.
Yes. We have me before, witch woman.
IT WAS A LONG TIME AGO, DREAM KING. I'M SURPRISED YOU REMEMBER.
There were more of you then.
YES. NOW IT'S ONLY ME.
Why aren' you dead
OH, LOOK, DON'T YOU START. IT'S A LONG STORY, AND I DON'T REALLY WANT TO GO INTO IT.
I see.
DREAM KING. THAT ONE THERE IS MY LEGITIMATE PREY-- SHE WHO CALLS HERSELF THE CUCKOO.
SHE ATTEMPTED TO HARM ME.
HER LIFE IS MINE.
No, her life is her own.
SHE WOULD HAVE HARMED ME, MORPHEUS. I DEMAND MY RIGHTS.
You DEMAND?
Thessalian. The moon has tumbled into sea, in this place cannot take you or followers back to waking worl
You are a trespasser, here without my consent.
I am ver displeas
WHAT'S HE SAYING, THESS?
I am saying, young lady, that you are here entirely--
HE'S SAYING WE'RE IN TROUBLE.
REAL TROUBLE?
Yes. Real trouble.
But then, you are far from alone in that...

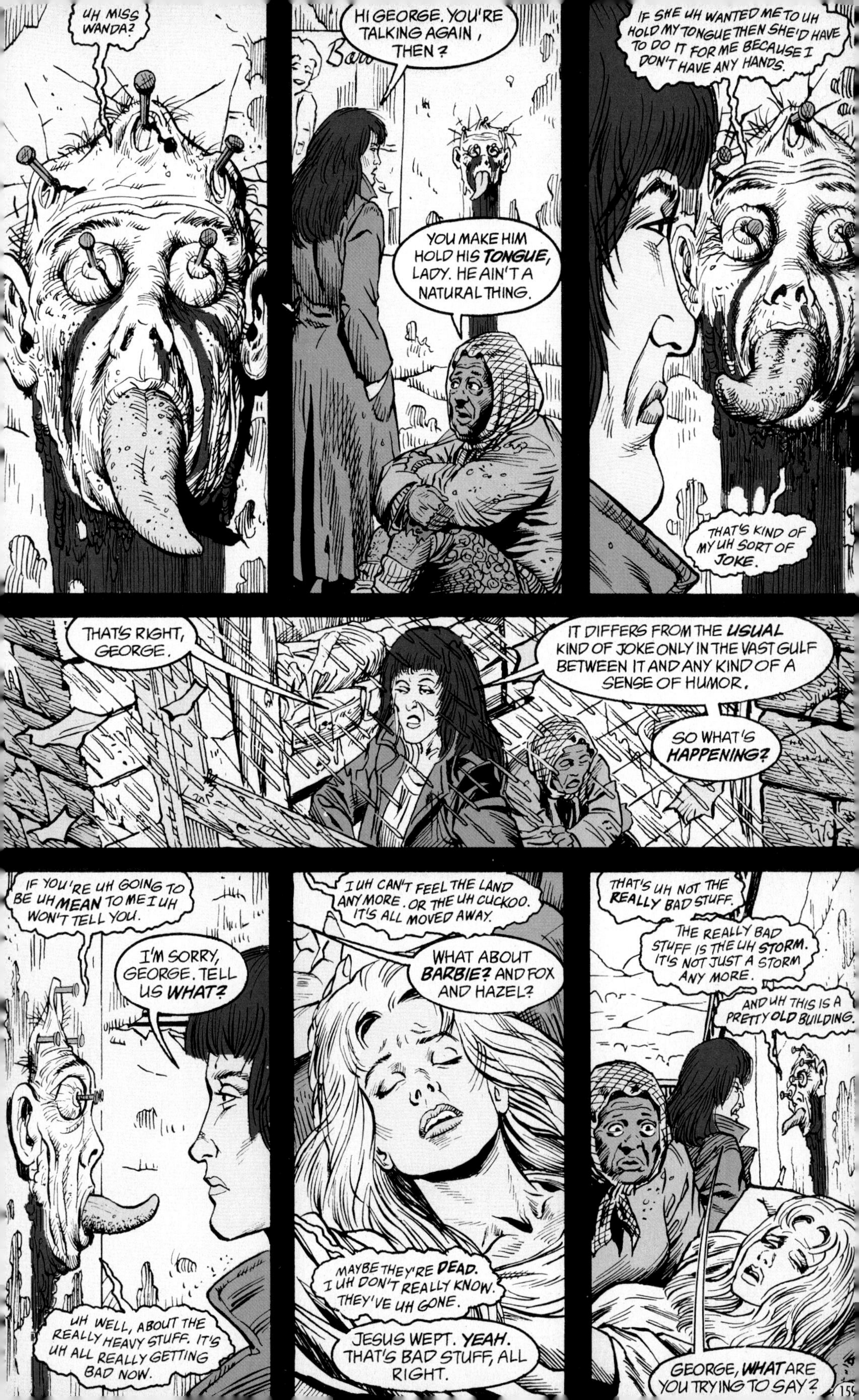
UH MISS WANDA?
HI GEORGE. YOU'RE TALKING AGAIN, THEN?
YOU MAKE HIM HOLD HIS TONGUE, LADY. HE AIN'T A NATURAL THING.
IF SHE UH WANTED ME TO UH HOLD MY TONGUE THEN SHE'D HAVE TO DO IT FOR ME BECAUSE I DON'T HAVE ANY HANDS.
THAT'S KIND OF MY UH SORT OF JOKE.
THAT'S RIGHT, GEORGE.
IT DIFFERS FROM THE USUAL KIND OF JOKE ONLY IN THE VAST GULF BETWEEN IT AND ANY KIND OF A SENSE OF HUMOR.
SO WHAT'S HAPPENING?
IF YOU'RE UH GOING TO BE UH MEAN TO ME I UH WON'T TELL YOU.
I'M SORRY, GEORGE. TELL US WHAT?
UH WELL, ABOUT THE REALLY HEAVY STUFF. IT'S UH ALL REALLY GETTING BAD NOW.
I UH CAN'T FEEL THE LAND ANY MORE. OR THE UH CUCKOO. IT'S ALL MOVED AWAY.
WHAT ABOUT BARBIE? AND FOX AND HAZEL?
MAYBE THEY'RE DEAD. I UH DON'T REALLY KNOW. THEY'VE UH GONE.
JESUS WEPT. YEAH. THAT'S BAD STUFF, ALL RIGHT.
THAT'S UH NOT THE REALLY BAD STUFF.
THE REALLY BAD STUFF IS THE UH STORM. IT'S NOT JUST A STORM ANY MORE.
AND UH THIS IS A PRETTY OLD BUILDING.
GEORGE, WHAT ARE YOU TRYING TO SAY?

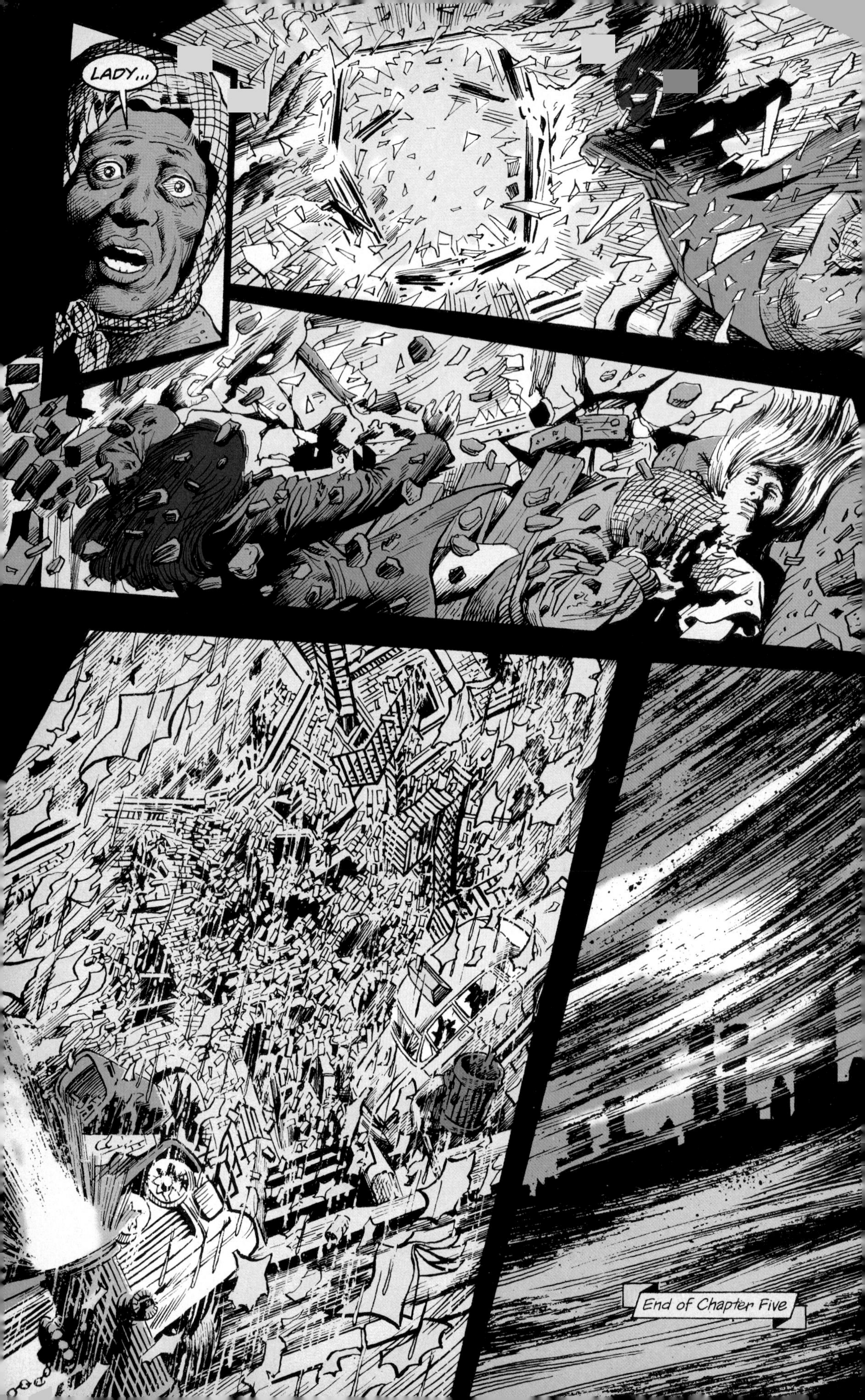
LADY...
End of Chapter Five

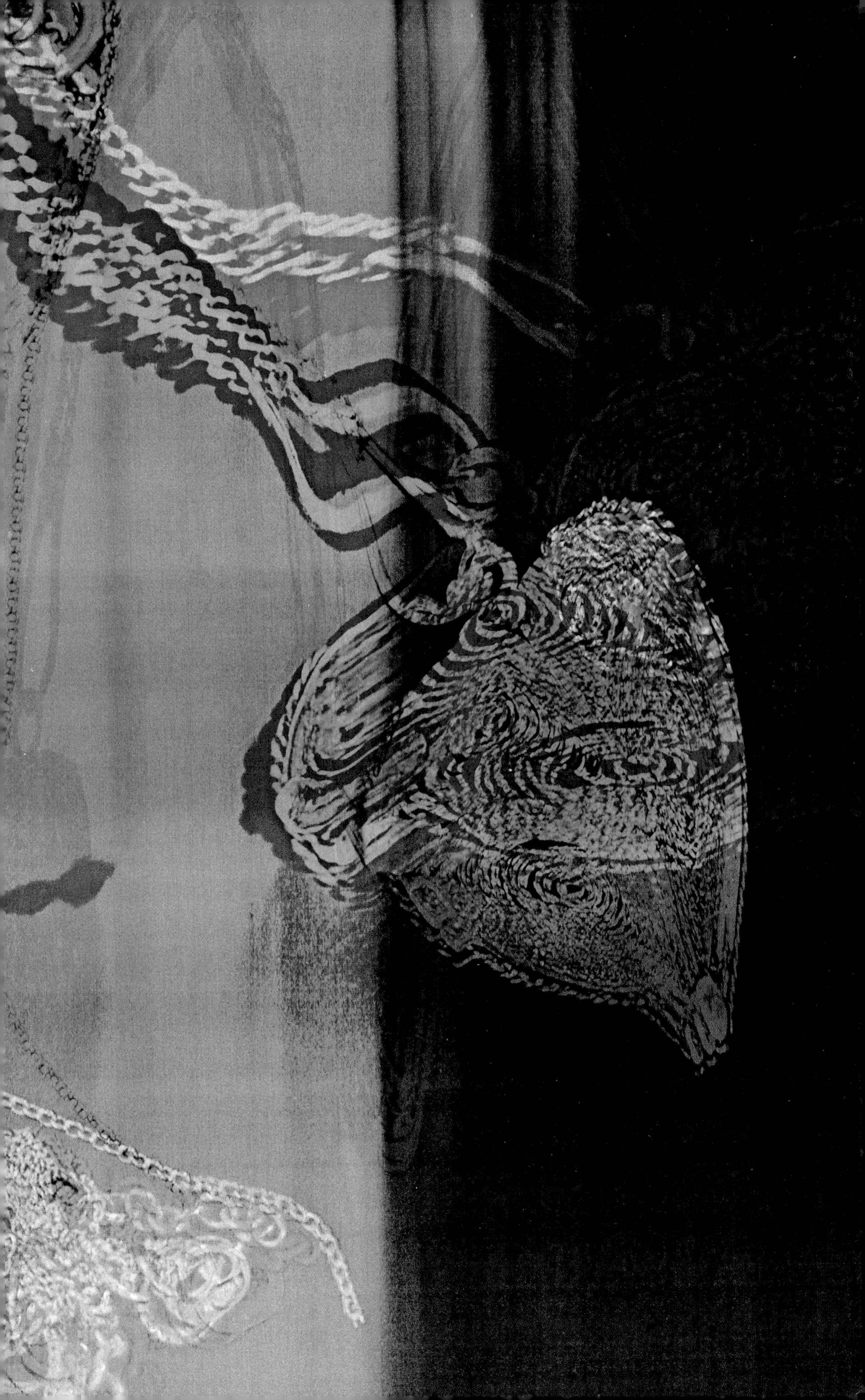

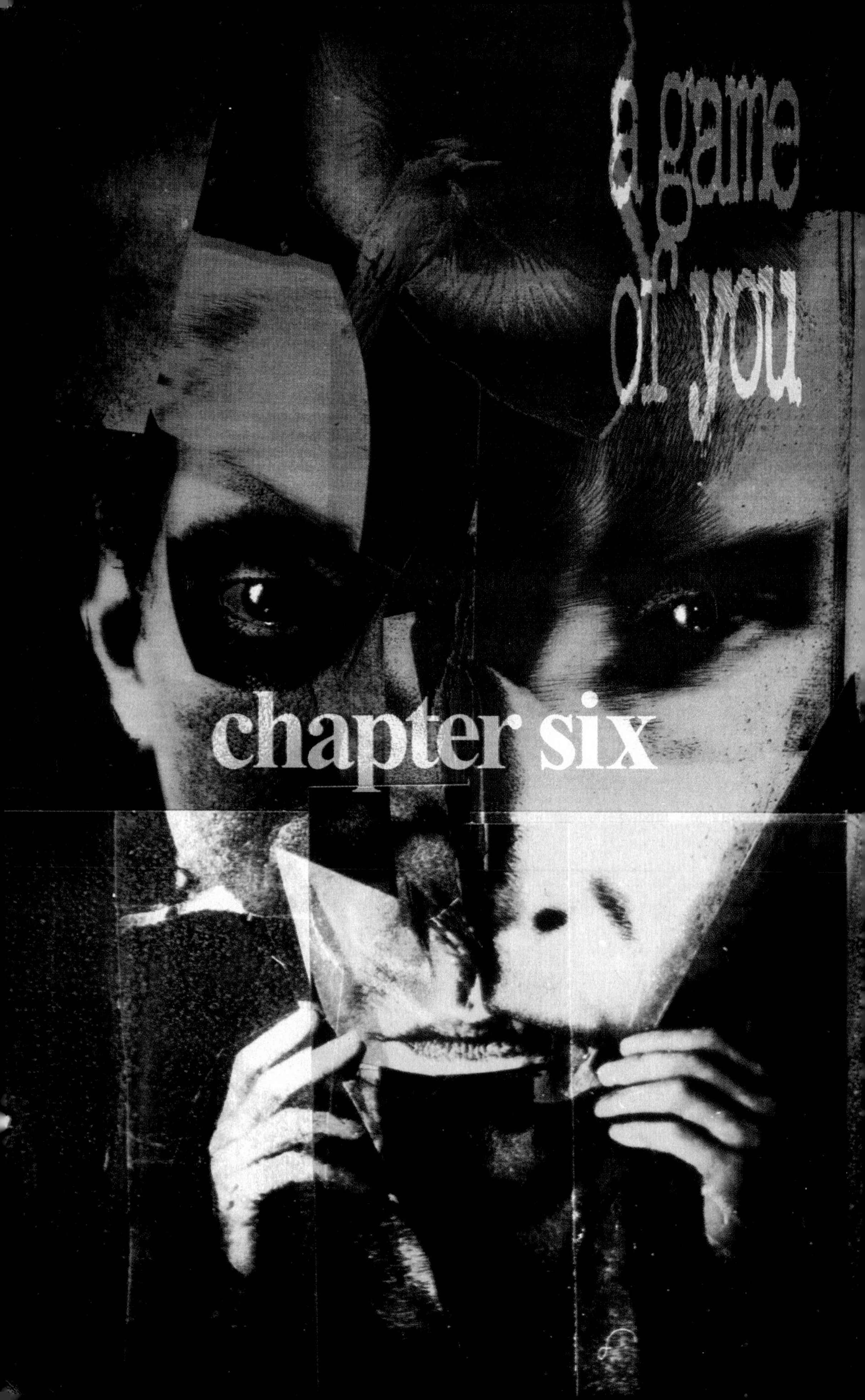
a game
of you
chapter six

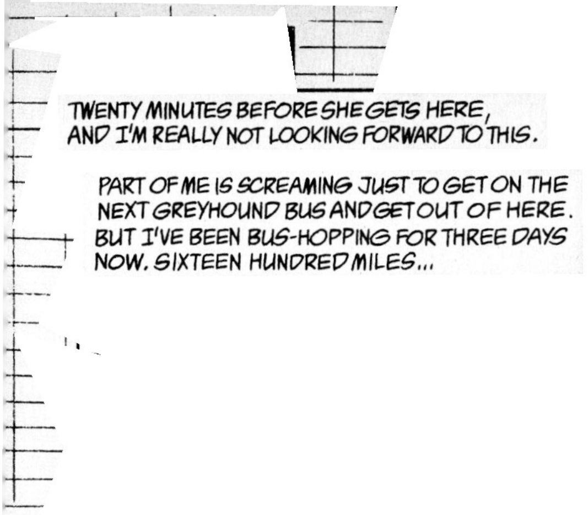
TWENTY MINUTES BEFORE SHE GETS HERE, AND I'M REALLY NOT LOOKING FORWARD TO THIS.
PART OF ME IS SCREAMING JUST TO GET ON THE NEXT GREYHOUND BUS AND GET OUT OF HERE. BUT I'VE BEEN BUS-HOPPING FOR THREE DAYS NOW. SIXTEEN HUNDRED MILES...

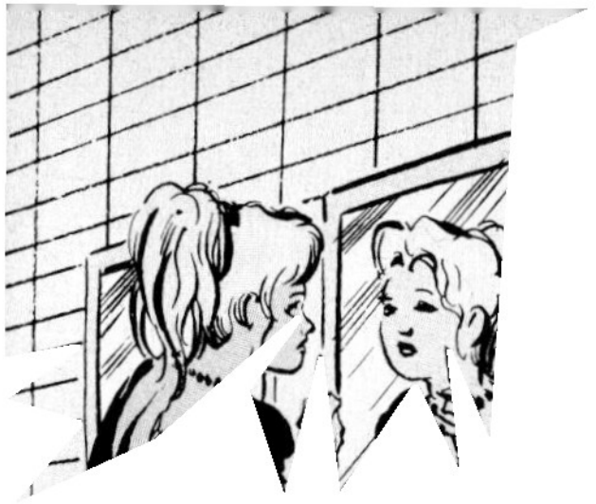

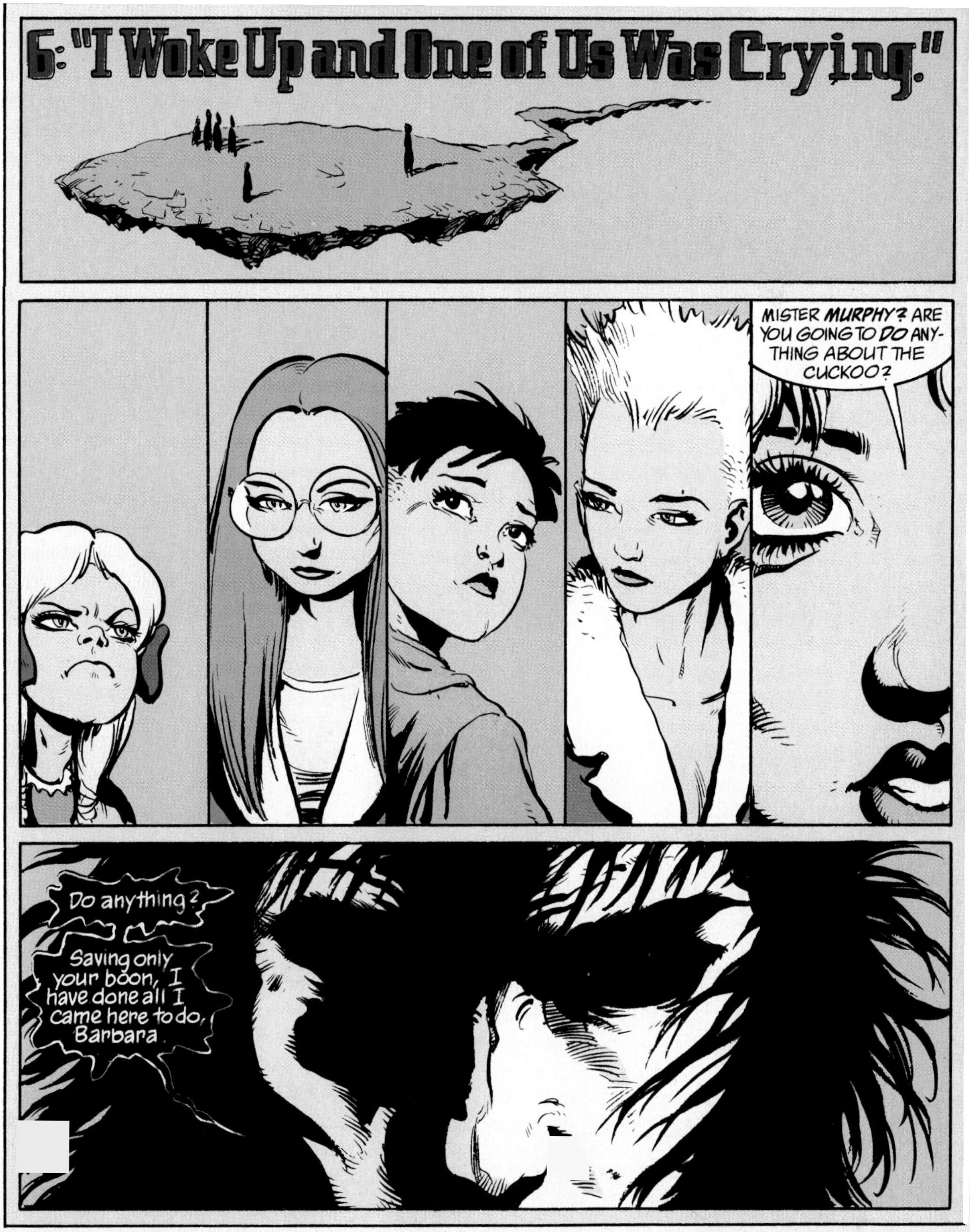
6: "I Woke Up and One of Us Was Crying."
MISTER MURPHY? ARE YOU GOING TO DO ANYTHING ABOUT THE CUCKOO?
Do anything?
Saving only your boon, I have done all I came here to do, Barbara.

BUT SHE STILL HAS TO BE *STOPPED*.

WHY?

WELL, SHE'S *DANGEROUS*. SHE'S *EVIL*.

Dangerous? Perhaps.

But evil? She acts according to her nature.

Is that evil?

LISTEN. SHE WAS GOING TO *KILL ME*.

And your Thessalian friend wanted to kill her. Should I kill Thessaly for you, also?

DON'T PUSH YOUR LUCK, DREAM KING.

I DON'T.

I, UH, I THINK HE WAS JOKING, THESS.

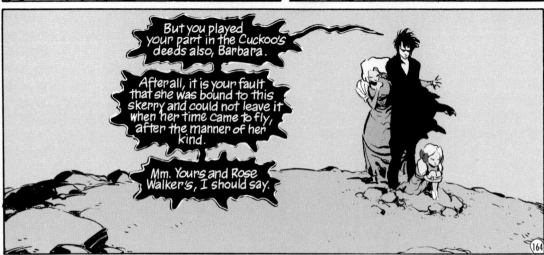

But you played your part in the Cuckoo's deeds also, Barbara.

Afterall, it is your fault that she was bound to this skerry and could not leave it when her time came to fly, after the manner of her kind.

Mm. Yours and Rose Walker's, I should say.

164

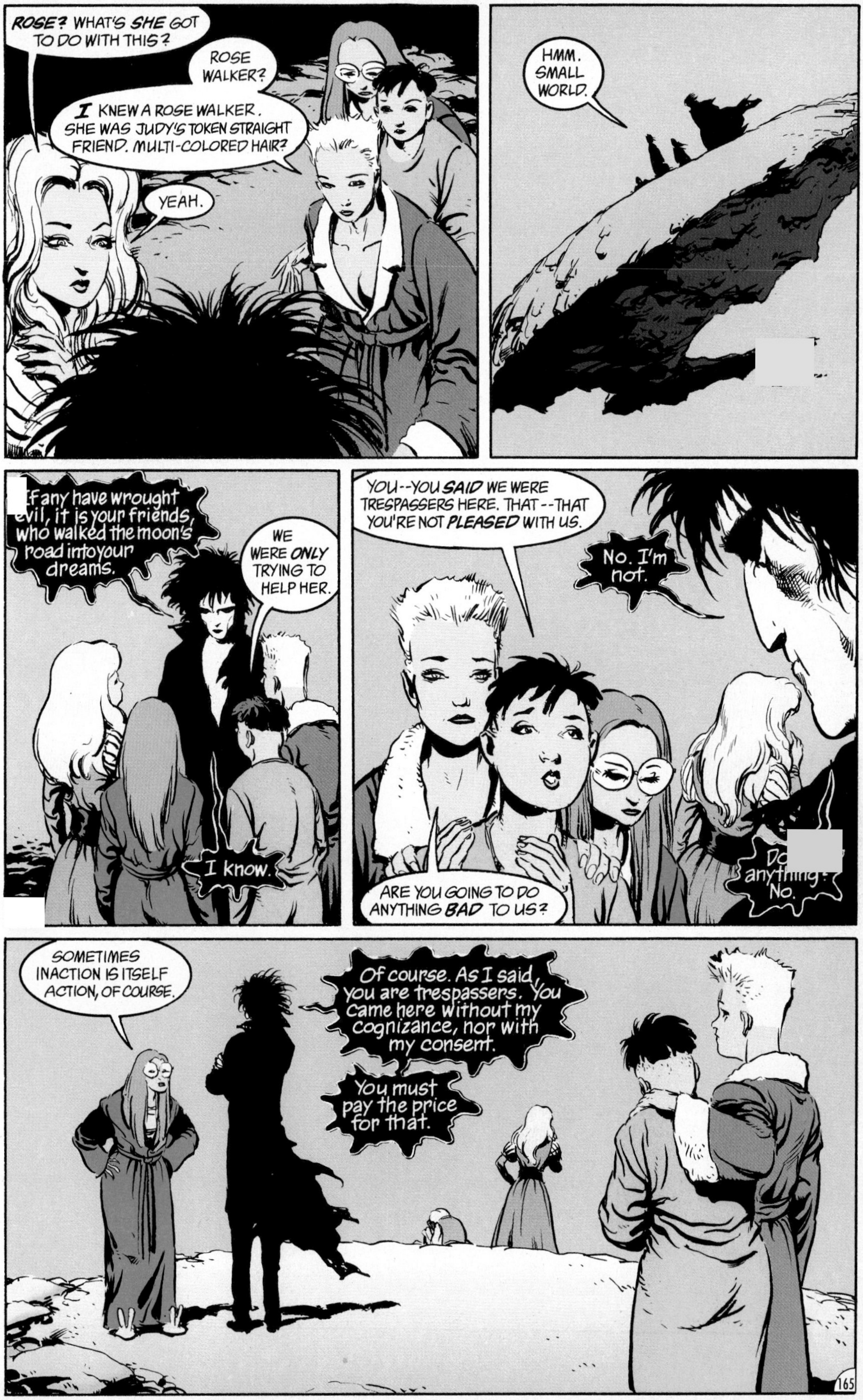
ROSE? WHAT'S SHE GOT TO DO WITH THIS?
ROSE WALKER?
I KNEW A ROSE WALKER. SHE WAS JUDY'S TOKEN STRAIGHT FRIEND. MULTI-COLORED HAIR?
YEAH.
HMM. SMALL WORLD.
If any have wrought evil, it is your friends, who walked the moon's road into your dreams.
WE WERE ONLY TRYING TO HELP HER.
I know.
YOU--YOU SAID WE WERE TRESPASSERS HERE. THAT--THAT YOU'RE NOT PLEASED WITH US.
No. I'm not.
ARE YOU GOING TO DO ANYTHING BAD TO US?
Do anything? No.
SOMETIMES INACTION IS ITSELF ACTION, OF COURSE.
Of course. As I said, you are trespassers. You came here without my cognizance, nor with my consent.
You must pay the price for that.

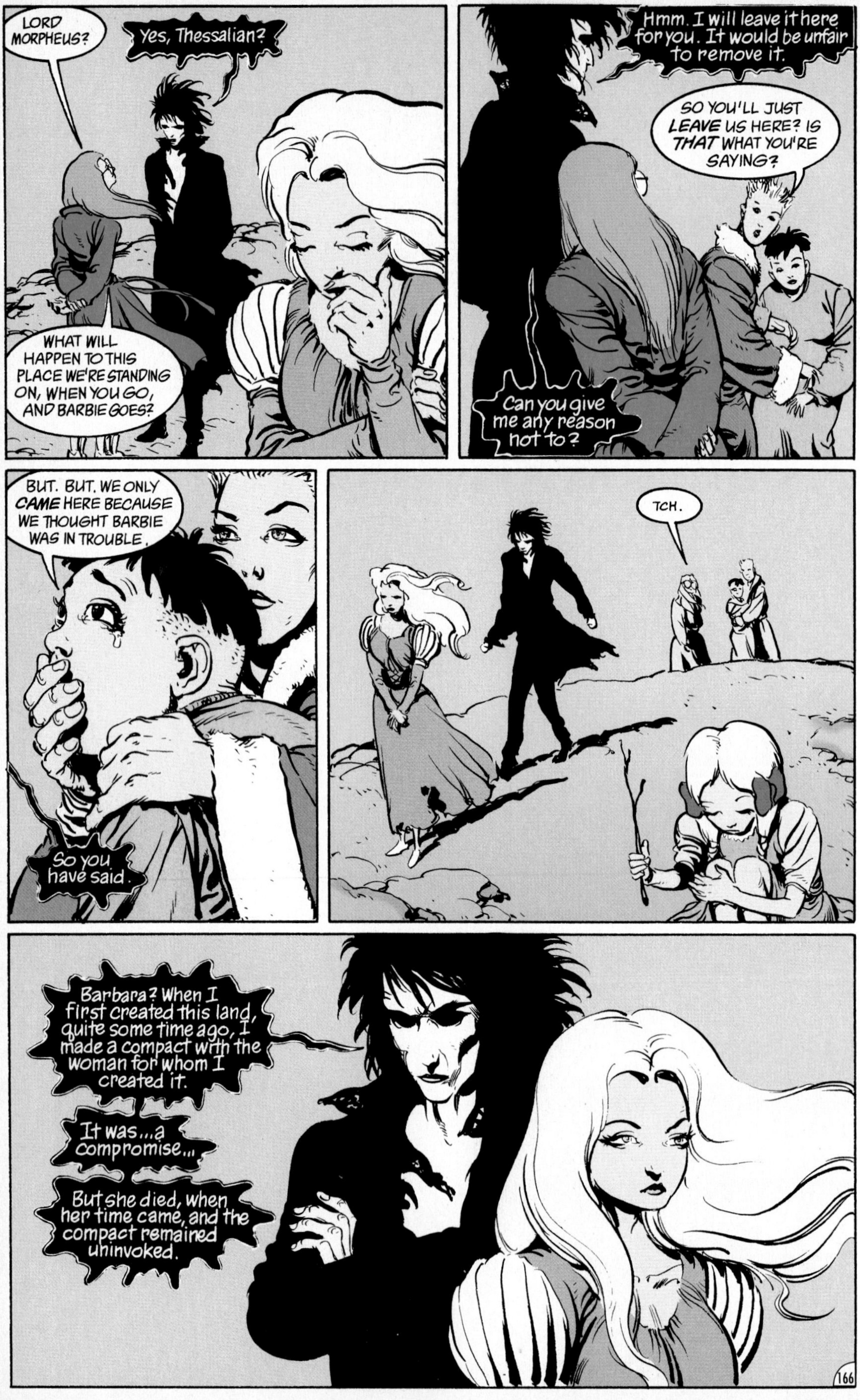
LORD MORPHEUS?
Yes, Thessalian?
WHAT WILL HAPPEN TO THIS PLACE WE'RE STANDING ON, WHEN YOU GO, AND BARBIE GOES?
Hmm. I will leave it here for you. It would be unfair to remove it.
SO YOU'LL JUST LEAVE US HERE? IS THAT WHAT YOU'RE SAYING?
Can you give me any reason not to?
BUT. BUT. WE ONLY CAME HERE BECAUSE WE THOUGHT BARBIE WAS IN TROUBLE.
So you have said.
TCH.
Barbara? When I first created this land, quite some time ago, I made a compact with the woman for whom I created it.
It was...a compromise...
But she died, when her time came, and the compact remained uninvoked.

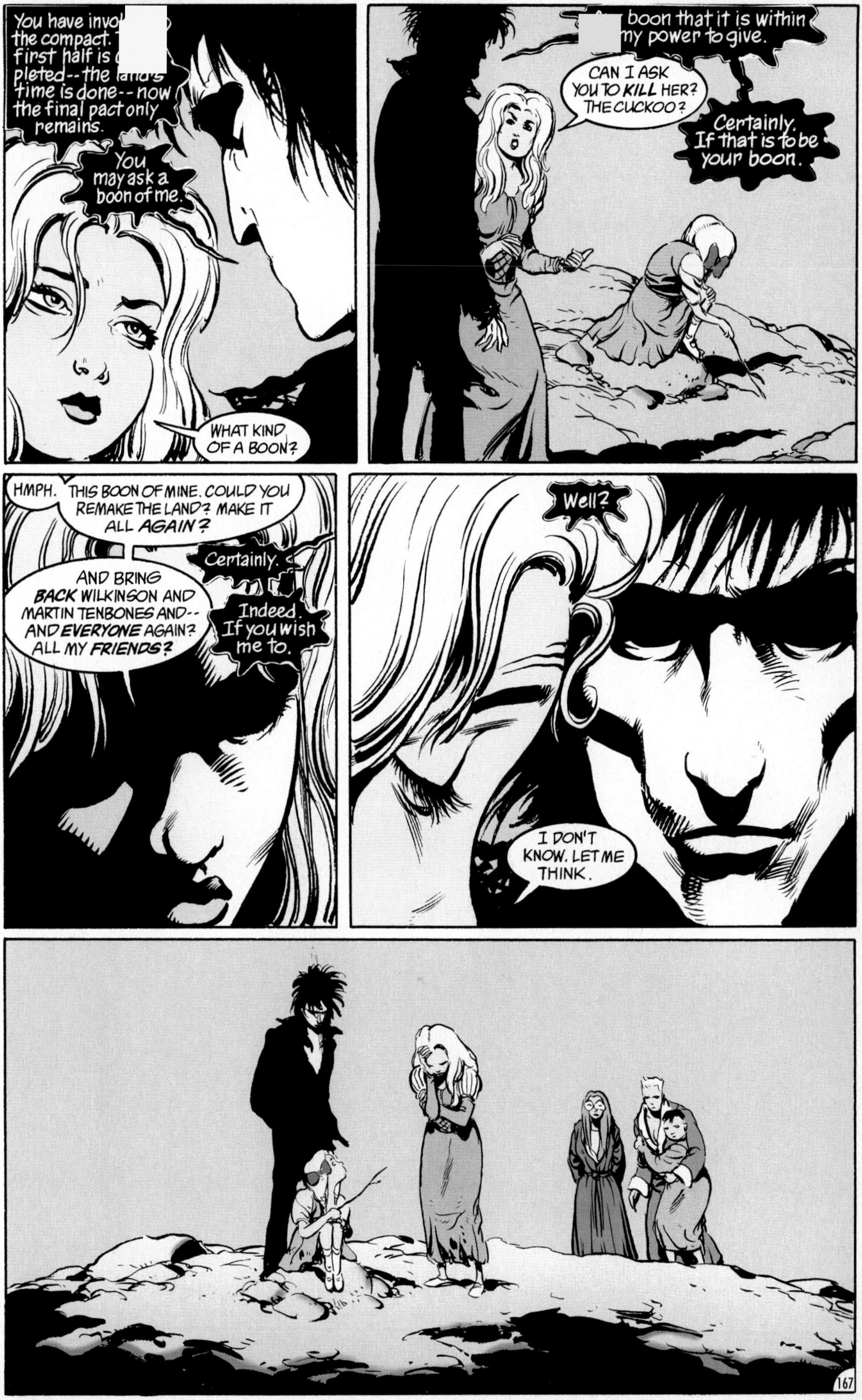

You have invo
the compact.
first half is
pleted--the land's
time is done--now
the final pact only
remains.
You may ask a boon of me.
WHAT KIND OF A BOON?
boon that it is within
my power to give.
CAN I ASK YOU TO KILL HER? THE CUCKOO?
Certainly. If that is to be your boon.
HMPH.
THIS BOON OF MINE. COULD YOU REMAKE THE LAND? MAKE IT ALL AGAIN?
Certainly.
AND BRING BACK WILKINSON AND MARTIN TENBONES AND--AND EVERYONE AGAIN? ALL MY FRIENDS?
Indeed. If you wish me to.
Well?
I DON'T KNOW. LET ME THINK.

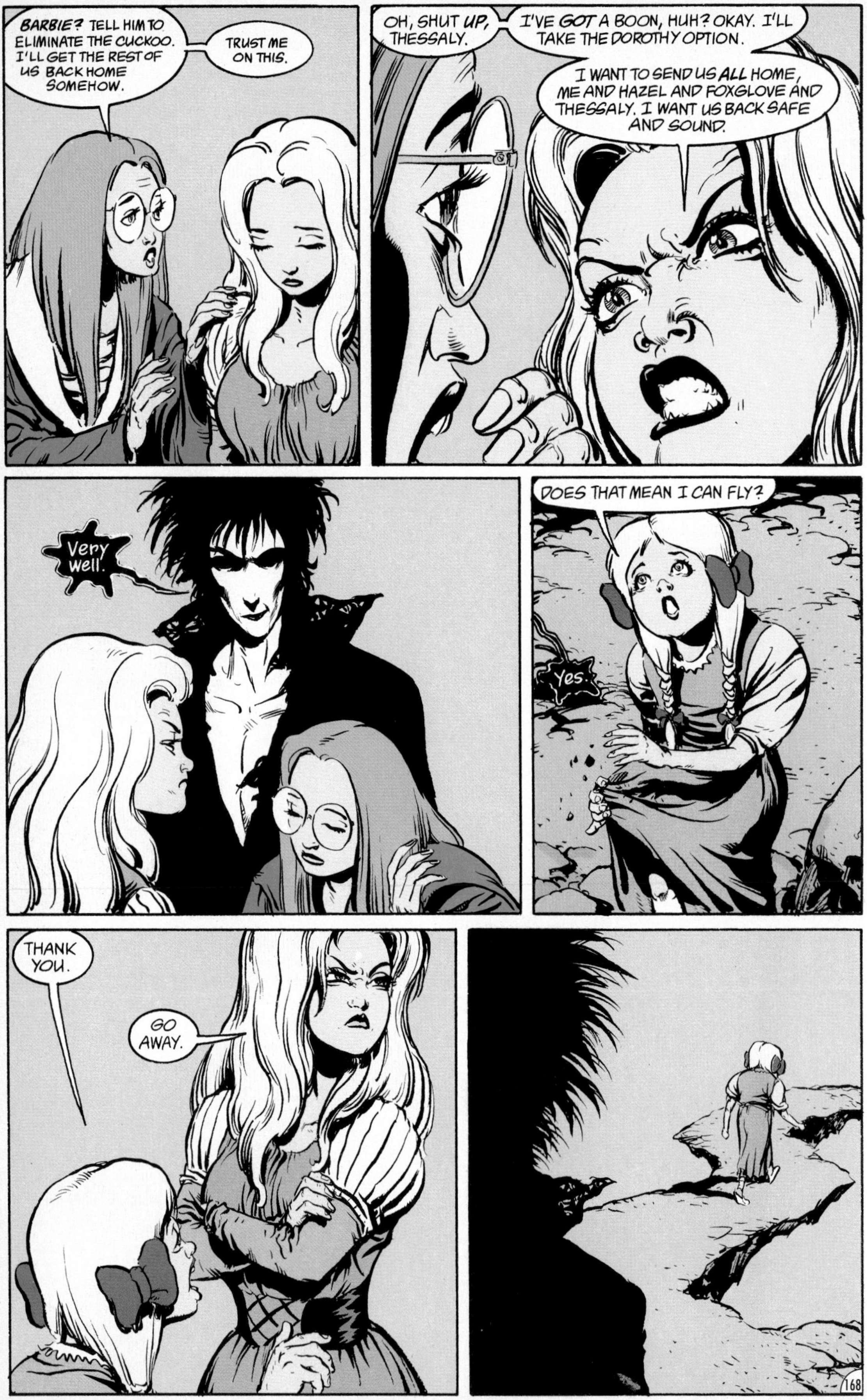
BARBIE? TELL HIM TO ELIMINATE THE CUCKOO. I'LL GET THE REST OF US BACK HOME SOMEHOW.
TRUST ME ON THIS.
OH, SHUT UP, THESSALY.
I'VE GOT A BOON, HUH? OKAY. I'LL TAKE THE DOROTHY OPTION.
I WANT TO SEND US ALL HOME, ME AND HAZEL AND FOXGLOVE AND THESSALY. I WANT US BACK SAFE AND SOUND.
Very well.
DOES THAT MEAN I CAN FLY?
Yes.
THANK YOU.
GO AWAY.

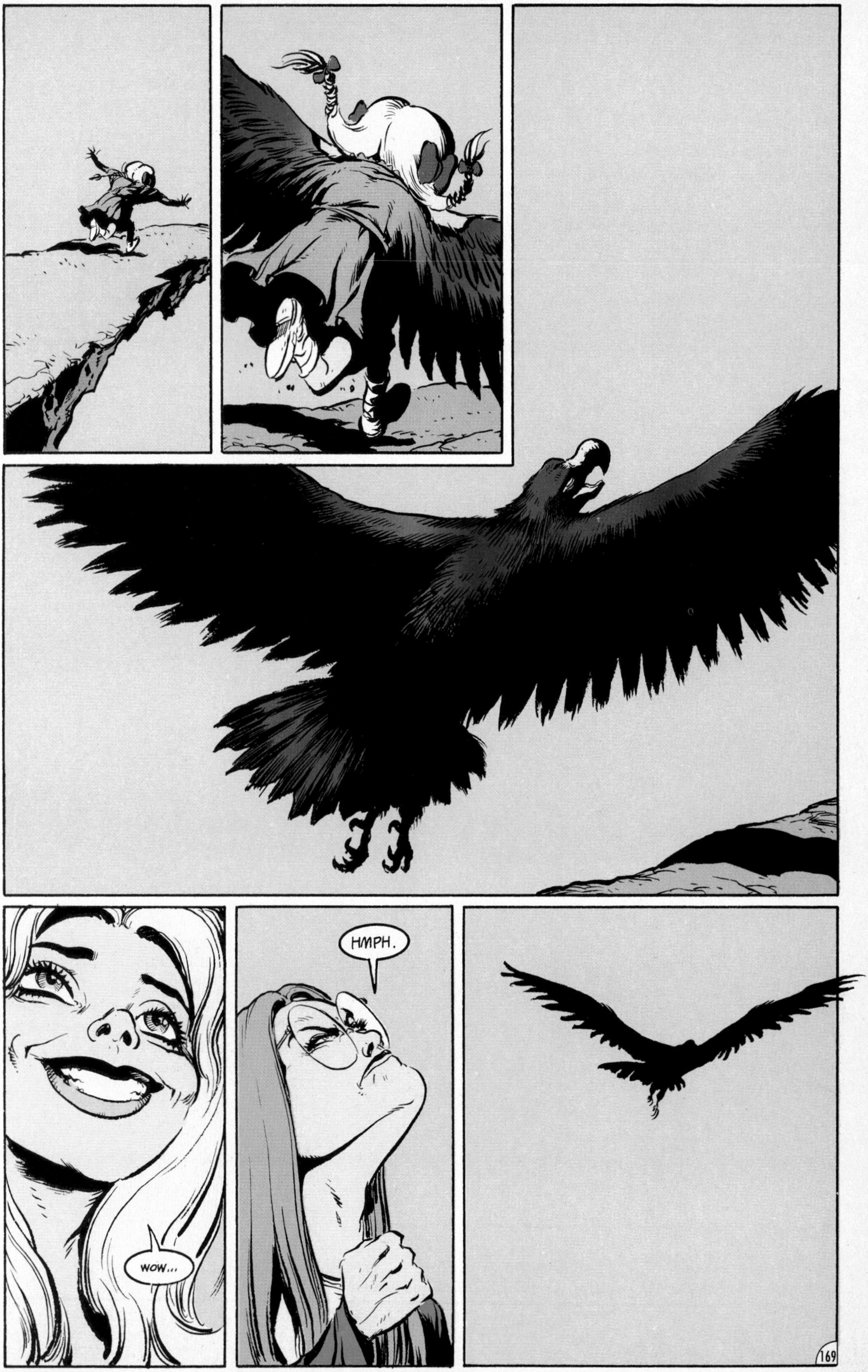
WOW...
HMPH.

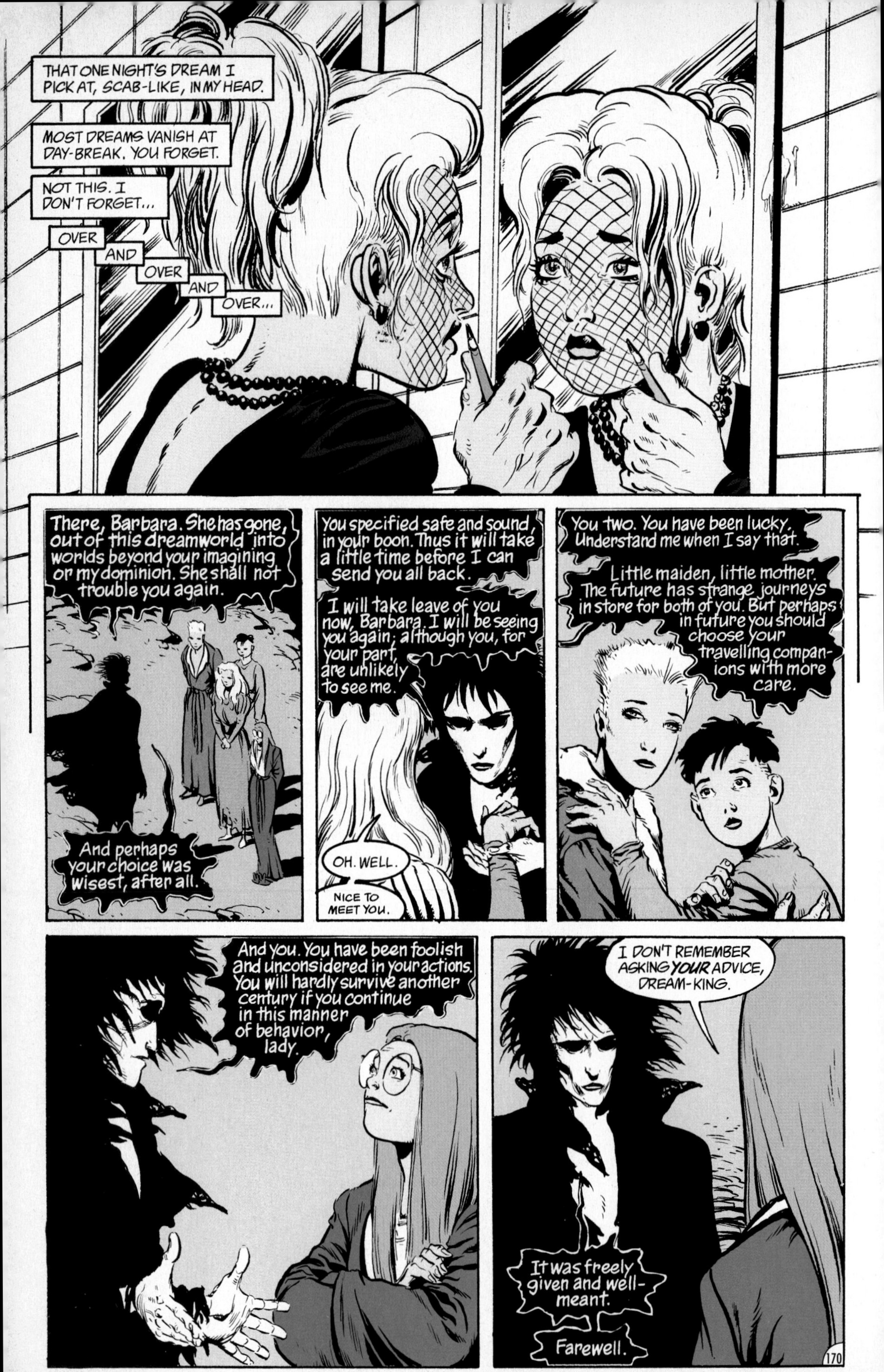
THAT ONE NIGHT'S DREAM I PICK AT, SCAB-LIKE, IN MY HEAD.
MOST DREAMS VANISH AT DAY-BREAK. YOU FORGET.
NOT THIS. I DON'T FORGET...
OVER
AND
OVER
AND
OVER...
There, Barbara. She has gone, out of this dreamworld into worlds beyond your imagining or my dominion. She shall not trouble you again.
And perhaps your choice was wisest, after all.
You specified safe and sound, in your boon. Thus it will take a little time before I can send you all back.
I will take leave of you now, Barbara. I will be seeing you again; although you, for your part, are unlikely to see me.
OH. WELL.
NICE TO MEET YOU.
You two. You have been lucky. Understand me when I say that.
Little maiden, little mother. The future has strange journeys in store for both of you. But perhaps in future you should choose your travelling companions with more care.
And you. You have been foolish and unconsidered in your actions. You will hardly survive another century if you continue in this manner of behavior, lady.
I DON'T REMEMBER ASKING YOUR ADVICE, DREAM-KING.
It was freely given and well-meant.
Farewell.

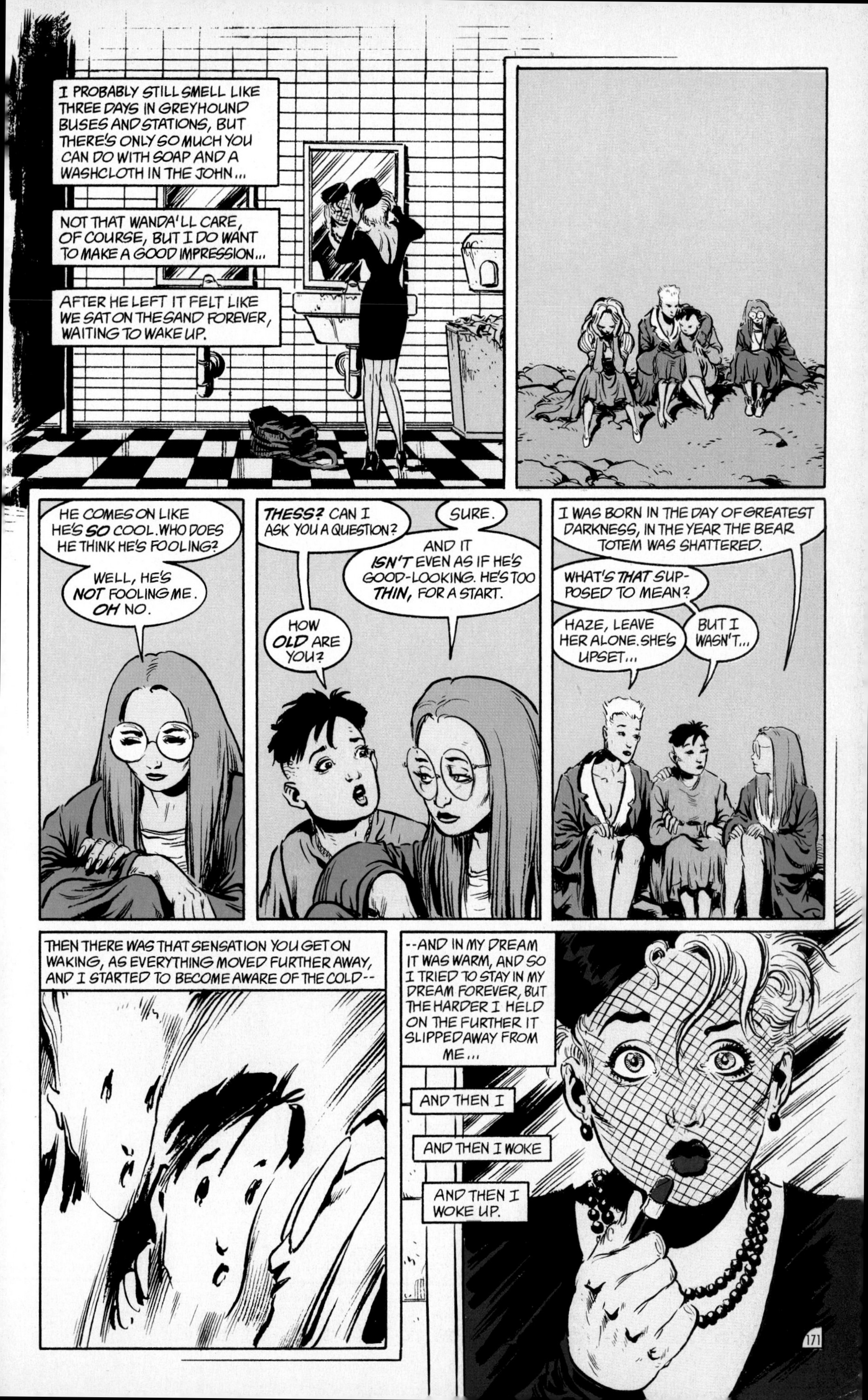
I PROBABLY STILL SMELL LIKE THREE DAYS IN GREYHOUND BUSES AND STATIONS, BUT THERE'S ONLY SO MUCH YOU CAN DO WITH SOAP AND A WASHCLOTH IN THE JOHN...
NOT THAT WANDA'LL CARE, OF COURSE, BUT I DO WANT TO MAKE A GOOD IMPRESSION...
AFTER HE LEFT IT FELT LIKE WE SAT ON THE SAND FOREVER, WAITING TO WAKE UP.
HE COMES ON LIKE HE'S SO COOL. WHO DOES HE THINK HE'S FOOLING?
WELL, HE'S NOT FOOLING ME. OH NO.
THESS? CAN I ASK YOU A QUESTION?
SURE.
AND IT ISN'T EVEN AS IF HE'S GOOD-LOOKING. HE'S TOO THIN, FOR A START.
HOW OLD ARE YOU?
I WAS BORN IN THE DAY OF GREATEST DARKNESS, IN THE YEAR THE BEAR TOTEM WAS SHATTERED.
WHAT'S THAT SUPPOSED TO MEAN?
HAZE, LEAVE HER ALONE. SHE'S UPSET...
BUT I WASN'T...
THEN THERE WAS THAT SENSATION YOU GET ON WAKING, AS EVERYTHING MOVED FURTHER AWAY, AND I STARTED TO BECOME AWARE OF THE COLD--
--AND IN MY DREAM IT WAS WARM, AND SO I TRIED TO STAY IN MY DREAM FOREVER, BUT THE HARDER I HELD ON THE FURTHER IT SLIPPED AWAY FROM ME...
AND THEN I
AND THEN I WOKE
AND THEN I WOKE UP.

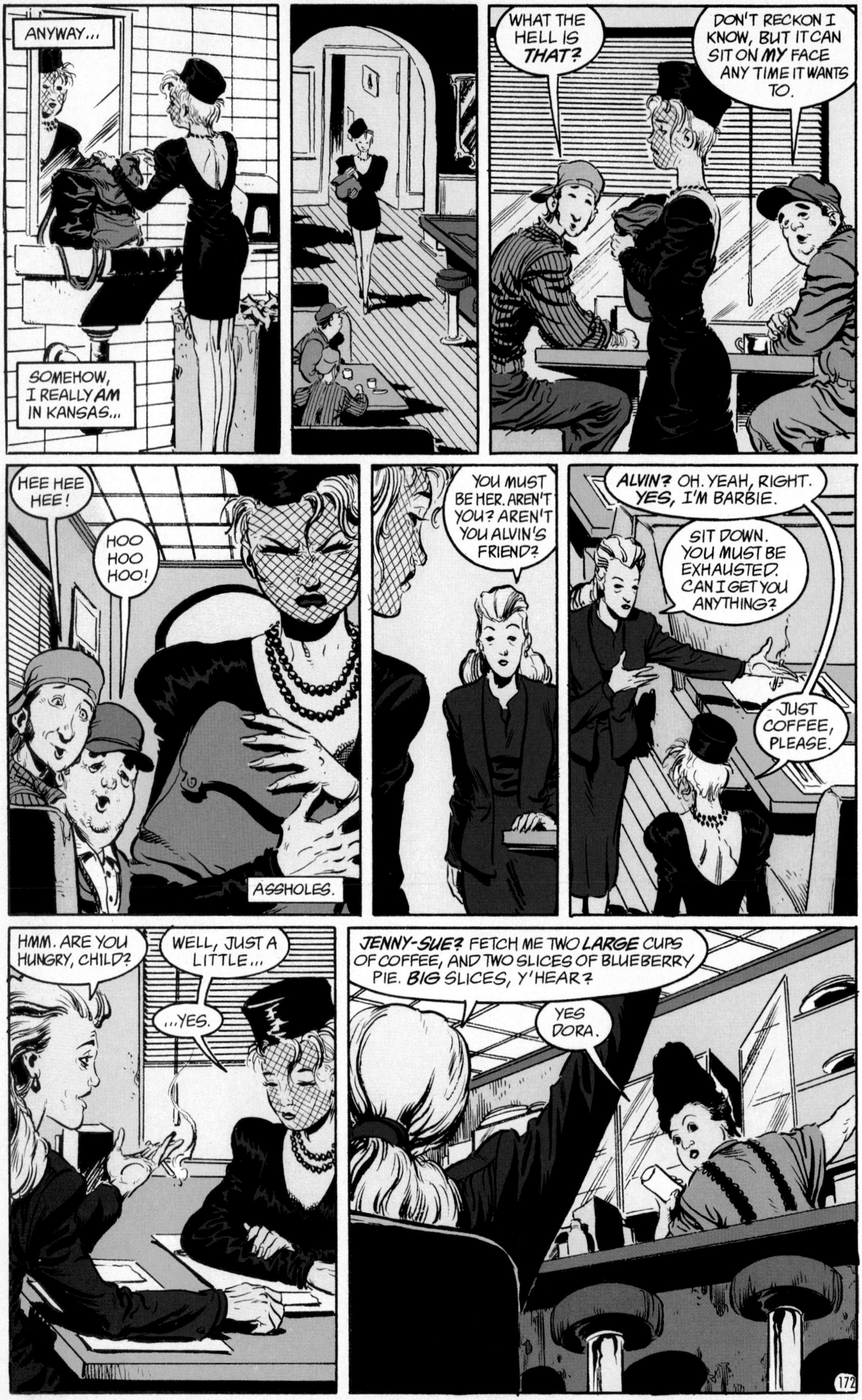
ANYWAY...
SOMEHOW, I REALLY AM IN KANSAS...
WHAT THE HELL IS THAT?
DON'T RECKON I KNOW, BUT IT CAN SIT ON MY FACE ANY TIME IT WANTS TO.
HEE HEE HEE!
HOO HOO HOO!
ASSHOLES.
YOU MUST BE HER. AREN'T YOU? AREN'T YOU ALVIN'S FRIEND?
ALVIN? OH. YEAH, RIGHT. YES, I'M BARBIE.
SIT DOWN. YOU MUST BE EXHAUSTED. CAN I GET YOU ANYTHING?
JUST COFFEE, PLEASE.
HMM. ARE YOU HUNGRY, CHILD?
WELL, JUST A LITTLE...
...YES.
JENNY-SUE? FETCH ME TWO LARGE CUPS OF COFFEE, AND TWO SLICES OF BLUEBERRY PIE. BIG SLICES, Y'HEAR?
YES DORA.
172

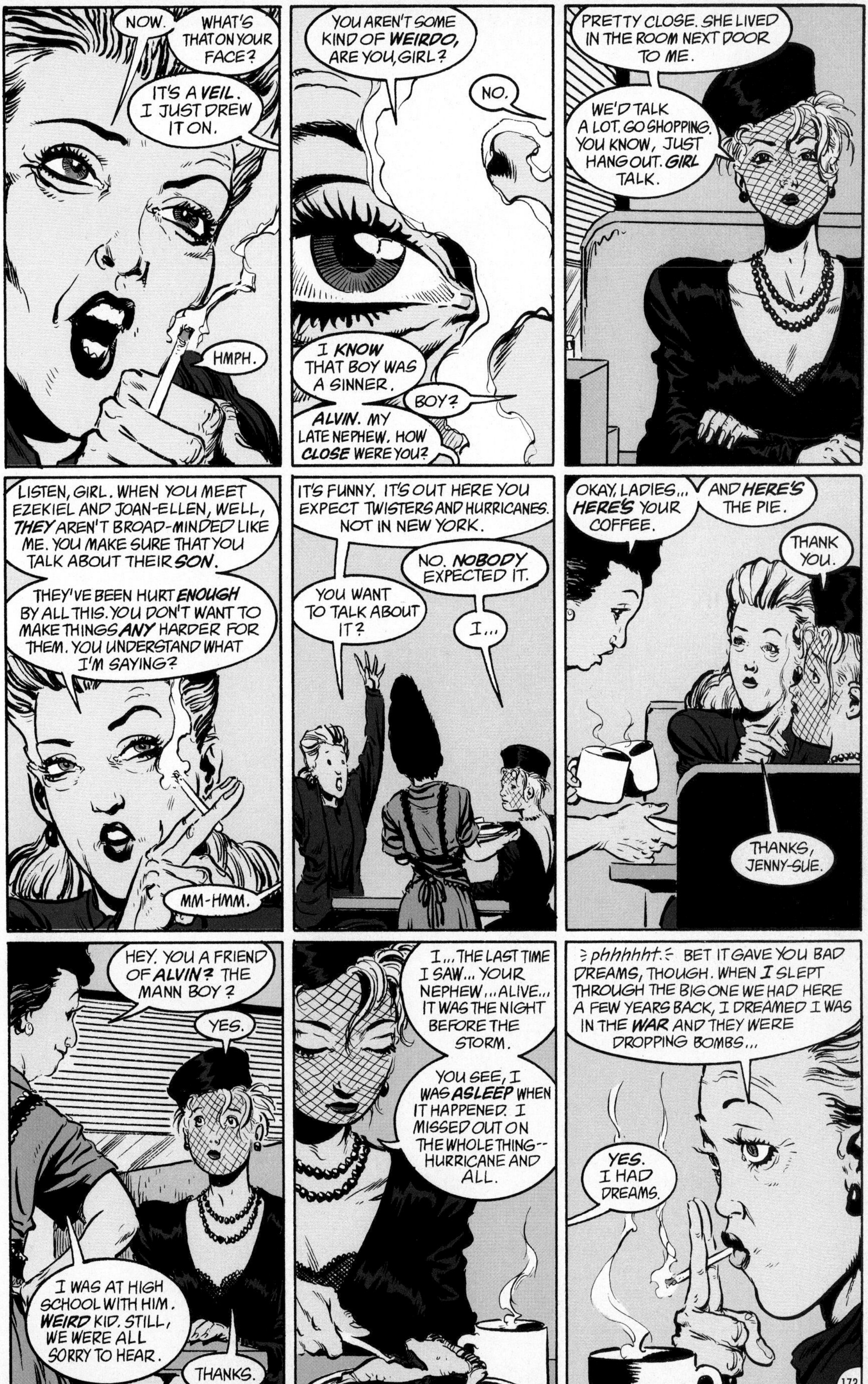
NOW.
WHAT'S THAT ON YOUR FACE?
IT'S A VEIL. I JUST DREW IT ON.
HMPH.
YOU AREN'T SOME KIND OF WEIRDO, ARE YOU, GIRL?
NO.
I KNOW THAT BOY WAS A SINNER.
BOY?
ALVIN. MY LATE NEPHEW. HOW CLOSE WERE YOU?
PRETTY CLOSE. SHE LIVED IN THE ROOM NEXT DOOR TO ME.
WE'D TALK A LOT. GO SHOPPING. YOU KNOW, JUST HANG OUT. GIRL TALK.
LISTEN, GIRL. WHEN YOU MEET EZEKIEL AND JOAN-ELLEN, WELL, THEY AREN'T BROAD-MINDED LIKE ME. YOU MAKE SURE THAT YOU TALK ABOUT THEIR SON.
THEY'VE BEEN HURT ENOUGH BY ALL THIS. YOU DON'T WANT TO MAKE THINGS ANY HARDER FOR THEM. YOU UNDERSTAND WHAT I'M SAYING?
MM-HMM.
IT'S FUNNY. IT'S OUT HERE YOU EXPECT TWISTERS AND HURRICANES. NOT IN NEW YORK.
NO. NOBODY EXPECTED IT.
YOU WANT TO TALK ABOUT IT?
I...
OKAY, LADIES... HERE'S YOUR COFFEE.
AND HERE'S THE PIE.
THANK YOU.
THANKS, JENNY-SUE.
HEY. YOU A FRIEND OF ALVIN? THE MANN BOY?
YES.
I WAS AT HIGH SCHOOL WITH HIM. WEIRD KID. STILL, WE WERE ALL SORRY TO HEAR.
THANKS.
I... THE LAST TIME I SAW... YOUR NEPHEW... ALIVE... IT WAS THE NIGHT BEFORE THE STORM.
YOU SEE, I WAS ASLEEP WHEN IT HAPPENED. I MISSED OUT ON THE WHOLE THING-- HURRICANE AND ALL.
phhhhht. BET IT GAVE YOU BAD DREAMS, THOUGH. WHEN I SLEPT THROUGH THE BIG ONE WE HAD HERE A FEW YEARS BACK, I DREAMED I WAS IN THE WAR AND THEY WERE DROPPING BOMBS...
YES. I HAD DREAMS.
173

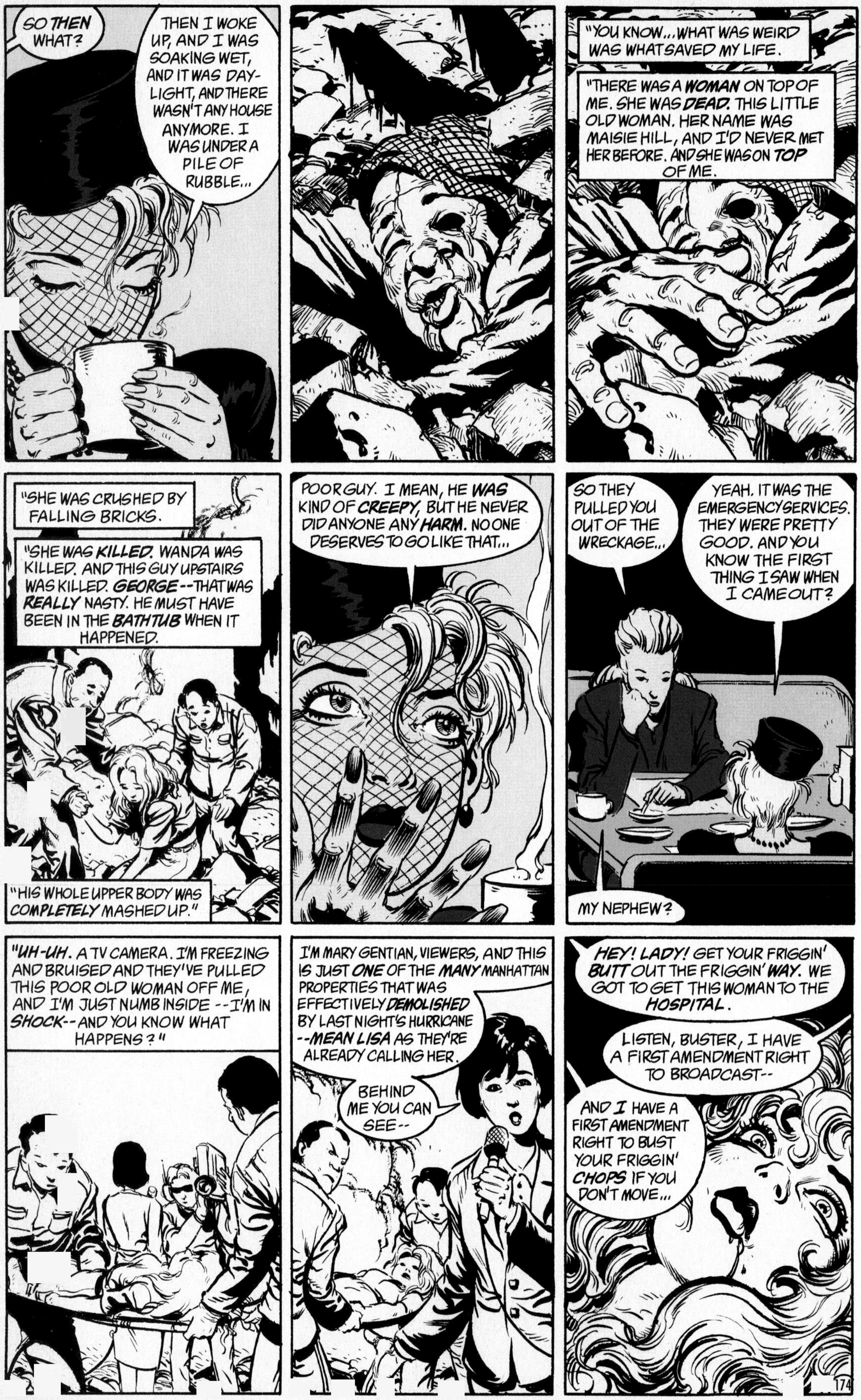
SO THEN WHAT?
THEN I WOKE UP, AND I WAS SOAKING WET, AND IT WAS DAY-LIGHT, AND THERE WASN'T ANY HOUSE ANYMORE. I WAS UNDER A PILE OF RUBBLE...
"YOU KNOW... WHAT WAS WEIRD WAS WHAT SAVED MY LIFE.
"THERE WAS A WOMAN ON TOP OF ME. SHE WAS DEAD. THIS LITTLE OLD WOMAN. HER NAME WAS MAISIE HILL, AND I'D NEVER MET HER BEFORE. AND SHE WAS ON TOP OF ME.
"SHE WAS CRUSHED BY FALLING BRICKS.
"SHE WAS KILLED. WANDA WAS KILLED. AND THIS GUY UPSTAIRS WAS KILLED. GEORGE--THAT WAS REALLY NASTY. HE MUST HAVE BEEN IN THE BATHTUB WHEN IT HAPPENED.
"HIS WHOLE UPPER BODY WAS COMPLETELY MASHED UP."
POOR GUY. I MEAN, HE WAS KIND OF CREEPY, BUT HE NEVER DID ANYONE ANY HARM. NO ONE DESERVES TO GO LIKE THAT...
SO THEY PULLED YOU OUT OF THE WRECKAGE...
YEAH. IT WAS THE EMERGENCY SERVICES. THEY WERE PRETTY GOOD. AND YOU KNOW THE FIRST THING I SAW WHEN I CAME OUT?
MY NEPHEW?
"UH-UH. A TV CAMERA. I'M FREEZING AND BRUISED AND THEY'VE PULLED THIS POOR OLD WOMAN OFF ME, AND I'M JUST NUMB INSIDE --I'M IN SHOCK-- AND YOU KNOW WHAT HAPPENS?"
I'M MARY GENTIAN, VIEWERS, AND THIS IS JUST ONE OF THE MANY MANHATTAN PROPERTIES THAT WAS EFFECTIVELY DEMOLISHED BY LAST NIGHT'S HURRICANE --MEAN LISA AS THEY'RE ALREADY CALLING HER.
BEHIND ME YOU CAN SEE--
HEY! LADY! GET YOUR FRIGGIN' BUTT OUT THE FRIGGIN' WAY. WE GOT TO GET THIS WOMAN TO THE HOSPITAL.
LISTEN, BUSTER, I HAVE A FIRST AMENDMENT RIGHT TO BROADCAST--
AND I HAVE A FIRST AMENDMENT RIGHT TO BUST YOUR FRIGGIN' CHOPS IF YOU DON'T MOVE...

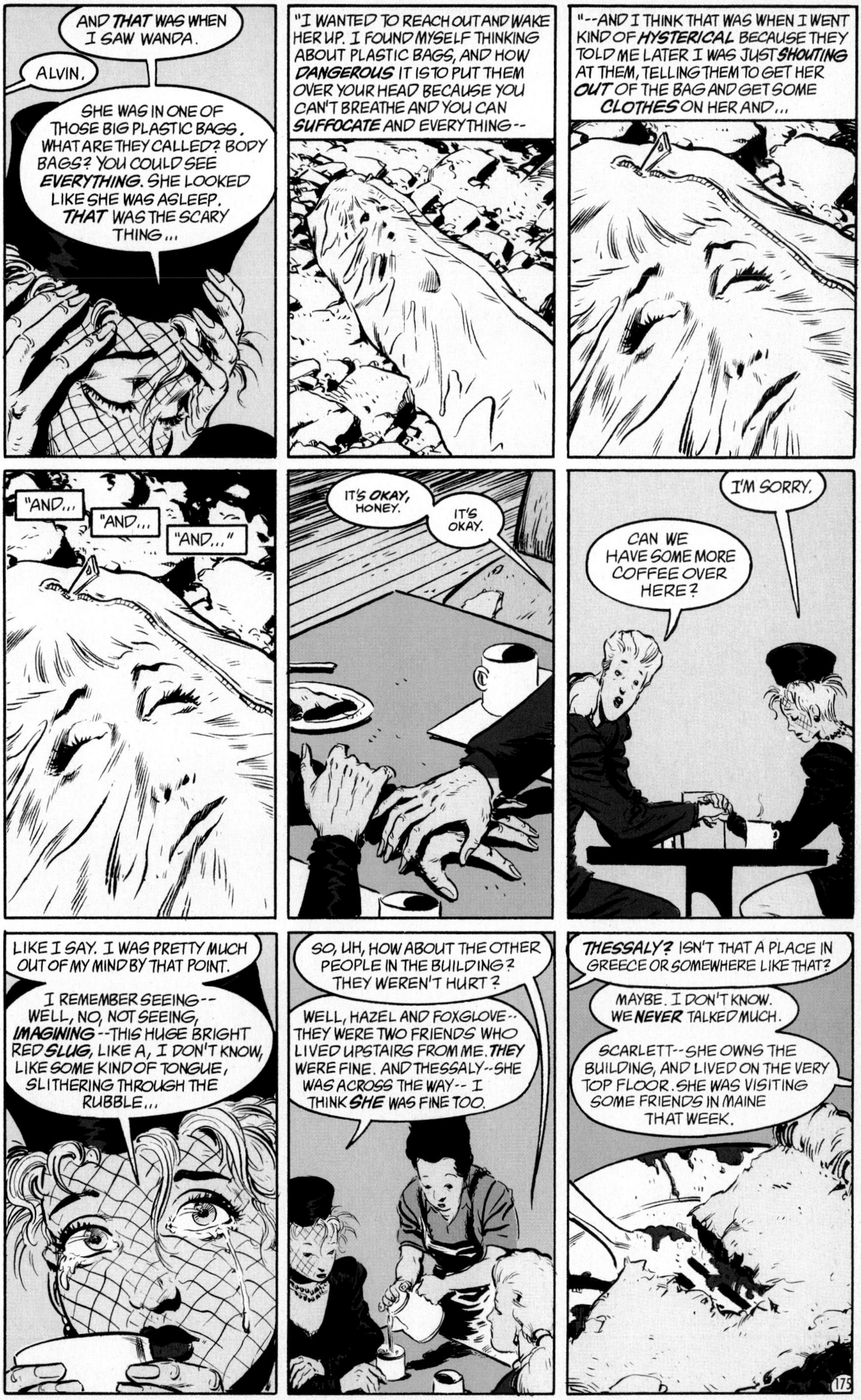

AND THAT WAS WHEN I SAW WANDA.
ALVIN.
SHE WAS IN ONE OF THOSE BIG PLASTIC BAGS. WHAT ARE THEY CALLED? BODY BAGS? YOU COULD SEE EVERYTHING. SHE LOOKED LIKE SHE WAS ASLEEP. THAT WAS THE SCARY THING...
"I WANTED TO REACH OUT AND WAKE HER UP. I FOUND MYSELF THINKING ABOUT PLASTIC BAGS, AND HOW DANGEROUS IT IS TO PUT THEM OVER YOUR HEAD BECAUSE YOU CAN'T BREATHE AND YOU CAN SUFFOCATE AND EVERYTHING--
"--AND I THINK THAT WAS WHEN I WENT KIND OF HYSTERICAL BECAUSE THEY TOLD ME LATER I WAS JUST SHOUTING AT THEM, TELLING THEM TO GET HER OUT OF THE BAG AND GET SOME CLOTHES ON HER AND...
"AND...
"AND...
"AND..."
IT'S OKAY, HONEY.
IT'S OKAY.
I'M SORRY.
CAN WE HAVE SOME MORE COFFEE OVER HERE?
LIKE I SAY. I WAS PRETTY MUCH OUT OF MY MIND BY THAT POINT.
I REMEMBER SEEING-- WELL, NO, NOT SEEING, IMAGINING--THIS HUGE BRIGHT RED SLUG, LIKE A, I DON'T KNOW, LIKE SOME KIND OF TONGUE, SLITHERING THROUGH THE RUBBLE...
SO, UH, HOW ABOUT THE OTHER PEOPLE IN THE BUILDING? THEY WEREN'T HURT?
WELL, HAZEL AND FOXGLOVE-- THEY WERE TWO FRIENDS WHO LIVED UPSTAIRS FROM ME. THEY WERE FINE. AND THESSALY--SHE WAS ACROSS THE WAY-- I THINK SHE WAS FINE TOO.
THESSALY? ISN'T THAT A PLACE IN GREECE OR SOMEWHERE LIKE THAT?
MAYBE. I DON'T KNOW. WE NEVER TALKED MUCH.
SCARLETT--SHE OWNS THE BUILDING, AND LIVED ON THE VERY TOP FLOOR. SHE WAS VISITING SOME FRIENDS IN MAINE THAT WEEK.

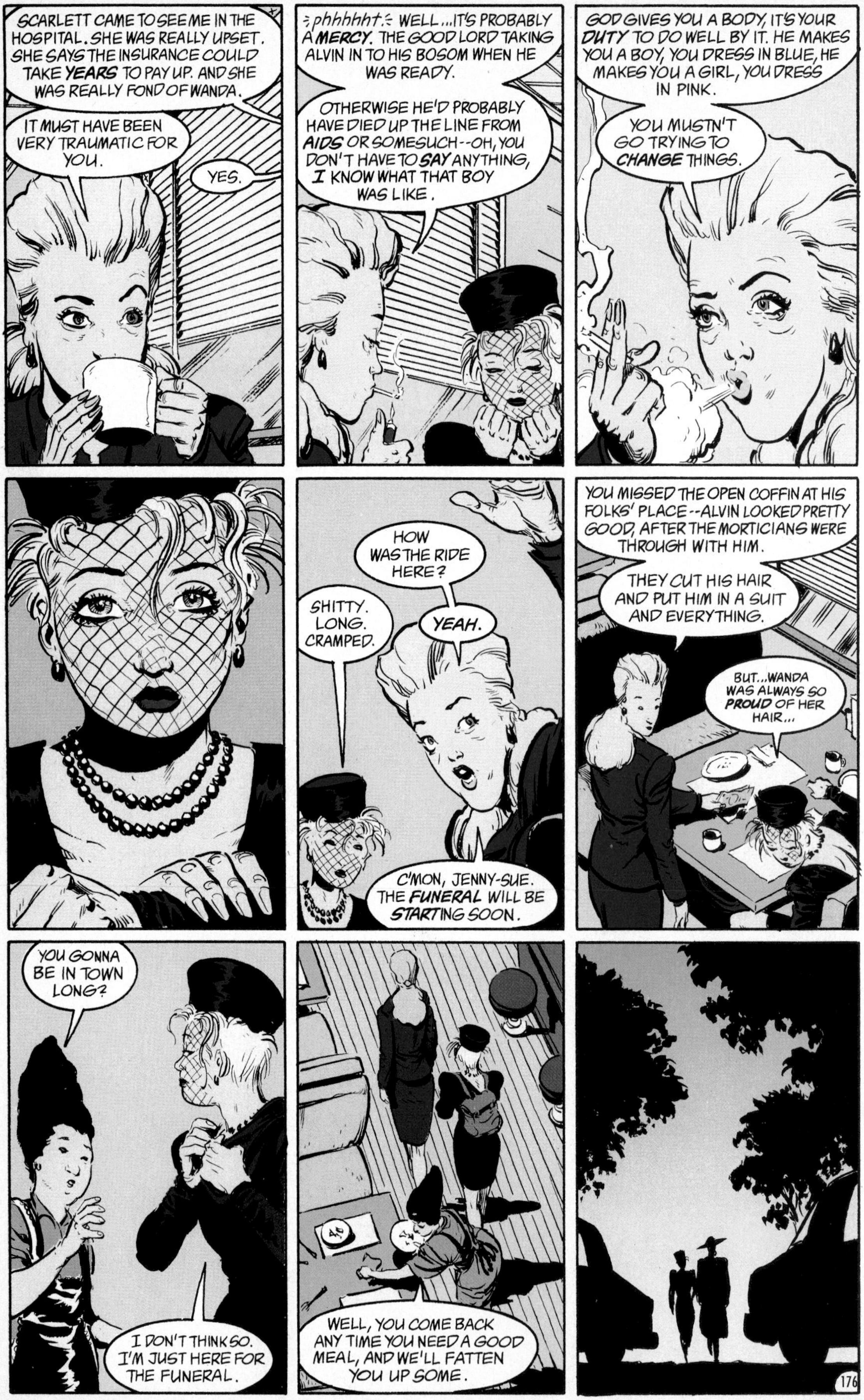
SCARLETT CAME TO SEE ME IN THE HOSPITAL. SHE WAS REALLY UPSET. SHE SAYS THE INSURANCE COULD TAKE YEARS TO PAY UP. AND SHE WAS REALLY FOND OF WANDA.
IT MUST HAVE BEEN VERY TRAUMATIC FOR YOU.
YES.
=phhhhht.= WELL...IT'S PROBABLY A MERCY. THE GOOD LORD TAKING ALVIN IN TO HIS BOSOM WHEN HE WAS READY.
OTHERWISE HE'D PROBABLY HAVE DIED UP THE LINE FROM AIDS OR SOMESUCH--OH, YOU DON'T HAVE TO SAY ANYTHING, I KNOW WHAT THAT BOY WAS LIKE.
GOD GIVES YOU A BODY, IT'S YOUR DUTY TO DO WELL BY IT. HE MAKES YOU A BOY, YOU DRESS IN BLUE, HE MAKES YOU A GIRL, YOU DRESS IN PINK.
YOU MUSTN'T GO TRYING TO CHANGE THINGS.
HOW WAS THE RIDE HERE?
SHITTY. LONG. CRAMPED.
YEAH.
C'MON, JENNY-SUE. THE FUNERAL WILL BE STARTING SOON.
YOU MISSED THE OPEN COFFIN AT HIS FOLKS' PLACE--ALVIN LOOKED PRETTY GOOD, AFTER THE MORTICIANS WERE THROUGH WITH HIM.
THEY CUT HIS HAIR AND PUT HIM IN A SUIT AND EVERYTHING.
BUT...WANDA WAS ALWAYS SO PROUD OF HER HAIR...
YOU GONNA BE IN TOWN LONG?
I DON'T THINK SO. I'M JUST HERE FOR THE FUNERAL.
WELL, YOU COME BACK ANY TIME YOU NEED A GOOD MEAL, AND WE'LL FATTEN YOU UP SOME.

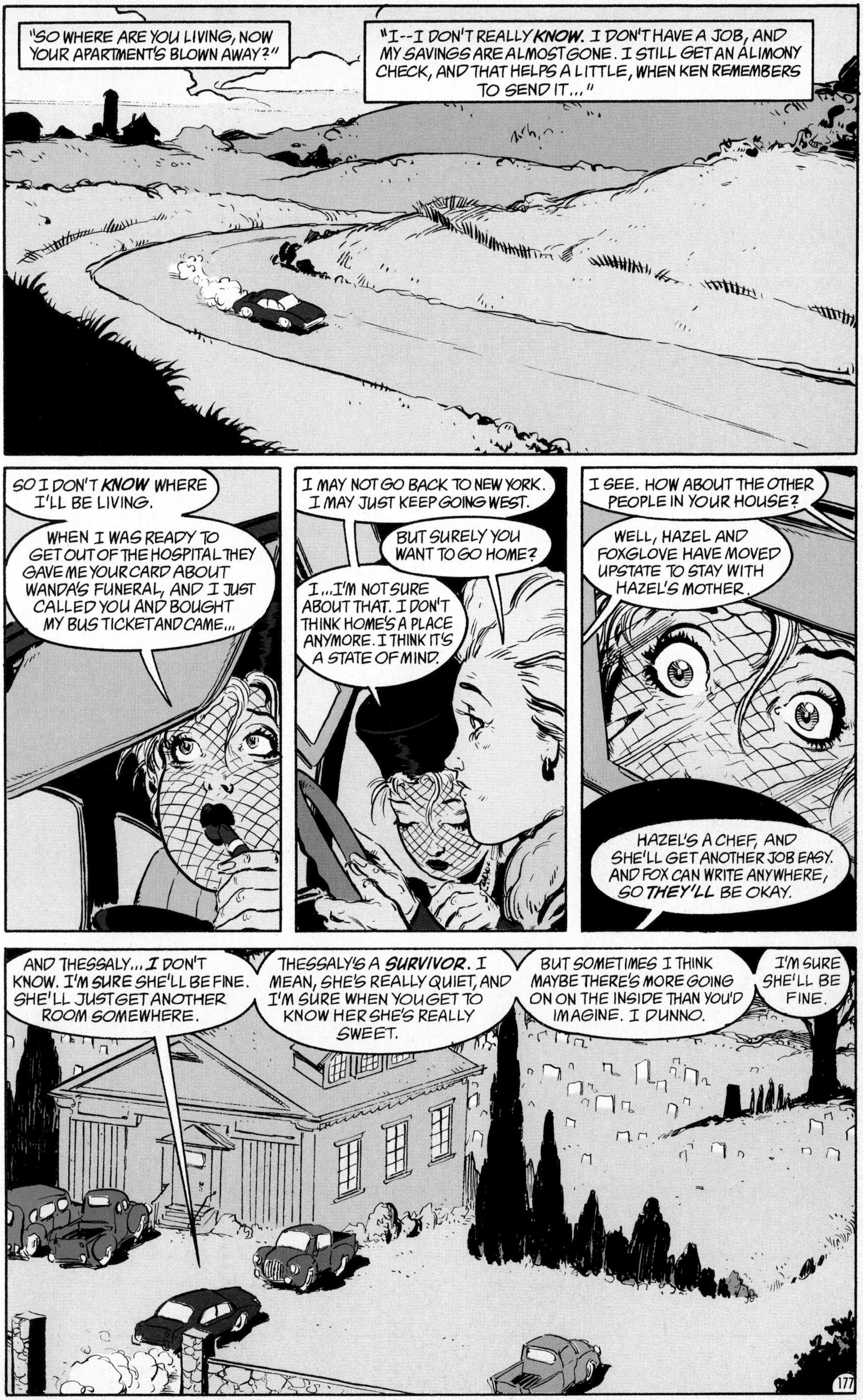
"SO WHERE ARE YOU LIVING, NOW YOUR APARTMENT'S BLOWN AWAY?"
"I--I DON'T REALLY KNOW. I DON'T HAVE A JOB, AND MY SAVINGS ARE ALMOST GONE. I STILL GET AN ALIMONY CHECK, AND THAT HELPS A LITTLE, WHEN KEN REMEMBERS TO SEND IT..."
SO I DON'T KNOW WHERE I'LL BE LIVING.
WHEN I WAS READY TO GET OUT OF THE HOSPITAL THEY GAVE ME YOUR CARD ABOUT WANDA'S FUNERAL, AND I JUST CALLED YOU AND BOUGHT MY BUS TICKET AND CAME...
I MAY NOT GO BACK TO NEW YORK. I MAY JUST KEEP GOING WEST.
BUT SURELY YOU WANT TO GO HOME?
I...I'M NOT SURE ABOUT THAT. I DON'T THINK HOME'S A PLACE ANYMORE. I THINK IT'S A STATE OF MIND.
I SEE. HOW ABOUT THE OTHER PEOPLE IN YOUR HOUSE?
WELL, HAZEL AND FOXGLOVE HAVE MOVED UPSTATE TO STAY WITH HAZEL'S MOTHER.
HAZEL'S A CHEF, AND SHE'LL GET ANOTHER JOB EASY. AND FOX CAN WRITE ANYWHERE, SO THEY'LL BE OKAY.
AND THESSALY... I DON'T KNOW. I'M SURE SHE'LL BE FINE. SHE'LL JUST GET ANOTHER ROOM SOMEWHERE.
THESSALY'S A SURVIVOR. I MEAN, SHE'S REALLY QUIET, AND I'M SURE WHEN YOU GET TO KNOW HER SHE'S REALLY SWEET.
BUT SOMETIMES I THINK MAYBE THERE'S MORE GOING ON ON THE INSIDE THAN YOU'D IMAGINE. I DUNNO.
I'M SURE SHE'LL BE FINE.

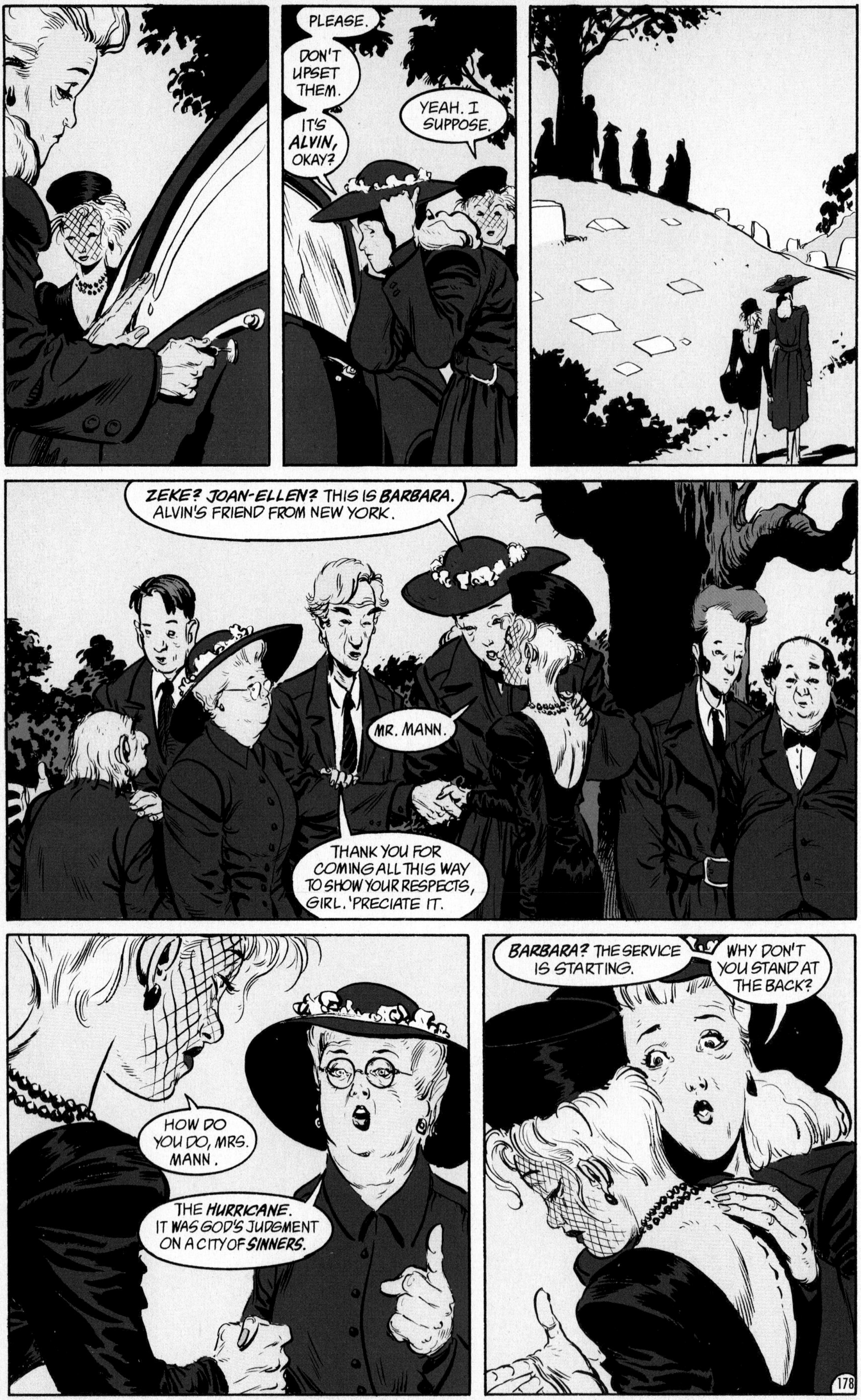
PLEASE.
DON'T UPSET THEM.
IT'S ALVIN, OKAY?
YEAH. I SUPPOSE.
ZEKE? JOAN-ELLEN? THIS IS BARBARA. ALVIN'S FRIEND FROM NEW YORK.
MR. MANN.
THANK YOU FOR COMING ALL THIS WAY TO SHOW YOUR RESPECTS, GIRL. 'PRECIATE IT.
HOW DO YOU DO, MRS. MANN.
THE HURRICANE. IT WAS GOD'S JUDGMENT ON A CITY OF SINNERS.
BARBARA? THE SERVICE IS STARTING.
WHY DON'T YOU STAND AT THE BACK?
178

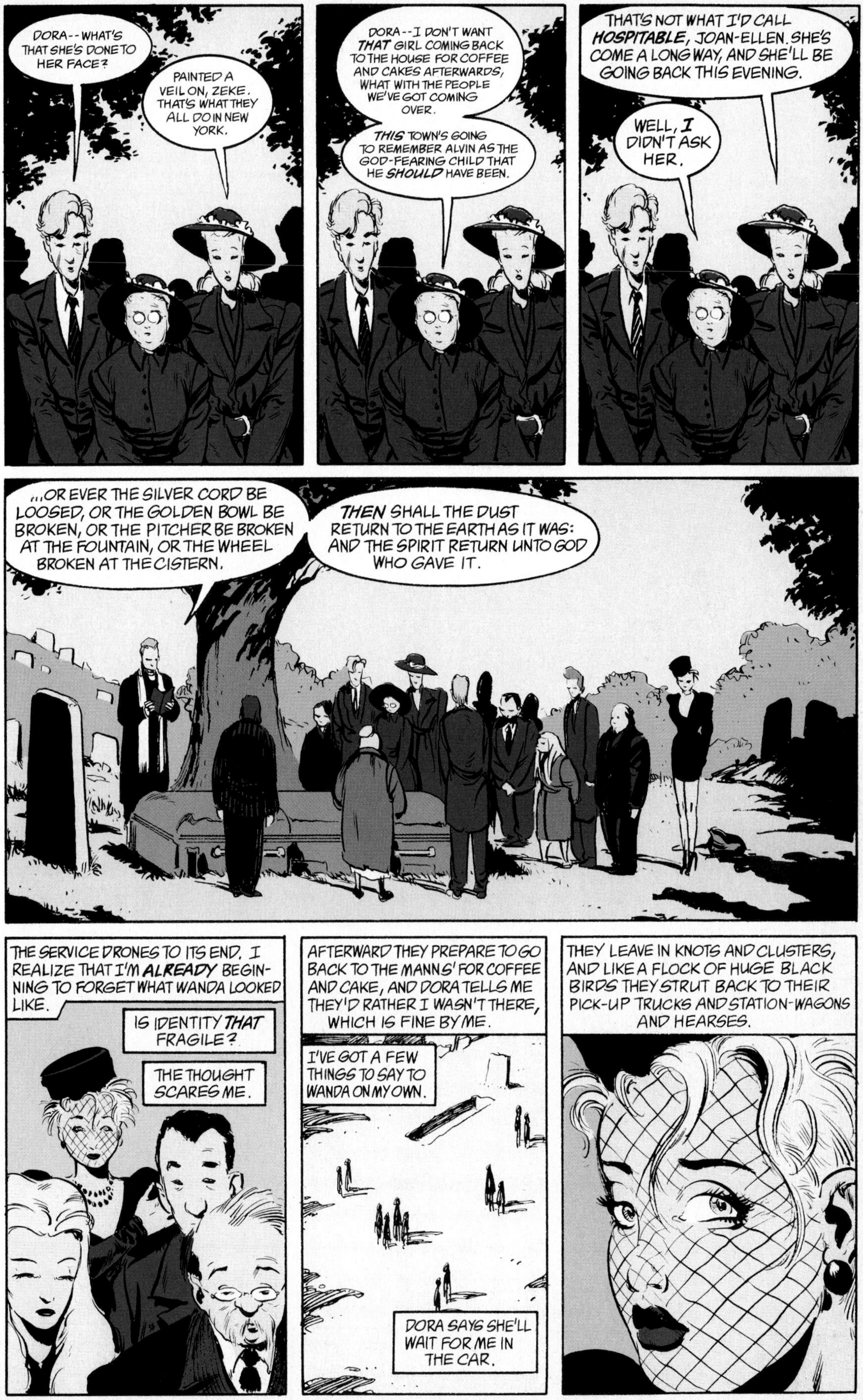
DORA--WHAT'S THAT SHE'S DONE TO HER FACE?
PAINTED A VEIL ON, ZEKE. THAT'S WHAT THEY ALL DO IN NEW YORK.
DORA--I DON'T WANT THAT GIRL COMING BACK TO THE HOUSE FOR COFFEE AND CAKES AFTERWARDS, WHAT WITH THE PEOPLE WE'VE GOT COMING OVER.
THIS TOWN'S GOING TO REMEMBER ALVIN AS THE GOD-FEARING CHILD THAT HE SHOULD HAVE BEEN.
THAT'S NOT WHAT I'D CALL HOSPITABLE, JOAN-ELLEN. SHE'S COME A LONG WAY, AND SHE'LL BE GOING BACK THIS EVENING.
WELL, I DIDN'T ASK HER.
...OR EVER THE SILVER CORD BE LOOSED, OR THE GOLDEN BOWL BE BROKEN, OR THE PITCHER BE BROKEN AT THE FOUNTAIN, OR THE WHEEL BROKEN AT THE CISTERN.
THEN SHALL THE DUST RETURN TO THE EARTH AS IT WAS: AND THE SPIRIT RETURN UNTO GOD WHO GAVE IT.
THE SERVICE DRONES TO ITS END. I REALIZE THAT I'M ALREADY BEGINNING TO FORGET WHAT WANDA LOOKED LIKE.
IS IDENTITY THAT FRAGILE?
THE THOUGHT SCARES ME.
AFTERWARD THEY PREPARE TO GO BACK TO THE MANNS' FOR COFFEE AND CAKE, AND DORA TELLS ME THEY'D RATHER I WASN'T THERE, WHICH IS FINE BY ME.
I'VE GOT A FEW THINGS TO SAY TO WANDA ON MY OWN.
DORA SAYS SHE'LL WAIT FOR ME IN THE CAR.
THEY LEAVE IN KNOTS AND CLUSTERS, AND LIKE A FLOCK OF HUGE BLACK BIRDS THEY STRUT BACK TO THEIR PICK-UP TRUCKS AND STATION-WAGONS AND HEARSES.

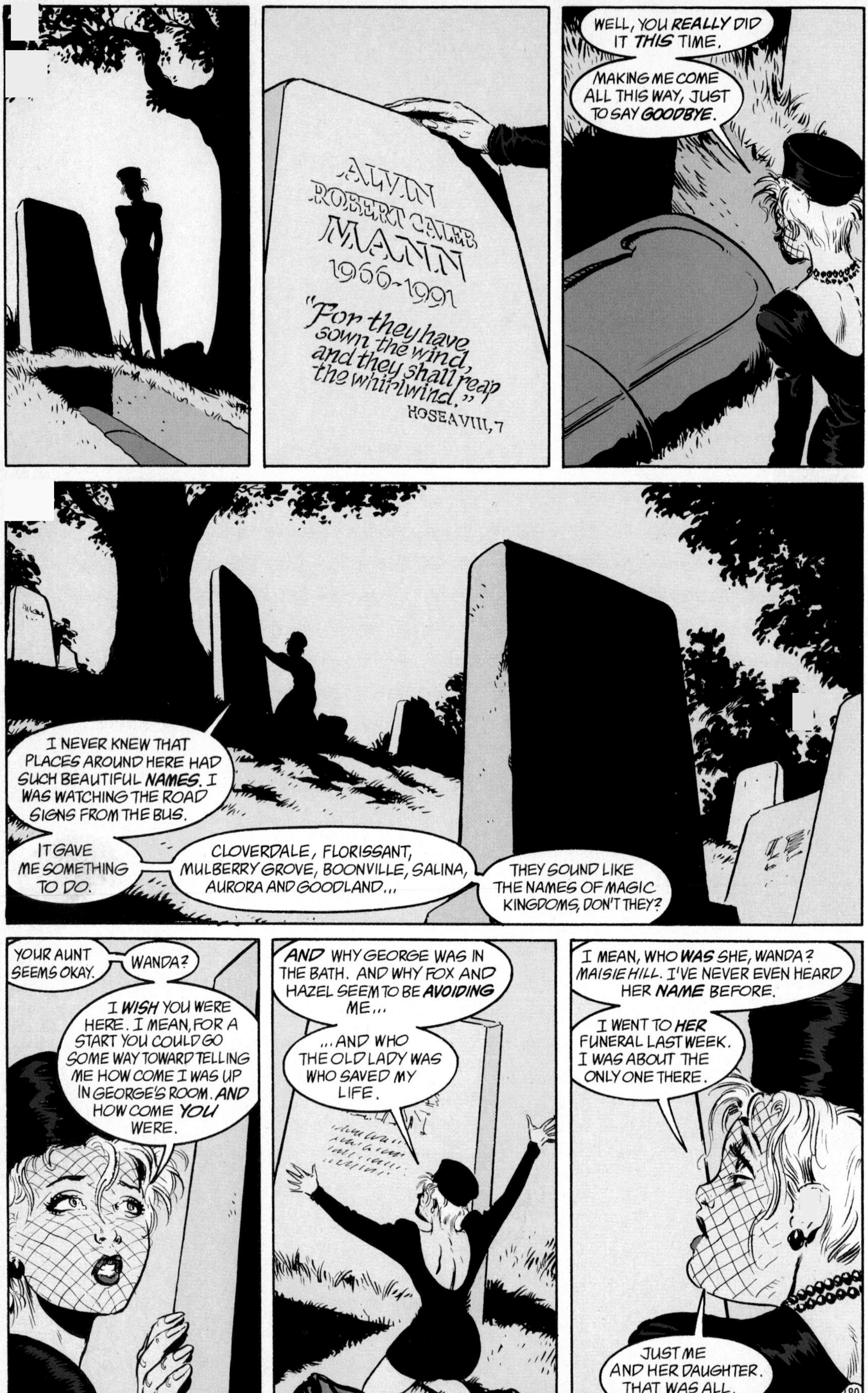

ALVIN
ROBERT CALEB
MANN
1966-1991
"For they have sown the wind, and they shall reap the whirlwind."
HOSEA VIII, 7
WELL, YOU REALLY DID IT THIS TIME.
MAKING ME COME ALL THIS WAY, JUST TO SAY GOODBYE.
I NEVER KNEW THAT PLACES AROUND HERE HAD SUCH BEAUTIFUL NAMES. I WAS WATCHING THE ROAD SIGNS FROM THE BUS.
IT GAVE ME SOMETHING TO DO.
CLOVERDALE, FLORISSANT, MULBERRY GROVE, BOONVILLE, SALINA, AURORA AND GOODLAND...
THEY SOUND LIKE THE NAMES OF MAGIC KINGDOMS, DON'T THEY?
YOUR AUNT SEEMS OKAY.
WANDA?
I WISH YOU WERE HERE. I MEAN, FOR A START YOU COULD GO SOME WAY TOWARD TELLING ME HOW COME I WAS UP IN GEORGE'S ROOM. AND HOW COME YOU WERE.
AND WHY GEORGE WAS IN THE BATH. AND WHY FOX AND HAZEL SEEM TO BE AVOIDING ME...
...AND WHO THE OLD LADY WAS WHO SAVED MY LIFE.
I MEAN, WHO WAS SHE, WANDA? MAISIE HILL. I'VE NEVER EVEN HEARD HER NAME BEFORE.
I WENT TO HER FUNERAL LAST WEEK. I WAS ABOUT THE ONLY ONE THERE.
JUST ME AND HER DAUGHTER. THAT WAS ALL.

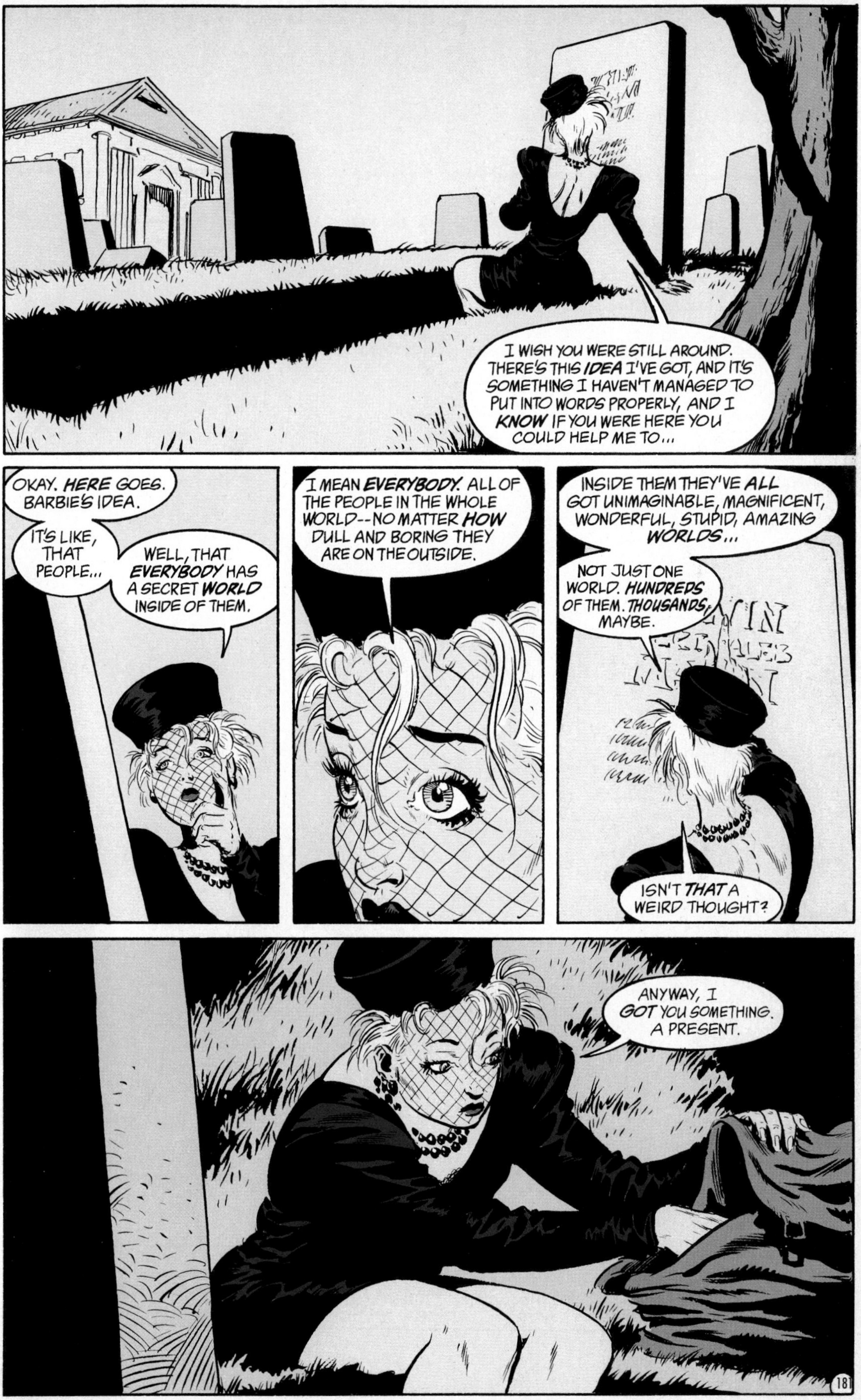
I WISH YOU WERE STILL AROUND. THERE'S THIS IDEA I'VE GOT, AND IT'S SOMETHING I HAVEN'T MANAGED TO PUT INTO WORDS PROPERLY, AND I KNOW IF YOU WERE HERE YOU COULD HELP ME TO...
OKAY. HERE GOES. BARBIE'S IDEA.
IT'S LIKE, THAT PEOPLE...
WELL, THAT EVERYBODY HAS A SECRET WORLD INSIDE OF THEM.
I MEAN EVERYBODY. ALL OF THE PEOPLE IN THE WHOLE WORLD--NO MATTER HOW DULL AND BORING THEY ARE ON THE OUTSIDE.
INSIDE THEM THEY'VE ALL GOT UNIMAGINABLE, MAGNIFICENT, WONDERFUL, STUPID, AMAZING WORLDS...
NOT JUST ONE WORLD. HUNDREDS OF THEM. THOUSANDS, MAYBE.
ISN'T THAT A WEIRD THOUGHT?
ANYWAY, I GOT YOU SOMETHING. A PRESENT.

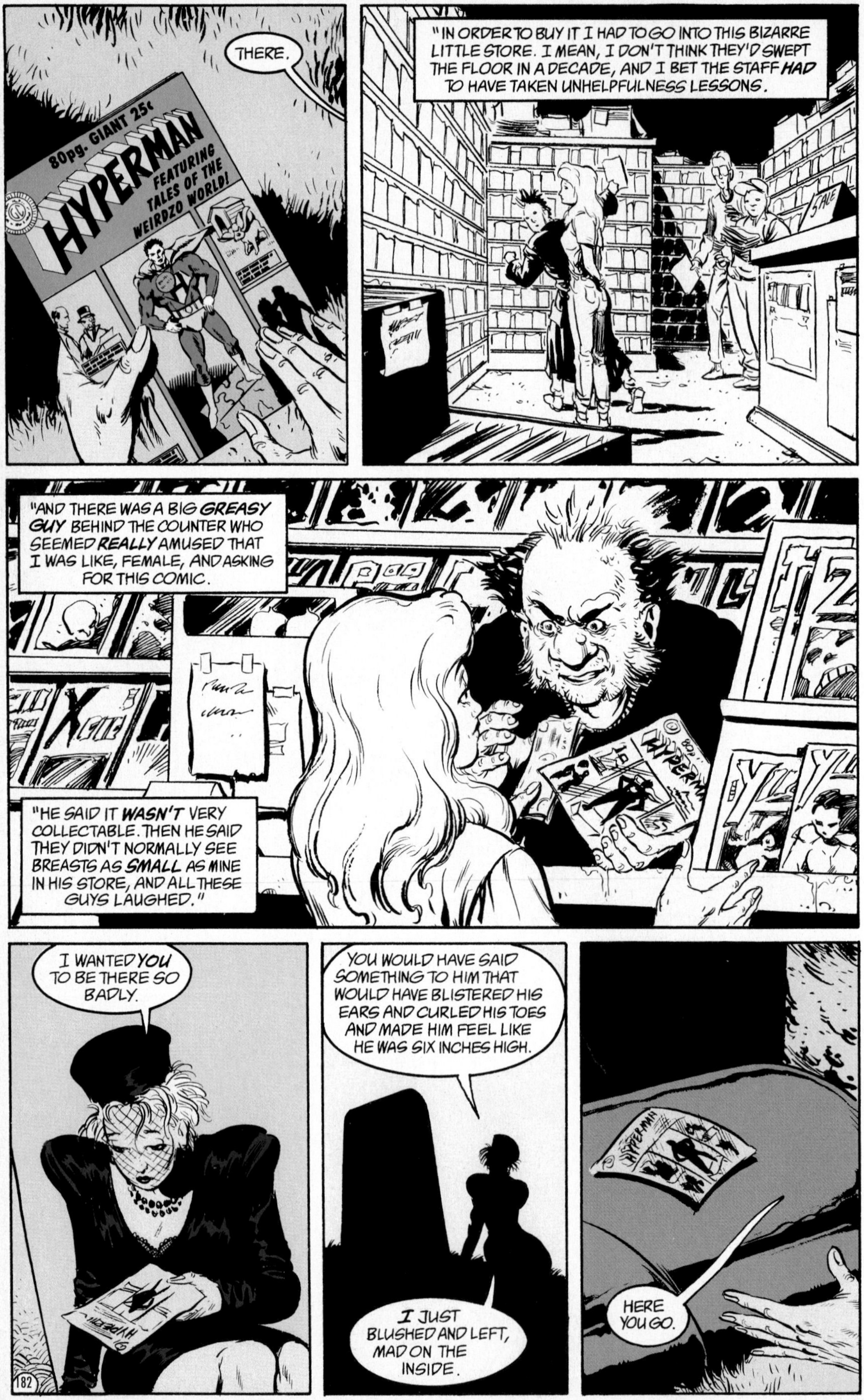
THERE.
80pg. GIANT 25¢
HYPERMAN
FEATURING TALES OF THE WEIRDZO WORLD!
"IN ORDER TO BUY IT I HAD TO GO INTO THIS BIZARRE LITTLE STORE. I MEAN, I DON'T THINK THEY'D SWEPT THE FLOOR IN A DECADE, AND I BET THE STAFF HAD TO HAVE TAKEN UNHELPFULNESS LESSONS.
SALE
"AND THERE WAS A BIG GREASY GUY BEHIND THE COUNTER WHO SEEMED REALLY AMUSED THAT I WAS LIKE, FEMALE, AND ASKING FOR THIS COMIC.
"HE SAID IT WASN'T VERY COLLECTABLE. THEN HE SAID THEY DIDN'T NORMALLY SEE BREASTS AS SMALL AS MINE IN HIS STORE, AND ALL THESE GUYS LAUGHED."
I WANTED YOU TO BE THERE SO BADLY.
YOU WOULD HAVE SAID SOMETHING TO HIM THAT WOULD HAVE BLISTERED HIS EARS AND CURLED HIS TOES AND MADE HIM FEEL LIKE HE WAS SIX INCHES HIGH.
I JUST BLUSHED AND LEFT, MAD ON THE INSIDE.
HYPERMAN
HERE YOU GO.

OH, YEAH. AND HERE...
I THOUGHT YOU'D LIKE IT. IT'S TACKY FLAMINGO, OR WHATEVER IT'S CALLED. YOUR FAVORITE COLOR.
WANDA
ALVIN
HEY, NO PROBLEM.
LEAST I COULD DO.

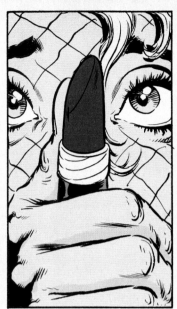

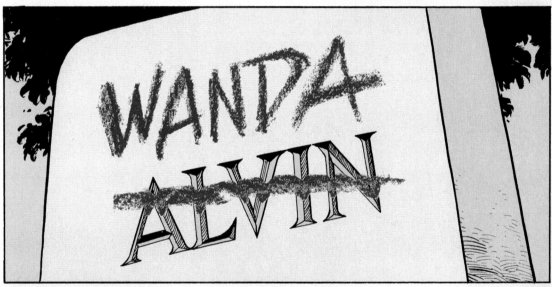

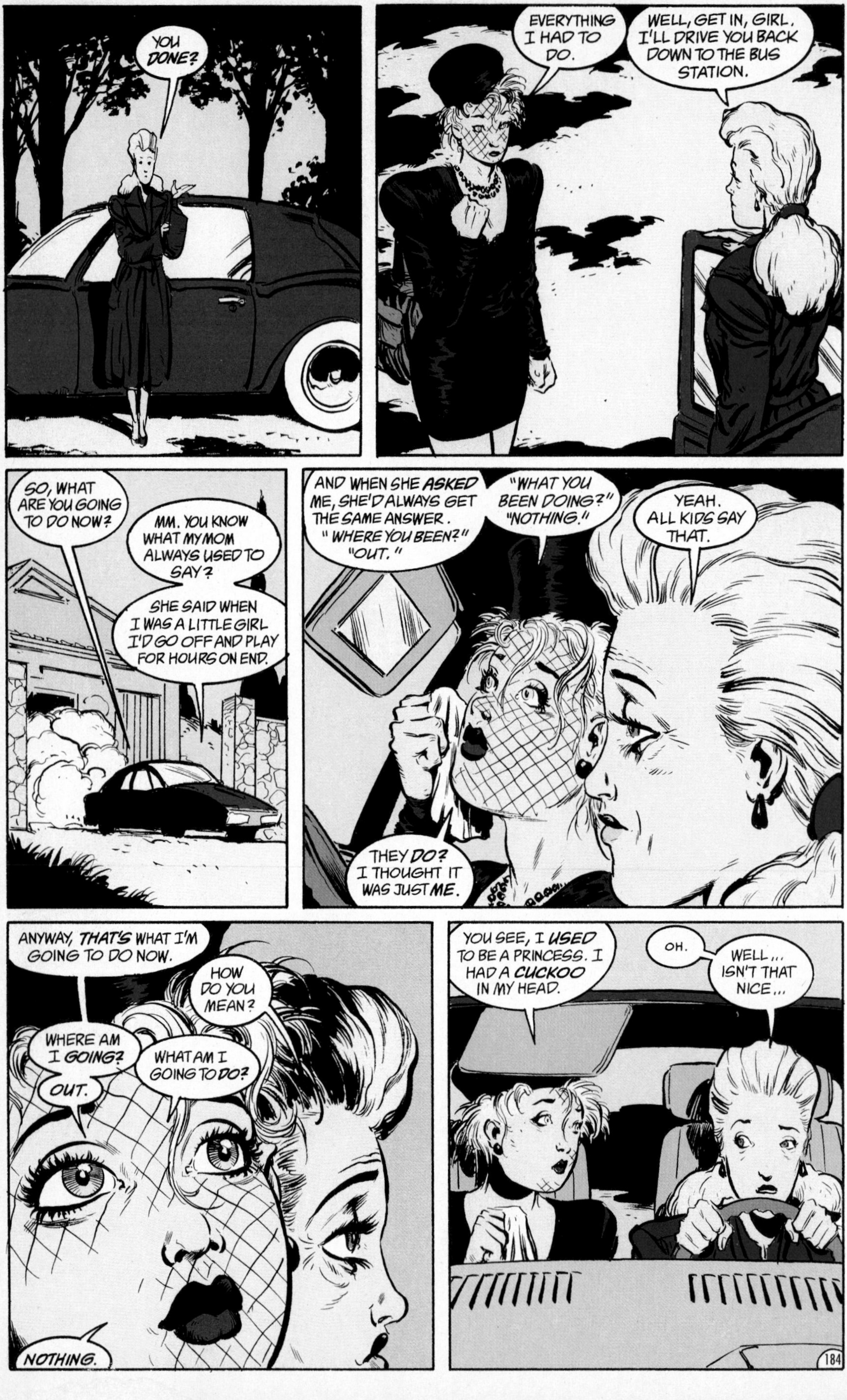

YOU DONE?
EVERYTHING I HAD TO DO.
WELL, GET IN, GIRL. I'LL DRIVE YOU BACK DOWN TO THE BUS STATION.
SO, WHAT ARE YOU GOING TO DO NOW?
MM. YOU KNOW WHAT MY MOM ALWAYS USED TO SAY?
SHE SAID WHEN I WAS A LITTLE GIRL I'D GO OFF AND PLAY FOR HOURS ON END.
AND WHEN SHE ASKED ME, SHE'D ALWAYS GET THE SAME ANSWER. "WHERE YOU BEEN?" "OUT."
"WHAT YOU BEEN DOING?" "NOTHING."
YEAH. ALL KIDS SAY THAT.
THEY DO? I THOUGHT IT WAS JUST ME.
ANYWAY, THAT'S WHAT I'M GOING TO DO NOW.
HOW DO YOU MEAN?
WHERE AM I GOING?
OUT.
WHAT AM I GOING TO DO?
NOTHING.
YOU SEE, I USED TO BE A PRINCESS. I HAD A CUCKOO IN MY HEAD.
OH.
WELL... ISN'T THAT NICE...

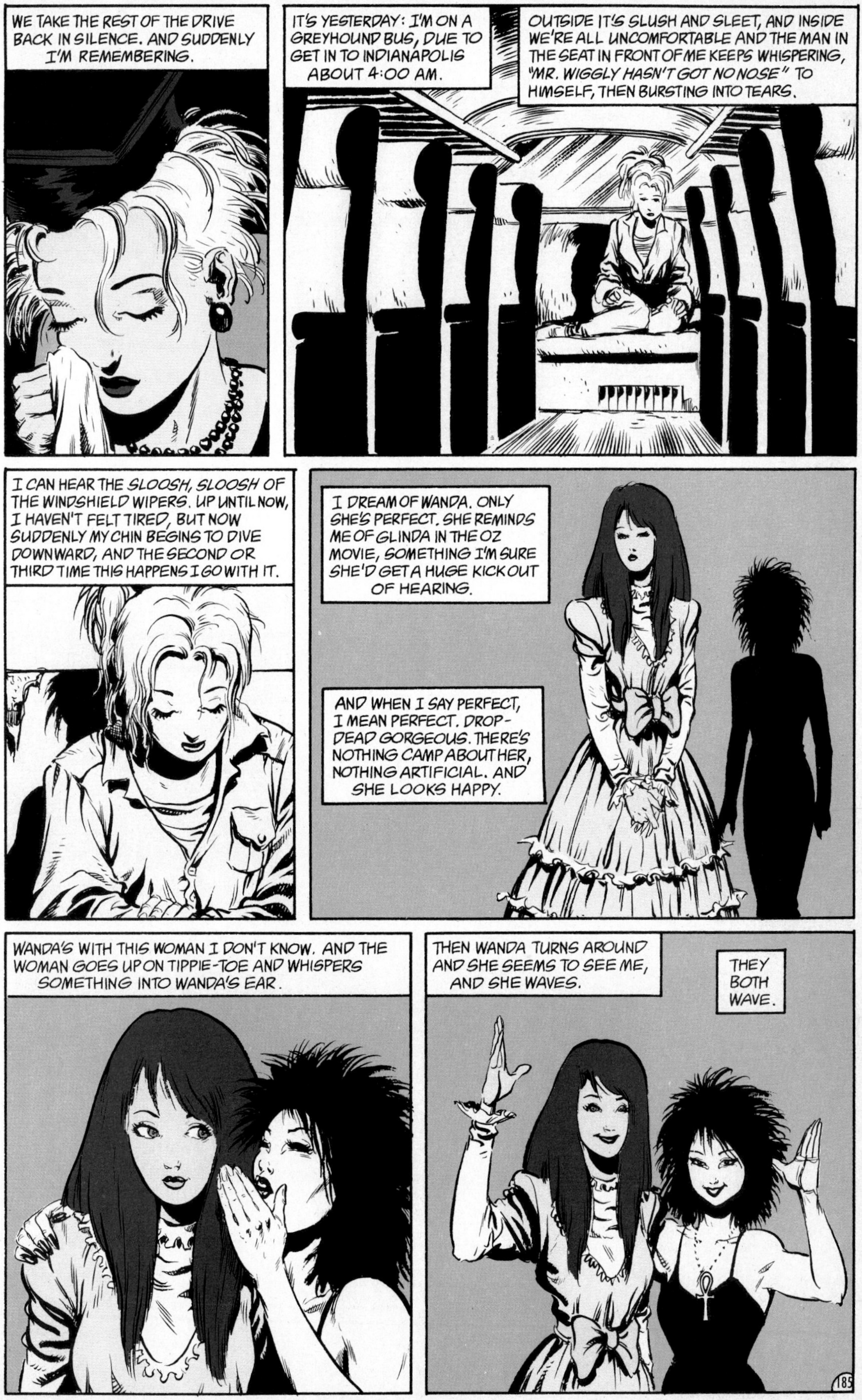
WE TAKE THE REST OF THE DRIVE BACK IN SILENCE. AND SUDDENLY I'M REMEMBERING.
IT'S YESTERDAY: I'M ON A GREYHOUND BUS, DUE TO GET IN TO INDIANAPOLIS ABOUT 4:00 AM.
OUTSIDE IT'S SLUSH AND SLEET, AND INSIDE WE'RE ALL UNCOMFORTABLE AND THE MAN IN THE SEAT IN FRONT OF ME KEEPS WHISPERING, "MR. WIGGLY HASN'T GOT NO NOSE" TO HIMSELF, THEN BURSTING INTO TEARS.
I CAN HEAR THE *SLOOSH, SLOOSH* OF THE WINDSHIELD WIPERS. UP UNTIL NOW, I HAVEN'T FELT TIRED, BUT NOW SUDDENLY MY CHIN BEGINS TO DIVE DOWNWARD, AND THE SECOND OR THIRD TIME THIS HAPPENS I GO WITH IT.
I DREAM OF WANDA. ONLY SHE'S PERFECT. SHE REMINDS ME OF GLINDA IN THE OZ MOVIE, SOMETHING I'M SURE SHE'D GET A HUGE KICK OUT OF HEARING.
AND WHEN I SAY PERFECT, I MEAN PERFECT. DROP-DEAD GORGEOUS. THERE'S NOTHING CAMP ABOUT HER, NOTHING ARTIFICIAL. AND SHE LOOKS HAPPY.
WANDA'S WITH THIS WOMAN I DON'T KNOW. AND THE WOMAN GOES UP ON TIPPIE-TOE AND WHISPERS SOMETHING INTO WANDA'S EAR.
THEN WANDA TURNS AROUND AND SHE SEEMS TO SEE ME, AND SHE WAVES.
THEY BOTH WAVE.
185

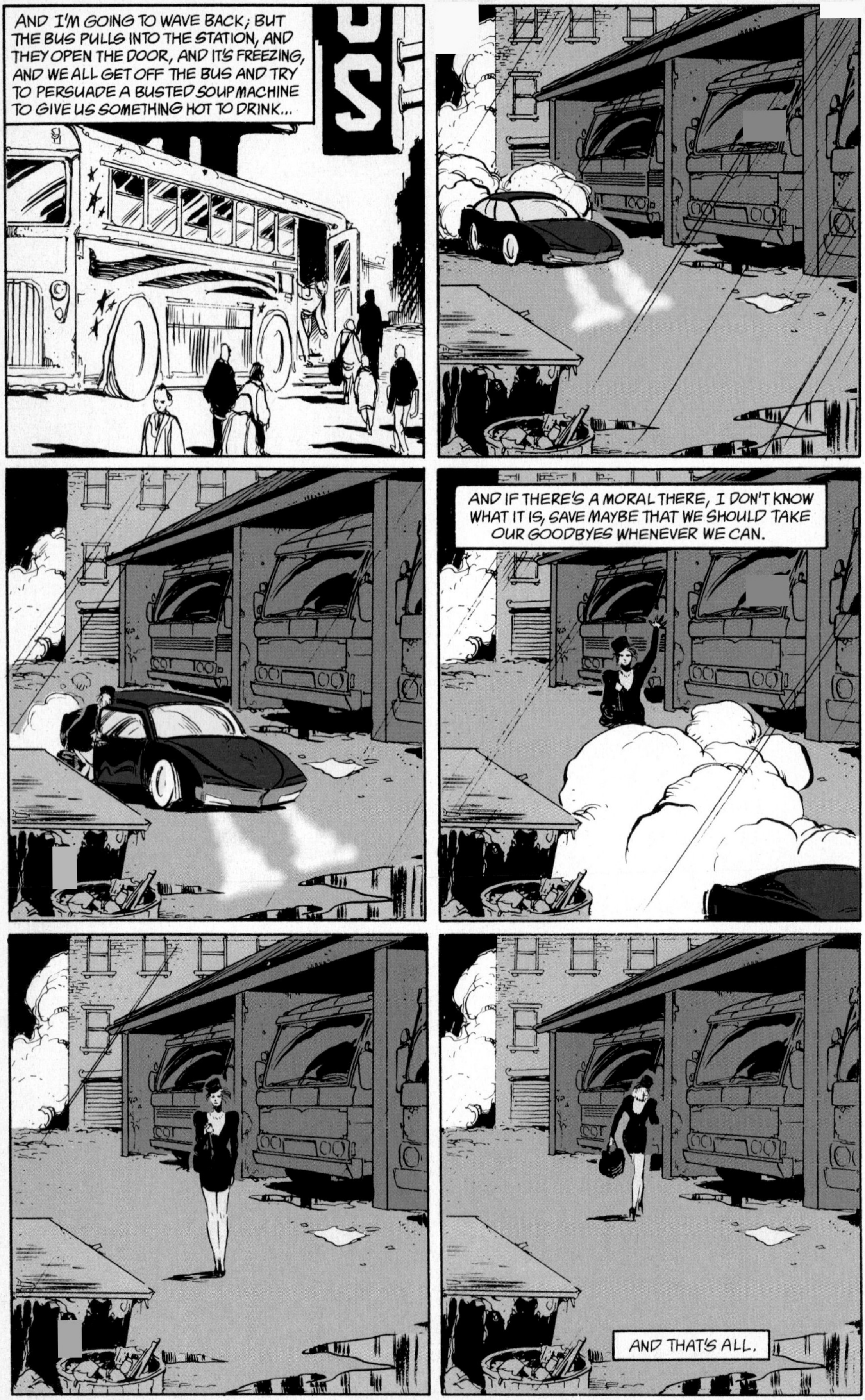
AND I'M GOING TO WAVE BACK; BUT THE BUS PULLS INTO THE STATION, AND THEY OPEN THE DOOR, AND IT'S FREEZING, AND WE ALL GET OFF THE BUS AND TRY TO PERSUADE A BUSTED SOUP MACHINE TO GIVE US SOMETHING HOT TO DRINK...
AND IF THERE'S A MORAL THERE, I DON'T KNOW WHAT IT IS, SAVE MAYBE THAT WE SHOULD TAKE OUR GOODBYES WHENEVER WE CAN.
AND THAT'S ALL.

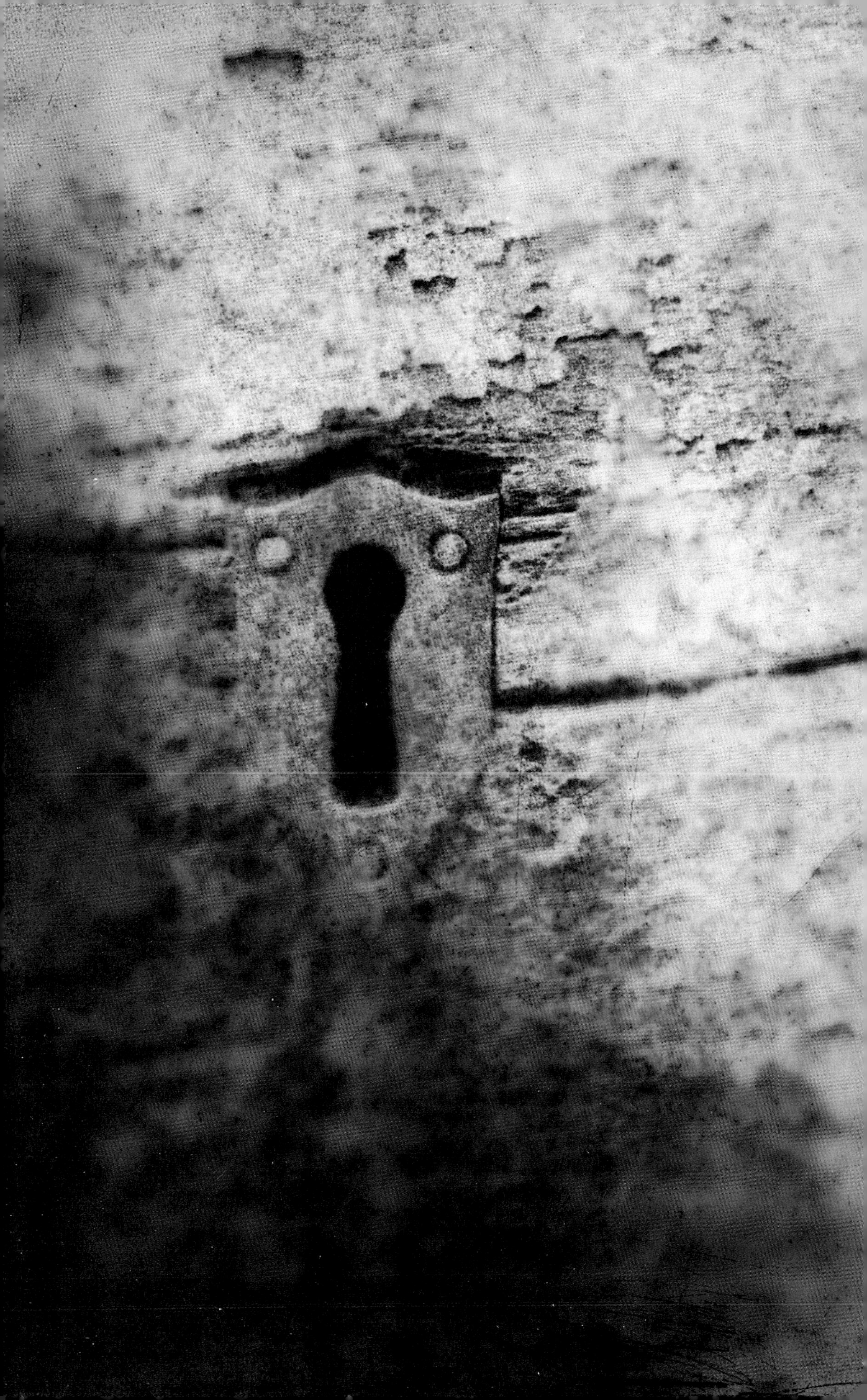

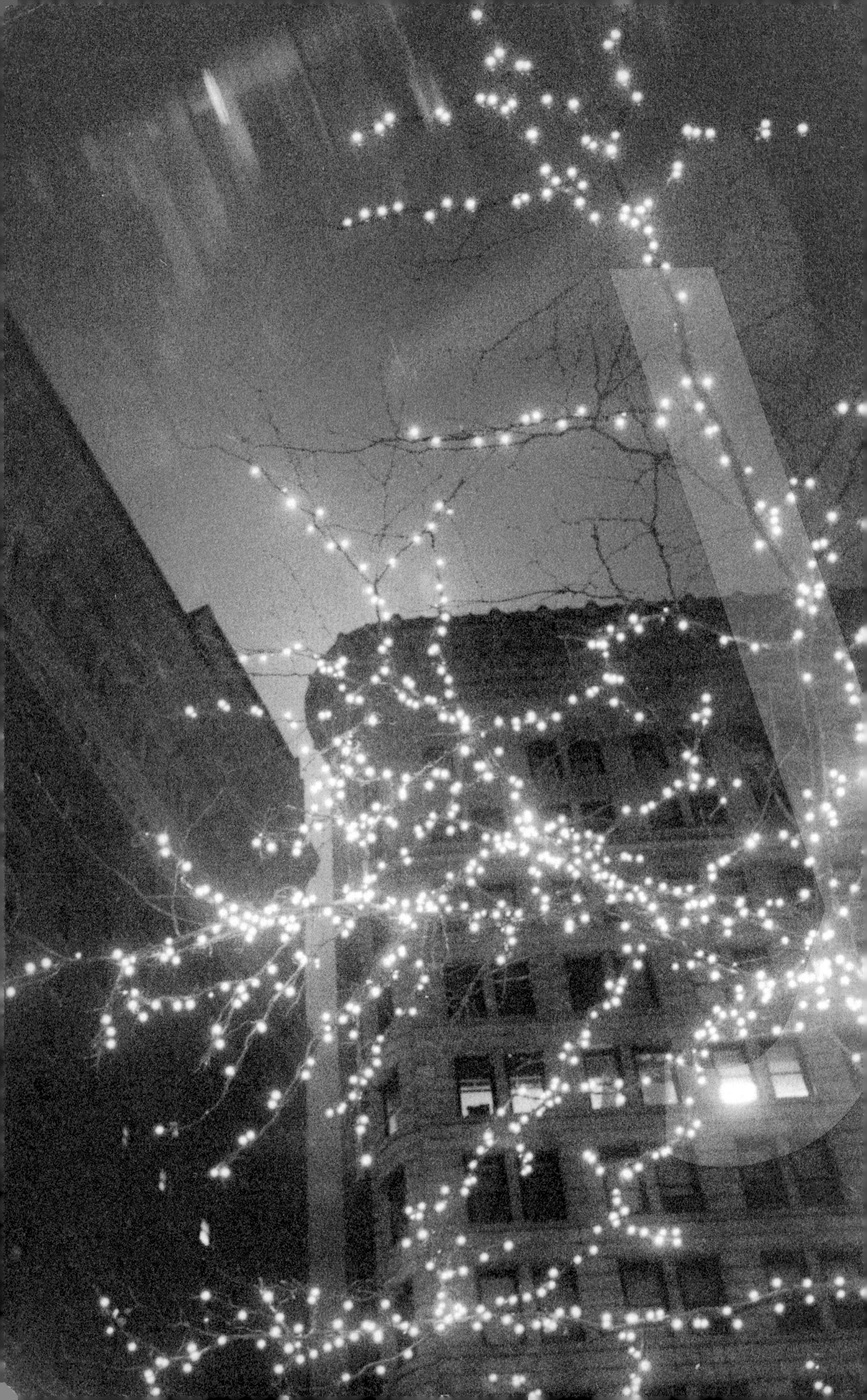

A BRIEF AFTERWORD

This story was written in a number of places, mostly in an office in Sussex, England, a hotel room in Wilmington, NC, and an apartment in Northampton, MA.

I couldn't and wouldn't have done it without Jonathan Carroll, who talked me into telling a story I had thought best left alone, and who taught me that one of the purposes of a writer is to write it new; the late Don Melia and his unnamed just-as-late roommate, who planted a seed that became Wanda.

Kevin Eastman gave me somewhere to hide while I was writing part of the story. Dolores Meeks and Susan Alston made sure I was fine, and Scott and Ivy McCloud took me out for ice cream.

Steve Bissette, Michael Zulli (who was there the day the story began), Rick Veitch and the rest of the Massachusetts mafia gave me support and encouragement.

On the home front I owe thanks to Mary Gaiman, our son Michael, and to Holly, our daughter, from whom I learned that cuckoos go *Lally Lally*.

My thanks to Shawn McManus, to Colleen Doran, and to Bryan Talbot (who rescued us at the last moment), and to Stan Woch, George Pratt and Dick Giordano. Todd Klein did his usual remarkable job, and Danny Vozzo made it happen in color. Karen Berger, my editor, kept editing despite having to go and give birth to Zachary Bruning in the middle (We were on the phone at the time. Honestly.); and Alisa Kwitney, assistant editor, dropped in at the deep end, did miracles.

Dave McKean is one of a kind, and it's hard to thank him enough for his vision or his friendship.

Bob Kahan brought to this collected edition the same dedication and obsession with detail he brought to *Season of Mists*. It's appreciated.

And there are other people without whom: Babs, Roz, Rachel, Ian and Anne, Patrick and Teresa, Steve Brust, Will and Emma, Steve Jones, Pete Atkins, Jim Chadwick, Tom Peyer, Jim Herbert...but that list's too long to print here and is, anyway, unfinished.

I spent more than half a year with Barbie and Wanda and Hazel and Foxglove and Wilkinson and Thessaly and the rest of them wandering around in my head.

Some nights I still miss them.

Neil Gaiman
4 March 1993

BIOGRAPHIES

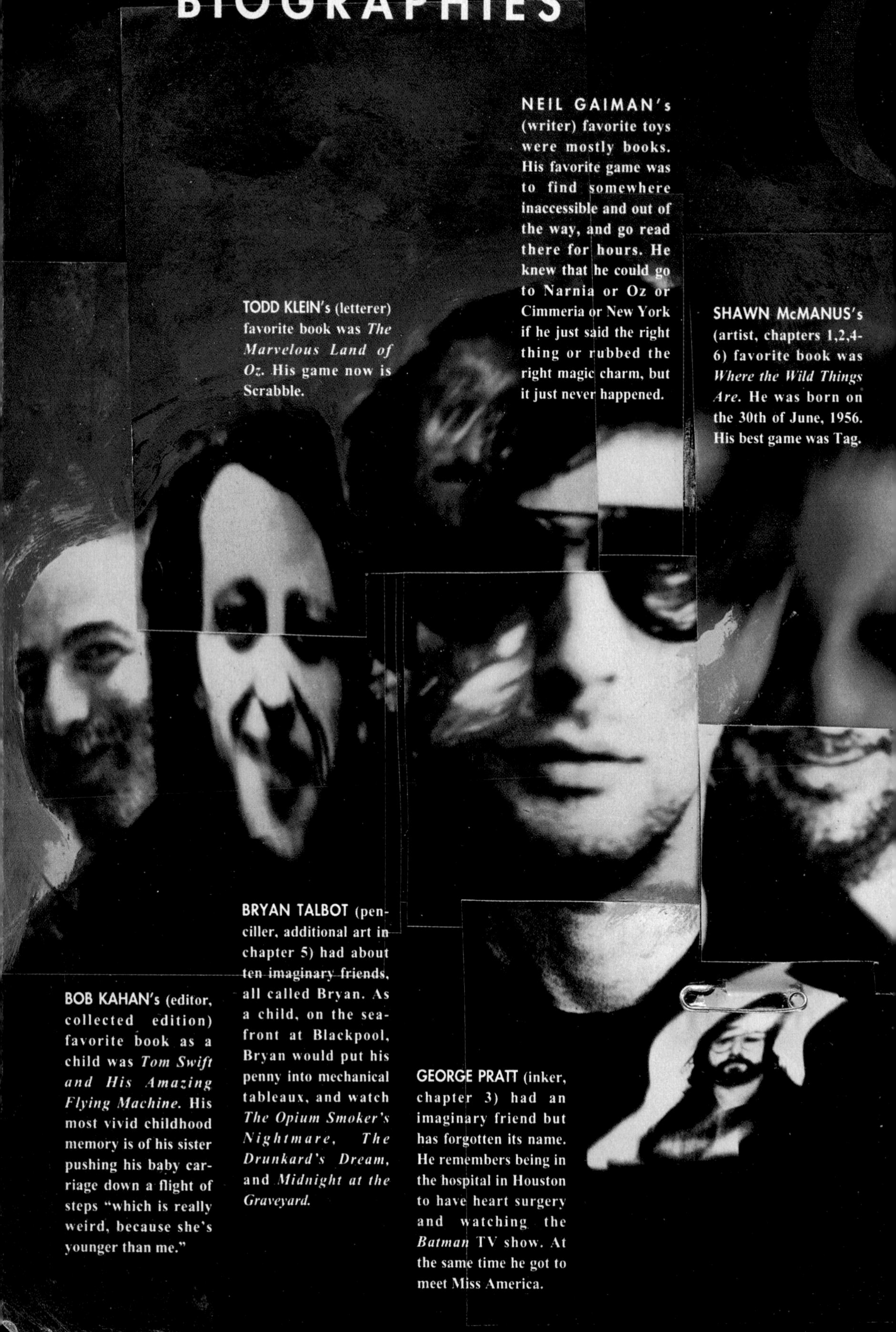

NEIL GAIMAN's (writer) favorite toys were mostly books. His favorite game was to find somewhere inaccessible and out of the way, and go read there for hours. He knew that he could go to Narnia or Oz or Cimmeria or New York if he just said the right thing or rubbed the right magic charm, but it just never happened.

TODD KLEIN's (letterer) favorite book was *The Marvelous Land of Oz.* His game now is Scrabble.

SHAWN McMANUS's (artist, chapters 1,2,4-6) favorite book was *Where the Wild Things Are.* He was born on the 30th of June, 1956. His best game was Tag.

BRYAN TALBOT (penciller, additional art in chapter 5) had about ten imaginary friends, all called Bryan. As a child, on the seafront at Blackpool, Bryan would put his penny into mechanical tableaux, and watch *The Opium Smoker's Nightmare, The Drunkard's Dream,* and *Midnight at the Graveyard.*

BOB KAHAN's (editor, collected edition) favorite book as a child was *Tom Swift and His Amazing Flying Machine.* His most vivid childhood memory is of his sister pushing his baby carriage down a flight of steps "which is really weird, because she's younger than me."

GEORGE PRATT (inker, chapter 3) had an imaginary friend but has forgotten its name. He remembers being in the hospital in Houston to have heart surgery and watching the *Batman* TV show. At the same time he got to meet Miss America.

ALISA KWITNEY (not pictured) (assistant editor) had a security blanket called Schmatta, and two imaginary friends named Roland and Syrup. Roland got his name from a small boy in Majorca who cracked open his head running full-tilt into a wall.

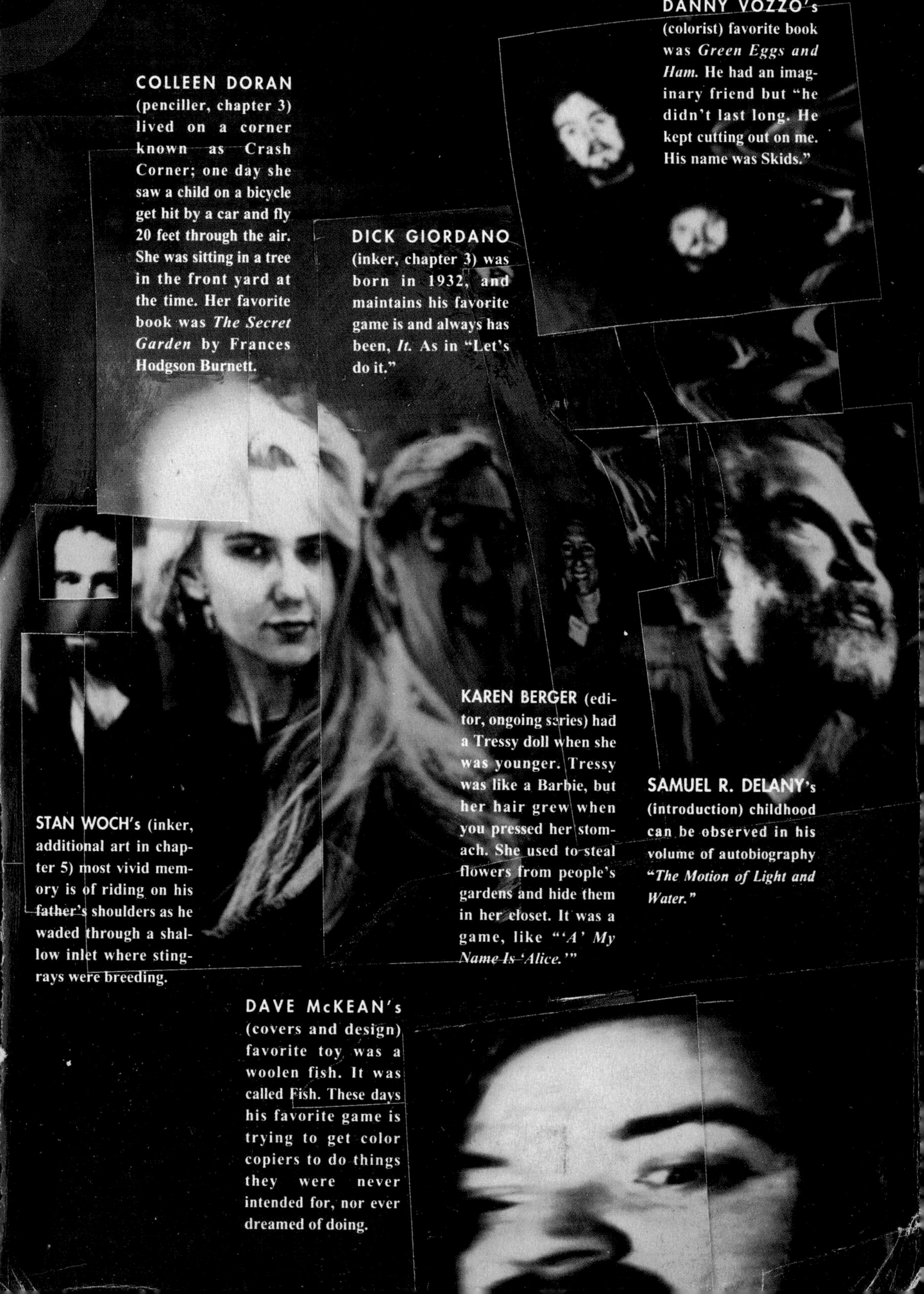

DANNY VOZZO's (colorist) favorite book was *Green Eggs and Ham.* He had an imaginary friend but "he didn't last long. He kept cutting out on me. His name was Skids."

COLLEEN DORAN (penciller, chapter 3) lived on a corner known as Crash Corner; one day she saw a child on a bicycle get hit by a car and fly 20 feet through the air. She was sitting in a tree in the front yard at the time. Her favorite book was *The Secret Garden* by Frances Hodgson Burnett.

DICK GIORDANO (inker, chapter 3) was born in 1932, and maintains his favorite game is and always has been, *It.* As in "Let's do it."

KAREN BERGER (editor, ongoing series) had a Tressy doll when she was younger. Tressy was like a Barbie, but her hair grew when you pressed her stomach. She used to steal flowers from people's gardens and hide them in her closet. It was a game, like "'*A' My Name Is 'Alice.'*"

SAMUEL R. DELANY's (introduction) childhood can be observed in his volume of autobiography *"The Motion of Light and Water."*

STAN WOCH's (inker, additional art in chapter 5) most vivid memory is of riding on his father's shoulders as he waded through a shallow inlet where stingrays were breeding.

DAVE McKEAN's (covers and design) favorite toy was a woolen fish. It was called Fish. These days his favorite game is trying to get color copiers to do things they were never intended for, nor ever dreamed of doing.

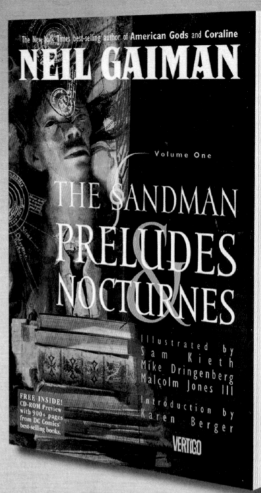
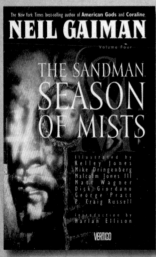